EARLY CHRISTIANS AND THEIR ART

EMORY STUDIES IN EARLY CHRISTIANITY

Vernon K. Robbins, General Editor
Roy R. Jeal, General Editor
Robert H. von Thaden Jr., Associate Editor
David B. Gowler, Associate Editor
Meghan Henning
Susan E. Hylen
Mikeal C. Parsons
Russell B. Sisson
Shively T. J. Smith

Number 27

EARLY CHRISTIANS AND THEIR ART

Edited by

Mikeal C. Parsons and Robin M. Jensen

Atlanta

Copyright © 2023 by SBL Press

Publication of this volume was made possible by the generous support of the Pierce Program in Religion of Oxford College of Emory University.

All rights reserved. No part of this work may be reproduced or transmitted in any form or by any means, electronic or mechanical, including photocopying and recording, or by means of any information storage or retrieval system, except as may be expressly permitted by the 1976 Copyright Act or in writing from the publisher. Requests for permission should be addressed in writing to the Rights and Permissions Office, SBL Press, 825 Houston Mill Road, Atlanta, GA 30329 USA.

Library of Congress Control Number: 2023952272

Cover design is an adaptation by Bernard Madden of Rick A. Robbins, Mixed Media (19" x 24" pen and ink on paper, 1981).

Contents

Editors' Preface vii
Abbreviations xi

Interpreting Select Early Sculptures Using Art-Historical
    Methodology
    Heidi J. Hornik 1

The Repudiation of Pagan Idols and the Rise of Christian
    Devotional Portraits
    Robin M. Jensen 25

Experiencing the Renewed Cosmos: The Significance of the
    Celestial Ceiling in the Baptistery at Dura-Europos
    Jeffrey M. Dale† 51

Seeing God at Mamre: Reconsidering the Early Visual Evidence
    Jeffrey M. Hubbard 79

Hope for Life after Death: Hebrews and the Origin of Christian
    Funerary Anchor Iconography in the Catacombs of Rome
    Jason A. Whitlark 107

Who Is the Good Shepherd? Answers from Early African Sources
    David E. Wilhite 143

Christian Children's Sarcophagi: Testaments to Grief and Hope
    Eric J. Brewer 175

Reimagining the Silver Casket of San Nazaro
    Zen Hess 203

A Christlike Tree: Personifying and Christomorphizing the Cross
in Early Christianity
  Christian Sanchez..233

Visualizing the *Adversus Judaeos* Tradition: Understanding
Ἰσραήλ as a *Nomen Sacrum* in Early Christian Manuscripts
  Mikeal Parsons, Gregory M. Barnhill, and Natalie Webb.................263

Early Christians and Their Theological Symbols in Ostia Antica
  Bruce W. Longenecker 301

Contributors..343
Ancient Sources Index...347
Modern Authors Index..362
Subject Index..367

Editors' Preface

Early Christians and Their Art is a collection of eleven essays that explore various aspects of the visual and material culture of early Christianity. The media analyzed range from sarcophagi to manuscripts and from architecture to catacombs across the several centuries in which early Christianity(ies) emerged and formed. Five of the papers (Brewer, Dale, Hess, Hubbard, and Sanchez) collected here were originally presented as part of the 2021–2022 New Testament Colloquium at Baylor University. The other six papers (Hornik; Jensen; Longenecker; Parsons, Barnhill, and Webb; Whitlark; and Wilhite) were prepared by persons who participated in the colloquium. Robin Jensen's contribution to the volume is a revised version of her Baylor public lecture, delivered as part of the New Testament Colloquium. The purpose of the colloquium, and thus these papers, was to mine the material culture of early Christians and their context(s) for insights into their beliefs and practices beyond the limits of the textual evidence. Each of the essays attempts to respond to the plea in the introductory essay, by art historian Heidi J. Hornik, for New Testament scholars, in their interdisciplinary ventures into the visual arts, to take the historical, cultural, political, and religious contexts of the material culture of early Christianity as seriously as they do for early Christian written texts.

New Testament Colloquium has been a vital part of the Baylor Graduate Program in Religion since 1995. Topics covered rotated on a three-year basis: Jewish, Greco-Roman, and early Christian (noncanonical). In the fall semester, doctoral students made presentations on the *status questionis* of various issues related to the subject matter; in the spring semester, they offered research papers exploring specific topics related to some aspect of the study of the New Testament/early Christianity. Guest specialists were brought to campus to give public lectures and to assist with refining and sharpening the focus of those papers. A broad range of texts and topics were covered, accompanied by a distinguished list of experts that included, inter alia: Jewish: Josephus (Steve Mason), Philo (Greg Sterling, Harold Attridge), Jewish apocalypses (Dale Allison), Jewish hermeneutics (Sidney White Crawford), the origin of evil in Second Temple Jewish literature (Kelly Coblentz Bautch), Mekilta de Rabbi Ishmael (Jonathan Kaplan); *Greco-Roman*: Plutarch's *Lives* (Bruce Winter), Greek novels (Ronald Hock, Edmund Cueva), Vesuvian towns (Carolyn Osiek), voluntary associations (John Kloppenborg); *early Christian*: Apostolic Fathers (Clayton Jefford), apocryphal acts (François Bovon), apocryphal gospels (Mark Goodacre), *adversus Ioudaios* traditions (Terence Donaldson). The guest expert for the 2021–2022 New Testament Colloquium on Early Christian Art was Robin Jensen, Patrick O'Brien Professor of Theology at the University of Notre Dame. Articles, dissertations, and other collections of essays have resulted from these colloquia over the years.

As it happens, the 2021–2022 New Testament Colloquium on Early Christian Art was the last iteration of the course. Changes in the graduate curriculum made it impossible for New Testament Colloquium to continue in its current form; therefore, we were delighted that the last year was among the best. It was made all the better by Jensen's virtual and online presence for the weekly sessions, in which she shared her expertise as a leading authority in the field. (Zoom was an inadvertent silver lining to the otherwise disruptive impact Covid has had on classroom instruction, not to mention the devastating toll on human life.)

We wish to express gratitude to Roy Jeal and Robert von Thaden, editors of Emory Studies in Early Christianity, for accepting the volume into that series, to the anonymous peer reviewers for their helpful comments on earlier drafts, and to Nicole L. Tilford and the staff at SBL Press for their excellent work in producing the printed volume. We also express gratitude to Dr. David Gowler (Pierce Professor of Religion, Oxford College, Emory University) for providing monies from the Pierce Fund to cover the copyright costs for images in the volume and to Dr. Douglas Weaver (chair, Department of Religion, Baylor University) for allocating a subvention from the George Alphin Fund for Research to cover the costs of printing most of those images in color.

We dedicate the volume to the memory of Jeffrey M. Dale, one of the volume's contributors and, at the time, a Baylor ABD in New Testament. Jeff died in a mountain-climbing accident while attempting to ascend to the summit of Mount Jefferson in Oregon's Cascade Range in July 2022. Jeff was working on a dissertation under the direction of Bruce Longenecker titled, "Microcosm of God's Final Victory: Paul's Vision in 1 Corinthians amid Cosmic Conflict in Greco-Roman Context." Jeff was exploring Paul's presentation of death as a cosmic power in God's good world; his family received a posthumous PhD from the university, awarded to Jeff in August 2022. His essay in this volume serves as a monument to the research trajectory that he was on. We will continue to remember Jeff as a beloved colleague whose friendship we were blessed to cherish for a while.

Mikeal C. Parsons and Robin M. Jensen

Abbreviations

General

ca.	circa
ch(s).	chapter(s)
cm	centimeter(s)
d.	died
fol(s).	folio(s)
frag(s).	fragment(s)
in	inch(es)
m	meter(s)

Primary Sources

1 Apol.	Justin, *Apologia i*
1–2 Clem.	1–2 Clement
1–2 Macc	1–2 Maccabees
Ab urb. cond.	Livy, *Ab urbe condita*
Abr.	Philo, *De Abrahamo*
Acts John	Acts of John
Acts Pet.	Acts of Peter
Acts Thom.	Acts of Thomas
Adv. Epiph.	Nicephorus, *Adversus Epiphanidem*
Adv. Jud.	Tertullian, *Adversus Judaeos*
Aeth.	Heliodorus, *Aethiopica*
A.J.	Josephus, *Antiquitates judaicae*
Ann.	Tacitus, *Annales*
Anth.	Joannes Stobaeus, *Anthologus*
Antichr.	Hippolytus, *De antichristo*
Antr. nymph.	Porphyry, *De antro nympharum*
Apoc. El.	Apocalypse of Elijah

Apoc. Pet.	Apocalypse of Peter
Apol.	*Apologia*
Aug.	Suetonius, *Divus Augustus*
b.	Babylonian Talmud
Barn.	Barnabas
Bell. civ.	Lucan, *De bello civili*
B.J.	Josephus, *Bellum judaicum*
B-S Ap.	Berlin-Strasbourg Apocryphon
C. Ar.	Athanasius, *Orationes contra Arianos*
C. Gent.	Athanasius, *Contra gentes*
C. Jul.	Augustine, *Contra Julianum*
Cal.	Suetonius, *Gaius Caligula*
Carm.	Paulinus, *Carmina*
Cels.	Origen, *Contra Celsum*
Civ.	Augustine, *De civitate Dei*
Comm. Aen.	Servius, *In Vergilii Aeneidos commentarii*
Comm. Cant.	Origen, *Commentarius in Canticum*
Comm. Diat.	Ephrem, *Commentary on the Diatessaron*
Comm. Gen.	Procopius of Gaza, *Commentarii in Genesim*
Comm. Isa.	Theodoret, *Commentarii in Isaiam*
Comm. Matt.	Jerome, *Commentariorum in Matthaeum libri IV*
Conf.	Augustine, *Confessionum libri XIII*
Cons.	Augustine, *De consensu evangelistarum*
Cons. ux.	Plutarch, *Consolatio ad uxorem*
Cor.	Tertullian, *De corona militis*
Dance Sav.	Dance of the Savior
Dem. ev.	Eusebius, *Demonstratio evangelica*
Dial.	Justin, *Dialogus cum Tryphone*
Did.	Didache
Did. apost.	Didascalia Apostolorum
Disc. Sav.	The Discourse of the Savior on the Mystery of the Cross
Eleem.	Cyprian, *De opera et eleemosynis*
Encom. Mar.	Encomium of Mary Magdalene
Ep.	*Epistula(e)*
Ep. Apost.	Epistle to the Apostles
Ep. fest.	Athanasius, *Epistulae festales*
Ep. Marcell.	Athanasius, *Epistula ad Marcellinum de interpretatione Psalmorum*
Epid.	Irenaeus, *Epideixis tou apostolikou kērygmatos*

Err. prof. rel.	Firmicus Maternus, *De errore profanarum religionum*
Exc.	Ambrose, *De excessu fratris sui Satyri*; Clement of Alexandria, *Excerpta ex Theodoto*
Flor.	Apuleius, *Florida*
Fort. Rom.	Plutarch, *De fortuna Romanorum*
Frag.	*Fragment(s)*
Fug.	Tertullian, *De fuga in persecutione*
Gos. Phil.	Gospel of Philip
Gos. Thom.	Gospel of Thomas
Hab. virg.	Cyprian, *De habitu virginum*
Haer.	Hippolytus, *Refutatio omnium haeresium*; Irenaeus, *Adversus haereses*
Hec.	Euripides, *Hecuba*
Hel.	Euripides, *Helena*
Her.	Philo, *Quis rerum divinarum heres sit*
Herm.	Shepherd of Hermas
Hist.	Herodotus, *Historiae*
Hist. eccl.	Eusebius, *Historia ecclesiastica*
Hist. rom.	Appian, *Historia romana*; Velleius Paterculus, *Historia romana*; Dio Cassius, *Historia romana*
Hom.	*Homilia(e)*
Hom. 1 Thess.	John Chrysostom, *Homiliae in epistulam i ad Thessalonicenses*
Hom. 2 Thess.	John Chrysostom, *Homiliae in epistulam ii ad Thessalonicenses*
Hom. cat.	Theodore of Mopsuestia, *Homiliae catecheticae*
Hom. Col.	John Chrysostom, *Homiliae in epistulam ad Colossenses*
Hom. Gen.	John Chrysostom, *Homiliae in Genesim*
Hom. Heb.	John Chrysostom, *Homiliae in epistulam ad Hebraeos*
Hom. Jo.	John Chrysostom, *Homiliae in Joannem*
Hom. Matt.	John Chrysostom, *Homiliae in Matthaeum*
Hom. Mel.	John Chrysostom, *Homily on Meletius*
Hom. Pass. Res.	[Evodius of Rome], *Homily on the Passion and Resurrection*
Hymn. Ep.	Ephrem, *Hymni de Epiphania*
Hymn. fid.	Ephrem, *Hymni de fide*
Hymn. ieiun.	Ephrem, *Hymni de ieiunio*
Hymn. nat.	Ephrem, *Hymni de nativitate*
Hymn. virg.	Ephrem, *Hymni de virginitate*

Idol.	Tertullian, *De idololatria*
Inc.	Athanasius, *De incarnatione*
Inst.	Calvin, *Institutes of the Christian Religion*
Instr. adv. gent.	Commodian, *Instructiones adversus gentium deos*
Invest. Abbat.	Investiture of Abbaton
IsP	[Hippolytus], *Paschal Homily*
Jupp. trag.	Lucian, *Juppiter tragoedus*
L	Martyrium Andraea Laudatio
Laps.	Cyprian, *De lapsis*
Laz.	John Chrysostom, *De Lazaro*
Leg.	Athenagoras, *Legatio pro Christianis*; Philo, *Legum allegoriae*; Plato, *Leges*
LXX	Septuagint
M	Martyrium Andreae prius
Mand.	Shepherd of Hermas, Mandate(s)
Marc.	Seneca the Younger, *Ad Marciam de consolatione*; Tertullian, *Adversus Marcionem*
Maxim.	Augustine, *Contra Maximinum Arianum*
Melet.	John Chrysostom, *De sancto Meletio Antiocheno*
Metam.	Apuleius, *Metamorphoses*
Mor. ecc.	Augustine, *De moribus ecclesiae catholicae*
MT	Masoretic Text
Nat.	Arnobius, *Adversus nationes*; Tertullian, *Ad nationes*
Noct. att.	Aulus Gellius, *Noctes atticae*
NRSV	New Revised Standard Version
Ob. Val.	Ambrose, *De obitu Valentianiani consolatio*
Oct.	Minucius Felix, *Octavius*
Off.	Ambrose, *De officiis ministrorum*
Or.	Gregory of Nazianzus, *Orationes*; Tertullian, *De oratione*
Or. Melet.	Gregory of Nyssa, *Oration on Meletius*
Paed.	Clement of Alexandria, *Paedagogus*
Paen.	Tertullian, *De paenitentia*
Pan.	Epiphanius, *Panarion (Adversus haereses)*
Pass. Perp.	The Passion of Perpetua and Felicity
P.Beatty	Kenyon, F. G., ed. *Chester Beatty Biblical Papyri*. London, 1933–1941.
P.Berol.	Papyrus Berolinensis. Ägyptisches Museum and Papyrussammlung, Staatliche Museen, Berlin

P.Bodmer	*Papyrus Bodmer*. Cologne: Bibliotheca Bodmeriana, 1954–1998.
Pirqe R. El.	Pirqe Rabbi Eliezer
P.Leipz.	Wessely, C., ed. *Die griechischen Papyri der Leipziger Universitätsbibliothek*. Leipzig, 1885.
Pol. *Phil.*	Polycarp, *To the Philippians*
Post.	Philo, *De posteritate Caini*
P.Oxy.	*The Oxyrhynchus Papyri*. Published by the Egypt Exploration Society in Graeco-Roman Memoirs. London, 1898–2010.
Praep. Ev.	Eusebius, *Praeparatio evangelica*
Praescr.	Tertullian, *De praescriptione haereticorum*
Princ.	Origen, *De principiis*
Protrep.	Clement of Alexandria, *Protrepticus*
Pud.	Tertullian, *De pudicitia*
Rep.	Cicero, *De republica*
Rerum nat.	Lucretius, *De rerum natura*
Sacr.	Ambrose, *De sacramentis*; Philo, *De sacrificiis Abelis et Caini*
Sent. Pyth.	Sententiae Pythagoreorum
Serm.	Augustine, *Sermones*
Shabb.	Shabbat
Sib. Or.	Sibylline Oracles
Sim.	Shepherd of Hermas, Similitude(s)
Sol.	Plutarch, *Solon*
Somn.	Philo, *De somniis*
Spect.	Tertullian, *De spectaculis*
Stat.	John Chrysostom, *Ad populam Antiochenum de statuis*
Strom.	Clement of Alexandria, *Stromateis*
Syn. libr.	Galen, *Synopsis librorum suorum de pulsibus*
Test.	Cyprian, *Ad Quirinum testimonia adversus Judaeos*
Theod. laps.	John Chrysostom, *Ad Theodorum lapsum*
Trin.	Augustine, *De Trinitate*
Unit. eccl.	Cyprian, *De catholicae ecclesiae unitate*
Ven.	Galen, *De venae sectione adversus Erasistratum*
Ver. rel.	Augustine, *De vera religione*
Virg.	Gregory of Nyssa, *De virginitate*
Vis.	Shepherd of Hermas, Vision(s)

Vit. Const.	Eusebius, *Vita Constantini*
Vulg.	Vulgate

Secondary Sources

AB	Anchor Bible
AC	*Arte Cristiana*
ActaCl	*Acta Classica*
ACW	Ancient Christian Writers
AH	*Artibus et Historiae*
AJA	*American Journal of Archaeology*
AJEC	Ancient Judaism and Early Christianity
AMCMRE	Art and Material Culture in Medieval and Renaissance Europe
ANF	Roberts, Alexander, and James Donaldson, eds. *The Ante-Nicene Fathers: Translations of the Writings of the Fathers Down to A.D. 325*. 10 vols. Repr., Peabody, MA: Hendrickson, 1994.
ANRW	Temporini, Hildegard, and Wolfgang Haase, eds. *Aufstieg und Niedergang der römischen Welt: Geschichte und Kultur Roms im Spiegel der neueren Forschung*. Part 2, *Principat*. Berlin: de Gruyter, 1972–.
ArtBul	*Art Bulletin*
ASR	Robert, Carl, Friedrich Matz, Gerhart Rodenwaldt, and Bernard Andreae, eds. *Die antiken Sarkophagreliefs*. Berlin: Manns, 1890–.
AT	*Antiquité Tardive*
AThR	*Anglican Theological Review*
AYBRL	Anchor Yale Bible Reference Library
BA	*Biblical Archaeologist*
BAC	Biblioteca de autores cristianos
BAC	*Bullettino di Archeologia Cristiana*
BCMA	*The Bulletin of the Cleveland Museum of Art*
BibInt	*Biblical Interpretation*
BM	*The Burlington Magazine*
BMCat	Walker, Susan. *Catalogue of Roman Sarcophagi in the British Museum*. London: British Museum Publications, 1990.
BollS	Bollingen Series

BSHJ	Baltimore Studies in the History of Judaism
CCARB	*Corsi di culture sull'arte Ravennate e Bizantina*
CCSA	Corpus Christianorum: Series Apocryphorum
CCSL	Corpus Christianorum: Series Latina
CEJL	Commentaries on Early Jewish Literature
CH	*Church History*
CHC	The Cambridge History of Christianity
CIL	Corpus Inscriptionum Latinarum
CR	*Christian Reflection*
CRBR	*Critical Review of Books in Religion*
CS	Cistercian Studies
CTC	Christian Theology in Context
CWS	Classics of Western Spirituality
DOML	Dumbarton Oaks Medieval Library
DOP	*Dumbarton Oaks Papers*
DOS	Dumbarton Oaks Studies
DRev	*Downside Review*
ECA	Eastern Christian Art
ECR	Eastern Churches Review
EDB	Epigraphic Database Bari. www.edb.uniba.it
EichstBeit	Eichstätter Beiträge
EL	*Ephemerides Liturgicae*
EpigA	Epigrafia e Antichità
EstBib	*Estudios bíblicos*
ExpTim	*Expository Times*
FC	Fathers of the Church
GBA	*Gazette des Beaux-Arts*
GCS	Die griechischen christlichen Schriftsteller der ersten [drei] Jahrhunderte
GD	Gorgias Dissertations
GN	*Geldgeschichtliche Nachrichten*
GR	*Greece and Rome*
GRBS	*Greek, Roman, and Byzantine Studies*
HabD	Habelts Dissertationsdrucke
HCSPTH	Holy Cross Studies in Patristic Theology and History
HdA	Handbuch der Archäologie
HDLLA	Handbuch der Lateinischen Literatur der Antike
HDR	Harvard Dissertations in Religion
HespSup	Hesperia Supplements

HSCP	*Harvard Studies in Classical Philology*
HTR	*Harvard Theological Review*
HTS	Harvard Theological Studies
ICUR	Rossi, Giovanni B. de, ed. *Inscriptiones christianae urbis Romae*. Rome: Officina Libraria Pontificia, 1857–1888.
IGER	Istituto grafico editoriale romano
IJHA	*International Journal of Historical Archeology*
IJRR	*Interdisciplinary Journal for Research on Religion*
JAC	*Jahrbuch für Antike und Christentum*
JAJ	*Journal of Ancient Judaism*
JBL	*Journal of Biblical Literature*
JBRec	*Journal of the Bible and Its Reception*
JECS	*Journal of Early Christian Studies*
JJMJS	*Journal of the Jesus Movement in Its Jewish Setting*
JL	Jerome Lectures
JÖB	*Jahrbuch der Österreichischen Byzantinistik*
JRA	*Journal of Roman Archaeology*
JRASup	Supplements to the Journal of Roman Archaeology
JRS	*Journal of Roman Studies*
JSJ	*Journal for the Study of Judaism in the Persian, Hellenistic, and Roman Period*
JSSSup	Supplements to the Journal of Semitic Studies
JTS	*Journal of Theological Studies*
LCL	Loeb Classical Library
LCPM	Letture Cristiane del Primo Millennio
LIMC	Ackerman, H. Christoph, and Jean-Robert Gisler, ed. *Lexicon Iconographicum Mythologiae Classicae*. 8 vols. Zurich: Artemis, 1981–1997.
LiSt	Liturgical Studies
LitTh	*Literature & Theology*
LNTS	The Library of New Testament Studies
LSJ	Liddell, Henry George, Robert Scott, Henry Stuart Jones. *A Greek-English Lexicon*. 9th ed. with revised supplement. Oxford: Clarendon, 1996
MEFR	*Mélanges de l'école française de Rome*
MFA	Monographs on the Fine Arts
MNTA	*More New Testament Apocrypha*
ModTheol	*Modern Theology*
NovT	*Novum Testamentum*

NovTSup	Supplements to Novum Testamentum
NPNF	Schaff, Philip, and Henry Wace, eds. *A Select Library of Nicene and Post-Nicene Fathers of the Christian Church*. 28 vols. in 2 series. Repr., Peabody, MA: Hendrickson, 1994.
NTApoc	Schneemelcher, Wilhelm, ed. *New Testament Apocrypha*. 2 vols. Rev. ed. English trans. ed. Robert McL. Wilson. Cambridge: Clarke; Louisville: Westminster John Knox, 2003.
NTOA	Novum Testamentum et Orbis Antiquus
NTS	*New Testament Studies*
NumC	*Numismatic Chronicle*
Numen	*Numen: International Review for the History of Religions*
OECT	Oxford Early Christian Texts
OGI	Dittenberger, Wilhelm, ed. *Orientis Graeci Inscriptiones Selectae*. 2 vols. Leipzig: Hitzel, 1903–1905.
OTM	Oxford Theological Monographs
OTP	Charlesworth, James H., ed. *Old Testament Pseudepigrapha*. 2 vols. New York: Doubleday, 1983, 1985.
PG	Migne, J.-P., ed. Patrologia Graeca. 162 vols. Paris, 1857–1886.
PL	Migne, J.-P., ed. Patrologia Latina. 217 vols. Paris, 1844–1855.
PMS	Patristic Monograph Series
PPS	Popular Patristics Series
ProEccl	*Pro Ecclesia*
PRSt	*Perspectives in Religious Studies*
RechAug	*Recherches augustiniennes*
Rep.	Deichmann, Friedrich Wilhelm, ed. *Repertorium der christlich-antiken Sarkophage*. 5 vols. Wiesbaden: Steiner, 1967–2018.
RIC	Roman Imperial Coinage
RS	Koch, Guntram, and Hellmut Sichtermann. *Römische Sarkophage*. HdA. Munich: Beck, 1982.
RSECW	Routledge Studies in the Early Christian World
SAAA	Studies on the Apocryphal Acts of the Apostles
SacEr	*Sacris Eruditi: Jaarboek voor Godsdienstwetenschappen*
SAŠ	*Studia Academica Šumenensia*
SBA	*Studies in the Bible and Antiquity*

SBLTT	Society of Biblical Literature Texts and Translations
ScRel	*Sciences Religieuses*
SCS	Septuagint and Cognate Studies
SD	Studies and Documents
SEG	Supplementum epigraphicum graecum
SFC	Selections from the Fathers of the Church
SFCBKEJ	Spätantike-Frühes Christentum-Byzanz Kunst im Ersten Jahrtausend, Reihe B, Studien und Perspektiven
SHCT	Studies in the History of Christian Thought
SNTSMS	Society for New Testament Studies Monograph Series
SP	Sacra Pagina
SPap	*Studies Papyrologica*
SPMed	Studia Patristica Mediolanensia
SR	*Studies in Religion*
StLit	*Studia Liturgica*
StPatr	Studia Patristica
StudRom	*Studi romani*
SUNT	Studien zur Umwelt des Neuen Testaments
TC	Traditio Christiana
TENTS	Texts and Editions for New Testament Study
ThTo	*Theology Today*
TLG	Berkowitz, Luci, and Karl A. Squitier, eds. *Thesaurus Linguae Graecae: Canon of Greek Authors and Works.* 3rd ed. New York: Oxford University Press, 1990.
TU	Texte und Untersuchungen
TUGAL	Texte und Untersuchungen zur Geschichte der altchristlichen Literatur
TZ	*Theologische Zeitschrift*
VC	*Vigiliae Christianae*
VCSup	Supplements to Vigiliae Christianae
VP	*Vox Patrum*
WGRW	Writings from the Greco Roman World
WS	Woodbrooke Studies
WSA	Works of Saint Augustine: A Translation for the Twenty-First Century
WUNT	Wissenschaftliche Untersuchungen zum Neuen Testament
ZTK	*Zeitschrift für Theologie und Kirche*

Interpreting Select Early Sculptures Using Art-Historical Methodology

Heidi J. Hornik

Introduction

For nearly thirty years, using art-historical methodology in the study of biblical art has been an interest of mine. Art historians, using a formal and content analysis of Christian art, frequently discuss and interpret the religious symbolism and narrative present in a work of art or narrative program. In this analysis, the object is situated in its cultural, political, social, historical, and religious contexts. Art-historical methodology also includes identifying sources and precedents. This is usually implemented through the comparison and contrast of objects. Biblical scholars usually seek a visual depiction of the scriptural text in sculpture or painting and often do not discuss the methodology outlined above.

Introduction to the Visual Arts

Entry-level art history courses often begin with a discussion of "Art and the Human Artist." What sets us apart as a critical-thinking species? Imagination, creativity, originality, meaning and style, self-expression and the audience, and tastes (likes and dislikes). Providing these human characteristics fosters agreement and recognition of the need to identify the abilities and talents of the individuals who create the works being studied. There is a way to look at art in an informed and critical manner by analyzing two areas (formal elements and content). Form consists of line, color, composition, light, shape, size, and medium. Content considers provenance (known or presumed locations), meaning, historical and social context, iconography of symbolism, and function. A formalist approach only considers the first area, and although it is the easiest way to begin a discussion of an image that is plopped into a discussion of biblical art, it is naive and superficial. Art historians organize works of art in styles. A style refers to the distinctive patterns or characteristics of some one thing (music, clothing, etc.). Art historians use style to place objects in a scheme or context and explain change. It is an important tool for allowing the art historian in the present to order past events. This leads to the zeitgeist or the spirit of the age of cultural values. These may coincide with historical periods (early Christian, medieval) or with movements within art (Renaissance, Impressionism).

Application of Art-Historical Methodology

The intention of this essay is to demonstrate how well-known Early Christian objects may be discussed using an art-historical methodology that includes an analysis of form and content with attention to sources and precedents through comparison and contrast. There are certainly more biblically informed discussions of the Good Shepherd, the Jonah story, and Christ teaching in published scholarship.[1] Here readers will find suggestions for teaching and research that cross disciplines.

The *Jonah Marbles*: A Group of Eleven Sculptures

Provenance and Origin

The Cleveland Museum of Art acquired eleven late Roman small marble sculptures and busts in 1965 (fig. 1.1).[2] Often objects from the early

---

1. This study is a continuation of my work on these objects, published as Heidi J. Hornik, "Freestanding Sculpture," in *Routledge Handbook of Early Christian Art*, ed. Robin M. Jensen and Mark D. Ellison (London: Routledge, 2018), 73–85.

2. Cleveland Museum of Art Object Files, reviewed 5 April 2017. Special thanks to Amanda Mikolic, curatorial assistant for medieval art, Cleveland Museum of Art, for allowing me to consult the museum's object files on all of the *Jonah Marbles*. The references included in this article are germane. They are a small representation of the voluminous scholarship published on the *Jonah Marbles*. For information related to the location of the marble, see the unpublished thesis by Donald A. McColl, "Early Christian Sculptures at Cleveland in Their Eastern Mediterranean Context" (MA thesis, Oberlin College, 1991); and McColl, "Signs of the Times: The Cleveland Marbles," Dumbarton Oaks, https://tinyurl.com/SBL4830a.

Fig. 1.1. *Jonah Marbles*. Cleveland Museum of Art, Cleveland, Ohio. Photograph by author.

Christian period have an unknown provenance and specific function, which, as defined above, would be considered part of the content discussion, but scientific and technical analysis (form) assists with that. Four of these sculptures depict specific events from the Jonah narratives and have become collectively known as the *Jonah Marbles*. There are three pairs of portrait busts of a Roman aristocratic couple and one sculpture of a youthful sheep-bearer that iconographically represents Christ. Although neither the exact location nor the place of production is known, it is believed that the eleven pieces were found buried together in a large pithos (jar). Technical analysis identified the source of the highly crystalline white marble as from the Roman imperial quarries at Dokimeion in ancient Phrygia (near the modern city of Afyon, Turkey).[3]

Function

The Cleveland Museum also suggests that these objects may have been situated in a funerary context given the popularity of the Jonah narrative as one of hope, salvation, and the redemptive powers of prayer and repentance. Another plausible possibility is that they decorated the home or garden of an affluent Christian Roman family. The Roman Gallery at the University of Pennsylvania Museum has recreated a villa from the fourth

---

3. William D. Wixom, "Early Christian Sculptures at Cleveland," *BCMA* (1967): 67–88; Wolfgang Wischmeyer, "Die vorkonstantinische christliche Kunst in neuem Licht. Die Cleveland-Statuetten," *VC* 35 (1981): 253–87; Cleveland Museum of Art Object Files.

century incorporating sculptures into fountains and atria.[4] Scholars debate the function of the *Jonah Marbles*, but recent studies argue that the group may have originally formed a domestic fountain group.[5] There are documented examples of marble sculptures in fountains, domestic and public, between 200 and 400 CE.[6] Eusebius writes a description of "fountains in the midst of the marketplace graced with figures of the Good Shepherd … and Daniel in the Lion's Den" in his biography of Constantine (*Vit. Const.* 3.49 [*NPNF* 2/1]). In the case of both the Jonah and Daniel narratives, Christians took Jewish Scriptures and gave them a christological focus. The water theme of the *Jonah Marbles* would have been appropriate to a fountain setting in a domestic garden.[7] The gardens in this period were places where family would take meals and congregate. Stephen N. Fliegel believes that the gardens were the focal point for piety in a variety of forms, so it is not difficult to imagine the *Jonah Marbles* in such a context.[8]

Portrait Busts

The same aristocratic couple appears in the three pairs of marble portrait busts (fig. 1.2). There are variations in their garments but not identifiable differences in age. It is believed that these busts were found together with the *Jonah Marbles* and that they represent the Christian patrons who commissioned the entire sculpture group.[9] Further study is needed to situate

---

4. Robert Milburn, *Early Christian Art and Architecture* (Berkeley: University of California Press, 1988), 80. For the Penn Museum Roman Gallery, see "Rome Gallery," Penn Museum, https://tinyurl.com/SBL4830b.

5. Stephen N. Fliegel, *A Higher Contemplation: Sacred Meaning in the Christian Art of the Middle Ages* (Kent, OH: Kent State University Press, 2012), 23, 191.

6. For more on this, see Brenda Longfellow, *Roman Imperialism and Civic Patronage: Form, Meaning, and Ideology in Monumental Fountain Complexes* (Cambridge: Cambridge University Press, 2011); Elisabeth Blair MacDougall and Wilhelmina F. Jashemski, eds., *Ancient Roman Gardens*, Dumbarton Oaks Colloquium on the History of Landscape Architecture VII (Washington, DC: Dumbarton Oaks, 1981); Elisabeth Blair MacDougall, ed., *Ancient Roman Villa Gardens*, Dumbarton Oaks Colloquium on the History of Landscape Architecture X (Washington, DC: Dumbarton Oaks, 1987).

7. For a model of a Roman villa with a fountain at the Penn Museum, see https://www.flickr.com/photos/leonandloisphotos/8458733151.

8. Fliegel, *Higher Contemplation*, 23.

9. See "Portrait Bust of an Aristocratic Man," Cleveland Museum of Art, https://tinyurl.com/SBL4830c; "Portrait Bust of an Aristocratic Woman," Cleveland Museum

Fig. 1.2. *Three Pairs of Portrait Busts of an Aristocratic Couple*, 280–290 CE. Asia Minor. Marble, ca. 33.4 x 18.5 x 10.7 cm. The Cleveland Museum of Art, John L. Severance Fund 1965.242–247. Photograph by the Cleveland Museum of Art.

these sculptures in the history of Roman busts.[10] This article focuses on the methodology applied to Christian-themed sculptures during the period.

Good Shepherd: Formal Analysis

Form

The *Good Shepherd* marble (fig. 1.3) is a small statuette, 19.5 x 10.25 x 6.375 inches. Beginning with a discussion of form, it should be noted that this is part of a visual type sharing common compositional traits such as being youthful, beardless, and having sheep draped over the shoulders. There are twenty-six extant marbles depicting the Good Shepherd. He wears a low-waisted tunic and holds the sheep with his left hand. The figure stands in *contrapposto*, a counterpoised body position created by the Greeks in the fifth century BCE. The *Doryphorus* (fig. 1.4) by Polykleitos is a life-size Roman marble copy of a Greek bronze original that had numerous copies and represents one example of the many sculptures in the *contrapposto* stance. It is a precedent for this sculpture and was a very likely source for

---

of Art, https://tinyurl.com/SBL4830d; "Portrait Bust of an Aristocratic Woman," Cleveland Museum of Art, https://tinyurl.com/SBL4830e; "Portrait Bust of an Aristocratic Man," Cleveland Museum of Art, https://tinyurl.com/SBL4830f; "Portrait Bust of an Aristocratic Woman," Cleveland Museum of Art, https://tinyurl.com/SBL4830g; "Portrait Bust of an Aristocratic Man," Cleveland Museum of Art, https://tinyurl.com/SBL4830h.

10. Nancy Ramage and Andrew Ramage, *Roman Art* (London: Pearson, 2014); Paul Zanker, *Roman Portraits* (New York: Metropolitan Museum of Art, 2016); Diana E. E. Kleiner, *Roman Art* (New Haven: Yale University Press, 1994).

Fig. 1.3. *Good Shepherd*, 280–290 CE. Asia Minor. Marble, 49.5 x 26 x 16.2 cm. Cleveland Museum of Art, John L. Severance Fund 1965.241. Photograph by Cleveland Museum of Art.

Fig. 1.4. *Doryphorus (Spear Bearer)*. Roman copy after Greek bronze original of ca. 450–440 BCE, by Polykleitos. Marble, 2 m. Source: public domain.

the artist. Three small sheep and a tree trunk are visible at the base of the sculpture. The unique qualities of this work include the use of a drill to add contrast of light and dark in the hair. This is a technical element shared by all the *Jonah Marbles* in Cleveland.

Sources and Precedents—Visual and Literary

The composition of the Good Shepherd can be discussed through comparing other contemporary works of art in painting and sculpture. *The Good Shepherd* fresco (fig. 1.5) in the catacomb of Saint Callixtus, Rome, also shows a male figure in *contrapposto* with a shepherd being carried across his shoulders. Another Roman catacomb fresco, Saints Pietro e Marcellino (fig. 1.6), also depicts a Good Shepherd figure (partially destroyed) in a roundel. What is quite interesting for this discussion is that four arms radiate from that roundel and culminate in four lunette (semicircular) shapes, each with a scene from the story of Jonah.

How does one explain the inclusion of the Christ figure as the Good Shepherd in these fresco paintings? This moves briefly to content. Early Christians interpreted Old Testament prophecies and events as announcing and prefiguring the ministry of Jesus or the church. What unites the Christ/Good Shepherd type with Jonah in the paintings and in the *Jonah Marbles*? Early Christian interpretation of the book of Jonah was inspired by Jesus's mysterious rebuke of some religious leaders demanding a prophetic sign: "You know how to interpret the appearance of the sky," Jesus warned them, "but you cannot interpret the signs of the times. An evil and adulterous generation asks for a sign, but no sign will be given to it except the sign of Jonah" (Matt 16:3–4).[11] In another passage, Jesus elaborates this typology by identifying his own ministry as the fulfillment of the sign of Jonah: "For just as Jonah was three days and three nights in the belly of the sea monster [Jonah 2:1], so for three days and three nights the Son of Man will be in the heart of the earth. The people of Nineveh will rise up at the judgment with this generation and condemn it, because they repented at the proclamation of Jonah, and see, something greater than Jonah is here!" (Matt 12:40–41; see Luke 11:29–32).

Another possible source for the Good Shepherd may be the Greek Hermes Criophorus figure; often he was shown bringing an offering to the

---

11. Unless otherwise noted, all biblical translations follow the NRSV.

Fig. 1.5. *The Good Shepherd*, third century CE. Mural. Catacomb of Saint Callixtus, Rome. Source: Public domain.

Fig. 1.6. *The Good Shepherd with Jonah and the Whale*, fourth century CE. Mural. Catacomb of Saints Pietro e Marcellino, Rome. Photograph by author.

altar, and, by the third century CE, he represented the ram bearer with its connotations of philanthropy and loving care.[12] Its adoption by Christians would probably have passed unnoticed by pagan neighbors.[13]

The literary source for the Good Shepherd appears in John 10:11–16, but it is more likely derived from the detailed passage in Luke 15:4–7:

> Which one of you, having a hundred sheep and losing one of them, does not leave the ninety-nine in the wilderness and go after the one that is lost until he finds it? When he has found it, he lays it on his shoulders and rejoices. And when he comes home, he calls together his friends and neighbors, saying to them, "Rejoice with me, for I have found my sheep that was lost." Just so, I tell you, there will be more joy in heaven over one sinner who repents than over ninety-nine righteous persons who need no repentance.

Content

A visual representation of Christ as the Good Shepherd bore rich meaning for early Christians during times of persecution because it symbolized a leader who would sacrifice his life for his flock; yet, as an already popular image among non-Christians, it did not draw attention to the persecuted believers.[14] Later, after the peace brought by Emperor Constantine in 306 CE, the Good Shepherd became the most popular symbol of Jesus Christ.

Four Sculptures from the Jonah Story: Formal Analysis

Introduction

There are four symbolic sculptures depicting events in the book of Jonah: *Jonah Swallowed* (fig. 1.7), *Jonah Praying to God* (fig. 1.8), *Jonah Cast Up* (fig. 1.9), and *Jonah under the Gourd Vine* (fig. 1.10). The thematic content of the *Jonah Marbles* can be found in the writing of Abraham Heschel, the great Jewish scholar. Heschel points out that Hebrew prophets were

---

12. "Hermes Kriophoros," World History Encyclopedia, https://tinyurl.com/SBL4830i.

13. Fliegel, *Higher Contemplation*, 20. For a discussion of Orpheus as a pagan source for the Good Shepherd type, see Hornik, "Freestanding Sculpture," 78.

14. For a discussion of the image of God as a shepherd watching over his flock, see Hornik, "Freestanding Sculpture," 79.

both *foretellers* and *forthtellers*, that is, their prophetic ministry included a predictive aspect of telling what God would do in the future (foretelling) as well as a social aspect wherein the prophet exposed the injustices of society (forthtelling).[15] Jonah was a reluctant prophet of God who initially rejected God's command to be foreteller and forthteller to the residents of Nineveh. His disobedience led him to spend three days in the belly of a whale before he finally, though still half-heartedly, agreed to deliver God's message to the residents of Nineveh.

Form, Sources, and Precedents

As freestanding sculptures, the *Jonah Marbles* are rare. All the figures are finished except for *Jonah under the Gourd Vine* (fig. 1.10) and were therefore probably seen in the round. The artist sculpted a *ketos*, or Greek sea monster, that is part land animal and part fish.[16] Its hybridity adds to its repulsiveness. The early Christian artist likely borrowed from the *ketea* found in Greek and Roman sculptures, wall paintings, and mosaics, but found a new narrative in which the sea monster could function. In *Jonah Swallowed* (fig. 1.7), the "large fish" (Jonah 1:17) is terrifying with a monstrous body, recoiling back on itself with its tail high above its head. This strong vertical representation, combined with the circularity of the two forms, helps to identify the two figures as one. The upper half of Jonah's body has disappeared into the body of the monster. Jonah's extended legs are placed side by side with thighs, knees, feet, and toes touching and parallel. This leg positioning creates a symmetrical form in an almost balletic pose. It certainly is a very graceful way of being swallowed. The sea monster has two front legs that resemble the paws of a lion, while the right rear leg is visible alongside the fish tail. The ears and snout of the monster are pronounced and alert like that of a boar. It may also have wings of a bird. There is a strange protrusion (another leg?) from the lower jaw–neckline area that is attached to the marble base between the paws. The two figures are united much like the mythological centaur. The centaur has the upper body of a man and the lower body of a horse.

---

15. Abraham J. Heschel, *The Prophets*, 2 vols. (New York: Harper & Row, 1962), 1:xii.

16. John Boardman, "'Very Like a Whale'—Classical Sea Monsters," in *Monsters and Demons in the Ancient and Medieval Worlds*, ed. Ann E. Farkas, Prudence O. Harperm and Evelyn B. Harrison (Mainz: von Zabern, 1987), 73–84.

Interpreting Select Early Sculptures

Fig. 1.7. *Jonah Swallowed*, 280–290 CE. Asia Minor. Marble, 50.4 x 15.5 x 26.9 cm. Cleveland Museum of Art, John L. Severance Fund 1965.237. Photograph by Cleveland Museum of Art.

Fig. 1.8. *Jonah Praying to God*, 280–290 CE. Asia Minor. Marble, 47.5 x 14.8 x 20.3 cm. Cleveland Museum of Art, John L. Severance Fund 1965.240. Photograph by Cleveland Museum of Art.

Fig. 1.9. *Jonah Cast Up*, 280–290 CE. Asia Minor. Marble, 41.5 x 36 x 18.5 cm. Cleveland Museum of Art, John L. Severance Fund 1965.238. Photograph by Cleveland Museum of Art.

Fig. 1.10. *Jonah under the Gourd Vine*, 280–90 CE. Asia Minor. Marble, 32.3 x 46.3 x 18 cm. Cleveland Museum of Art, John L. Severance Fund 1965.239. Photograph by Cleveland Museum of Art.

In the third scene in the narrative, *Jonah Cast Up* (fig. 1.9), there is a visual complement to *Jonah Swallowed*. In this sculpture, Jonah emerges from the same monster. The circular composition is now stretched more laterally than the strong vertical orientation of *Jonah Swallowed*. Jonah is bearded and raises his hands above his head as his abdomen is clearly still clenched by the teeth of the monster. Once again there is a protrusion from the right side of the head of the monster. Now it appears to be coming out of the cheek instead of jaw or neck. The right rear leg is now beneath the front leg. The fur that unites the animal body with the tail of the fish is more pronounced and almost looks like a wing. The tail of the fish wraps up and over itself and almost touches Jonah's right hand.

There is no sculpture depicting Jonah inside the belly of the monster. That would be a quite difficult subject to portray. Instead one imagines what happens in the belly of the monster. This evokes the second scene of the narrative, *Jonah Praying to God* (fig. 1.8). The sculptor portrays the sole figure of Jonah in the gesture of an orant, with arms outstretched and palms up, as he prays to God for deliverance. He has the same bearded face and hairstyle as in the other sculptures. The sculptor has created a Jonah type that viewers recognize. Jonah maintains the *contrapposto* stance, as seen in the *Good Shepherd* marble (fig. 1.3), evoking a figure at rest. Although one might think there would be anxiety while trapped in the monster, Jonah's calm demeanor and body position offer a reminder of the calming and saving power of prayer as well as the intensity of Jonah's devotion to God through prayer. He is a believer.

In *Jonah under the Gourd Vine* (fig. 1.10), the prophet reclines and relaxes. He raises his right arm over his head, while the left arm supports his weight as he leans on his side. A thematic source might be Endymion, the shepherd boy in Greek mythology who slept eternally underneath a tree. Endymion symbolized repose, peace, and well-being. Here Jonah has received peace and rests in the calm after the events of the story. Beneath a creeping gourd, which symbolized resurrection in Roman art, Jonah contemplates the miracle of his salvation. The bearded Jonah wears the same tunic as in the marble showing him praying to God (fig. 1.8).

Art-historical methodology also allows consideration of objects that include shared sources with those being discussed. The body position recalls river-god types known throughout the Greek and Roman world. This type was revived during the Italian Renaissance, when artists returned to Greek and Roman sculptures for sources and precedents. Michelangelo

(1475–1564) sculpted a *Study for a River God* (fig. 1.11), in marble, circa 1526–1527. Raphael (1483–1520) modified this reclining type by placing the figure on steps, holding a folio in the *School of Athens* (fig. 1.12), a fresco in the Vatican papal apartments painted circa 1515–1517. This transforms the river-god type into a Diogenes figure (named after the philosopher he is believed to portray), which served as a source for numerous later artists.[17]

It is possible to consider the marbles as one compositional narrative with message and movement. The *Good Shepherd*, *Jonah Praying to God*, and *Jonah under the Gourd Vine* convey a sense of relaxation, meditation, and prayer, in contrast to the scenes with the fish (*Jonah Swallowed* and *Jonah Cast Up*), which are heightened in drama and action. This alternation of action and calm reflects the biblical story and creates a narrative flow among the five marbles.

Fig. 1.11. Michelangelo, *Study for a River God*, ca. 1526–1527. Clay, earth, sand, plant and animal fibers, and casein model built around iron wire core, 64 x 140 x 70 cm. Accademia delle Arti del Disegno, Florence. Photograph by author.

---

17. See Alice Correia, "*Reclining Figure* 1951 by Henry Moore OM, CH," catalogue entry, January 2014, in *Henry Moore: Sculptural Process and Public Identity* (Tate Research Publication, 2015), https://tinyurl.com/SBL4830j.

Fig. 1.12. Raphael, Diogenes figure, *School of Athens*, ca. 1515–1517. Fresco. Vatican papal apartments, Rome. Source: public domain.

The forceful regurgitation of Jonah indicates the power of God as Jonah is expelled from the sea monster. The force is not Jonah's alone but rather God's action in answer to Jonah's prayers.

Content, Meaning, Significance

The christological interpretation of the Jonah story mentioned above in the discussion of the Good Shepherd continued in the patristic period. In a letter to Deogratias in 409 CE, Augustine expounds on the Jesus/Jonah typology:

> As to the question, what was prefigured by the sea monster restoring alive on the third day the prophet whom it swallowed? Why is this asked of us, when Christ Himself has given the answer.... As, therefore, Jonah passed from the ship to the belly of the whale, so Christ passed from the cross to the sepulchre, or into the abyss of death. And as Jonah suffered this for the sake of those who were endangered by the storm, so Christ suffered for the sake of those who are tossed on the waves of this world. And as the command was given at first that the word of God should be preached to the Ninevites by Jonah, but the preaching of Jonah did not come to them until

after the whale had vomited him forth, so prophetic teaching was addressed early to the Gentiles, but did not actually come to the Gentiles until after the resurrection of Christ from the grave. (*Ep.* 102 [*NPNF* 1/1, par. 34])

In the *Jonah Marbles* we glimpse Christian life before its official acceptance in the Roman Empire. When, during the third and early fourth centuries, Christians were threatened by persecution and death, they found hope in the sign of Jonah, which promised life would follow death. The parallels between the three-day period of Jonah in the fish and Jesus in the tomb allowed believers to understand the prophecy of Jonah in a new way, as pointing toward the resurrected Christ, who was their shepherd and savior.

After Christianity became an accepted religion in the empire by the Edict of Milan in 313, artists also portrayed Christ as a Caesar, with royal attributes such as a halo, purple robe, and throne. This type became known as Christos Pantokrator. A separation occurred between Jonah and Christ in the visual art and theology of Christianity. As Christ became more regal, the popularity of Jonah's story decreased significantly. Perhaps the concerns of the Christians expanded from uncertainty about their own death, which had been a very real issue during the early centuries, to the eternal kingdom of God after resurrection. Jonah's words were not less important to this next generation of Christians, but Christ's triumphant rule over the powers became prevalent.[18]

Christ Teaching: Formal Analysis

Form

The marble, known as *Christ Teaching* or *Cristo Docente* (fig. 1.13), whose provenance is unknown, is housed in the Museo Nazionale (Palazzo Massimo) in Rome. The sculpture has been dated to the second century based on style and was originally referred to as the "seated poetess."[19]

The seated figure wears contemporary Roman dress and holds a scroll in his left hand. He has youthful, delicate, and somewhat effeminate facial features. His soft, curly hair falls to the shoulders. He wears an undergown as well as a mantle that wraps around his left shoulder and rests across his waist. The mantle drapes over his thighs, revealing his knees and lower calf

---

18. This paragraph is taken from Hornik, "Freestanding Sculpture," 80–81.
19. For a discussion of this inaccurate dating, see Hornik, "Freestanding Sculpture," 81.

Fig. 1.13. *Christ Teaching*, statuette 61565, 370–380 CE. Marble, 72 cm. Museo Nazionale, Rome. Photograph by Scala/Ministero per i Beni e le Attività culturali / Art Resource, New York.

muscles in seated *contrapposto*. The right hand has been lost but clearly would have extended out in an oratorial gesture as he addresses the crowd seated before him. The figure is seated on a claw-footed, four-legged stool, visible beneath the drapery and behind the sandaled feet. Although the figure is seated, his body is not completely at rest. His left foot pulls back as if to lean in or move forward ever so gently while the right foot is firmly on the ground for stability. The soft lines and drapery contours contribute to an early date. It is highly likely that the drapery would have been painted with bright, garish colors.[20] This would have been a vibrant sculpture of a youthful Christ.

Content

A sculptural representation of Christ as teacher without a beard is likely to be a fourth-century convention, at least when applying a comparison-and-contrast method of analysis, along with a discussion of the subject. The depiction of Christ as youthful, beardless, and curly-haired appears on many early Christian sarcophagi, including the sarcophagus of Junius Bassus and the Passion Sarcophagus in the Vatican.[21] These are both securely dated circa 360 CE, and *Christ Teaching* should be considered a contemporary work and share this dating. A youthful Christ may be a reference to Jesus among the doctors, a popular theme across the history of Christian art. Drawing on Luke 2:41–52, the only canonical Gospel text that describes Jesus as a child, artists used the scene to foreshadow Jesus's impending role as an adult as "Lord of the Temple."[22] Scholars now date

---

20. For a brief but informative essay on the painting of Roman sculptures, see Mark B. Abbe, "Polychromy of Roman Marble Sculpture," The Met, April 2007, https://tinyurl.com/SBL4830k; see also Janet Burnett Grossman, *Looking at Greek and Roman Sculpture in Stone* (Los Angeles: Getty Museum, 2003).

21. For a comparison of these two Good Shepherd sculptures, see Hornik, "Freestanding Sculpture," 78. For background and history of the Junius Bassus sarcophagus, see Allen Farber, "Sarcophagus of Junius Bassus," Smart History, 8 August 2015, https://tinyurl.com/SBL4830l. For the Passion of Christ Sarcophagus in the Pius-Christian Museum (Vatican), see "Sarcophagus with Scenes from the Passion of Christ," Musei Vaticani, https://tinyurl.com/SBL4830m.

22. Heidi J. Hornik and Mikeal C. Parsons, "Christ among the Doctors (Luke 2:41–52) in the Exegetical Tradition and Select Florentine Renaissance Paintings," in *Anatomies of the Gospels and Beyond: Essays in Honor of R. Alan Culpepper* (Leiden: Brill, 2018), 191–210.

Christ Teaching (fig. 1.13) to the third century, concluding that the "second century" style continued into the third century in aristocratic and religious circles.²³

Comparison and Contrast

The *Christ with Sts. Peter and Paul* (fig. 1.14) on the Junius Bassus sarcophagus offers an effective comparison with the *Christ Teaching* figure. A beardless Christ sits between the two bearded figures of Peter on his right (the favored side) and Paul on his left. Peter and Paul could pass as twins to further differentiate them in appearance from Christ. Christ's right hand has been lost, but he holds an unraveled scroll in his left. Peter has a rolled scroll in his left hand, while his right hand is clenched tightly, holding something (the top of a key?) firmly to his chest.²⁴ Neither of Paul's hands is visible. The facial features of the Junius Bassus Christ are older than the *Christ Teaching*, and he looks downward in thought rather than outward toward the people in front of him. The Junius Bassus Christ is not an orator but rather a figure in conversation or giving direction to his two disciples. Both depictions of Christ serve to identify him as a teacher and wise individual at a young age.

Influences on Later Works of Art: The Beardless Christ

It seems appropriate to conclude a study on how art historians often look forward to see how a type changes in the visual tradition. Earlier types influence and evolve in subsequent works of art, often crossing into other media—in this case sculpture into painting. Here we see two examples of the use of a beardless-Christ type in Christian art of the high Renaissance and the baroque, both by Italian painters.

The use of a beardless Christ became a way to depict Christ in another manner or in an altered state later, in the high Renaissance of the sixteenth century and the Italian Baroque in the seventeenth century. Michelangelo Buonarotti (1475–1564) painted a beardless Christ (fig. 1.15) in the *Last Judgment* fresco on the wall of the Sistine Chapel behind the altar. This is

---

23. Milburn, *Early Christian Art and Architecture*, 80.
24. Although it is not possible to identify the object in Peter's right hand, a key would be appropriate given the Matt 16:18–19 apostolic succession, symbolized by the keys given from Christ to Peter.

Fig. 1.14. *Christ with Saint Peter and Paul*, Junius Bassus sarcophagus, 359 CE. Marble, 120 x 140 x 120 cm. Treasury of Saint Peter's Basilica, Rome. Photograph by Art Resource, NY.

Interpreting Select Early Sculptures 21

Fig. 1.15. Michelangelo (1475–1564), *Last Judgment*, 1536–1541. Fresco. Sistine Chapel, Vatican, Rome. Source: public domain.

no longer a portrayal of youth. The beardless Christ is in the central area of the painting, the best-lit area, from the natural light of the chapel windows. Often considered a "damning" figure, he draws up the dead with his left arm and casts down those consigned to hell with his right arm. Christ is in a role of judgment and is intended to look different than he appears in the numerous frescoes on the north and south walls of the chapel, painted in the 1480s. Christ's proportions and exaggerated gestures reflect *La Maniera*, the Mannerist style, which flourished between the High Renaissance and Baroque styles of art. Mary is seated on the favored right side of Christ. Michelangelo's self-portrait is believed to be located on the flayed skin of the martyred apostle Bartholomew, held by the figure in the lower right, who now looks up in terror at his Judge.[25]

Another example of the use of a beardless Christ was painted by Caravaggio (1571–1610) in the *Supper at Emmaus*, held in the National Gallery, London.[26] Christ appears bearded in all other supper at Emmaus paintings.

---

25. Heidi J. Hornik, "The Final Judgment in Christian Art," *CR* 3 (2002): 48.
26. For an illustration of Caravaggio's *Supper at Emmaus* at the National Gallery, London, see "The Supper at Emmaus," National Gallery, https://tinyurl.com/SBL4830n. For a more extensive discussion of Caravaggio's *Supper at Emmaus*, see

Here Caravaggio invents a new way of solving the formal compositional problem of painting a "moment of recognition" of a Christ who to this point had not been recognizable. Mark 16:12 says that Christ "appeared in another form to two of them, as they were walking into the country." This point in Mark made its way into the comment on Luke 24 in the Glossa Ordinaria, so that anyone consulting the Gloss about the supper at Emmaus would encounter this reference to *alia effigie*, without ever having to turn the page to the comments at the end of Mark's Gospel.[27] For Caravaggio, in *alia effigie* translates visually into a beardless Christ.

Conclusion

The value of situating a work of art in its historical, cultural, political, and religious contexts must always be recognized in scholarship that includes Christian art. Illustrations alone without form and content significantly denigrate scholarly study. Background of the artist, when known, further contributes to this art-historical methodology. All these components combined with biblical insights and innovative thoughts allow the object to have a voice that is rich, confident, and worthy of being heard. Anything less is a dishonor to the disciplines of both art history and biblical studies.

Works Cited

Abbe, Mark B. "Polychromy of Roman Marble Sculpture." The Met. April 2007. https://tinyurl.com/SBL4830k.

Boardman, John. "'Very Like a Whale'—Classical Sea Monsters." Pages 73–84 in *Monsters and Demons in the Ancient and Medieval Worlds*. Edited by Ann E. Farkas, Prudence O. Harper, and Evelyn B. Harrison. Mainz: von Zabern, 1987.

Correia, Alice. "*Reclining Figure* 1951 by Henry Moore OM, CH." Catalogue entry January 2014 in *Henry Moore: Sculptural Process and Public Identity*. Tate Research Publication, 2015. https://tinyurl.com/SBL4830j.

Heidi J. Hornik and Mikeal C. Parsons, *Illuminating Luke: The Passion and Resurrection Narratives in Italian Renaissance and Baroque Painting*, 3 vols. (London: T&T Clark International, 2007), 3:119–49.

27. Hornik and Parsons, *Illuminating Luke*, 3:131.

Farber, Allen. "Sarcophagus of Junius Bassus." Smart History. 8 August 2015. https://tinyurl.com/SBL4830l.
Fliegel, Stephen N. *A Higher Contemplation: Sacred Meaning in the Christian Art of the Middle Ages*. Kent, OH: Kent State University Press, 2012.
Grossman, Janet Burnett. *Looking at Greek and Roman Sculpture in Stone*. Los Angeles: Getty Museum, 2003.
Heschel, Abraham J. *The Prophets*. 2 vols. New York: Harper & Row, 1962.
Hornik, Heidi J. "Freestanding Sculpture." Pages 73–85 in *Routledge Handbook of Early Christian Art*. Edited by Robin M. Jensen and Mark D. Ellison. London: Routledge, 2018.
———. "The Final Judgment in Christian Art." CR 3 (2002): 46–49.
Hornik, Heidi J., and Mikeal C. Parsons. "Christ among the Doctors (Luke 2:41–52) in the Exegetical Tradition and Select Florentine Renaissance Paintings." Pages 191–210 in *Anatomies of the Gospels and Beyond: Essays in Honor of R. Alan Culpepper*. Leiden: Brill, 2018.
———. *Illuminating Luke: The Passion and Resurrection Narratives in Italian Renaissance and Baroque Painting*. Vol. 3. London: T&T Clark, 2007.
Kleiner, Diana E. E. *Roman Art*. New Haven: Yale University Press, 1994.
Longfellow, Brenda. *Roman Imperialism and Civic Patronage: Form, Meaning, and Ideology in Monumental Fountain Complexes*. Cambridge: Cambridge University Press, 2011.
MacDougall, Elisabeth Blair, ed. *Ancient Roman Villa Gardens*. Dumbarton Oaks Colloquium on the History of Landscape Architecture X. Washington, DC: Dumbarton Oaks, 1987.
MacDougall, Elisabeth Blair, and Wilhelmina F. Jashemski, eds. *Ancient Roman Gardens*. Dumbarton Oaks Colloquium on the History of Landscape Architecture, VII. Washington, DC: Dumbarton Oaks, 1981.
McColl, Donald A. "Early Christian Sculptures at Cleveland in Their Eastern Mediterranean Context." MA thesis, Oberlin College, 1991.
———. "Signs of the Times: The Cleveland Marbles." Dumbarton Oaks. https://tinyurl.com/SBL4830a.
Milburn, Robert. *Early Christian Art and Architecture*. Berkeley: University of California Press, 1988.
Ramage, Nancy, and Andrew Ramage. *Roman Art*. London: Pearson, 2014.
"Rome Gallery." Penn Museum. https://tinyurl.com/SBL4830b.

Wischmeyer, Wolfgang. "Die vorkonstantinische christliche Kunst in neuem Licht. Die Cleveland-Statuetten." *VC* 35 (1981): 253–87.

Wixom, William D. "Early Christian Sculptures at Cleveland." *BCMA* (1967): 67–88.

Zanker, Paul. *Roman Portraits*. New York: Metropolitan Museum of Art, 2016.

The Repudiation of Pagan Idols and the Rise of Christian Devotional Portraits

Robin M. Jensen

> Little children, keep yourselves from idols.
> —1 John 5:21

Christian theologians have often characterized other religions' cult images as pagan idols and offer them as evidence of ignorant, primitive, or superstitious worship of inanimate objects. Idol worship even has been posited as a defining feature of ancient Greco-Roman polytheism. Those same theologians regard the adherence to the biblical prohibitions against making graven images (see Exod 20:4, Deut 5:8) as a fundamental tenet in Jewish and Christian monotheism. While this issue might seem to be limited to images of the divine being, theologians of the past have extended the biblical prohibition of graven images to denounce sacred pictorial art generally. John Calvin's censure of such work is a case in point. According to him, true Christians would eschew all sacred images, as he insists that an imageless form of Christianity existed for the first five hundred years (Calvin, *Inst.* 1.11.13). Calvin was certain that Christian visual art only appeared when church leadership had degenerated, godliness was lost, and the faithful slid headlong into pagan superstition.

Similarly, Edward Gibbon's classic work, *The Decline and Fall of the Roman Empire*, reflects an attitude that still rings familiar, even though it was written more than two centuries ago:

> Primitive Christians were possessed with an unconquerable repugnance to the use and abuse of images, and this aversion may be ascribed to their descent from the Jews and their enmity to the Greeks. The Mosaic law severely proscribed all representations of the Deity; and that precept was firmly established in the chosen people's principles and practices.

> The wit of Christian apologists was pointed against the foolish idolaters, who bowed before the workmanship of their own hands; the brass and marble images which, had they been endowed with sense and motion, should have stepped off their pedestals to adore the creative powers of the artist.[1]

Yet, Christians were making and using pictorial art by the early third century and even offering veneration and prayers to portraits of the saints no later than fourth. Even though this practice apparently worried some church leaders, for the most part the use of sacred images became well established long before they were condemned by iconoclastic councils in the eighth and ninth centuries. This essay briefly explores the attitudes of early Christian writers toward cult images of the pagan gods, proposes that their concerns about idolatry were almost never about pictorial art as such, and explores the transition in Christian iconography from narrative subjects to sacred portraits during the third century through the early fifth century.

Biblical Condemnation of Idols and the Belief in an Invisible God

While many Christians, like Calvin and Gibbon, assume that the laws summarized in the Decalogue, as found in the books of Exodus and Deuteronomy, are often taken to forbid any kind of pictorial art, others interpret them to forbid only those divine images humans might inappropriately venerate. For this reason, Roman Catholics and many Lutherans align the prohibition of graven images with the commandment to have no other gods and the subsequent proscription against bowing down to or worshiping idols (Exod 20:3–5a, Deut 5:7–9). This accords with other biblical texts that assert that paying undue homage to an object made from wood, stone, or metal—no matter how beautifully handcrafted—is both irrational and shameful. For example, Ps 115 proclaims that idols made by human hands have mouths but cannot speak, ears that cannot hear, and noses that cannot smell (Ps 115:4). Isaiah 44 declares that anyone who fashions the image of a god will be ridiculed and put to shame (Isa 44:9).

The famous incident in which the Israelites beseeched Aaron to fashion the image of a calf from contributed golden jewelry in order to worship

---

1. Edward Gibbon, *The Decline and Fall of the Roman Empire* (London: Strahan & Cadell, 1776–1788), 3:359.

it with burnt offerings is not only related at length in Exodus and Deuteronomy (Exod 32:1–25, Deut 9:15–21) but also referred to either directly or indirectly in several other places in both the Old and New Testaments (Ps 106:19–20, Neh 9:18, Acts 7:39–43, 1 Cor 10:7). In Judges, God raises up judges to repudiate the Israelites for transgressing the covenant and disobeying the divine commandment by lapsing into the idolatrous worship of Baal and Astarte (Judg 2:16–23).

Biblical references to idols vary according to whether they refer to existing or nonexisting entities. The Wisdom of Solomon, a deuterocanonical book written in Greek sometime between 30 BCE and 70 CE, delivers an especially detailed discourse on the folly of idol makers who make perishable objects to be honored and so construct traps for the unwary, but along with this the poet claims that the images honored as gods are merely the representations of long-deceased men or living-but-distant kings wishing to be flattered (Wis 14:8–31).

A slightly different aspect of the condemnation of idols affirms that the true God is invisible and so cannot be depicted or even imagined. However, this idea is not consistent across both Testaments. Whereas the Hebrew Scriptures suggest that God actually has a form that is extremely dangerous for humans to see (see Exod 33:20), it is mainly in the New Testament where one finds explicit declarations of God's essential invisibility. For example, the author of 1 Timothy praises God as immortal and invisible and insists that no one has ever seen or can see God (1 Tim 1:17, 6:16). While Exodus indicates that Moses was ultimately permitted to see God face-to-face (Exod 33:11), the author of Hebrews grants only that Moses's faith in God allowed him to persevere *as though* he saw the one who is invisible (Heb 11:27). And though he does not actually assert God's invisibility, when Paul addresses the Athenians from the Areopagus, he declares that the Christian God is unlike those pagan deities whose images mortals fabricate from their imagination from gold, silver, or stone (Acts 17:24–29).

This difference between the Old and New Testament treatment of God's visibility may be due to the influence of Hellenistic philosophy on first-century Judaism and subsequently on early Christianity, which placed little emphasis on Israelite taboos against graven images while stressing the futility of trying to envision the transcendent divine being. Consequently, for most early Christian theologians, God was essentially a purely intelligible and spiritual divine being, not a material or visible one. Even the text of Col 1:15, which declares Christ to be the visible image of the invisible God, basically affirms that fundamental principle. The Colossians text, however, accords with Jesus's words to Philip in John 14:9, "whoever who has seen me has seen the Father," which could be regarded as a provisional condescension of God's image to human beings, so long as Jesus appeared on earth in a human body and likeness.[2]

Early Christian Apologists on Idolatry

In the last century, modern art historians, though not precisely echoing Gibbon's judgments, drew similar conclusions about early Christian attitudes toward sacred images. For example, in one of his 1950s articles, Ernst Kitzinger proclaims that Christianity was persistently aniconic until the second half of the fourth century.[3] Kitzinger's assessment probably influenced church historians, such as the greatly respected Henry Chadwick, whose 1967 handbook includes a chapter on Christian art in which he extends early Christian aniconism to include figurative art in general and asserts that this was anchored in Christian obedience to the so-called second commandment: "The second of the Ten Commandments forbade the making of any graven image. Both Tertullian and Clement of Alexandria regarded this prohibition as absolute and binding on Christians. Images and statues belonged to the demonic world of paganism."[4] Chadwick then goes on to assert that the only early Christians who possessed images of Christ were radical gnostics, the followers of the licentious Carpocrates.

Chadwick's reference to the writings of Tertullian and Clement is significant. Early Christian apologists, such as the two that Chadwick cites, were among those who regularly railed against pagan cult images. However, neither Tertullian or Clement of Alexandria made the biblical prohibition of graven images an essential part of their argument.[5] Remark-

---

2. Unless otherwise noted, biblical translations follow the NRSV.

3. Ernst Kitzinger, "The Cult of Images in the Age before Iconoclasm," *DOP* 8 (1954): 86. For similar analysis by other art historians, see Paul Corby Finney, *The Invisible God: The Earliest Christians on Art* (Oxford: Oxford University Press, 1994), 7–10.

4. Henry Chadwick, *The Early Church* (Penguin: London, 1967), 277. On Carpocrates's image specifically, see below.

5. Rare references are found in Tertullian, *Idol.* 3–4; *Spect.* 23; and in Clement, *Strom.* 5.5.

ably, Clement also asserted that the Decalogue's prohibition of graven images was actually intended to discourage overattachment to worldly things and redirect attention to the invisible, transcendent, and uncreated being. Depending on the sense of sight inhibits reverence for what is truly divine, and worshiping the immaterial by material is to dishonor it. It seems that only early third-century father Origen of Alexandria actually suggested that Christians should emulate Jewish aniconism (*Cels.* 4.31).

For the most part, these early Christian apologists argued that the divine being was beyond representation. God could not be perceived with the eyes or fully comprehended by the mind. They insisted that material things, unlike divine beings, were subject to disintegration, rust, and decay. They might have started out as mere saucepans or worse (e.g., chamber pots), and they were liable to become infested with mice and spiders.

For example, in the third century, African/Latin writer Marcus Minucius Felix constructed a dialogue between a Roman polytheist and a Christian. In this work, among his other accusations, the polytheist character claims that Christians are ashamed to display their god's images publicly. In response, the Christian protagonist explains that Christians lack altars, temples, and divine images because Christians believe in and worship an *invisible* God. He adds that simpleminded folks who worship images are dazzled by the objects' beauty or their precious materials, and that they deludedly regard the thing as a god *merely* because they wish it to be so (Minucius Felix, *Oct.* 24.5–8).

This idea has a more basic parallel, espoused by another Christian apologist, Justin Martyr, who like these others almost never cited the biblical condemnations of idols and instead claimed that the pagan gods were nonexistent and their images were invented, inanimate, and soulless representations of imagined beings (Justin Martyr, *1 Apol.* 9).

Even though Christian apologists asserted the impossibility of visually depicting the divine being and ridiculed polytheists for trying, they did not dismiss pagan cult images as merely ludicrous. Christian persecution narratives often centered on martyrs' refusal to venerate the pagan gods' images or to honor the emperor's statues or portraits. Episodes of Christian heroes attempting to interrupt sacrifices or kicking over altars in the midst of actual trials are recounted.[6] Spitting on or hissing at cult

---

6. Hissing or spitting on idols in Tertullian, *Idol.* 11.7; *Apol.* 23.16; also Minucius Felix, *Oct.* 8.4; and later in Augustine, *C. Jul.* 6.23(7).

images was a way to express contempt but could result in one's arrest. And while the images themselves were depictions of nonentities, they were not necessarily benign lumps of stone or metal. Justin Martyr, Minucius Felix, Tertullian, Athenagoras, and Origen all conceded that they could be dangerous, inhabited by demons who took advantage of the gullible by usurping the figures and names of the gods, consumed the sacrifices offered to them, and sometimes drove their devotees mad.[7]

Sometimes the arguments drew on well-entrenched, pre-Christian philosophical teachings that denounced attitudes and misplaced values more than idolatrous objects. For instance, early third-century Christian writer Clement of Alexandria, influenced by Platonic ideals, argues that since all images are derived from (and thus inferior to) their prototypes, regarding any visual representation as existent or truthful is to mistake earthly and impermanent objects for transcendent and eternal realities—to fail to distinguish the mundane from the sacred. Clement also insists that sensory perception is altogether unreliable, in contrast to knowledge apprehended by the mind. He compares this to the difference between the artist's work and the artist's conception. The first is the inferior product of the second (Clement, *Protrep.* 4; see also Athenagoras, *Leg.* 15).

Tertullian of Carthage similarly argues that the real problem with idols lies not so much in their being mistaken for something they are not but rather in that they are improperly valued. For Tertullian, idols were anything that received unwarranted reverence, not only certain types of cult objects or gods' images. Luxurious goods and ostentatious displays of wealth or social status were, to him, a particular kind of idolatry (*Idol.* 4, 8). Those who made such things were certainly guilty of promoting idolatry, even if they were only fancy slippers or nice dishware. Tertullian, however, clearly condemns images as illusory and false, but this is not altogether different from other forms of mendacity and fraud, such as that carried on by deceivers who cheat in their actions, speech, and writing (*Spect.* 23).

Thus, early Christian theologians' objections to idols reveal certain assumptions about pagan religious practices. First, those who offered veneration to cult images of the gods believed the objects were in themselves powerful and so confused material and immaterial realities. Second, the divine Being was essentially invisible and so, by nature, unable to be

---

7. On the problem of demons, see Tertullian, *Apol.* 22.6, 23.14; *Idol.* 1, 15, 21–22; *Spect.* 8.10; Minucius Felix, *Oct.* 27; Firmicus Maternus, *Err. prof. rel.* 13.4

depicted in any image. Third, those who appreciated beautiful objects had misplaced values and were distracted from what was truly worthy. Fourth, while the idols were nothing in themselves, they could harbor dangerous spirits who could do actual harm to naive devotees. A fifth point, however, often missed by modern readers is that to early Christians, pagan cult images were idolatrous primarily because they depicted the wrong gods. In other words, the conflict was not about images per se but about which deity or deities were worthy or true. Tertullian makes this explicit when he objects to pagan cult images because of the danger they pose to viewers who get entangled with false gods, which he equates with fornication and adultery (e.g., consorting with someone else's deities; Tertullian, *Idol.* 1.1).

Yet, despite their critical and often mocking denunciations of the practices and cult objects belonging to traditional polytheism, most early Christian writers knew perfectly well that polytheists did not *actually* worship gods' statues. This suggests that their condemnations were essentially unfair—perhaps even deliberately defamatory—rhetorical tropes. They were also aware of long-standing intellectual critiques of anthropomorphic depictions of the gods, and standard defenses that merely affirmed that the images were not intended to be actual likenesses. In that regard, they insisted the Christian position was not all that different from that taught by pagan philosophers.[8] Undoubtedly, many polytheists esteemed certain ancient or especially illustrious artifacts and may even have imputed a kind of intrinsic sacrality or power to particular ones. Nevertheless, when they responded to Christian accusations of their idol worship, they explained that any attention they paid to gods' images was meant to be redirected to their divine models, and many—if not most—of these disparaging Christians clearly knew this was the case (e.g., Arnobius, *Nat.* 8.8.9–10).

Thus, one might ask whether Christian apologists merely wished to mock their adversaries by disingenuously characterizing them as believing that inanimate images of gods possessed some intrinsic power or whether those apologists had a different aim altogether. Were they, as figures such as Calvin, Gibbon, and others contended, worried that making any kind of sacred visual art was simply capitulation to pagan practices?

---

8. For some examples, see Justin Martyr, *1 Apol.* 9, 20; Tertullian, *Apol.* 46.4; Clement of Alexandria, *Protrep.* 4–7; Minucius Felix, *Oct.* 19.

The Rise of Early Christian Pictorial Art and the Emergence of the Portrait Icon

Around the same time that these apologists were railing against idols, ordinary Christians were producing pictorial art for their tombs, homes, churches, and personal objects (e.g., rings, lamps, dishware) that depicted scenes from the Bible (both Old Testament and New Testament) and images of Jesus as well as of God the Father. The incorporation of figurative iconography in these contexts suggests that many Christians sought—and their leaders and teachers tolerated or even approved—the production of certain types of sacred images. Moreover, representative authorities such as Clement of Alexandria actually recommended appropriate designs for Christian signet rings (e.g., a fisher, dove, anchor, or ship at full sail; Clement of Alexandria, *Paed.* 3.11). He explicitly instructed that certain subjects be avoided (e.g., weapons, drinking cups, or pagan gods' images), so that Christians could distinguish themselves from non-Christians. If we do not regard these instances as indicating that Christians had succumbed to idolatrous pagan practices, how should we understand them?

First, the earliest surviving examples of early Christian visual art consisted of simple symbols (e.g., doves, anchors, or fish) or abbreviated scenes drawn from Bible stories, at first primarily from the Hebrew Scriptures (e.g., Adam and Eve, Abraham and Isaac, Noah, Jonah, Moses) and then also from the New Testament (e.g., Jesus's baptism, Jesus raising the dead and healing the sick, multiplying loaves, and changing water to wine; see figs. 2.1 and 2.2).

Additionally, most surviving third- or early fourth-century Christian artworks are two-dimensional, either wall paintings or relief sculptures. Freestanding statues or even two-dimensional portraits of saints, biblical characters, sacred persons, or divine beings depicted apart from a narrative context exist but are rare (fig. 2.3).[9]

In other words, insofar as early Christians can be described as aniconic, it is not because they produced no images but because the sacred images they produced were initially quite different in both style and subject matter from the pagan cult images they derided.

---

9. On portraits and statues, see Katherine Marsengill, "The Christian Reception of Sculpture in Late Antiquity and the Historical Reception of Late Antique Christian Sculpture," *JBRec* 1 (2014): 67–101; and Heidi J. Hornik "Freestanding Sculpture," in *The Routledge Handbook of Early Christian Art*, ed. Robin M. Jensen and Mark D. Ellison (London: Routledge, 2018), 73–85.

Most of the pictorial art that Christians produced from the third through the mid-fourth century would not have prompted worship. Such art might have been edifying or inspiring, perhaps helpful for meditating on sacred stories, but little evidence suggests that viewers typically

Fig. 2.1. Noah with Moses striking the rock and Adam and Eve, fourth century. Catacomb of Peter and Marcellinus. Source: Joseph Wilpert, *Die Malereien der Katakomben Roms* (Freiburg: Herder, 1903), pl. 186.

Fig. 2.2. Jesus raising Lazarus, adoration of the magi, the paralytic, Peter striking the rock, and other scenes, fourth century. Catacomb of Domitilla, Rome. Source: Joseph Wilpert, *Die Malereien der Katakomben Roms* (Freiburg: Herder, 1903), pl. 239.

Fig. 2.3. Bronze statuette of Saint Peter holding a cross, fourth–fifth century. Rome. 9.5 x 5 x 4.4 cm. Berlin State Museum. Photograph by Art Resource, New York.

prayed or made offerings to these mostly narrative subjects. Attending to this distinction between portrait-type and narrative images is crucially important for understanding the nature and function of earliest Christian iconography, which consisted mainly of symbols and pictorial renderings of biblical figures and scenes. These biblical figures and scenes may have been intended to be exegetical or didactic, perhaps even expressive, but they were not designed to be objects of veneration, much less to suggest the presence of the represented deity.

Certainly, rare surviving documents refer to early Christian portraits that may have been treated like cult objects. In each case, however, the texts reflect disapproval of such treatment. For example, a story from the second-century apocryphal Acts of John recounts the case of the Ephesian official Lycomedes, who commissioned the apostle's portrait in gratitude for his miraculous healing, placed it on an altar, lit lamps before it, and draped garlands on it (Acts John 26–27). John severely reproached Lycomedes for his pious but misguided act because, although the image might resemble his external appearance, it could not depict his (John's) inner character.

Late second-century bishop Irenaeus of Lyons similarly complained that the heretical Carpocratian sect possessed an image of Christ made from life by (or possibly for) Pontius Pilate. According to Irenaeus, the Carpocratians treated this image, along with those of certain revered philosophers, in the same way that polytheists customarily venerated idols—by offering them garlands and lit tapers (Irenaeus, *Haer.* 1.25.6).

Nevertheless, neither of these instances implies objecting to visual art in general. Rather, they object to portrait types of images that were treated like pagan cult images.[10]

In sum, despite their rhetoric, early Christian apologists or church authorities virtually never condemned art in general, whether merely decorative adornments for homes, gardens, or public buildings or more explicitly religious narrative images that Christians displayed in their tombs or churches. Rather, they condemned cult statues of the Greco-Roman gods, primarily because they were explicitly linked to and entangled with false gods.

Then a dramatic change occurred. At some point, around the end of the fourth century, Christians began making their own cultic images—of the right god for devotional purposes. This change coincided with the toleration of the faith and its patronage by the emperor, which radically changed the church's political, social, and economic circumstances as well as the ways by which Christians engaged pictorial images. Contrary to Paul's and Minucius Felix's insistence that Christians had no altars, shrines, and images, shrines, images, and altars began to spring up in abundance. Along with this, the belief that physical matter could facilitate encounters with transcendent realities gradually became widely accepted. The senses—touch, taste, smell, hearing, and especially sight—were integrated into public Christian liturgies as well as private devotions. Almost overnight, saints' tombs, holy relics, and sacred places became foci for personal and corporate prayer and even veneration.[11]

This rapidly developing role for material objects in Christian practice also affected the style, content, and treatment of Christian visual art. The earlier narrative-based subjects, mostly showing abbreviated scenes from the Bible, began to be joined and eventually surpassed in popularity by individual or group portraits of the apostles, saints, the Virgin Mary, and Christ (figs. 2.4–5). At the same time, such portraits gradually became prominent in the apses of Christian churches and basilicas (fig. 2.6).

---

10. The story is repeated in later works, including Hippolytus, *Haer.* 7.32.7; Epiphanius, *Pan.* 27.6.9–10.

11. On the material turn in the fourth century, see Patricia Cox Miller, *The Corporeal Imagination: Signifying the Holy in Late Antique Christianity* (Philadelphia: University of Pennsylvania Press, 2009), 3–7, 14–19. On the rise of the cult of relics, see Robert Wiśniewski, *The Beginnings of the Cult of Relics* (Oxford: Oxford University Press, 2019), 8–27.

Fig. 2.4. Christ with Peter and Paul and four martyrs, fourth century. Catacomb of Peter and Marcellinus, Rome. Photograph by DeA Picture Library / Art Resource, NY.

Fig. 2.5. Fresco of Saint Januarius, fifth century. Catacomb of San Gennaro, Naples. Photograph by DeA Picture Library / Art Resource, NY.

Fig. 2.6. Mosaic apse, Christ with saints, ca. 530. Basilica of Saints Cosmas and Damian, Rome. Photograph by Scala / Luciano Romano / Art Resource, NY.

This alteration in both Christian art's content and context was momentous. While the earlier, abbreviated narrative scenes were unlikely to prompt veneration, these new types of images—mostly front-facing, full-length figures or bust portraits apart from a narrative context—invited contemplation more than comprehension. The episode was less significant than the actor. Viewers would have been prompted to gaze reverently on the holy persons' portraits, gaze into their eyes, and offer their prayers to those whose images they engaged. Moreover, as the evolution of this new kind of art was roughly simultaneous with the veneration of saints' remains, they functioned in certain respects in a similar manner. Along with their relics, the likenesses of holy men and women (whether imagined or rendered from life) likewise became devotional objects.

One instance of the similarities and even direct connections between the veneration of saints, their relics, and their portrait images appears in John Chrysostom's eulogy for Meletius, bishop of Antioch (ca. 360–381):

> And what you did with the names you also did the same with his image: for many people inscribed that hallowed image on ring-heads, on stamps, on plates, on the walls of rooms, and everywhere, so that it was not only possible to hear that holy name, but also to see everywhere the figure of

his body, and have a double means of consolation for his absence. (*Hom. Mel.* 3 [Rizos])

Chrysostom evidently sees the value in gazing on their portraits as a way of making connection to departed holy persons. By impressing the saint's likeness on their signet rings, bedroom walls, drinking cups, or other objects, the pious mourners would be inspired by the saint's example of holiness and be comforted in their grief.

According to Gregory of Nyssa's eulogy for the same bishop, given five years earlier (at the time of Meletius's death), this practice would have had an additional purpose. Gregory assures his audience that, as a saint, Meletius had the power to intercede with Christ for them from his place in heaven. Thus, gazing at his portrait would help viewers sense the saint's presence as they prayed to him for aid (*Oration on Meletius*).

Early Christian Criticism of Devotional Portraits

Although John Chrysostom, Gregory of Nyssa, and others obviously approved of devotional images such as those of Meletius and Saint Theodore, other fourth- and fifth-century bishops regarded them as dangerously similar to pagan cult images. However, the fourth-century critics evince a somewhat different perspective from those given by their second- and third-century predecessors. Rather than emphasize the problem of confusing material with spiritual realities, the potential for the images' demonic inhabitation, or the concern about misplaced values, these critics often turned to doctrinal arguments.

Perhaps the best-known example of this comes from a letter attributed to Eusebius of Caesarea and included in a dossier later assembled by eighth-century iconoclasts. In this letter, Eusebius replies to the request of Emperor Constantine's sister for a portrait of Christ and explains that what Constantia asks for is impossible and probably heretical. Showing almost prescient cognizance of the complex arguments that would be deployed in fifth-century christological debates, Eusebius frames the problem somewhat like the apostle John did in his rebuke of Lycomedes. Depicting only Christ's external appearance heretically divides his inseparable human and divine natures. Because no artist could depict Christ's invisible, uncircumscribable divine nature but could show him only in his external appearance, the portrait can be no more than an inanimate imitation of the temporally conditioned form he assumed in his incarnation:

What sort of image of Christ are you seeking? Is it the true and unalterable one which bears his essential characteristics, or the one which he took up for our sakes when he assumed the form of a servant? [Phil 2.7].... Granted, he has two forms, but even I do not think your request has to do with his divine form.... Surely, then, you are seeking his image as a servant, that of the flesh which he put on for our sake. But that too, we have been taught, was mingled with the glory of his divinity, so that the mortal part was swallowed up by life [2 Cor 5.4].... How can one paint an image of so wondrous and unattainable a form—if the term "form" is even applicable to the divine and spiritual essence—unless, like unbelieving pagans, one is to represent things that bear no possible resemblance to anything...? For they, too, make such idols when they wish to mold the likeness of what they consider to be a god or, as they might say, one of the heroes or anything else of the kind, yet are unable even to approach a resemblance, and so delineate and represent some strange human shapes. Surely, even you will agree that such practices are not lawful for us. (Mango)[12]

Eusebius adds an interesting detail to his denial of Constantia's request. He reports that a certain woman once presented him with a picture of two men in philosopher's robes, insisting that they depicted Paul and Christ. Declaring he had no idea where she had obtained the image or *why* she believed the two figures depicted the apostle and the Savior, he determined it was best to confiscate the offending object. He went on to ask how anyone could presume to depict any saint or apostle—or even Christ—without some direct knowledge of their earthly appearance.

The authenticity of Eusebius's letter has been challenged, largely because his response anticipates subsequent christological debates over Christ's inseparable but distinct human and divine natures, the one visible but the other invisible. Although the scholarly consensus tilts in favor of the letter's being genuine, scholars have registered legitimate doubts.[13]

---

12. Text in Jean B. Pitra, *Spicilegium Solesmense Sanctorum Patrum* (Paris, 1852), 1:383–86; and PG 20:1545–49.

13. See Claudia Sode and Paul Speck, "Ikonoklasmus vor der Zeit? Der Brief des Eusebius von Kaisareia an Kaiserin Konstantia," *JÖB* 54 (2004): 113–34. Among those who questioned the authenticity of this letter are Mary Charles Murray, "Art and the Early Church," *JTS* 28 (1977): 335–36. Murray revised her opinion based on the challenge by Stephen Gero, "The True Image of Christ: Eusebius' Letter to Constantia Reconsidered," *JTS* 32 (1981): 460–70. Gero's support for authenticity is on the basis of style and vocabulary, which a good forger could obviously copy. Some

Surviving documents record that another fourth-century writer, Epiphanius of Salamis, also objected to devotional images of Christ and the saints, even reprising Irenaeus's critique that such things were being treated like pagan idols. Problematically, most of Epiphanius's complaints have been reconstructed from much later sources, including acts from the iconoclastic council of 754, and John of Damascus's *First Apology* against the iconoclasts. Thus, like Eusebius's letter to Constantia, this has caused some historians to question the works' authenticity. The scholarly debate is too complicated to replicate here in detail, but briefly, the consensus tends toward acceptance of some, if not all, of the works as authentic.[14] Nevertheless, as in the purported Eusebian letter to Constantia, Epiphanius's arguments show some apparent anachronisms and echo arguments raised by eighth-century iconoclasts (among them Epiphanius's insistence that the incarnation did not justify making portraits of Christ).[15]

---

who presume that the letter is genuinely Eusebian include Georges Florovsky, "Origen, Eusebius, and the Iconoclastic Controversy," *CH* 19.2 (1950): 77–96; and Christoph von Schönborn, *God's Human Face: The Christ-Icon*, trans. Lothar Krauth (San Francisco: Ignatius, 1994), 57–59. Florovsky insists that there is "no reason whatsoever to question its authenticity" ("Origen, Eusebius," 84). Von Schönborn simply takes it for granted. Among scholars who dismiss the letter's authenticity are Timothy Barnes, *Constantine and Eusebius* (Cambridge: Harvard University Press, 1984), 401 n. 82; and Steven Bigham, *Early Christian Attitudes toward Images* (Rollingsford, NH: Orthodox Research Institute, 2004), 193–99.

14. Among those who accept the authenticity of Epiphanius's works are Karl Holl, "Die Schriften des Epiphanius gegen die Bilderverehrung," in *Gesammelte Aufsätze zur Kirchengeschichte* (Darmstadt: Wissenschaftliche Buchgesellschaft, 1916), 1:351–87; Kitzinger, "Cult of Images," 93 n. 28; and Murray, "Art and the Early Church," 336–38, which outlines the discussion up to the time of her writing. Murray notes that George Ostrogorsky initially accepted only the *Treatise* (or *Testament*) as authentic but after severe critique allowed also that the *Letter to John of Jerusalem* could be as well. Georg Ostrogorsky's change of mind is evident in his *Studien zur Geschichte des byzantinischen Bilderstreits* (Breslau, Marcus, 1929), 61–113. Also accepting are Paul J. Alexander, "Church Councils and Patristic Authority: The Iconoclastic Council of Hiereia (754) and St. Sophia (815)," *HSCP* 63 (1958): 493–505; and Pierre Maraval, "Épiphane, 'Docteur des Iconoclasts,' Nicée II, 787–1987. Douze siècles d'images religieuses," in *Actes du colloque international Nicée II tenu au Collège de France, Paris les 2, 3, 4 Octobre 1986*, ed. François Boespflug and Nicolas Lossky (Paris: Cerf, 1987), 51–62.

15. On this see Leslie Brubaker and John Haldon, *Byzantium in the Iconoclast Era* (Cambridge: Cambridge University Press, 2010), 46–47.

As they stand, the fragments express Epiphanius's opinion that no early church authority would have permitted portraits of Christ, biblical figures, or saints in their houses of worship. Furthermore, he added, artists "lie by representing the appearance of saints in different forms according to their whim, sometimes delineating the persons as old men, sometimes as youths, and so intruding into that which they have not seen" (Nicephorus, *Adv. Epiph.* 18.79 [Mango]).[16] Epiphanius likens depictions of Peter, Paul, and John, made in colors on plaster walls of private homes, to abominations similar to the pagan idols. He dismisses the explanation that the images were meant to honor the apostles and remind viewers of them, saying that images are merely false.

In the epistle, said to be from Epiphanius to Emperor Theodosius, Epiphanius flatly denies that any orthodox Christian teacher could have painted an image of Christ either for a display in a church or in a private house. Epiphanius then complains that he has often but without success urged his fellow clergy to remove such images. He entreats the emperor to act, ordering the whitewashing of paintings on walls and removal of any curtains bearing holy portraits, which, he suggests again, could be given to the poor as burial shrouds. Here Epiphanius also alleges that painters have invented the apostles' images entirely from their own imaginations: "They represent the holy apostle Peter as an old man with hair and beard cut short; some represent St. Paul as a man with receding hair, others as being bald and bearded, and the other apostles as being closely cropped" (*Letter to Theodosius* [Mango]). This description matches the two founding apostles' depictions from fourth- and fifth-century iconography, which present those very same physical attributes (fig. 2.7). Epiphanius concludes his letter by allowing that the single salutary sign of Christ (i.e., the empty cross) should suffice for doors and everywhere else.

Authentic or not, both Eusebius's alleged query regarding how one could possibly make a verifiable likeness of Paul or Christ and Epiphanius's note about the variations in representations of Peter and Paul have echoes in a fifth-century passage from a work of Augustine of Hippo. In his treatise *On the Trinity*, Augustine refers somewhat sarcastically to portraits of Peter, Paul, the Virgin Mary, and Christ and notes the vast discrepancies

---

16. Citing Epiphanius's so-called *Letter to the Emperor Theodosius* (Ostrogorsky, *Studien zur Geschichte*, 71–72).

Fig. 2.7. Gold glass with Peter and Paul, fourth century. Rome. Metropolitan Museum, New York.

in their depictions. He seems less concerned about their existence or their treatment than that they at least show Jesus as having a human appearance:

> Anyone, surely, who has read or heard what the apostle Paul wrote or what was written about him, will fabricate a face for the apostle in his imagination and for everybody else whose name is mentioned in these texts. And every one of the vast number of people to whom these writings are known will think of their physical features and lineaments in a different way, and it will be quite impossible to tell whose thoughts are nearest the mark in this respect.... Even the physical face of the Lord is pictured with infinite variety by countless imaginations, though whatever it was like he certainly had only one. Nor as regards the faith we have in the Lord Jesus Christ is it in the least relevant to salvation what our imaginations picture him like, which is probably quite different from the reality.... What does matter is that we think of him as a man; for we have embedded in us a standard notion of the nature of a man.... Nor do we know what the Virgin Mary looked like, from whom he was marvelously born.... And so, without prejudice to faith it is permissible to say, "Perhaps she had a face like this, perhaps she did not." (*Trin.* 8.7 [Hill])[17]

Augustine mentions the existence of saints' portraits also in his work *The Harmony of the Gospels*, where he remarks that many assume that

---

17. The critical edition is William J. Mountain and Frater Glorie, eds., *Sancti Augustini: De Trinitate Libri XV, Libri I–XV*, CCSL 50 (Turnhout: Brepols, 2001).

Christ also wrote directly to Peter and Paul because in many places they had seen these two apostles depicted with Christ. This caused those people to fall into error, Augustine insists, not only because they attributed magical arts to Christ but also because they sought to encounter Christ and his apostles on painted walls instead of in the Holy Scriptures. Moreover, he worries that the painters were deceiving these viewers by suggesting that during his earthly life, Christ actually had contact with Paul (Augustine, *Cons.* 1.10.15–16).[18] This comment may relate to a popular fourth- and fifth-century depiction of Christ standing between Peter and Paul and handing the scroll of the new law to Paul (fig. 2.8).

Fig. 2.8. *Traditio Legis* (Christ between Peter and Paul), detail from fourth-century sarcophagus. Museo Pio Cristiano, Vatican Museums, Vatican State. Photograph by Vanni Archive / Art Resource, New York.

---

18. See Goulven Madec, "Le Christ des païens d'après le De consensus Evangelistarum de Saint Augustin," *RechAug* 26 (1992): 5–67, esp. 46–47.

In other places, Augustine expressly warns members of his flock against the veneration of both tombs and pictures—probably saints' martyria augmented with their portraits (*Mor. ecc.* 1.34). In one of his sermons, Augustine even allows that some pagans had accused Christians themselves of adoring columns (or perhaps images set on columns) in the church as if they were sacred objects (*Serm.* 198.10).[19] In any case, Augustine evidently was less concerned about his flock confusing material with spiritual realities and more about misunderstandings that might arise from inaccurate or doctrinally deficient representations.

Thus for various reasons, fourth- and early fifth-century writers such as Eusebius, Epiphanius, and Augustine all raised questions about how any artist could produce faithful images of Christ or, in fact, of any holy person whom they had not seen in life. True portraits of Christ present the particular problem of rendering his invisible divine nature along with his human likeness. Yet, in addition to anguishing about confusing material and spiritual realities, these writers doubt human artists' ability to produce theologically justifiable, scripturally accurate, or visually authentic likenesses of Christ or holy persons.

Notwithstanding these various purported objections, these texts testify that Christians were making, using, and even venerating saints' images by the late fourth or early fifth century. Their rapid popularity and that portrait icons largely displaced earlier iconographic types belong to the larger transition to accepting the mediatorial potential of certain material objects, including saints' relics.

The Mediating Image: From Idols to Icons

Despite evidence that some ecclesial authorities worried about this development, the ordinary Christian faithful evidently began to regard holy portraits as devotional aids and desired to view them in prominent positions within saints' shrines, in churches, and on personal and household objects (e.g., rings and drinking cups).

Although much later writers such as Gibbon regarded this development as evidence of backsliding converts and indulgent bishops, classicist and art historian Jaś Elsner proposes a different theory, that Christians

---

19. It may be that images were attached to columns, but he may also refer here to the text of Lev 26:1, "You shall make for yourselves no idols and erect no carved images on pillars."

adopted these new artistic forms as an effective strategy for pagan evangelization. Elsner suggests that Christianity (in his words, "originally a non-iconic cult") became a "master manipulator of material objects in the fourth century" and that developing their icon pictorial art was a "brilliant" effort by Christians to "upstage" paganism by employing the very strategies that their competitors had "mastered and pioneered." In other words, Christians adopted a popular pagan tactic to "outplay their polytheistic rivals."[20]

To some degree, one could argue that pictorial art was an attraction that bishops used to lure the reluctant into their churches. At the outset of the fifth century, Paulinus of Nola acknowledges that he commissioned painters to adorn his cathedral church with sacred images in order to draw an audience. While he explicitly denies that such images were sacred in themselves and refers to them as "empty figures," he also claims they are edifying, insofar as they might entice those who prefer to feast and drink outside at the local martyr's (Saint Felix's) tomb, and thereby nurture their faith and elevate their piety (Paulinus, *Carm.* 27.542–597).

Paulinus's images appear to have mostly been biblical subjects, but they also included saints' portraits. Captions to aid their identification were included on both types of images. According to Paulinus, a depiction of Saint Martin was included in the baptistery of a church founded by his friend Severus at Primulacum, and Paulinus describes it as the image of a heavenly man who was worthy of imitation. Severus apparently included the portrait of Paulinus himself, which made him uncomfortable, as he declared that he was unworthy of the honor—being a lowly figure, shrouded in mental darkness, at best merely a comfort for wretched sinners. Despite his misgivings, he composed a poem to accompany the image, and in this poem he identifies both Martin and himself as the subjects of the viewer's gaze (Paulinus, *Ep.* 32.2–4).

Although the incorporation of cult images into Christian practice could make sense as a competitive religious stratagem, the simpler answer might just be that once the competition from other gods abated, Christians felt less compunction about having their own sacred cult images to which they might offer their prayers, intended, of course, to be received by the model. The image even permitted the sense of a shared gaze, the image

---

20. Jaś Elsner, "Inventing Christian Rome: The Role of Early Christian Art," in *Rome: The Cosmopolis*, ed. Catharine Edwards and Greg Woolf (Cambridge: Cambridge University Press, 2003), 71–72.

acting as a way to communicate with the holy person as if he or she were actually present.

Two conditions might explain this shift from narrative to portrait images. First, from a more materialist perspective, the church's increasing security and wealth following its legalization and gradual establishment would have underwritten the inclusion of elaborate images to adorn walls, apses, and pavements. However, this change in the church's political and social status alone does not account for the change in the content of Christian iconography. Second, from a theological perspective, a renewed emphasis on the Christian doctrine of the incarnation—the invisible God made visible—could have arisen from the fourth- and fifth-century Trinitarian and christological controversies and found its expression in visual culture as well as dogmatic debate. The insistence on the importance of seeing a holy person's embodied representation might have been guided by the affirmation that Christ himself had a human face and form. Yet, maintaining that God became incarnate in a human (and therefore corruptible) physical body was also initially important for combatting docetism and other antimaterialist heresies at a time long before portraits became a preeminent form of pictorial art.

Nevertheless, a short section taken from Athanasius of Alexandria's treatise *On the Incarnation* (ca. 319) links the material context with the theological argument. In this work, Athanasius propounds a theology of visuality in which he affirms that God's nature is manifest in myriad ways and forms, including creation's beauties (see Rom 1:20), observing that because mortals are often tricked into mistaking the false for the true, God condescended to become corporeal—physically and visibly present to the world. He also insists that when the Word became incarnate in a mortal body, humanity could recognize its original image. In this following passage Athanasius compares this recognition to an artist's restoration of an actual damaged portrait:

> For as when a figure painted on wood has been soiled by dirt from outside, it is necessary for him whose figure it is to come again, so that the image can be renewed on the same material, because of his portrait even the material on which it is painted is not cast aside, but the portrait is re-inscribed on it. In the same way the all-holy Son of the Father, being the Image of the Father, came to our place to renew the human being made according to himself. (*Inc.* 14 [Behr])[21]

---

21. The critical edition is Eginhard P. Meijering, *Athanasius: De Incarnatione Verbi: Einleitung, übersetzung, Kommentar* (Amsterdam: Gieben, 1989).

Elsewhere Athanasius compares the renewed soul's vision of itself to an instance of beholding God's true image—the Word—as if in a mirror, thereby recognizing its own divine capacity (*C. Gent.* 2.34). Christ came to be sensibly (visibly) present to creation, so that it could realize its original beauty. This is why God made himself visible: not in order to come down and fix things or to figure out, at close range, how they had come to be broken. In other words, the invisible became visible in order for humans to recognize the truth both of God's being and of God's redemptive plan for their deliverance. In this way, Athanasius makes a distinction between God's absolute nature, which is invisible, and God's visible, bodily incarnation and earthly deeds.

Eventually, the polytheists' defense, that they honored images in order to express their devotion to the model (whether an emperor or a god), also justified Christian holy portraits. While they were not the objects of adoration themselves, they were a means by which reverence could be expressed to the divine being or holy person they represented. Those who paid them such honors realized that they were only representations and not realities, and this was essentially how polytheists described their actions.

Ultimately, whether the mediating representation is helpful or harmful derives from the model's worthiness. This is why the validity of sacred portraits came to have more to do with who they depicted than with how they were regarded. Whether one venerated images of Christ or the saint or images of other—false—gods became the important distinction between the idol and the icon.

Through the next centuries, Christians developed new devotional practices that included gazing on portraits of Christ, the Virgin Mary, and the saints (fig. 2.9). These images came to be regarded as more than simply aids to contemplation and a focus of prayers, but even to be means of encountering the saints, not in their images but *by means* of their images. In this sense, what Christians did with these holy images was not all that different from what pagans had done with their cult statues. The biggest difference, one could say, is that Christian holy images did not dupe their devotees into worshiping false deities—because an authentic representation, whether an artist's painted portrait or a verified relic depicted a true sacred being and therefore not an idol. Moreover, correctly understood (as it always had been), the images were not divine beings in themselves, but like the sacred Scriptures that were venerated as instantiations of God's words, these portraits mediated visual engagement with holy persons.

Fig. 2.9. Mosaic apse and arch, Christ with apostles and Virgin Mary with angels and saints, sixth century. Euphrasian Basilica, Porec. Photograph by Cameraphoto Arte, Venice / Art Resource, New York.

In summary, from the early third to the late fifth century, Christian art developed from simple symbolic figures, to narrative and dogmatic representations, and finally to iconic images. The function and place of art had become increasingly varied and complex along with the materials and venues for its creation and display. At first pictorial art served many purposes, including edification, adornment, and inspiration. By the end of the early Christian period, visual art also provided a means by which viewers were invited to encounter the holy presence itself.

Works Cited

Alexander, Paul J. "Church Councils and Patristic Authority: The Iconoclastic Council of Hiereia (754) and St. Sophia (815)." *HSCP* 63 (1958): 493–505.

Athanasius. *On the Incarnation*. Translated by John Behr. Yonkers, NY: Saint Vladimir's Seminary Press, 2011.
———. *The Trinity*. Translated by Edmund Hill. WSA. Brooklyn: New City, 1991.
Barnes, Timothy. *Constantine and Eusebius*. Cambridge: Harvard University Press, 1984.
Bigham, Steven. *Early Christian Attitudes toward Images*. Rollingsford, NH: Orthodox Research Institute, 2004.
Brubaker, Leslie, and John Haldon. *Byzantium in the Iconoclast Era*. Cambridge: Cambridge University Press, 2010.
Chadwick, Henry. *The Early Church*. London: Penguin, 1967.
Elsner, Jaś. "Inventing Christian Rome: The Role of Early Christian Art." Pages 71–99 in *Rome: The Cosmopolis*. Edited by Catharine Edwards and Greg Woolf. Cambridge: Cambridge University Press, 2003.
Epiphanius. *Letter to Theodosius*. Pages 41–42 in *Art of the Byzantine Empire 312–1453: Sources and Documents*. Translated by Cyril A. Mango. Toronto: University of Toronto Press, 1997.
Eusebius. *Letter to Constantia*. Translated by Cyril A. Mango. Pages 16–18 in *Art of the Byzantine Empire, 312–1453, Sources and Documents*. Toronto: University of Toronto Press, 1997.
Finney, Paul Corby. *The Invisible God: The Earliest Christians on Art*. Oxford: Oxford University Press, 1994.
Florovsky, Georges. "Origen, Eusebius, and the Iconoclastic Controversy." *CH* 19 (1950): 77–96.
Gero, Stephen. "The True Image of Christ: Eusebius' Letter to Constantia Reconsidered." *JTS* 32 (1981): 460–70.
Gibbon, Edward. *The Decline and Fall of the Roman Empire*. 6 vols. London: Strahan & Cadell, 1776–1788.
Holl, Karl. "Die Schriften des Epiphanius gegen die Bilderverehrung." Pages 351–87 in *Gesammelte Aufsätze zur Kirchengeschichte*. Vol. 1. Darmstadt: Wissenschaftliche Buchgesellschaft, 1916.
Hornik, Heidi J. "Freestanding Sculpture." Pages 73–85 in *The Routledge Handbook of Early Christian Art*. Edited by Robin M. Jensen and Mark D. Ellison. London: Routledge, 2018.
John Chrysostom. *De sancto Meletio Antiocheno*. Translated by Efthymios Rizos. Cult of Saints in Late Antiquity database. https://tinyurl.com/SBL4830o.
Kitzinger, Ernst. "The Cult of Images in the Age before Iconoclasm." *DOP* 8 (1954): 83–150.

Madec, Goulven. "Le Christ des païens d'après le De consensu Evangelistarum de Saint Augustin." *RechAug* 26 (1992): 5–67.
Mango, Cyril A. *The Art of the Byzantine Empire, 312–1453: Sources and Documents*. Toronto: University of Toronto Press, 1997.
Maraval, Pierre. "Épiphane, 'Docteur des Iconoclasts.'" Pages 51–62 in *Nicée II, 787–1987. Douze siècles d'images religieuses: Actes du colloque international Nicée II tenu au Collège de France, Paris les 2, 3, 4 Octobre 1986*. Edited by François Boespflug and Nicolas Lossky. Paris: Cerf, 1987.
Marsengill, Katherine. "The Christian Reception of Sculpture in Late Antiquity and the Historical Reception of Late Antique Christian Sculpture." *JBRec* 1 (2014): 67–101.
Meijering, Eginhard P. *Athanasius: De Incarnatione Verbi: Einleitung, übersetzung, Kommentar*. Amsterdam: Gieben, 1989.
Miller, Patricia Cox. *The Corporeal Imagination: Signifying the Holy in Late Antique Christianity*. Philadelphia: University of Pennsylvania Press, 2009.
Mountain, William J., and Frater Glorie, eds. *Sancti Augustini: De Trinitate Libri XV, Libri I–XV*. CCSL 50. Turnhout: Brepols, 2001.
Murray, Mary Charles. "Art and the Early Church." *JTS* 28 (1977): 303–45.
Ostrogorsky, Georg. *Studien zur Geschichte des byzantinischen Bilderstreits*. Breslau: Marcus, 1929.
Pitra, Jean B. *Spicilegium Solesmense Sanctorum Patrum*. Vol. 1. Paris, 1852.
Schönborn, Christoph von. *God's Human Face: The Christ-Icon*. Translated by Lothar Krauth. San Francisco: Ignatius, 1994.
Sode, Claudia, and Paul Speck. "Ikonoklasmus vor der Zeit? Der Brief des Eusebius von Kaisareia an Kaiserin Konstantia." *JÖB* 54 (2004): 113–34.
Wilpert, Joseph. *Die Malereien der Katakomben Roms*. Freiburg: Herder, 1903.
Wiśniewski, Robert. *The Beginnings of the Cult of Relics*. Oxford: Oxford University Press, 2019.

Experiencing the Renewed Cosmos: The Significance of the Celestial Ceiling in the Baptistery at Dura-Europos

Jeffrey M. Dale†

The city of Dura-Europos (hereafter Dura) has yielded extraordinary insights into life in ancient Syria ever since teams of archaeologists in the 1920s–1930s began excavations.[1] One structure that has received extensive attention is a building used for Christian worship.[2] After having been constructed as a private house in 232/233 CE, it was converted to a space suitable for Christian gatherings (a house-church or *domus ecclesiae*) in the 240s. The most significant changes took place in a room to the north of the courtyard that became the baptistery: a new floor was added, the

---

Editors' note: Before his accidental death in July 2022, Jeffrey Dale was working on revisions for this essay, including interacting more directly with Michael Peppard, *The World's Oldest Church: Bible, Art, and Ritual at Dura-Europos, Syria*, Synkrisis (New Haven: Yale University Press, 2016). Had he survived, he would have revised his essay to deal more extensively with the stimulating work of Peppard.

1. The history of the excavations is traced extensively in Clark Hopkins, *The Discovery of Dura-Europos*, ed. Bernard Goldman (New Haven: Yale University Press, 1979).

2. See, e.g., Carl H. Kraeling, *The Christian Building, The Excavations at Dura-Europos, Final Report VIII, Part II* (New Haven: Dura Europos, 1967); L. Michael White, *Texts and Monuments for the Christian Domus Ecclesiae in Its Environment*, vol. 2 of *The Social Origins of Christian Architecture*, HTS 42 (Valley Forge, PA: Trinity Press International, 1996), 123–31; Graydon F. Snyder, *Ante Pacem: Archaeological Evidence of Church Life before Constantine*, rev. ed. (Macon, GA: Mercer University Press, 2003), 128–34; Robin M. Jensen, *Living Water: Images, Symbols, and Settings of Early Christian Baptism*, VCSup 105 (Leiden: Brill, 2011), 182–84; Edward Adams, *The Earliest Christian Meeting Places: Almost Exclusively Houses?*, LNTS 450 (London: Bloomsbury, 2013), 89–95.

ceiling was lowered, a basin and canopy were constructed as the baptismal font, and the walls were adorned with frescoes featuring scenes from the Old and New Testaments.[3] Although scholars have discussed this space and its art extensively, one element of the artistic program has received relatively little treatment: the depiction of the starry sky (eight-pointed white stars on a blue background) on the canopy above the baptismal font as well as on the ceiling of the entire room (fig. 3.1). Everett Ferguson briefly suggests that this feature gave "a cosmic setting to the baptismal event" and then further refines this suggestion with a parenthetical question: "Has the baptized become part of a new creation?"[4]

In this paper, I provide evidence and context for Ferguson's suggestions, arguing that the star imagery gives a cosmic significance to the entire artistic program and reflects a cosmic understanding of baptism held by the Christian group at Dura. This group saw baptism as a ritual in which initiates renounced the powers of evil and became part of God's new creation, and one way they communicated this understanding was through the art that initiates would see as they experienced the ritual.[5]

---

3. The south wall contained an image of a woman at a well and one depicting David and Goliath. On the east wall, frescoes from the upper register are no longer extant, while all that has been preserved from the lower register is a few sets of feet. The feet in this procession continue to the lower register of the north wall, where it is evident that they are women carrying lamps toward a structure. Scholars take this procession to represent either the women coming to Christ's tomb or the virgins from Christ's parable. Above this image, on the upper register of the north wall, are scenes from the ministry of Christ: walking on water and healing the paralyzed man. On the west wall, where the baptismal font was located, a depiction of the good shepherd is featured. An image of Adam, Eve, and the serpent is also present at the bottom left, probably a later addition. See Adams, *Earliest Christian Meeting Places*, 94.

4. Everett Ferguson, *Baptism in the Early Church: History, Theology, and Liturgy in the First Five Centuries* (Grand Rapids: Eerdmans, 2009), 441.

5. Some scholars in recent years—notably Lucinda Dirven and Michael Peppard—have argued for interpretations of the artistic program that are somewhat along these lines, with initiates participating in a drama of redemption leading to the reattainment of paradise. I draw on their work and seek to emphasize the cosmic dimension. See Lucinda Dirven, "Paradise Lost, Paradise Regained: The Meaning of Adam and Eve in the Baptistery of Dura-Europos," *ECA* 5 (2008): 43–57; Michael Peppard, "New Testament Imagery in the Earliest Christian Baptistery," in *Dura-Europos: Crossroads of Antiquity*, ed. Lisa R. Brody and Gail L. Hoffman (Chestnut Hill, MA: McMullen Museum of Art, 2011), 169–87.

Fig. 3.1. Reconstruction of baptistery in Christian building from Dura-Europos, 240s CE. Brick, mortar, rubble, stone, plaster, and paint, 6.80–6.87 x 3.132–3.16 x 3.45 m. Yale University Art Gallery. Photograph by Yale University Art Gallery, Dura-Europos Collection.

I pursue my argument from two comparative angles. First, I situate the Christian building in the context of two other religious sites at Dura (the Jewish synagogue and a site for Mithras devotion) and consider cosmic imagery at those sites. Second, I explore the theme of baptism in four texts or writers from third- and fourth-century Syria (Acts of Thomas, Didascalia Apostolorum, Ephrem the Syrian, and Theodore of Mopsuestia), focusing on scriptural and cosmic motifs in these literary sources from the same general region as Dura in order to find language that complements the visual evidence. I find these two comparative angles to be helpful in shedding light on the significance of the celestial imagery, but my intention is not to exclude other potential contexts. I acknowledge that there is some ambiguity in the imagery and that it could be multivalent.

Cosmic Imagery at Two Other Dura Religious Sites

The Dura Synagogue

A few blocks north of the Christian building stood a Jewish synagogue. Both structures were located along Dura's western wall and were fortuitously preserved, in part, by an embankment added during the Sasanian siege of the 250s CE. Chad Spigel has recently argued on the basis of a recalculation of the seating capacity that this community was larger and more significant than previously thought.[6] The synagogue underwent two phases of development: it was first converted from a house sometime between 165 CE (when the Romans took control of the city) and 200 CE, and then renovated and enlarged in 244/245.[7] During each of the two phases, Spigel argues for a significantly larger seating capacity than Carl H. Kraeling initially calculated.[8] The Jewish population was certainly still a minority in Dura; Spigel estimates that it was never much larger than two hundred people.[9] Yet comparison with Mithraic and Christian structures suggests that the Jewish group was not only the largest of the three but also the fastest growing among them during the final decades before the city's fall.[10]

It is not surprising, then, that the synagogue's assembly hall displayed an artistic program that has been described as "elaborate," particularly in comparison with other sites at Dura.[11] The clearest example of an image

---

6. Chad Spigel, "The Jewish *Minority* of Dura-Europos," *JAJ* 10 (2019): 211–55.

7. Spigel, "Jewish *Minority*," 218–26.

8. His revised calculation exceeds Kraeling's by up to 80 percent for the first phase and 50 percent for the second phase, and is based on a methodology for determining seating capacity that was worked out in detail elsewhere (see Spigel, "Jewish *Minority*," 232–35). For the earlier calculation, see Carl H. Kraeling, *The Synagogue: The Excavations at Dura-Europos, Final Report VIII, Part I* (New York: Ktav, 1979), 328 n. 36, 335.

9. Spigel, "Jewish *Minority*," 236–38. As he points out, various factors make it difficult to use seating capacity to determine the Jewish population of Dura. For instance, the Jewish community could be smaller if space were included in the synagogue for gentile Godfearers, or it could be larger since the entire community might not be expected to attend at the same time.

10. Spigel, "Jewish *Minority*," 244–48. See also Charles B. McClendon, "The Articulation of Sacred Space in the Synagogue and Christian Building at Dura-Europos," in Brody and Hoffman, *Dura-Europos*, 157.

11. Kurt Weitzmann and Herbert L. Kessler, *The Frescoes of the Dura Synagogue and Christian Art*, DOS 28 (Washington, DC: Dumbarton Oaks Research Library and

Experiencing the Renewed Cosmos 55

Fig. 3.2. Sun, moon, and stars above standing male figure, 250s CE. Dura-Europos synagogue assembly hall. Fresco. National Museum of Damascus. Photograph by Yale University Art Gallery, Dura-Europos Collection.

with a cosmic orientation is one depicting the sun, moon, and seven stars above a male figure (fig. 3.2). Scholarly identifications of this figure have included Abraham, Jacob, Moses, Joshua, and Isaiah.[12] Several factors support identifying the figure as Abraham. According to Jewish tradition, Abraham was the first man to have white hair, a physical sign of the honor of advanced age (Pirqe R. El. 52). The depiction of crossed and covered hands is the gesture of accepting a promise (b. Shabb. 10a) and could reflect the ancestral promise given to Abraham (Gen 12). Finally, in this context, the sun, moon, and stars might allude to the promise that Abraham would be the "ancestor of a multitude of nations" (Gen 17:4 NRSV).

A focus on the Hebrew Scriptures was made clear not only through the many biblical scenes depicted but also through the prominence of an

---

Collection, 1990), 153. The most detailed account of the synagogue's artistic program can be found in Kraeling, *Synagogue*, 34–254.

12. Weitzmann and Kessler, *Frescoes of the Dura Synagogue*, 127.

Fig. 3.3. Reconstruction of assembly hall in Jewish synagogue from Dura-Europos, 240s–250s CE. Brick, mortar, tile, plaster, and paint, 13.65 x 7.68 x 7.00 m. National Museum of Damascus. Photograph by Yale University Art Gallery, Dura-Europos Collection.

arched niche, presumably for holding Torah scrolls, on the west wall (fig. 3.3).[13] Temple imagery on a blue background appears directly above the niche, and several other frescoes also feature temples. One depicts the pagan temple of Dagon, illustrating the narrative of the God of Israel triumphing over the god of the Philistines. Another shows Aaron as a priest wearing Parthian garb that had associations with cosmic worship. For Edwin R. Goodenough, this depiction "seems to announce that the true cosmic priesthood sought by the gentiles presents itself in Aaron; he presides over a worship that is one with the worship which the universe itself offers to God."[14]

---

13. Since this niche is relatively small, McClendon argues that it would not have been large enough to hold all the Torah scrolls belonging to the group and thus it likely served an honorific function for select scrolls on particular occasions ("Articulation of Sacred Space," 157).

14. Erwin R. Goodenough, *Jewish Symbols in the Greco-Roman Period*, abridged ed., ed. Jacob Neusner, BollS (Princeton: Princeton University Press, 1988), 219.

The Dura Mithraeum

Continuing northward along the city's western wall, several blocks north of the synagogue, archaeologists discovered a site for devotion to Mithras. This mithraeum underwent three stages of construction.[15] The early mithraeum, dated to a time not long after the city came under Roman control (165 CE), consisted simply of one room in an already-existing house, the rest of which remained a domestic space. Following a period when the building was mostly destroyed, perhaps due to disuse during a time of waning military presence, the mithraeum was reconstructed and significantly enlarged (ca. 209–211).[16] During this phase the decorative program became much more elaborate. Around what had been a simple square niche—into which were set two reliefs of Mithras—an arched recess was constructed, and plaster was added to the niche to match the contours of this arch. The final phase of construction, or the late mithraeum, began ca. 240. At this time a vaulted canopy was added above the arch, and the platform at the front was made larger and more impressive.

The mythology and rituals of the Mithraic mysteries focused on the cosmic dimension, and sites for Mithras devotion were designed to reflect this focus. The core narrative about Mithras—his slaying of the bull—associates him with the sun, while the bull represents the moon. This event is one that brings about cosmic death and rebirth; the cave in which it took place seems to have been a representation of the cosmos, with the cave's vault representing the dome of the heavens.[17] Accordingly, when devotees of Mithras gathered in literal caves or mithraea made to resemble caves, they were participating in this drama.[18] As Manfred Clauss explains,

---

15. My discussion here follows White, *Texts and Monuments*, 261–71. See also Maarten J. Vermaseren, *Corpus Inscriptionum et Monumentorum Religionis Mithriacae* (The Hague: Nijhoff, 1956–1960), 1:57–72.

16. Since a substantial portion of Dura's population was part of the military and since Mithraism was especially popular among Roman soldiers, it makes sense that the mithraeum's success would be tied to a strong military presence. On the importance of soldiers to the spread of Mithraism, see Manfred Clauss, *The Roman Cult of Mithras: The God and His Mysteries*, trans. Richard Gordon (New York: Routledge, 2000), 34–37.

17. For discussion of the narrative and its significance, see Clauss, *Roman Cult of Mithras*, 62–101.

18. This understanding is confirmed by literary evidence from Porphyry, who declared that the mithraeum bore "the image of the cosmos which Mithras had cre-

"Mithraists thus created for themselves an image of the kosmos, the dwelling-place of humankind, which then became, as the locus of the encounter with Mithras, a new and better home."[19]

The architecture and art of the Dura mithraeum were like mithraea elsewhere and as such had a distinctly cosmic orientation. This mithraeum was not a cave, of course, but in its successive renovations it gained features (arch and then canopy) that caused it to resemble a cave more closely. The paintings that adorned the mithraeum may have been somewhat basic in terms of artistic skill, but they are of immense value in attesting to conceptions of Mithraic mythology and its cosmic setting.[20] Wrapping around the central depictions of Mithras slaying the bull in the niche reliefs were separate images of the twelve signs of the zodiac, each of which was framed with an individual rectangle.[21] Beginning with the middle phase of the Dura mithraeum, the starry heavens were depicted with eight-pointed white stars on a blue background in the arch's soffit. The motif became even more prominent in the late mithraeum, with the blue sky and stars featured on the vaulted canopy (fig. 3.4).[22] A microcosm of the Mithraic drama had indeed been created at Dura.

Comparing the Jewish, Mithraic, and Christian Sites

A number of similarities can be noted between these three religious sites along Dura's western wall, suggesting some form of borrowing among them. All three were former domestic spaces that were converted for use by these religious communities, and in their modified form they displayed certain similarities in their arrangement.[23] Each included an arched niche

---

ated" (*Antr. nymph.* 6). See Roger Beck, "Ritual, Myth, Doctrine, and Initiation in the Mysteries of Mithras: New Evidence from a Cult Vessel," *JRS* 90 (2000): 147.

19. Clauss, *Roman Cult of Mithras*, 60–61.

20. The characterization comes from Franz Cumont, "The Dura Mithraeum," trans. Eric D. Francis, in *Mithraic Studies: Proceedings of the First International Congress of Mithraic Studies*, ed. John R. Hinnells (Manchester: Manchester University Press, 1975), 1:169. Cumont provides an extensive description and analysis of the paintings (1:169–94).

21. Cumont, "Dura Mithraeum," 1:182.

22. See White, *Texts and Monuments*, 270–71; see also Cumont, "Dura Mithraeum," 1:164. For re-creations of the starry heavens in other mithraea, see Clauss, *Roman Cult of Mithras*, 51.

23. See McClendon, "Articulation of Sacred Space."

Fig. 3.4. Reconstruction of naos in mithraeum from Dura-Europos, 240s CE. Brick, mortar, plaster, and paint. Yale University Art Gallery. Photograph by Yale University Art Gallery, Dura-Europos Collection.

or canopy of some sort in a prominent position; in the synagogue it held Torah scrolls, in the mithraeum it created a cave over the platform, and in the Christian building it contained the baptismal font. The parallels continue when the artistic programs of these sites are considered.[24] The Christian art has an affinity to the Jewish art in that both focus on scenes from biblical narratives, but, perhaps surprisingly, the Christian artistic program appears at least as similar to the Mithraic one. Both are relatively rudimentary in terms of artistic execution, and the uniformity in celestial imagery is striking—the mithraeum and Christian building display the same eight-pointed stars on a blue background. At the same time, the

---

24. It is quite possible that different groups at Dura employed painters from the same workshop. See Robin M. Jensen, "The Dura Europos Synagogue, Early-Christian Art, and Religious Life in Dura Europos," in *Jews, Christians, and Polytheists in the Ancient Synagogue: Cultural Interaction during the Greco-Roman Period*, ed. Steven Fine, BSHJ (London: Routledge, 1999), 184–87.

synagogue also contains the same shade of blue above the Torah niche, and the image that does include stars also has them as eight-pointed.[25]

What might such parallels indicate about the self-understanding of the Christian group and how it viewed itself in relation to other groups? While it makes sense to see a degree of borrowing between various religious communities at Dura, we should probably not frame this borrowing as syncretism. The reality is more complex; thematic features might be shared but take on different significance for each community. Cosmic imagery might be present at different religious sites, but the real question is how different groups interpreted such imagery. To gain an understanding of what significance the Christian group might have attached to this imagery in a baptismal context, we turn to Christian literary sources from Syria.

Baptism in Third- and Fourth-Century Syrian Writings

Acts of Thomas

The third-century Acts of Thomas proclaims salvation through a return to a state of purity (104, 139) that is saturated in a heavenly or cosmic light (149–153). Various passages refer to initiatory rituals, and it appears that baptism generally takes place after an anointing with oil and before one celebrates the Eucharist.[26] This sequence is particularly clear in the narrative of Thomas baptizing Mygdonia (121), and it is later alluded to when Thomas is accused of bewitching people with "oil and water and bread" (152).[27]

An earlier passage that presents initiation as a sealing seems to reverse the order of anointing and baptism, but it is at least as notable for the significance it attaches to initiatory rituals. Thomas prays on behalf of King Gundaphorus and his brother:

---

25. See Patricia Deleeuw, "A Peaceful Pluralism: The Durene Mithraeum, Synagogue, and Christian Building," in Brody and Hoffman, *Dura-Europos*, 194–96. Still, one might note the slight variation in the pattern of the stars (e.g., the baptistery does not have lines in the smaller stars, whereas the mithraeum does).

26. For further discussion of baptism in the Acts of Thomas, see Ferguson, *Baptism in the Early Church*, 429–35. On early Syrian practices of anointing in connection with baptism, see Gabriele Winkler, "The Original Meaning of the Prebaptismal Anointing and Its Implications," *Worship* 52 (1978): 24–45.

27. Translations of the Acts of Thomas follow *NTApoc*.

And now as I beseech and supplicate thee, receive the king and his brother and unite them with thy flock, cleansing them with thy washing and anointing them with thy oil from the error which surrounds them. Preserve them also from the wolves, leading them in thy pastures. Give them to drink from thine ambrosial spring which neither is turbid nor dries up. For they pray thee and implore and desire to become thy ministers and thy servants, and for this cause they are content even to be persecuted by thine enemies, and for thy sake to be hated by them and be despitefully used and put to death, even as thou for our sakes didst suffer all these things that thou mightiest preserve us, who art Lord and truly a *good shepherd*. (Acts Thom. 25)

Here washing precedes anointing, and this sequence may also be in view in the narrative that follows, in which the king and his brother are sealed and then receive "the additional sealing" (27).[28] Regardless of the precise steps of the ritual, what is clear is its significance, expressed metaphorically as becoming part of God's flock. The initiatory ritual is crucial because God "knows his own sheep by his seal" (26). The passage quoted above develops the metaphor at length, alluding to scriptural passages such as Ps 23 and John 10.

Elsewhere the theological significance of the baptismal ritual is further unfolded. At one point Thomas offers the following instruction: "This baptism is forgiveness of sins. It brings to new birth a light that is shed around" (Acts Thom. 132). In this densely packed statement, the author puts forward a theology of baptism that associates it with forgiveness, new birth, and light.

Didascalia Apostolorum

Another third-century document pertaining to church order, the Didascalia Apostolorum, or Teaching of the Apostles, presents a much different

---

28. There is significant debate on this passage. Albertus F. J. Klijn agrees that baptism followed by anointing is what is indicated by the Greek text's "seal" and "additional seal," but he follows the Syriac, in which the language is significantly different and explicitly indicates anointing and then baptism. See Klijn, *The Acts of Thomas: Introduction, Text, and Commentary*, 2nd ed., NovTSup 108 (Leiden: Brill, 2003), 78. Susan E. Myers uses this text to argue that at an early stage of Syrian Christianity anointing-only initiation (no water baptism) was an option, if not the norm. See Myers, "Initiation by Anointing in Early Syriac-Speaking Christianity," *StLit* 31 (2001): 150–70.

practice from that described in the Acts of Thomas.[29] Rather than calling for sexual abstinence as the way of salvation, it declares (in a polemic against Jewish views of impurity) that the Holy Spirit is given through baptism and does not leave someone "by reason of natural issues and the intercourse of marriage" (Did. apost. 26).[30] Despite the different outlook as compared with the Acts of Thomas, certain language and ritual practices overlap. The Didascalia also employs the language of a "seal" to refer to initiation that is a prerequisite for receiving the Eucharist (10) and assumes that anointing precedes baptism (16). For the Didascalia, anointing takes place in two stages (the bishop anoints the head while others are authorized to perform a whole-body anointing[31]) and is cast in the light of Old Testament tradition. The text states, "As of old the priests and kings were anointed in Israel, do thou in like manner" (16).[32]

The Didascalia declares that baptism involves a double departure, a separation from both gentile and Jewish observances: "But you through baptism have been set free from idolatry, and from the Second Legislation, which was (imposed) on account of idols, you have been released" (26). This document displays a polemical attitude toward Judaism and its ritual law, which it refers to as the "Second Legislation." As part of the polemic, it proclaims complete forgiveness gained through a one-time baptismal ritual, in contrast with Jewish purifications that must be repeated with each new case of impurity (24, 26).[33] The Christian initiate turns away not only from gentile idolatry but also from this Jewish ritual system.

---

29. For a fuller discussion of baptism in this document, see Ferguson, *Baptism in the Early Church*, 436–40.

30. Translations of the Didascalia follow R. Hugh Connolly, *Didascalia Apostolorum: The Syriac Version Translated and Accompanied by the Verona Latin Fragments, with an Introduction and Notes* (Oxford: Clarendon, 1969).

31. The context for this passage is the role of deaconesses. Their role is important for the whole-body anointing of women initiates.

32. Regarding the kingship motif in this and other Syriac texts, see Winkler, "Original Meaning," 31–36. She concludes, "Therefore the main theme of this pre-baptismal anointing is the entry into the eschatological kingship of the Messiah, being in the true sense of the word assimilated to the Messiah-King through this anointing" (36).

33. "And as for baptism also, one is enough for you, even that which has perfectly forgiven you your sins" (Did. apost. 24).

Ephrem the Syrian

Although Ephrem the Syrian (ca. 306–373) was born a half-century after the fall of Dura, his writings can still provide useful data for interpreting the cosmic significance of the Dura baptistery.[34] Ephrem's writings demonstrate continuities with the third-century sources discussed above and are tremendously helpful in bringing to light additional elements of Syrian baptismal theology and practice that seem to be reflected in the Christian art at Dura. As Michael Peppard puts it, "Ephrem never set foot in the house-church at Dura-Europos, but his hymns would have felt right at home."[35]

Poetic allusions in Ephrem's hymns attest to practices connected with baptism as it was known to him. *Hymns on Virginity* 7 is especially rich in baptismal allusions, with several aspects brought together in the following line: "April revives fasters, anoints, dips and whitens" (7.2). This brief statement apparently refers to baptism taking place during the paschal season and bringing an end to a period of fasting. It also suggests that anointing precedes baptism (see 7.6, 8). A Trinitarian formula perhaps connected with a triple immersion is an important part of the ritual; Ephrem speaks of "three labor pangs" connected with "the three glorious names of Father and Son and Holy Spirit" (7.5; for language of immersion, see 7.10). Ritual actions for the purpose of sanctifying the water seem to be referenced when Ephrem mentions a cross being placed in the water (*Hymn. virg.* 15.6). A sequence of removing garments and then being clothed after leaving the water also seems to be an important part of the ritual and is probably in view when Ephrem speaks of pearl divers stripping themselves (*Hymn. fid.* 5.3–4).[36]

---

34. In doing so, I follow others, such as Lucinda Dirven and Michael Peppard, and seek to build on their work (see Dirven, "Paradise Lost, Paradise Regained"; Peppard, "New Testament Imagery"; Peppard, *World's Oldest Church*). One must consult a plethora of sources to find English translations of Ephrem's writings. Translations of *Hymns on Epiphany* and *Hymns on the Pearl* follow *NPNF* 2/13. Translations of *Hymns on the Nativity* and *Hymns on Virginity* follow Kathleen E. McVey, *Ephrem the Syrian: Hymns*, CWS (New York: Paulist, 1989). Translations of Ephrem's Commentary on the Diatessaron follow Carmel McCarthy, *Saint Ephrem's Commentary on Tatian's Diatessaron: An English Translation of Chester Beatty Syriac MS 709*, JSSSup 2 (Oxford: Oxford University Press, 1993).

35. Peppard, *World's Oldest Church*, 203.

36. For discussion of these and other texts, see Ferguson, *Baptism in the Early Church*, 506–8.

When discussing baptism, Ephrem habitually draws on scriptural narratives in typological fashion. In *Hymn. Ep.* 5, he moves through several Old Testament narratives, all of which he takes as prefiguring elements of baptism: Naaman's cleansing, the Red Sea, David's anointing, and Moses striking the rock.[37] New Testament scenes from Christ's ministry, including the narratives of the Samaritan woman at the well and the paralyzed man beside the pool, also illuminate the meaning of baptism:

> Blessed are you, O Shechem, for upon your well
> today is built a holy church:
> For behold, "I baptize with living water
> for which your mouth asked there.
> Whoever drank from your well thirsted again and returned to it;
> My baptism needs no repetition." (*Hymn. virg.* 17.10; see *Comm. Diat.* 12.17)

> For, if they believe that an angel can heal illnesses through *the waters of Shiloah*, how much more can the Lord of angels purify the stains [of sin] through baptism? (*Comm. Diat.* 13.1; see *Hymn. Ep.* 11.6)

Ephrem also relates Christ's own baptism to his role as shepherd and with his walking on the water:

> John was at the gate of the sheepfold where the Israelite flock was gathered together in unity. [The Lord] entered into the flock not by his power but by his justice. The Spirit which rested on him during his baptism attested that he was the shepherd, for he had received the prophecy and priesthood through John. (*Comm. Diat.* 4.3)

> How wonderful your footsteps, walking on the waters!
> You subdued the great sea beneath your feet.
> [Yet] to a little stream you subjected your head,
> bending down to be baptized in it. (*Hymn. fid.* 10.20)[38]

---

37. It should be noted that the authenticity of the *Hymns for Epiphany* is disputed. According to Kees den Biesen, the editor of the major critical edition considered only numbers 1, 2, 5, and 11 to come from Ephrem. See des Biesen, *Annotated Bibliography of Ephrem the Syrian: Student Edition* (N.p.: Kees den Biesen, 2011). My discussion draws only from numbers 1 and 5.

38. Translation follows Robert Murray, "A Hymn of St Ephrem to Christ on

These last two examples may not qualify as typologies in the strict sense, but they are at least scriptural narratives or motifs that are used for illustrative purposes.

The cosmic nature of his theology is evident in his work generally. As Kathleen McVey explains, "Ephrem's world is permeated by the divine presence. His poetry is based upon a vision of the created order as a vast system of symbols or mysteries. No person, thing or event in the world exists without a mysterious relation to the whole."[39] Such knowledge of God's presence, however, is possible only because God has crossed the chasm between divinity and humanity to make himself known.[40] Accordingly, Christ's incarnation is crucial for Ephrem and paradoxically does not diminish Christ's cosmic rule:[41]

> The Power that governs all dwelt in a small womb.
> While dwelling there, He was holding the reins of the universe.
> His Parent was ready for His will to be fulfilled.
> The heavens and all creation were filled by Him.
> The Sun entered the womb, and in the height and depth
> His rays were dwelling. (*Hymn. nat.* 21.6)

The imagery of celestial light is not limited to this passage. In many other places Ephrem speaks of Christ as a star or other heavenly light in connection with his birth, referencing scriptural texts such as Balaam's prophecy of a star or the magi following the star to Bethlehem (*Hymn. nat.* 1.5–6, 24.12–13, *Hymn. virg.* 5.3, *Comm. Diat.* 2.21c).

Ephrem's vision of redemption has to do with cosmic renewal and the restoration of what was lost through the actions of Adam and Eve. He explicitly speaks of the renewal of heaven and earth: "He renewed the sky

---

the Incarnation, the Holy Spirit, and the Sacraments: Translation and Notes," *ECR* 3 (1970): 142–50.

39. Kathleen E. McVey, "Ephrem the Syrian," in *The Early Christian World*, ed. Philip F. Esler (London: Routledge, 2000), 2:1232. As an example, Ephrem declares, "In every place, if you look, His symbol is there" (*Hymn. virg.* 20.12).

40. Sebastian Brock, "St Ephrem the Syrian on Reading Scripture," *DRev* 438 (2007): 39.

41. Kees den Biesen explains that for Ephrem "the paradox of the Incarnation captures in an archetypal way the paradoxical, and therefore symbolical, nature of all reality." See Kees den Biesen, *Simple and Bold: Ephrem's Art of Symbolic Thought*, GD 26 (Piscataway, NJ: Gorgias, 2006), 55.

since fools worshipped all the luminaries. He renewed the earth that had grown old because of Adam" (*Hymn. nat.* 17.12). Exactly what this cosmic renewal looks like concretely is not spelled out, but the poetic imagery makes clear that Ephrem imagines Christ's new creation to encompass even the heavenly luminaries. Elsewhere Ephrem depicts Christ and the Virgin Mary as a new Adam and Eve through whom God's plan for restoration is accomplished (*Hymn. nat.* 1.15–16, *Comm. Diat.* 2.2). Christ comes to find lost Adam "and in the garment of light to return him to Eden" (*Hymn. virg.* 16.9). The fall involved losing the garments of light, so Christ himself becomes a "robe of glory" for redeemed humanity:[42]

> Eve became a cave and grave
> for the accursed serpent, for his evil counsel
> entered and dwelt in her; she who became dust
> became bread for him. [But] You are our bread,
> and you are our bridal chamber and the robe of glory. (*Hymn. nat.* 17.6)

The imagery of garments, light, and a wedding are joined to one another for Ephrem in Christ's parable of the virgins. As they go to the wedding, they are "clothed with the light of their lamps" (*Hymn fid.* 3.4).

Many of the points sketched above find expression in a cosmic understanding of baptism for Ephrem. The language about the renewal of heaven and earth in response to Adam's failure and ongoing false worship is echoed in *Hymn. Ep.* 1.1, and then in 1.4 there is discussion of "a sign of baptism." The action of putting on clothing as the baptized initiate comes forth from the water seems to have symbolic value. Ephrem tells initiates to "put on from the waters of baptism the Holy Spirit" (*Hymn. nat.* 5.1). Finally, the fasting that is practiced prior to baptism is significant for more than just spiritual preparation; it also has the function of making the baptism itself a wedding feast (*Hymn. ieiun.* 5.1).[43] Baptism for Ephrem, then, is a cosmic ritual in which the initiate enters the divine reality of a new heaven and earth. Becoming part of this reality must necessarily entail

---

42. For further discussion, see Sebastian Brock, "Clothing Metaphors as a Means of Theological Expression in Syriac Tradition," in *Typus, Symbol, Allegorie Bei den Östlichen Vätern und Ihren Parallelen im Mittelalter*, ed. Margot Schmidt and Carl-Friedrich Geyer, EichBeit 4 (Regensburg: Pustet, 1982), 11–38.

43. For this text, see Sebastian Brock, *The Luminous Eye: The Spiritual World Vision of Saint Ephrem*, rev. ed., CS 124 (Kalamazoo, MI: Cistercian, 1992), 122–23.

rejecting the false worship of the old existence and embracing the light of the new cosmos.

Theodore of Mopsuestia

Even further removed temporally from the church at Dura is Theodore of Mopsuestia (ca. 350–428), but it is worth briefly discussing his perspective because of his important description of a ceremony preceding baptism that has to do with renouncing the cosmic powers of evil.[44] The one coming to receive baptism stands barefoot on rough sackcloth and then adopts a posture of prayer, with knees bowed and body erect. After praying for deliverance, the candidate then receives words of assurance from those presiding over the ritual. Next the candidate utters a solemn pledge: "I abjure Satan and all his angels, and all his service, and all his deception, and all his worldly glamour; and I engage myself, and believe, and am baptised in the name of the Father, and of the Son, and of the Holy Spirit" (*Hom. cat.* 13).[45] Theodore proceeds to spell out in specific terms what each of these phrases mean. Of interest is his comment that the service of Satan to be renounced includes "that a person should follow astrology and watch the positions and motions of the sun, the moon and the stars for the purpose of travelling, going forth, or undertaking a given work, while believing that he is benefited or harmed by their motion and their course" (*Hom. cat.* 13). Baptism thus includes the rejection of a certain stance toward the cosmos, but it also can be said to involve a cosmic perspective for Theodore in that the initiate becomes a cosmic citizen: "We expect to be enrolled in heaven through the gift of

---

44. According to Ferguson, most scholars date Theodore's baptismal homilies to the late fourth century (*Baptism in the Early Church*, 519). Theodore believes himself to be following an "early tradition" (*Hom. cat.* 13), and indeed, we find attestation of a similar renunciation ceremony much earlier, from Tertullian: "When we are going to enter the water, but a little before, in the presence of the congregation and under the hand of the president, we solemnly profess that we disown the devil, and his pomp, and his angels" (*Cor.* 3 [ANF 3]). Theodore offers the first evidence from Syria, however. For other ancient sources discussing this practice, see Robin M. Jensen, *Understanding Early Christian Art* (London: Routledge, 2000), 178, 213 nn. 72–73.

45. Regarding the numbering of Theodore's *Catechetical Homilies*, see Ferguson, *Baptism in the Early Church*, 520 n. 7. Translations follow Alphonse Mingana, *Commentary of Theodore of Mopsuestia on the Lord's Prayer and on the Sacraments of Baptism and the Eucharist*, WS 6 (Piscataway, NJ: Gorgias, 2009).

the holy baptism" (*Hom. cat.* 12). Finally, those being baptized enact the drama of redemption: they become naked like Adam in his innocence, and after a whole-body anointing and baptism they are clothed with "radiant" garments as an eschatological sign pointing to future resurrection (*Hom. cat.* 14).[46]

A Brief Synthesis of the Syrian Writings

While the above discussion has been far from exhaustive for any of the third- and fourth-century Christian texts from Syria (and admittedly has focused especially on elements that seem promising for comparison with Dura), it has provided at least a glimpse into perspectives on baptism in that region. While these texts display many differences, they also reveal certain points of commonality. In each of the four documents or authors discussed above, anointing is a crucial part of the initiatory ritual and appears to precede baptism in almost all cases. Although a renunciation ceremony is explicit only in Theodore, all sources reject this earthly life, past and present, in favor of the heavenly one. Scriptural types and motifs abound in the writings of Ephrem but can be seen in each of the others as well. Ephrem is also the one who makes cosmic themes most explicit, but most of the other sources seem to display some sort of cosmic orientation. The table on the following page summarizes the data gathered from these literary sources.

Envisioning Baptism at Dura in Cosmic Context

In this section I seek to make the picture of baptism at Dura concrete: by using the comparative data discussed above, I offer an imaginative account of a baptismal candidate's encounter with the art in the Christian building. Through the connections that can be drawn between the understandings of baptism found in the Syrian Christian authors and the physicality of the Dura baptistery, including the art that surrounded participants in the ceremony, one can envision what the experience may have been like for an initiate. The baptismal ritual truly was an embodied one that engaged the senses.[47]

---

46. A more detailed discussion of Theodore's perspective can be found in Ferguson, *Baptism in the Early Church*, 519–32.

47. Ulrich Mell observes that only one image (David and Goliath) contains an inscription that would aid in interpretation and concludes that the rest should be

Select Comparison of Third- and Fourth-Century Syrian Perspectives on Baptism

	Acts of Thomas	Didascalia Apostolorum	Ephrem the Syrian	Theodore of Mopsuestia
Rituals connected with baptism	anointing	anointing	fasting, anointing, consecrating water, unclothing/clothing	renunciation of evil, anointing, unclothing/clothing
Evil to be renounced	sexual desire	Jewish rituals and gentile idolatry	existence in the old creation	satanic powers and service
Scriptural motifs	shepherd/flock	kingly/priestly anointing	Adam/Eve, Moses, Naaman, David, woman at well, paralyzed man, shepherd, walking on water	Adam/Eve
Cosmic motifs	light		heavens/earth, light/stars, cosmic Christ, garments of light, wedding feast	enrolled in heaven, radiant garments

---

considered self-explanatory (*selbsterklärend*) for those viewing. See Mell, *Christliche Hauskirche und Neues Testament: die Ikonologie des Baptisteriums von Dura Europos und das Diatessaron Tatians*, NTOA/SUNT 77 (Göttingen: Vandenhoeck & Ruprecht, 2010), 155. I suggest that one reason we can assume candidates would have readily been able to make sense of the art is the period of catechesis that would have preceded their entrance to the room. Presumably during this period they would have been instructed as to the significance of baptism, including scriptural motifs that they then observed in the art.

Fig. 3.5. Canopy, in situ, 240s CE. Dura-Europos baptistery. Brick, mortar, stone, plaster, and paint, 1.583–1.830 x 1.74 x 3.20 m. Yale University Art Gallery. Photograph by Yale University Art Gallery, Dura-Europos Collection.

I imagine a female baptismal candidate being ushered into the room where her initiation into the Christian community is about to take place.[48] She immediately finds herself underneath a celestial expanse. The starry sky above her sets the context for the ritual that is about to take place and indicates something of its momentousness. It may take place in a small room of a house-church, but its significance is truly cosmic. The lowered ceiling of the room brings the starry sky especially close to the candidate (fig. 3.5).[49]

The candidate is led to a place in front of a niche in the south wall, from which a flask of oil is taken. There she receives an anointing as she gazes at a depiction of David holding a sword, about to kill Goliath. She

---

48. Peppard's *World's Oldest Church* engages in a similar imaginative exercise.

49. The ceiling was lowered considerably during the renovation, from 5.22 m (as in the other rooms) to 3.2 m (Adams, *Earliest Christian Meeting Places*, 93). While the lowered ceiling created an additional space above, it was too small to be usable for much, suggesting the modification was primarily for "aesthetic purposes" (Snyder, *Ante Pacem*, 133). This fact reinforces the notion that the ceiling played a role in the sensory experience of the room and thus in the interpretation of the art.

remembers that in the biblical narrative the future king of Israel goes forth to engage in battle against the giant following his anointing. In a similar way, her own anointing is preparing her to participate in a struggle against cosmic evil forces.[50] She knows that by participating in this ceremony she is renouncing allegiance to Satan and other powers of evil.[51] From the place of anointing, the candidate begins to move around the room in a counterclockwise fashion as she takes in the artistic panorama.[52] It is as if she is joining in a procession as she encounters a depiction of women with lamps moving toward a structure. She understands them to be the virgins of Christ's parable, on their way to the bridal chamber.[53] This night scene connects with the night sky on the ceiling, reminding the one experiencing this ceremony that the spiritual wedding in which she is participating is a cosmic event. Following the procession, she moves around the room from the east wall to the north one. Above the processional image are scenes from Christ's ministry that attest to his power, particularly as exercised in the context of water. The Christ who walks on

---

50. In Ephrem's *Hymn. Ep.* 5.9–11, the sequence of David's anointing and then fighting the giant is compared to baptismal candidates being anointed and baptized and thereby receiving "armour" for contending against "the haughtiness of the Evil One."

51. Regardless of whether the specific renunciation ceremony described by Theodore was practiced at Dura, the notion of renouncing evil as part of baptism can be assumed.

52. As Dominic E. Serra explains, a counterclockwise reading of the room seems to be required by the art. This is the direction the women are arguably moving in procession, and the two scenes in the image of the paralyzed man proceed from right to left. See Serra, "The Baptistery at Dura-Europos: The Wall Paintings in the Context of Syrian Baptismal Theology," *EL* 120 (2006): 73–74.

53. The scriptural referent for this scene is a matter of significant debate. Through Kraeling's influence, the interpretation of the woman as those coming to Christ's tomb became dominant. Serra, however, revived an early suggestion that they are the virgins of Christ's parable, and others have found significant explanatory power in this understanding. See Serra, "Baptistery at Dura-Europos," 69–71; Peppard, "New Testament Imagery"; Michael Peppard, "Illuminating the Dura-Europos Baptistery: Comparanda for the Female Figures," *JECS* 20 (2012): 543–74; Sanne Klaver, "The Brides of Christ: 'The Women in Procession' in the Baptistery of Dura-Europos," *ECA* 9 (2012–2013): 63–78. I find the reasoning laid out by Peppard to be quite persuasive: (1) the depiction seems to have been of ten women, five on each wall; (2) the structure toward which they are moving seems to be a building rather than a sarcophagus; (3) iconographic analysis suggests the women are depicted as virgins ("New Testament Imagery," 175–76).

Fig. 3.6. Canopy with painted stars above wall painting of shepherd and sheep (the shepherd is standing left of center), 240s CE. Dura-Europos baptistery, west wall. Fresco, 130.81 x 153.67 cm. Yale University Art Gallery. Photograph by Yale University Art Gallery, Dura-Europos Collection.

the sea and brings healing to a paralyzed man at a pool is also disclosing his power in the waters of baptism.[54]

As the candidate turns to the western wall, where the baptismal font is located, she encounters a representation of the cosmic Christ. Beneath a canopy of stars, Christ is represented as a shepherd caring for his flock (fig. 3.6). The candidate believes that through participating in this ritual she is becoming one of the sheep in that flock. Christ the Shepherd is engaged in a work of cosmic redemption, and a smaller image at the lower left of Adam, Eve, and the serpent gives context for Christ's work. Adam and Eve, the candidate has been taught, are figures who evoke the whole drama of redemption, from humanity's fall, which marred the cosmos, to humanity's restoration in a renewed cosmos.[55] With this understanding, she then

---

54. As discussed above, Ephrem connects these narratives with baptism (*Comm. Diat.* 13.1, *Hymn. Ep.* 11.6, *Hymn. fid.* 10.20).

55. See Jensen, *Understanding Early Christian Art*, 178. Ephrem's theology con-

experiences the water of baptism. She believes herself to be renouncing the old existence and to be entering into life in God's new creation. As she goes forth from the font, the final image she sees is a woman at a well. Like the woman of John 4, she too finds joy in having experienced "living water."[56] The newly baptized one is then clothed and goes forth to partake in the eucharistic feast.

The imaginative interpretation I have just sketched has a strong affinity to interpretations of the Dura baptistery's pictorial focus on redemption and new-creation program offered by Lucinda Dirven and Peppard; I have sought to build on their work and to stress the cosmic dimension that is present especially through the celestial ceiling that stands over the room. Both Dirven and Peppard, however, dichotomize between the baptismal theology implied by the art at Dura and the baptismal theology expressed by Paul in the New Testament. Dirven argues against "a Pauline notion of baptism" at Dura and asserts that "it is extremely unlikely that Paul's teaching of redemption was ever popular here."[57] Peppard argues that "the Pauline interpretation of baptism as death and resurrection" is absent from Dura.[58]

While I agree that the understanding of baptism as dying and rising with Christ expressed in Rom 6 does not seem to be reflected at Dura, it is a mistake to limit Paul's understanding of baptism to Rom 6. In fact, I contend that Paul's baptismal theology in Galatians resonates strongly with a cosmic view of baptism. This is evident when baptismal formula of 3:27–28 is seen in relation to his new-creation theology of 6:15 (and see also 2 Cor 5:17). In the first passage Paul declares, "As many of you as were baptized into Christ have clothed yourselves with Christ. There is no longer Jew or Greek, there is no longer slave or free, there is no longer male and female; for all of you are one in Christ Jesus" (Gal 3:27–28 NRSV).

---

nects Adam and Eve with the drama of redemption and renewal of the cosmos (*Hymn. nat.* 1.15–16; 17.6, 12).

56. The identification of the woman in this image as the woman of John 4 was nearly universal until Serra proposed that she is Mary, referring to the "annunciation at the well" passage in the Protoevangelium of James ("Baptistery at Dura-Europos," 77–78). I do not wish to completely dismiss that possibility, but I still find the woman of John 4 to be a more likely possibility since there is evidence that her narrative was associated with baptism (Ephrem, *Hymn. virg.* 17.10; *Comm. Diat.* 12.17). The language of "living water" was significant in early Christian baptismal contexts (see Did. 7.1).

57. Dirven, "Paradise Lost, Paradise Regained," 46, 53.

58. Peppard, *World's Oldest Church*, 119.

The clothing language that became prominent in Syrian descriptions of baptism is part of Paul's vocabulary here, and the description of polarities of the old order losing their significance implies that God's new creation is the framework for Pauline baptism as well—the new creation in which Jewish and Greek identity are inconsequential: "For neither circumcision nor uncircumcision matters; the only thing that matters is new creation" (6:15, my translation).[59]

Concluding Summary

In this paper I have given attention to a neglected dimension of the artistic program of the Christian baptistery at Dura—the starry sky on the canopy and ceiling—and have argued that it contributes to the cosmic orientation of the baptistery. I do not claim that this study is exhaustive; probing the significance of the celestial imagery through other comparative contexts might prove fruitful as well.[60] But I suggest that the two comparative angles I have explored above have shed light on the role of the baptistery's star imagery in supporting a cosmic view of baptism. First, comparison with the art and architecture of the Dura synagogue and mithraeum demonstrates that artistic features, including cosmic imagery, were shared among various religious sites. Residents of Dura would not have found such imagery unusual. What the imagery meant to the different groups, however, varied considerably. Second, possibilities for what cosmic imagery meant to the Christian group can be found by tracing perspectives on baptism in Christian Syrian writers. Many connections can be drawn between these literary sources and the visual evidence from Dura, suggesting a view of baptism that highlights the drama of redemption involving the renewal of heaven and earth. Christian initiates found themselves caught up in this cosmic drama, benefiting from the redemption secured by Christ and experiencing what it means to live within the renewed cosmos.

---

59. Peppard, it should be noted, acknowledges that this perspective can be seen in Galatians (*World's Oldest Church*, 208).

60. One might consider exploring similar celestial imagery in early Christian art from other regions and/or somewhat later periods. For instance, a mosaic in the fifth-century Galla Placidia Mausoleum in Ravenna contains hundreds of eight-pointed stars surrounding a cross. See Robin M. Jensen, *The Cross: History, Art, and Controversy* (Cambridge: Harvard University Press, 2017), 106.

Works Cited

Adams, Edward. *The Earliest Christian Meeting Places: Almost Exclusively Houses?* LNTS 450. London: Bloomsbury, 2013.

Beck, Roger. "Ritual, Myth, Doctrine, and Initiation in the Mysteries of Mithras: New Evidence from a Cult Vessel." *JRS* 90 (2000): 145–80.

Biesen, Kees den. *Annotated Bibliography of Ephrem the Syrian: Student Edition.* N.p.: Kees den Biesen, 2011.

———. *Simple and Bold: Ephrem's Art of Symbolic Thought.* GD 26. Piscataway, NJ: Gorgias, 2006.

Brock, Sebastian. "Clothing Metaphors as a Means of Theological Expression in Syriac Tradition." Pages 11–38 in *Typus, Symbol, Allegorie Bei Den Östlichen Vätern Und Ihren Parallelen Im Mittelalter*. Edited by Margot Schmidt and Carl-Friedrich Geyer. EichstBeit 4. Regensburg: Pustet, 1982.

———. *The Luminous Eye: The Spiritual World Vision of Saint Ephrem.* Rev. ed. CS 124. Kalamazoo, MI: Cistercian, 1992.

———. "St Ephrem the Syrian on Reading Scripture." *DRev* 438 (2007): 37–50.

Clauss, Manfred. *The Roman Cult of Mithras: The God and His Mysteries.* Translated by Richard Gordon. New York: Routledge, 2000.

Connolly, R. Hugh. *Didascalia Apostolorum: The Syriac Version Translated and Accompanied by the Verona Latin Fragments, with an Introduction and Notes.* Oxford: Clarendon, 1969.

Cumont, Franz. "The Dura Mithraeum." Translated by Eric D. Francis. Pages 151–214 in *Mithraic Studies: Proceedings of the First International Congress of Mithraic Studies.* Vol. 1. Edited by John R. Hinnells. Manchester: Manchester University Press, 1975.

Deleeuw, Patricia. "A Peaceful Pluralism: The Durene Mithraeum, Synagogue, and Christian Building." Pages 189–99 in *Dura-Europos: Crossroads of Antiquity.* Edited by Lisa R. Brody and Gail L. Hoffman. Chestnut Hill, MA: McMullen Museum of Art, 2011.

Dirven, Lucinda. "Paradise Lost, Paradise Regained: The Meaning of Adam and Eve in the Baptistery of Dura-Europos." *ECA* 5 (2008): 43–57.

Ferguson, Everett. *Baptism in the Early Church: History, Theology, and Liturgy in the First Five Centuries.* Grand Rapids: Eerdmans, 2009.

Goodenough, Erwin R. *Jewish Symbols in the Greco-Roman Period.* Edited by Jacob Neusner. Abridged ed. BollS. Princeton: Princeton University Press, 1988.

Hopkins, Clark. *The Discovery of Dura-Europos*. Edited by Bernard Goldman. New Haven: Yale University Press, 1979.

Jensen, Robin M. *The Cross: History, Art, and Controversy*. Cambridge: Harvard University Press, 2017.

———. "The Dura Europos Synagogue, Early-Christian Art, and Religious Life in Dura Europos." Pages 174–89 in *Jews, Christians, and Polytheists in the Ancient Synagogue: Cultural Interaction during the Greco-Roman Period*. Edited by Steven Fine. BSHJ. London: Routledge, 1999.

———. *Living Water: Images, Symbols, and Settings of Early Christian Baptism*. VCSup 105. Leiden: Brill, 2011.

———. *Understanding Early Christian Art*. London: Routledge, 2000.

Klaver, Sanne. "The Brides of Christ: 'The Women in Procession' in the Baptistery of Dura-Europos." *ECA* 9 (2012–2013): 63–78.

Klijn, Albertus F. J. *The Acts of Thomas: Introduction, Text, and Commentary*. 2nd ed. NovTSup 108. Leiden: Brill, 2003.

Kraeling, Carl H. *The Christian Building: The Excavations at Dura-Europos, Final Report VIII, Part II*. New Haven: Dura Europos, 1967.

———. *The Synagogue: The Excavations at Dura-Europos, Final Report VIII, Part I*. New York: Ktav, 1979.

McCarthy, Carmel. *Saint Ephrem's Commentary on Tatian's Diatessaron: An English Translation of Chester Beatty Syriac MS 709*. JSSSup 2. Oxford: Oxford University Press, 1993.

McClendon, Charles B. "The Articulation of Sacred Space in the Synagogue and Christian Building at Dura-Europos." Pages 155–67 in *Dura-Europos: Crossroads of Antiquity*. Edited by Lisa R. Brody and Gail L. Hoffman. Chestnut Hill, MA: McMullen Museum of Art, 2011.

McVey, Kathleen E. "Ephrem the Syrian." Pages 1228–50 in *The Early Christian World*. Vol. 2. Edited by Philip F. Esler. London: Routledge, 2000.

———. *Ephrem the Syrian: Hymns*. CWS. New York: Paulist, 1989.

Mell, Ulrich. *Christliche Hauskirche und Neues Testament: die Ikonologie des Baptisteriums von Dura Europos und das Diatessaron Tatians*. NTOA/SUNT 77. Göttingen: Vandenhoeck & Ruprecht, 2010.

Mingana, Alphonse. *Commentary of Theodore of Mopsuestia on the Lord's Prayer and on the Sacraments of Baptism and the Eucharist*. WS 6. Piscataway, NJ: Gorgias, 2009.

Murray, Robert. "A Hymn of St Ephrem to Christ on the Incarnation, the Holy Spirit, and the Sacraments: Translation and Notes." *ECR* 3 (1970): 142–50.

Myers, Susan E. "Initiation by Anointing in Early Syriac-Speaking Christianity." *StLit* 31 (2001): 150–70.

Peppard, Michael. "Illuminating the Dura-Europos Baptistery: Comparanda for the Female Figures." *JECS* 20 (2012): 543–74.

———. "New Testament Imagery in the Earliest Christian Baptistery." Pages 169–87 in *Dura-Europos: Crossroads of Antiquity*. Edited by Lisa R. Brody and Gail L. Hoffman. Chestnut Hill, MA: McMullen Museum of Art, 2011.

———. *The World's Oldest Church: Bible, Art, and Ritual at Dura-Europos, Syria*. Synkrisis. New Haven: Yale University Press, 2016.

Serra, Dominic E. "The Baptistery at Dura-Europos: The Wall Paintings in the Context of Syrian Baptismal Theology." *EL* 120 (2006): 67–78.

Snyder, Graydon F. *Ante Pacem: Archaeological Evidence of Church Life before Constantine*. Rev. ed. Macon, GA: Mercer University Press, 2003.

Spigel, Chad. "The Jewish *Minority* of Dura-Europos." *JAJ* 10 (2019): 211–55.

Vermaseren, Maarten J. *Corpus Inscriptionum et Monumentorum Religionis Mithriacae*. 2 vols. The Hague: Nijhoff, 1956–1960.

Weitzmann, Kurt, and Herbert L. Kessler. *The Frescoes of the Dura Synagogue and Christian Art*. DOS 28. Washington, DC: Dumbarton Oaks Research Library and Collection, 1990.

White, L. Michael. *Texts and Monuments for the Christian Domus Ecclesiae in Its Environment*. Vol. 2 of *The Social Origins of Christian Architecture*. HTS 42. Valley Forge, PA: Trinity Press International, 1996.

Winkler, Gabriele. "The Original Meaning of the Prebaptismal Anointing and Its Implications." *Worship* 52 (1978): 24–45.

Seeing God at Mamre:
Reconsidering the Early Visual Evidence

Jeffrey M. Hubbard

Introduction

The LORD appeared to Abraham by the oaks of Mamre, as he sat at the entrance of his tent in the heat of the day. He looked up and saw three men standing near him. When he saw them, he ran from the tent entrance to meet them, and bowed down to the ground. He said, "My lord, if I find favor with you, do not pass by your servant. Let a little water be brought, and wash your feet, and rest yourselves under the tree. Let me bring a little bread, that you may refresh yourselves, and after that you may pass on—since you have come to your servant." So they said, "Do as you have said." (Gen 18:1–5)[1]

These first five verses of Gen 18 present their interpreter with a conundrum. While this famous episode of Abraham's hospitality to three strangers is introduced as an appearance of the Lord (יהוה in the MT, ὁ θεός in the LXX), the text proceeds to introduce three men. The waters are further muddied when Abraham's initial address switches back to a singular referent, only to give way to the plural once again. How many persons is Abraham seeing? Because it is virtually certain that the text's vacillation between singular and plural is not attributable to the presence of multiple sources in Gen 18, interpreters must attempt to resolve the discrepancies at the narrative and theological levels.[2]

---

1. Unless otherwise noted, biblical translations follow the NRSV.
2. Gerhard von Rad, *Genesis: A Commentary* (Philadelphia: Westminster John Knox, 1973), 204; Gordon Wenham, *Genesis 16–50* (Dallas: Word, 2002), 44.

Numerous such attempts have been made, and the task of cataloguing just the ancient reception of this enigmatic text has generated an extensive secondary bibliography.[3] In one of the most recent and detailed treatments of the scene's reception in early Christian exegesis, Bogdan Bucur identifies an interpretive trajectory that moves from christological interpretations (especially popular in the second and third centuries) to the more symbolic Trinitarian readings that became "normative in doctrinal and exegetical writings after the fourth century."[4] Bucur makes his case persuasively, but includes a caveat to his argument: unlike the "doctrinal and exegetical writings" he surveys, Bucur believes that the few Christian artistic depictions of Gen 18 that date from the fourth, fifth, and sixth centuries favor a christological interpretation over a Trinitarian one. In fact, he claims that the iconography does not shift from christological to Trinitarian until "the middle of the second millennium."[5]

Bucur, however, uses little space to substantiate this claim about the ancient Christian visual interpretations of Gen 18, which he treats in just

---

3. Important voices include Lars Thunberg, "Early Christian Interpretation of the Three Angels in Gen. 18," StPatr 7 (1966): 560–70; Andrew Louth, "The Oak of Mamre, the Fathers and St. Andrei Rublev: Patristic Interpretation of the Hospitality of Abraham and Rublev's Icon of the Trinity," in *The Trinity-Sergius Lavra in Russian History and Culture*, ed. Vladimir Tsurikov (Jordanville, NY: Holy Trinity Seminary Press, 2005), 90–100; Marie-Odile Boulnois, "'Trois hommes et un Seigneur': Lectures trinitaires de la théophanie de Mambré dans l'exégèse et l'iconographie," StPatr 39 (2006): 194–201; Gabriel Bunge, *The Rublev Trinity: The Icon of the Trinity by the Monk-Painter Andrei Rublev* (Crestwood, NY: Saint Vladimir's Seminary Press, 2007), 23–57; Robin Jensen, "Early Christian Images and Exegesis," in *Picturing the Bible: The Earliest Christian Art*, ed. Jeffrey Spier (New Haven: Yale University Press, 2007), 65–85; Emmanouela Grypeou and Helen Spurling, "Abraham's Angels: Jewish and Christian Exegesis of Genesis 18–19," in *The Exegetical Encounter between Jews and Christians in Late Antiquity*, ed. Grypeou and Spurling (Leiden: Brill, 2009), 181–202; Boulnois, "L'exégèse de la théophanie de Mambré dans le De Trinitate d'Augustin: enjeux et ruptures," in *Le De Trinitate de saint Augustin: Exégèse, logique et noétique*, ed. Emmanuel Bermon and Gerard O'Daly (Paris: Études Augustiniennes, 2012), 35–65; Bogdan Gabriel Bucur, "The Early Christian Reception of Genesis 18: From Theophany to Trinitarian Symbolism," JECS 23 (2015): 245–72; Bucur, *Scripture Re-envisioned: Christophanic Exegesis and the Making of a Christian Bible*, BAC 13 (Leiden: Brill, 2018), 42–70.

4. Bucur, *Scripture Re-envisioned*, 64. The distinction will be explored further below.

5. Bucur, *Scripture Re-envisioned*, 62.

one paragraph.⁶ The purpose of this essay is to test Bucur's conclusions via a detailed examination of three early depictions of Gen 18 in Christian art: a fresco from Cubiculum B in the Via Latina catacombs (late fourth century), a mosaic from the wall of the nave in the church of Santa Maria Maggiore in Rome (fifth century), and a mosaic from the church of San Vitale in Ravenna (sixth century). Closer attention to the larger iconographic program of each piece's setting may challenge Bucur's analyses.⁷

The paper proceeds in three parts. First, I briefly summarize the literary evidence for christological and Trinitarian interpretations of Gen 18 in early Christian writers. Next, I offer detailed analyses of the fresco from Via Latina, the mosaic from Santa Maria Maggiore, and the mosaic from San Vitale. Contra Bucur, I argue that only the mosaic from Santa Maria Maggiore should be identified as a christological interpretation. The mosaic from San Vitale offers more evidence for Trinitarian exegesis than christological, and importantly, the fresco from Via Latina offers neither. Finally, I compare these observations with Bucur's conclusions and offer some reflections on the task of evaluating early Christian art in light of our literary sources.

Reading Genesis 18: Christological and Trinitarian Interpretations

Far more ancient Christian writers comment on the narrative of Gen 18 than can be surveyed here.⁸ The important matter for our evaluation of Bucur's claims is to note that in the second and third centuries we find a greater concentration of christological readings of the Mamre episode. In such interpretations, one of the three men whom Abraham sees is interpreted as a preincarnate Christ, while the other two are usually taken to be angelic beings. Justin (mid-second century) may be the earliest Christian writer to espouse such a view: "One of these three is God and is called an

---

6. Bucur, *Scripture Re-envisioned*, 60–61.

7. At least in the case of Santa Maria Maggiore, I am by no means the first to problematize a simple christological interpretation (see Boulnois, "Trois hommes et un Seigneur," 199; Jensen, "Early Christian Images and Exegesis," 65). Nevertheless, Bucur's recent arguments warrant renewed attention to the strengths and weaknesses of this position.

8. See again the bibliographic information in note 3, especially Grypeou and Spurling, "Abraham's Angels"; Bunge, *Rublev Trinity*, 23–57; Bucur, *Scripture Re-envisioned*, 42–57.

angel…. He appeared on earth to Abraham in human form, just like the two angels who were with him, and was God before the creation of the world…. He is other than God who made all things—other in number, though not in will" (Justin, *Dial.* 56.10–11).[9] As the broader context of Justin's *Dialogue* makes clear, Justin takes this other God to be the preincarnate Son, who he maintains is the only "God" who appears to mortals in Israel's Scriptures: "Therefore, neither Abraham, nor Isaac, nor Jacob, nor any other person saw the Father and Ineffable Lord of all things and of Christ Himself, but simply him who, by the will of God, is also God, his Son" (*Dial.* 127.4).[10] Justin's christological reading rests on a thoroughly literal interpretation of the pentateuchal texts, one that presumes that the text records a historical event in which the preincarnate Christ participated. For Justin, the historicity of the Son's appearances in the patriarchal period renders his eventual incarnation more plausible.[11]

Irenaeus offers a similar interpretation: "Now two of the three were angels, but one was the Son of God, with whom Abraham spoke, pleading on behalf of the inhabitants of Sodom" (*Epid.* 44).[12] Like Justin, Irenaeus advances this interpretation as part of a larger attempt to demonstrate that "there is a Son to God, and He is, not only before His appearance in the world, but also before the world came to be" (*Epid.* 43). The text's mention of a "God" who appeared to humans offers Irenaeus the perfect opportunity to prove the existence of the Son, committed as he is to the total

---

9. Translations of Justin are my own. The text follows Philippe Bobichon, *Justin Martyr, Dialogue avec Tryphon: édition critique, traduction, commentaire* (Fribourg: Academic Press Fribourg, 2003).

10. The sources that might have influenced Justin's rather novel conclusions have been widely debated. On the possibility of a relationship with Philo, see Erwin R. Goodenough, *The Theology of Justin Martyr* (Jena: Frommann, 1923), 139–73; Leslie Barnard, *Justin Martyr: His Life and Thought* (Cambridge: Cambridge University Press, 1967), 85–100; Demetrios Christ Trakatellis, *The Preexistence of Christ in the Writings of Justin Martyr*, HDR 6 (Missoula, MT: Scholars Press, 1976), 53–84; Oskar Skarsaune, *The Proof from Prophecy: A Study in Justin Martyr's Proof-Text Tradition; Text-Type, Provenance, Theological Profile*, NovTSup 56 (Leiden: Brill, 1987), 409–24; David Rokéah, *Justin Martyr and the Jews* (Leiden: Brill, 2002), 22–28; Jeffrey M. Hubbard, "Does Justin Argue with Jews? Reconsidering the Relevance of Philo," *VC* 77 (2022): 237–56.

11. See Hubbard, "Does Justin Argue with Jews?," 254.

12. Translations follow Irenaeus, *On the Apostolic Preaching*, trans. John Behr (Crestwood, NY: St. Vladimir's Seminar Press, 1997).

transcendence of the Father (*Epid.* 45). The interpretations of Justin and Irenaeus are consonant with the broader subordinationist tendencies of pre-Nicene Christology.

By contrast, some early Christian writers saw an even deeper meaning in the story of Abraham's three visitors. Trinitarian readings of the Mamre theophany are more diverse, but the idea that the text's vacillation between three and one could be explained by appealing to the Trinity is at least as old as Origen (*Comm. Cant.* 2.8.8).[13] For Ambrose, "Abraham … saw the Trinity in a type; he added religious duty to hospitality, when beholding Three he worshiped One, and preserving the distinction of the Persons, yet addressed one Lord, he offered to Three the honor of his gift, while acknowledging one Power.… He sees Three, but worships the Unity" (*Exc.* 2.96 [*NPNF* 2/10]). Trinitarian readings such as that of Ambrose usually entailed a different hermeneutic from the one employed by christological interpreters. It is uncommon to find such interpreters arguing that all three persons of the Trinity became visible to Abraham in a literal sense.[14] Far more often, Trinitarian interpreters acknowledge that the literal meaning of the story relates the visit of three angels to Abraham, but that the Christian reader is meant to discern in the text the symbol of the Trinity. Thus Ambrose asserts that Abraham sees the Trinity "in a type."

As Bucur acknowledges, christological interpretations of Gen 18 by no means disappear after the fourth century. Eusebius offers one famous example of such a reading:

> And he is no angel who is named in the previous passage, but One greater than an angel, the God and Lord who was seen beside the before-mentioned oak with the two angels in human form. Nor can it be thought that Almighty God Himself is meant. For it is impious to suggest that the Divine changes and puts on the shape and form of a man. And so it remains for us to own that it is the Word of God who in the preceding passage is regarded as divine. (*Dem. ev.* 5.9)[15]

---

13. See Bucur, *Scripture Re-envisioned*, 52.

14. Bucur does not identify such an interpretation until the tenth century (*Scripture Re-envisioned*, 57).

15. Translations of *Demonstratio evangelica* follow Eusebius, *The Proof of the Gospel, Being the Demonstratio Evangelica*, trans. W. J. Ferrar, 2 vols. (New York: Macmillan, 1920).

The christological interpretation also occurs in numerous other later writers.[16] There are also several authors (including Ambrose and Origen) who know and use both interpretations.[17] But at least in some circles, the christological reading came to be understood as standing in tension, even conflict, with the Trinitarian reading. Augustine in multiple places explicitly sets his reading against a christological one (e.g., *Civ.* 16.29, *Maxim.* 2.26.5), arguing that the two other men who go to visit Lot are also implicated in divine activity (the destruction of Sodom). The important issue for Augustine is the Son's complete equality with the Father, which was not always emphasized by exegetes such as Justin and Irenaeus, who sometimes treated the Son as an intermediary between the transcendent God and humanity.[18] Augustine thus denies that one of the three men was the preincarnate Christ and believes instead that the Trinity is depicted figurally in a story about three angels (*Trin.* 2.11.20).[19]

The tradition of opposing the Trinitarian and christological readings comes to a head in Procopius of Gaza (sixth century), who attributes the christological interpretation to the (heterodox) Judaizers: "Some take the three men as three angels; the Judaizers, however, say that one of the three is God, while the other two are angels; others still deem them to bear the type of the holy and consubstantial Trinity, who are addressed as 'Lord' in the singular" (*Comm. Gen.* 18).[20] For at least Augustine and Procopius, then, the two interpretations were not equally valid or even equally pious readings of Gen 18. For these later writers, to suggest that only Christ is signified in the Mamre theophany ran afoul of Nicene theology, either by unduly subordinating the Son to the Father (Augustine's concern) or by denying the Trinity altogether (Procopius's concern).[21] While some Christian writers used both the christological and Trinitarian interpreta-

---

16. For a detailed list, see Bucur, *Scripture Re-envisioned*, 49–51.

17. Bucur, *Scripture Re-envisioned*, 52–54.

18. For a full treatment of Augustine's exegesis of theophanies, see Kari Kloos, *Christ, Creation, and the Vision of God: Augustine's Transformation of Early Christian Theophany Interpretation*, BAC 7 (Leiden, Brill: 2011).

19. "But since three men appeared, and no one of them is said to be greater than the rest either in form, or age, or power, why should we not here understand, as visibly intimated by the visible creature, the equality of the Trinity, and one and the same substance in three persons?" (*Trin.* 2.11.20 [*NPNF* 1/3]).

20. Translation follows Bucur, *Scripture Re-envisioned*, 56.

21. Noted also by Grypeou and Spurling ("Abraham's Angels," 196).

tions quite freely, some later exegetes (including the massively influential Augustine) did not believe they could coexist; to claim one was to deny the other.

These diverse approaches to Gen 18 are chronologically intertwined, and there is no clear point at which we can safely speak of the complete abandonment of the christological interpretation in ancient Christianity. Nevertheless, as Bucur has demonstrated persuasively, the literary evidence generally tends toward an increased opposition between the two readings in the fourth, fifth, and sixth centuries.[22]

Visual Interpretations of Genesis 18

Trying to read the visual evidence alongside these literary approaches invites some initial questions. Most importantly: How can contemporary viewers determine whether a given piece exhibits christological or Trinitarian leanings? Art is a different medium from written exegesis, and it is not difficult to imagine an artistic depiction of Gen 18 that preserves the ambiguity of the text itself (by depicting just Abraham and three men) without offering much hint of further commentary.[23]

However, at least when it comes to a christological artistic depiction, we are fortunate enough to have some ancient evidence. We have already noted that in book 5 of his *Demonstratio Evangelica*, Eusebius provides a fourth-century example of a christological interpretation of the Mamre scene. On its own, his interpretation is unremarkable and sounds a good deal like the earlier readings of Justin and Irenaeus. Just a few lines later, however, Eusebius adds further support to his exegesis by appealing to a (now apparently lost) visual depiction of the scene at the site of Mamre itself:

> The place is even to-day honored by those who live in the neighborhood as a sacred place in honor of those who appeared to Abraham, and the terebinth can still be seen there. For they who were entertained by Abraham, as represented in the picture [γραφή], sit one on each side, and he in the midst surpasses them in honor. This would be our Lord and Savior. (*Dem. ev.* 5.9)

---

22. As noted above, Bucur believes that the early artistic depictions of the scene are an exception to this trend.

23. As we will see below, this is very close to the situation for the Via Latina fresco.

Eusebius here provides invaluable evidence for what a christological image might look like: three seated men are depicted, but the central figure "surpasses [the other two] in honor." The means by which this picture distinguished the Lord's honor remains unclear, though we can perhaps draw some inferences from later iconography, where the central figure is sometimes identified as Christ with a cross nimbus.[24]

Trinitarian artistic depictions of the scene also have a rich history in later iconography, a history that culminates in the transcendence of Andrei Rublev's *Trinity* (fifteenth century). Common to this iconographic tradition is the presence of three indistinguishable angels (though there is some ambiguity to such a depiction). Again, Augustine's comment on the scene in *Trin.* 2.11.20 may prove instructive. There, Augustine emphatically defends the position that the literal meaning of the story refers to angels. But Augustine also understands their total equality in "form, age, and power" as a figure of the Trinity. As we will see, portraying the men as identical is not necessarily enough to establish a Trinitarian agenda within a given piece, but it is certainly an informative starting point. With these methodological issues in mind, we can turn to the evidence itself.

Via Latina Cubiculum B

The earliest extant visual depiction of Abraham's three visitors occurs on a wall fresco in Cubiculum B of the Via Latina catacombs (fig. 4.1). Abraham is seated under a tree, with his right arm raised in a greeting gesture. Behind him is a calf, presumably an anticipation of the calf he will slaughter to feed his guests (Gen 18:7). Across from Abraham are the three visitors, each with right arm raised. They are very similar youthful figures, with short, curly hair and matching garments.[25]

It is frequently noted that the Via Latina fresco offers few clues when it comes to identifying a christological or Trinitarian interpretation of the three visitors.[26] This has not, however, prevented some scholars from

---

24. E.g., the eleventh-century Barberini Psalter (372, fol. 85v). For detailed photos see Bunge, *Rublev Trinity*, 32; Bucur, *Scripture Re-envisioned*, 65.

25. They are dressed in the traditional *pallium*. Erwin R. Goodenough notes that this article of clothing is ubiquitous in the catacomb art of Via Latina and refers to it simply as "the Robe." See Goodenough, "Catacomb Art," *JBL* 81 (1962): 117.

26. See Jensen, "Early Christian Images and Exegesis," 65–66. Bucur calls it "somewhat ambiguous" (*Scripture Re-envisioned*, 61).

Fig. 4.1. *Abraham's Hospitality*, late fourth century CE. Wall fresco. Via Latina Catacomb Cubiculum B, Rome. Photograph by Pontificia Commissione di Archeologia Sacra.

trying. Erwin Goodenough memorably grouped the Via Latina catacomb alongside christological interpretations by noting that "the central figure is distinguished by being slightly smaller than the other two."[27] But this attempt at a christological reading has not proven persuasive.[28] A "slightly smaller" central figure does not sound much like the one described by Eusebius, who surpassed the other two in honor.

Bucur is reluctant to provide any extensive interpretation of the "somewhat ambiguous" Via Latina fresco.[29] By contrast, Gabriel Bunge asserts that "on the typological level, we have here ... an early representation of the Holy Trinity."[30] Bunge supports this conclusion by appealing to

---

27. Erwin R. Goodenough and Jacob Neusner, *Jewish Symbols in the Greco-Roman Period*, abridged ed. (Princeton: Princeton University Press, 1988), 244.

28. See the contrary judgments of Jensen ("Early Christian Images and Exegesis," 65) and Bunge (*Rublev Trinity*, 25). Goodenough himself seems to have later softened his position ("Catacomb Art," 119).

29. Bucur, *Scripture Re-envisioned*, 61.

30. Bunge, *Rublev Trinity*, 47.

the identical appearance of the three men, which he notes is "something which cannot be ascertained from the biblical text."³¹ Of course, one might reply (with Goodenough) that the three men are not exactly identical, given that the central figure is noticeably shorter. Further, such a specific interpretation may be asking too much of our fourth-century catacomb artists, who seem to rely on this particular figure as a model for portraying any angelic being.³² Another fresco (fig. 4.2) from the same section of Cubiculum B (the right arcosolium/wall) is a helpful example.

The scene depicts Jacob's vision of a ladder (Gen 28:10–19), on which he sees "the angels of God … ascending and descending" (Gen 28:12). In

Fig. 4.2. *Jacob's Ladder*, late fourth century CE. Wall fresco. Via Latina Catacomb Cubiculum B, Rome. Photograph by Pontificia Commissione di Archeologia Sacra.

---

31. Bunge, *Rublev Trinity*, 47.

32. We cannot be certain that only one artist produced all the frescoes in Cubiculum B. William Tronzo argues that two styles are present in Via Latina Cubicula A–C, indicating two artists who would have been employed by the same workshop. See Tronzo, *The Via Latina Catacomb: Imitation and Discontinuity in Fourth-Century Roman Painting*, MFA 38 (University Park: Pennsylvania State University Press and the College Art Association of America, 1986), 24–25. In any case, the artist(s) most likely would have carried out the artistic vision of a patron or patrons.

the Via Latina fresco, Jacob sits to the right, and two figures are on the ladder, only one of whom is fully visible. This fully visible figure looks strikingly like the three visitors in the Mamre scene. Like them, he is a youthful, beardless male with short, curly hair, wearing the *pallium*. His right arm may even be raised in the same greeting gesture that the three visitors made.

The value of this comparison is that the Jacob's ladder fresco depicts a biblical scene that explicitly identifies some of its characters as angels. This, combined with the close similarity between this figure and Abraham's visitors, make it very likely that this fresco depicts Abraham's three visitors as angels. If this is simply the model used by the artist(s) to portray angelic figures, Bunge's attempt to find a Trinitarian interpretation based only on the similarities between the three men appears less persuasive.

To be sure, identifying the fresco as a depiction of three angels by no means excludes a Trinitarian reading. After all, the three seated angels of Gen 18 eventually became the most popular way to depict the Trinity in Christian iconography. But we should be cautious before imposing these later developments onto this fourth-century fresco. Any study of the purpose of this image should first attend to the artistic context in which it occurs. Such attention to the larger iconographic program of the right arcosolium of Cubiculum yields a rather different interpretation.

As Catherine Taylor shows, the right and left walls and arcosolia of Cubiculum B each seem to trace a distinct theological motif.[33] The left side "includes scenes of the mortal fall, earthly trial and toil, physical dependency and vulnerability, the necessity for deliverance, and physical transiency."[34] Among these scenes are Adam and Eve's exit from Eden, the discovery of the baby Moses, and Lot fleeing Sodom. A rather different set of images from the Old Testament appears on the right. These include, in addition to Abraham's visitors and Jacob's ladder, Elijah's ascension on the fiery chariot, Rebekah conspiring to get Isaac's blessing for Jacob instead of Esau, Jacob's blessing of Ephraim over Manasseh, and Balaam encountering the angel of the Lord.

Many of the scenes in this cycle are connected by the presence of some kind of angelic or otherwise visionary experience (especially Jacob's ladder, Elijah's ascension, and Balaam). But this is less explicitly the case for the scene of Rebekah and Jacob's conspiracy and Jacob's blessing of Ephraim. What all of these biblical scenes do have in common is the depiction of

---

33. Catherine C. Taylor, "The Matrilineal Cord of Rahab in the Via Latina Catacomb," *SBA* 8 (2016): 189–90.

34. Taylor, "Matrilineal Cord," 189.

divine prophecy at work in Israel's history. Jacob's visionary experience is the first time the Abrahamic prophecy of many descendants is extended to Jacob, and Balaam's episode represents the prophetic (even inevitable) blessing of God's people. Even Rebekah and Jacob's deception marks the fulfillment of an earlier prophecy (that Rebekah's elder son would serve the younger; see Gen 25:23), and a similar prophetic reversal is at play in Jacob's blessing of Ephraim (Gen 48:12–20).[35]

We should not be surprised to discover that the Mamre episode of Gen 18 fits very nicely within the right wall's emphasis on prophetic moments in Israel's history. Interest in the *identity* of the three men can sometimes distract from the *mission* of the three men, which is to prophesy the birth of Isaac (Gen 18:10).[36] It is this feature of the Gen 18 narrative more than any other that connects this fresco to those surrounding it. Every fresco on the right arcosolium and wall of Cubiculum B signifies the utterance or the fulfillment of a prophecy from the Scriptures, including the fresco depicting Abraham's angelic guests. Notably, none of these frescoes depict a vision of God, not even the fresco of Jacob's vision, which leaves off any depiction of God at the top of the ladder despite his appearance in the biblical text (Gen 28:13).

The right arcosolium and wall of Cubiculum B invite their viewers into a biblical history replete with prophetic annunciations and fulfillments. This evidence needs to be considered carefully before we begin to speculate about christological or Trinitarian readings of the three visitors at play in this wall painting. Any type of theophanic portrayal of Abraham's visitors in Cubiculum B would make this fresco a significant theological outlier when it comes to the surrounding material. This is a case where the traditional lines of scholarly inquiry have been motivated too much by priorities set by literary evidence. In fact, the artistic context of Cubiculum B suggests that, unlike some early Christian writers, the artist (or more likely the artist's patrons) had little interest in portraying the event as a theophany at all.

Santa Maria Maggiore

The next extant depiction of Abraham's three visitors from Christian antiquity is from the fifth-century mosaics of the church of Santa Maria

---

35. Taylor's illuminating study underappreciates the degree to which prophecy links every fresco on the right arcosolium and wall.

36. This is the first time such a prophecy is made to Sarah, and the second time to Abraham (see Gen 17:21).

Maggiore in Rome.[37] This mosaic (fig. 4.3) is divided into an upper and a lower register. At the top, Abraham bows to three visitors, each of whom is beardless, with long, curly hair and dressed in a white garment. Each has a halo. In fact, the three men would be identical were it not for the presence of a mandorla surrounding the central figure. In the bottom register, Abraham speaks to Sarah during the baking of three loaves of bread, and Abraham offers the prepared calf to the three men, now seated behind a table. Curiously, in this lower register, any differentiation between the three men is gone, and they appear completely identical.

As Robin Jensen notes, this mosaic may be the ancient depiction that corresponds best to Eusebius's description of the icon at fourth-century Mamre.[38] Eusebius spoke of a central figure who "surpassed the other two in honor," a characterization that may correspond well to the presence of the mandorla in the upper register of the Santa Maria Maggiore mosaic. Indeed, this feature of the mosaic is frequently invoked as evidence of a christological interpretation of Gen 18. Bucur confidently asserts that "the exegesis [that is, christological exegesis] of the upper register of the Santa Maria Maggiore mosaic is evident: the central figure among the three visitors is clearly set off from the other two by its imposing mandorla."[39] The same conclusion is reached by William C. Loerke, who cites the mandorla as proof that one of the men is portrayed as the preincarnate Christ.[40]

To be sure, the correspondence to Eusebius's picture is compelling. Nonetheless, the situation is a bit more complicated than some scholars

---

37. Relevant discussions of the composition and historical situations of the art at Santa Maria Maggiore can be found in Suzanne Spain, "The Program of the Fifth Century Mosaics of Santa Maria Maggiore" (PhD diss., New York University, 1968); Beat Brenk, *Die frühchristlichen Mosaiken in Santa Maria Maggiore zu Rom* (Wiesbaden, 1975); Spain, "'The Promised Blessing': The Iconography of the Mosaics of Santa Maria Maggiore," *ArtBul* 61 (1979): 518–40; Allan Braham, "The Emperor Sigismund and the Santa Maria Maggiore Altarpiece," *BM* 122 (1980): 106–12; Brandon Strehlke and Mark Tucker, "The Santa Maria Maggiore Altarpiece: New Observations," *AC* 728 (1987): 105–24; Margaret R. Miles, "Santa Maria Maggiore's Fifth-Century Mosaics: Triumphal Christianity and the Jews," *HTR* 86 (1993): 155–75.

38. Jensen, "Early Christian Images and Exegesis," 66.

39. Bucur, *Scripture Re-envisioned*, 61.

40. William C. Loerke, "Observations on the Representation of Doxa in the Mosaics of S. Maria Maggiore, Rome, and St. Catherine's, Sinai," *Gesta* 20 (1981): 19; see also Bunge, *Rublev Trinity*, 29.

Fig. 4.3. *Abraham and the Angels*, from *Scenes of the Life of Abraham*, fifth century CE. Early Christian mosaic. Santa Maria Maggiore, Rome. Photograph by Scala / Art Resource, New York.

suggest. To begin with, the absence of the mandorla in the bottom register must be reckoned with. Why is the central figure emphasized in one scene but not in the next?[41] As Marie-Odile Boulnois and Bunge independently note, the identical appearance of the visitors in the lower register, along with the presence of three identical loaves of bread on the table, may gesture toward a Trinitarian interpretation.[42]

Perhaps more importantly, there is less certainty over the meaning of the mandorla than many suppose. By some reckonings, this is the earliest appearance of the mandorla in Christian art.[43] We should exercise at least some caution before equating this mosaic with later Christian uses of the mandorla, which do regularly focus on the risen Christ and the Virgin Mary.[44] As Rostislava Todorova notes, the mandorla is used early on in a variety of contexts and is best explained as "a representation of the "Glory of God … [which] points to those rare cases in the Old and the New Testaments when God decided to reveal His essence in front of humans."[45] While early Christians certainly did apply this artistic device to Christ, it could be used in other contexts.[46]

Another mosaic from the nave at Santa Maria Maggiore illustrates this well. The mosaic relates the attempted stoning of Moses from Num 14:10,

---

41. A question raised also by Jensen ("Early Christian Images and Exegesis," 65–66) and Boulnois ("Trois hommes et un Seigneur," 199).

42. Boulnois, "Trois hommes et un Seigneur," 199; Bunge, *Rublev Trinity*, 51. However, the placement of the basin at the feet of the central angel may be meant to distinguish him from the other two, making a Trinitarian reading of the bottom register less likely.

43. See Rostislava Todorova, "New Religion—New Symbolism: Adoption of Mandorla in The Christian Iconography," in *Collection of Scientific Works Nis and Byzantium: Towards the Celebration of the Edict of Milan anniversary (Nish)*, 9, (Nis, 2011), 54; Todorova, "The Aureole and the Mandorla: Aspects of the Symbol of the Sacral from Ancient Cultures to Christianity," *SAŠ* 3 (2016): 215.

44. For a summary of scholarly opinions on the origin of this mysterious artistic tool, see Todorova, "The Aureoloe and the Mandorla," 200–206; Otto Brendel, "Origin and Meaning of the Mandorla," *GBA* 25 (1944): 5–24.

45. Todorova, "New Religion—New Symbolism," 47.

46. Contra Wolfgang Braunfels et al., who claim, "cette distinction iconographique ne peut désigner que le Christ." See Braunfels et al., *Les Voies de la création en iconographie chrétienne* (Paris: Champ, 1979), 104. For an example of early Christians applying this artistic device to Christ, see the transfiguration mosaic on the apse of Saint Catherine's at Mount Sinai. For discussion see Loerke, "Observations on the Representation," 20–21.

where at the last moment, "the glory of the L‍ord appeared at the tent of meeting to all the Israelites." The mosaicist vividly portrays this by means of a mandorla that surrounds Moses and his companions and seems to be generated by the hand of God descending from the upper right corner of the mosaic.

It is clear that this use of the mandorla (as a sort of protective force field) is motivated by the presence of the "glory of the Lord" in the biblical text and is not an attempt to portray a Christophany.[47] We can cautiously conclude that for the artisans of Santa Maria Maggiore, the mandorla was a flexible artistic device that could be used to capture a range of divine activity found in the biblical text. Its presence in the Gen 18 mosaic almost certainly indicates an attempt to convey the sense of 18:1, that God appeared to Abraham. It may be that the disappearing mandorla was intended to imitate the vacillation and ambiguity of the text itself. Where the text emphasizes both theophany and "oneness" (18:1), the mandorla directs the viewer's attention to one of the otherwise identical men. When the text more clearly has the three men in view (18:6–9), the disappearance of the mandorla highlights the visitors as a triad.[48] In any case, contra Bucur and Bunge, we should probably not invoke the mandorla as the *definitive* proof of a christological reading at work in this mosaic, especially given its absence in the lower register.

However, there is overlooked evidence that supports the identification of this mosaic as christological. This evidence comes from the larger iconographic program of the Santa Maria Maggiore mosaics, a program that has been thoroughly explicated by both Suzanne Spain and Margaret Miles.[49] The crucial element of Spain's analysis (which is followed and built on by Miles) is the degree to which the mosaics of Santa Maria Maggiore

---

47. Loerke, "Observations on the Representation," 20; Todorova, "New Religion—New Symbolism," 54.

48. This is not unlike Philo's interpretation in *Abr.* 119–122. Something similar may be at play in the medieval mosaics of this scene found at the cathedral of Monreale and from Cappella Palatina. These each depict Abraham greeting three angels (identified as such by their wings) with the caption, "Abraham saw three and worshiped one." They also each include a separate register for the hospitality scene. The inclusion of the famous phrase alongside three indistinguishable angels may suggest a Trinitarian interpretation at work, where the artists used the caption to highlight the singular God/Lord emphasized in Gen 18:1–2.

49. Spain, "Promised Blessing," 518–40; Miles, "Santa Maria Maggiore's Fifth-Century Mosaics," 155–75.

emphasize "the harmony of the Testaments."[50] Miles calls it "a systematic and comprehensive articulation of the relationship of the Hebrew Bible and the Christian scriptures as one in which the Hebrew Bible foreshadows Christianity."[51]

Indeed, the architecture of the church mimics the trajectory of the Christian Bible. Only scenes from the Hebrew Bible appear along both walls of the nave, but these lead into the church's central arch, which is richly decorated with Christ-focused scenes. Some of these arch scenes are from the New Testament, but some resist easy identification. Spain argues persuasively that several of these arch scenes actually depict meetings between Christ and Old Testament patriarchs, such as David and Isaiah or Abraham and Sarah.[52] These mosaics underline the thematic unity of the Christian Bible, portraying Christ as the fulfillment of the prophecies and figures of the Old Testament.[53]

This theological agenda appears in at least one other mosaic from the nave: Abraham's meeting with Melchizedek (fig. 4.4). This mosaic appears adjacent to the mosaic of Abraham's three visitors. In it, Abraham receives gifts of bread and wine from Melchizedek, while a bearded Christ presides over the exchange from heaven. While we cannot say precisely what sort of theological interpretation of Gen 14 is at play here, it clearly evinces an interest in demonstrating Christ's supernatural involvement in an especially evocative and enigmatic patriarchal narrative.[54]

Between the figurally suggestive nave scenes and the explicit theologizing of the arch, the fifth-century mosaics of Santa Maria Maggiore present a resolutely christocentric iconographic program. With that data

---

50. Spain, "Promised Blessing," 539.

51. Miles, "Santa Maria Maggiore's Fifth-Century Mosaics," 160. Brenk also recognizes a kind of salvation history at work in the mosaics, which he relates to Ambrose's five stages of theological history (*Die frühchristlichen Mosaiken*, 112–13).

52. Spain, "Promised Blessing," 520.

53. As Miles puts it, "in the iconographical program of Santa Maria Maggiore, scenes from the Hebrew Bible receive their contextualization and interpretation as the prologue to the Christian saga" ("Santa Maria Maggiore's Fifth-Century Mosaics," 161–62).

54. Various early Christian approaches to the figure of Melchizedek are helpfully catalogued by Fred L. Horton Jr., though he offers no discussion of the visual evidence. See Horton, *The Melchizedek Tradition: A Critical Examination of the Sources to the Fifth Century A.D. and in the Epistle to the Hebrews*, SNTSMS 30 (Cambridge: Cambridge University Press, 1976), 87–114.

Fig. 4.4. *Abraham and Melchisedek*, fifth century CE. Early Christian mosaic. Santa Maria Maggiore, Rome. Photograph by Nimatallah / Art Resource, NY.

in mind, the christological reading of the Mamre scene put forward by Bucur is rendered significantly more plausible. Concerned as these mosaics are with portraying Christ as the content of patriarchal faith and the fulfillment of scriptural promises, reading the central figure as the preincarnate Son would situate the Mamre mosaic nicely within the theological agenda of Santa Maria Maggiore. However (and against many recent commentators), the presence of the mandorla is insufficient evidence for the christological interpretation. Such a reading becomes much more secure by considering the mosaic's iconographic context.

San Vitale at Ravenna

Finally, we come to a sixth-century mosaic from the church of San Vitale at Ravenna (fig. 4.5).[55] It is noticeably similar to the lower register of the mosaic at Santa Maria Maggiore.[56] Here, Abraham offers a calf to three identical men, who are seated together behind a four-legged table. Just as at Santa Maria Maggiore, each has a halo. On the table are three identical loaves of bread. On the left, Sarah watches from the house. Unlike the mosaic of Santa Maria Maggiore, the central figure is not surrounded by a mandorla. This absence notwithstanding, recent interpreters have commonly identified this mosaic as a christological interpretation of Gen 18.[57]

As at Santa Maria Maggiore (and to a lesser extent Via Latina), one of the key arguments for identifying a christological agenda in this mosaic rests on the respective appearances of the three men. There is some contestation over just how identical the three visitors are. Jensen says that they are "represented as equals" and are "indistinguishable."[58] Quite a different interpretation is offered by Goodenough, who believed that at San Vitale, the central figure

---

55. Like those of Santa Maria Maggiore, the style and background of the mosaics of San Vitale (and the church more generally) have received much discussion, especially because of the presence of imperial iconography from the Justinianic period. For introductions to relevant issues, see Angelo Lipinsky, "Oreficerie e gioielli nei mosaici Ravennati Romani," *CCARB* 9 (1962): 367–403; Katherine R. Brown, "The Mosaics of San Vitale: Evidence for the Attribution of Some Early Byzantine Jewelry to Court Workshops," *Gesta* 18 (1979): 57–62; Irina Andreescu-Treadgold and Warren Treadgold, "Procopius and the Imperial Panels of S. Vitale," *ArtBul* 79 (1997): 708–23; Sarah E. Bassett, "Style and Meaning in the Imperial Panels at San Vitale," *AH* 29 (2008): 49–57; Lamberto Tronchin and David J. Knight, "Revisiting Historic Buildings through the Senses: Visualizing Aural and Obscured Aspects of San Vitale, Ravenna," *IJHA* 20 (2016): 127–45.

56. Goodenough identifies the beginnings of a shared iconographical tradition (*Jewish Symbols*, 244–45).

57. Bunge, *Rublev Trinity*, 29; Bucur, *Scripture Re-envisioned*, 61.

58. Jensen, "Early Christian Images and Exegesis," 65.

Fig. 4.5. Mosaic of Abraham and three angels at the sacrifice of Isaac, sixth century CE. Byzantine wall mosaic. San Vitale, Ravenna. Photograph by HIP / Art Resource, New York.

"sits well in front of the other two."[59] Bunge softens Goodenough's judgment slightly and speaks of the central figure's "restrained prominence," a reading that Bucur cites approvingly.[60] Goodenough and Bucur both use this observation as evidence that this is a christological mosaic.

However, the arguments for an emphasized middleman fail to persuade. Goodenough's position is clearly an overstatement, but the "restrained prominence" of Bunge and Bucur should also be subjected to scrutiny. To begin with, while portions of the central figure's anatomy may be foregrounded compared to his companions, this is not true for his entire body. The figure on the left is noticeably leaning forward, positioning his arm and upper shoulder in front of the central figure. The figure on the right sits too far away from the other two and at too much of an angle to create a backgrounded effect.[61] More importantly, the differences are so slight that any actual differentiation is more likely due to the compositional

---

59. Goodenough, *Jewish Symbols*, 245.
60. Bunge, *Rublev Trinity*, 29; Bucur, *Scripture Re-envisioned*, 61.
61. Note that below the table his feet are even with (or maybe in front of) those of the central figure.

difficulty of portraying three men sitting very close together in the mosaic medium; some texture is bound to emerge. Especially compared to the otherworldly mandorla that surrounds the central figure at Santa Maria Maggiore, the San Vitale mosaic hardly seems to correlate with Eusebius's description of a middleman who surpassed the other two in honor. It is safest to say, with Jensen, that the three men are portrayed as identical.[62]

Bunge introduces another argument for the christological interpretation of this scene, which must be taken seriously. Bunge helpfully draws attention to the mosaic's iconographic setting above the altar of the church at San Vitale.[63] The other mosaics that surround the altar all depict well-known figures from the Old Testament making sacrifices or offerings. Abraham's offering of Isaac can be seen alongside the hospitality mosaic (fig. 4.5). Directly opposite this mosaic, Melchizedek and Abel offer bread and a lamb (respectively; see fig. 4.6).

Fig. 4.6. *Sacrifice of Abel and Melchizedek*, sixth century CE. Byzantine wall mosaic. S. Vitale, Ravenna, Italy. Photograph by Scala / Art Resource, NY.

---

62. Jensen, "Early Christian Images and Exegesis," 65.
63. Bunge, *Rublev Trinity*, 27–28, 49.

Because of the position of these offering scenes around the church's altar, Bunge reasons that "the Old Testament scenes of sacrifice are therefore quite clearly to be understood as 'types' or figures of the New Testament sacrificial meal of the Eucharist."[64] Thus, the Abraham mosaic should be understood "in a Christological/eucharistic way."[65] Bucur (relying on Bunge) makes a similar argument: "Within the iconographic program of the cathedral, the meal at Mamre functions as a foreshadowing of the Eucharist, so that the central angel corresponds in some fashion to Christ."[66]

That there is eucharistic significance to these altar mosaics seems beyond dispute, and Bunge never explicitly articulates in what way he believes the mosaic is christological.[67] But Bucur's move from recognizing a eucharistic theme to identifying the central angel as Christ demands further scrutiny. As we will see, there is no reason that a eucharistic interpretation of this mosaic entails a christological identification for the central figure.

If we leave out the scene of Abraham's hospitality for the moment, we are left with three scenes that depict some kind of offering. Each scene shares three basic elements: an offering, an offeror, and God. The offerings and offerors differ. Abel offers a sheep, Melchizedek bread, Abraham Isaac. Common to each mosaic is the reverent depiction of the offering's recipient, God, in the form of the divine hand (visible in figs. 4.5 and 4.6). What can we infer from this pattern? First, we should note that the divine recipients in these mosaics are not Christ. As Robert Couzin persuasively demonstrates, the hand of God is not a technique used of Christ in early Christian art and even seems to have developed specifically as a way to portray God without resorting to a Christophanic interpretation.[68] This observation might not exclude a christological reference in these images, but it does make it difficult to locate such a christological reference within the divine-recipient element of each scene.

Any christological and/or eucharistic element would most naturally be found in the other two elements of each scene, the offerings and

---

64. Bunge, *Rublev Trinity*, 28.
65. Bunge, *Rublev Trinity*, 49.
66. Bucur, *Scripture Re-envisioned*, 61.
67. Contra Bucur (*Scripture Re-envisioned*).
68. Robert Couzin, *Right and Left in Early Christian and Medieval Art*, AMCMRE 16 (Leiden: Brill, 2021), 49.

the offerors. As Bunge notes, each biblical figure (Abraham, Abel, and Melchizedek) is the source of significant christological interpretation in the tradition.[69] Theological speculation could connect Christ to each scene in terms of the offeror (Abraham's faithfulness, Melchizedek's priesthood, and Abel's innocence all foreshadow Christ) and in terms of the thing offered (Isaac, Abel's acceptable lamb, and Melchizedek's bread and wine all foreshadow Christ).

The mosaics at San Vitale could be evoking either or both of these potential christological/eucharistic connections, though we cannot be certain. What we can say most definitively is that all the scenes depict acceptable offerings to God. This theme resonates nicely with their placement above the altar and is paralleled by the almost contemporary first eucharistic prayer of the Roman canon (seventh century). There, the priest implores God to accept the offering of the Eucharist just as he accepted the offerings of Abel, Melchizedek, and Abraham.[70] In the eucharistic prayer, no explicitly christological interpretation of the patriarchal offerings is invoked. Instead, the emphasis is simply on God's favorable inclination toward both offeror and offering. While we cannot say whether this form of the eucharistic prayer was used in sixth-century Ravenna, we do have exactly the same constellation of figures in the altar mosaics of San Vitale. Given this correspondence, we should admit the possibility that the figures at San Vitale are meant to focus similarly on acceptable offerings and less on explicitly christological interpretations of the characters.

If we apply these insights from the other three mosaics to the scene of Abraham's three visitors, we can discern the same threefold pattern. Abraham functions as the offeror, bowing his head as he presents his offering of the fattened calf on a platter. But where is God? If this mosaic is meant to be viewed in harmony with its iconographic program, the three holy visitors who all receive the offering together surely stand in his place. It is no accident that this is the only offering scene at San Vitale that does not include the mysterious hand-of-God device. Where the other eucharistic foreshadowings portray God via the hand, the text of Gen 18 supplies a more natural option: when Abraham offered food to three men, he was actually offering to God.

---

69. Bunge, *Rublev Trinity*, 27–38.
70. Noted by Jensen ("Early Christian Images and Exegesis," 82).

In the place where surrounding iconography leads us to expect a non-Christophanic depiction of God (the hand), this mosaic portrays three identical men who together receive Abraham's faithful offering. In this way, the San Vitale mosaic is the most Trinitarian of any of the three surveyed in this essay. While Abraham's offering almost certainly does have eucharistic overtones, they do not justify identifying the central figure as Christ. Instead it seems that at San Vitale, the image of the three identical men symbolically intimates the mystery of the Trinity, as Augustine claimed a century before (*Trin.* 2.11.20).[71]

Concluding Reflections

A few words of summary are in order. Of the three depictions of Genesis 18 analyzed above, only the mosaic at Santa Maria Maggiore can be securely identified as a christological interpretation of the episode. The mosaic at San Vitale is best understood as a Trinitarian interpretation, and the fresco in Cubiculum B of the Via Latina catacombs evinces no interest in either theological agenda. Instead, the scene of Abraham's three visitors is invoked because of its link to an important scriptural prophecy, the birth of Isaac.

What implications might we draw out of the foregoing arguments? First, Bucur's claim that the iconography was slow to transition from christological to Trinitarian readings needs to be tempered by the sixth-century evidence from San Vitale, in which a christological interpretation of the central angel is not present. It may also be significant that in the case of San Vitale, the iconographic program seems to exclude the kind of irenic, flexible position taken by Ambrose and others, wherein the christological and Trinitarian readings can sit alongside each other.[72] Because of the iconographic logic of San Vitale (offerings were made to God just as Christ/Eucharist is offered to God), it is unlikely that Christ could at the

---

71. A Trinitarian agenda is more likely in light of Justinian's reconquest of Ravenna in 540. The city had previously been ruled by the Arian Ostrogoth Theodoric, and Justinian's regime change included the promotion of Nicene, anti-Arian Trinitarianism. The completion of the interior design and the dedication of the church at Ravenna probably took place in the spring of 547. See Judith Herrin and Jinty Nelson, "Introduction," in *Ravenna: Its Role in Earlier Medieval Change and Exchange*, ed. Judith Herrin and Jinty Nelson (London: Institute of Historical Research, 2016), 9; Carola Jäggi, "Ravenna in the Sixth Century: the Archaeology of Change," in Herrin and Nelson, *Ravenna*, 94.

72. Contra Bunge (*Rublev Trinity*, 49).

same time be depicted as the recipient of Abraham's offering. This choice of a Trinitarian reading *over* a christological one may reflect the already significant influence of Augustine in sixth-century Italy.

The most important implication of this study is a methodological one. In each of the cases considered, the most helpful interpretive key to each piece of art proved to be not external literary sources but the larger iconographic program in which each occurred. For example, Eusebius's description of a more glorious central figure is a misleading guide to the mosaic of San Vitale, and it has caused many to seize on the slightest variation among the three men in an attempt to substantiate a christological agenda there. This is all the more the case with the Via Latina fresco. Consideration of its artistic context reveals an apparent lack of interest in the theological dialogues between christological and Trinitarian readings that proliferate in our literary sources from the same time. Even at Santa Maria Maggiore, where Bucur's christological reading was substantiated, it was the larger theological agenda of the mosaics as a whole that provided the most compelling evidence.

This is not to reassert an outdated false binary by pitting the written evidence against the material.[73] After all, in two out of three cases the ancient art is found to resonate nicely with one of the two major theological positions known to us from literary sources. Nonetheless, these conclusions do caution us against appealing to a literary comparandum before taking the time to appreciate deeply the way a piece of art is contributing to the motifs and movements of its broader iconographic setting.

Works Cited

Andreescu-Treadgold, Irina, and Warren Treadgold, "Procopius and the Imperial Panels of S. Vitale." *ArtBul* 79 (1997): 708–23.

Barnard, Leslie. *Justin Martyr: His Life and Thought*. Cambridge: Cambridge University Press, 1967.

Bassett, Sarah E. "Style and Meaning in the Imperial Panels at San Vitale." *AH* 29 (2008): 49–57.

Bobichon, Philippe. *Justin Martyr, Dialogue avec Tryphon: édition critique, traduction, commentaire*. Fribourg: Academic Press Fribourg, 2003.

---

73. See the brief but nuanced discussion of this issue in Jensen, "Early Christian Images and Exegesis," 68–69.

Boulnois, Marie-Odile. "L'exégèse de la théophanie de Mambré dans le De Trinitate d'Augustin: enjeux et ruptures." Pages 35–65 in *Le De Trinitate de saint Augustin: Exégèse, logique et noétique*. Edited by Emmanuel Bermon and Gerard O'Daly. Paris: Études Augustiniennes, 2012.

———. "'Trois hommes et un Seigneur': Lectures trinitaires de la théophanie de Mambré dans l'exégèse et l'iconographie." StPatr 39 (2006): 194–201.

Braham, Allan. "The Emperor Sigismund and the Santa Maria Maggiore Altarpiece." *BM* 122 (1980): 106–12.

Braunfels, Wolfgang, Guglielmo Matthiae, Beat Brenk, and André Grabar. *Les Voies de la creation en iconographie chrétienne*. Paris: Champ, 1979.

Brendel, Otto. "Origin and Meaning of the Mandorla." *GBA* 25 (1944): 5–24.

Brenk, Beat. *Die frühchristlichen Mosaiken in Santa Maria Maggiore zu Rom*. Wiesbaden, 1975.

Brown, Katherine R. "The Mosaics of San Vitale: Evidence for the Attribution of Some Early Byzantine Jewelry to Court Workshops." *Gesta* 18 (1979): 57–62.

Bucur, Bogdan Gabriel. "The Early Christian Reception of Genesis 18: From Theophany To Trinitarian Symbolism." *JECS* 23 (2015): 245–72.

———. *Scripture Re-envisioned: Christophanic Exegesis and the Making of a Christian Bible*. BAC 13. Leiden: Brill, 2018.

Bunge, Gabriel. *The Rublev Trinity: The Icon of the Trinity by the Monk-Painter Andrei Rublev*. Crestwood, NY: St. Vladimir's Seminary Press, 2007.

Couzin, Robert. *Right and Left in Early Christian and Medieval Art*. AMCMRE 16. Leiden: Brill, 2021.

Eusebius. *The Proof of the Gospel, Being the Demonstratio Evangelica*. Translated by William J. Ferrar. 2 vols. New York: Macmillan, 1920.

Goodenough, Erwin R. "Catacomb Art." *JBL* 81 (1962): 113–42.

———. *The Theology of Justin Martyr*. Jena: Frommann, 1923.

Goodenough, Erwin R., and Jacob Neusner. *Jewish Symbols in the Greco-Roman Period*. Abridged ed. Princeton: Princeton University Press, 1988.

Grypeou, Emmanouela, and Helen Spurling, "Abraham's Angels: Jewish and Christian Exegesis of Genesis 18–19." Pages 181–202 in *The Exegetical Encounter between Jews and Christians in Late Antiquity*. Edited by Grypeou and Spurling. Leiden: Brill, 2009.

Herrin, Judith, and Jinty Nelson. "Introduction." Pages 1–14 in *Ravenna: Its Role in Earlier Medieval Change and Exchange*. Edited by Herrin and Nelson. London: Institute of Historical Research, 2016.

Horton, Fred L., Jr. *The Melchizedek Tradition: A Critical Examination of the Sources to the Fifth Century A.D. and in the Epistle to the Hebrews*. SNTSMS 30. Cambridge: Cambridge University Press, 1976.

Hubbard, Jeffrey M. "Does Justin Argue with Jews? Reconsidering the Relevance of Philo." *VC* 77 (2022): 237–56.

Irenaeus. *On the Apostolic Preaching*. Translated by John Behr. Crestwood, NY: Saint Vladimir's Seminar Press, 1997.

Jäggi, Carola. "Ravenna in the Sixth Century: the Archaeology of Change." Pages 87–110 in *Ravenna: Its Role in Earlier Medieval Change and Exchange*. Edited by Judith Herrin and Jinty Nelson. London: Institute of Historical Research, 2016.

Jensen, Robin. "Early Christian Images and Exegesis." Pages 65–85 in *Picturing the Bible: The Earliest Christian Art*. Edited by Jeffrey Spier. New Haven: Yale University Press, 2007.

Kloos, Kari. *Christ, Creation, and the Vision of God: Augustine's Transformation of Early Christian Theophany Interpretation*. BAC 7. Leiden, Brill: 2011.

Lipinsky, Angelo. "Oreficerie e gioielli nei mosaici Ravennati Romani." *CCARB* 9 (1962): 367–403.

Loerke, William C. "Observations on the Representation of Doxa in the Mosaics of S. Maria Maggiore, Rome, and St. Catherine's, Sinai." *Gesta* 20 (1981): 15–22.

Louth, Andrew. "The Oak of Mamre, the Fathers and St. Andrei Rublev: Patristic Interpretation of the Hospitality of Abraham and Rublev's Icon of the Trinity." Pages 90–100 in *The Trinity-Sergius Lavra in Russian History and Culture*. Edited by Vladimir Tsurikov. Jordanville, NY: Holy Trinity Seminary Press, 2005.

Miles, Margaret R. "Santa Maria Maggiore's Fifth-Century Mosaics: Triumphal Christianity and the Jews." *HTR* 86 (1993): 155–75.

Rad, Gerhard von. *Genesis: A Commentary*. Philadelphia: Westminster, 1973.

Rokéah, David. *Justin Martyr and the Jews*. Leiden: Brill, 2002.

Skarsaune, Oskar. *The Proof from Prophecy: A Study in Justin Martyr's Proof-Text Tradition; Text-Type, Provenance, Theological Profile*. NovTSup 56. Leiden: Brill, 1987.

Spain, Suzanne. "The Program of the Fifth Century Mosaics of Santa Maria Maggiore." PhD diss., New York University, 1968.

———. "'The Promised Blessing': The Iconography of the Mosaics of Santa Maria Maggiore." *ArtBul* 61 (1979): 518–40.

Strehlke, Brandon, and Mark Tucker. "The Santa Maria Maggiore Altarpiece: New Observations." *AC* 728 (1987): 105–24.

Taylor, Catherine C. "The Matrilineal Cord of Rahab in the Via Latina Catacomb." *SBA* 8 (2016): 182–214.

Thunberg, Lars. "Early Christian Interpretation of the Three Angels in Gen. 18." StPatr 7 (1966): 560–70.

Todorova, Rostislava. "The Aureole and the Mandorla: Aspects of the Symbol of the Sacral from Ancient Cultures to Christianity." *SAŠ* 3 (2016): 199–223.

———. "New Religion—New Symbolism: Adoption of Mandorla in the Christian Iconography." Pages 47–63 in *Collection of Scientific Works Nis and Byzantium: Towards the Celebration of the Edict of Milan Anniversary (Nish)* 9. Nis, 2011.

Trakatellis, Demetrios Christ. *The Preexistence of Christ in the Writings of Justin Martyr*. HDR 6. Missoula, MT: Scholars Press, 1976.

Tronchin, Lamberto, and David J. Knight. "Revisiting Historic Buildings through the Senses: Visualizing Aural and Obscured Aspects of San Vitale, Ravenna." *IJHA* 20 (2016): 127–45.

Tronzo, William. *The Via Latina Catacomb: Imitation and Discontinuity in Fourth-Century Roman Painting*. MFA 38. University Park: Pennsylvania State University Press and the College Art Association of America, 1986.

Wenham, Gordon. *Genesis 16–50*. Dallas: Word, 2002.

Hope for Life after Death: Hebrews and the Origin of Christian Funerary Anchor Iconography in the Catacombs of Rome

Jason A. Whitlark

Funerary Anchors in Rome

Some of the earliest identifiable Christian art comes from the catacombs of Rome. The first Christian art forms in these funerary settings are rudimentary symbols of fish, palms, doves, and anchors. There are more than 550 funerary anchors identified among the catacombs used by Christ-followers in Rome, dating to the beginning of the third century.[1]

An earlier and condensed version of this essay was first published as "Funerary Anchors of Hope and Hebrews: A Reappraisal of the Origins of the Anchor Iconography in the Catacombs of Rome," *PRSt* 48 (2021): 219–41. Gratitude is expressed to the editors for permission to reuse that material in this essay.

1. A search of "(ancora)" in the EDB turned up 551 inscriptions distributed across the catacombs in Rome. The epigraphic evidence from the catacombs in Rome is cataloged in ICUR. This evidence can be searched in the EDB (www.edb.uniba.it), where 40,566 inscriptions of 40,815 items have been added at the time this search was done. There are some sixty to eighty catacombs identified in Rome. The Christian burial complexes begin toward the end of the second century and continued in use until the early fifth century. The major expansions occurred from the mid-third to the mid-fourth centuries. For dating of the catacombs, see Vincenzo Fiocchi Nicolai and Jean Guyon, eds., *Origine delle catacombe romane: Atti della giornata tematica dei Seminari di Archeologia Cristiana (Roma, 21 marzo 2005)* (Vatican City: Pontificio Istituto di Archeologia Cristiana, 2006). For initial radiocarbon studies on dating the catacombs, see Leonard V. Rutgers et al., "Further Radiocarbon Dates from the Catacombs of St. Callixtus in Rome," *Radiocarbon* 49 (2007): 1221–29. One of the conclusions reached from this study was that "the Liberian region in its entirety is likely to have been in use from at least the middle of the 3rd century AD onwards—that is, one century prior to

Possibly the earliest extant funerary anchors date to the second half of the second century and are found in the Piazzuola of San Sebastiano.[2] A study by Emanuele Castelli on the Catacomb of Priscilla gives us a sense of the frequency and importance of this symbol for Christians in third-century Rome. After examining 200 of the 370 inscriptions found in situ in the earliest parts of the upper floor of the Catacomb of Priscilla, Castelli identifies sixty-four figures: one lamb, three doves, five fish, ten palms, and forty-five anchors. The anchor constitutes 70 percent of these images. In the first floor, Castelli notes that the image of the anchor stands alone most of the time. From the second floor of the catacomb there are twenty-three figures, with eleven of them being anchors, thus constituting 48 percent of the images.[3] The anchor, then, occurs with higher frequency than other Christian symbols in the earliest areas of the Catacomb of Priscilla.

Funerary anchors are also widely distributed among Christian burials in Rome. The distribution of funerary anchors in Rome can be seen in table 5.1. This table represents 76 percent of all anchors from the Epigraphic Database Bari, targeting the areas with the largest concentration of anchors.[4] The table begins in the north of Rome and moves clockwise to the south of Rome.

---

the reign of Pope Liberius (AD 352–366), whose name has been associated with this region since the 19th century."

2. Paul Corby Finney discusses the early presence of three funerary inscriptions with anchors (ICUR 5.12891, 5.12892, 5.12900) in the Piazzuola of San Sebastiano. See Finney, *The Invisible God: The Earliest Christians on Art* (New York; Oxford University Press, 1994), 231–46. Christian presence among these burials dates from ca. 150–244 (see esp. the upper chamber of Tomb i, which contains the *ichthys* acrostic with an inserted *tau*). The burials in the Piazzuola, however, are diverse and not indicative of ecclesial oversight. According to the EDB, some of the other potentially earliest inscriptions of anchors are from the catacombs on the Via Appia: ICUR 5.15360 (ca. 190–225); and on the Via Cornelia: ICUR 2.4212 (ca. 190–225).

3. Emanuele Castelli, "The Symbols of Anchors and Fish in the Most Ancient Parts of the Catacomb of Priscilla: Evidence and Questions," StPatr 59 (2011): 13–14.

4. It should be noted that some funerary anchor icons have uncertain origins. The largest concentrations of anchors are found both in the northern and southern areas of Rome: from the catacombs on Via Salaria Nova in the north of Rome (147 anchors) and from the catacombs on the Via Appia/Ardeatina in the south of Rome (215 anchors).

Table. 5.1. Distribution of Funerary Anchors in Rome

Via Salaria Vetus	Catacomb of Saint Hermes or Bassilla	14 anchors
Via Salaria Nova	Catacomb of Priscilla	123 anchors
Via Nomentana	Cemetery Maius	47 anchors
Via Tiburtina	Catacomb of Cyriaca or Saint Lawrence	11 anchors
Via Labicana	Catacomb of Saints Peter and Marcellinus	23 anchors
Via Appia	Catacomb of Praetextatus	59 anchors
	Catacomb of Saint Callixtus	68 anchors
	Catacomb of Saint Sebastian	3 anchors
Via Ardeatina	Catacomb of Domitilla	75 anchors

The regular and widespread use of anchors in Rome undergirds stylistic analyses that conclude that a limited number of workshops in Rome were responsible for Christian art.[5]

Rome is not a littoral city, so why does the anchor appear repeatedly and widely among the earliest identifiable Christian burials?[6] The funerary-anchor phenomenon has been traditionally interpreted in light of Heb 6:18–20a, where Christian hope is compared to an anchor: "So that by two unchangeable things, in which it is impossible for God to lie, we have strong encouragement—we who have fled to take a hold of the hope [ἐλπίδος] set before us, which is as an anchor [ὡς ἄγκυραν] for the soul, secure and reliable, and enters inside the curtain where Jesus the forerunner entered on our behalf."[7] In the history of interpretation, Castelli identifies Heb 6:18–20a as the most important passage in the quest for the origin of the meaning of this symbol among early Christians.[8] During the past fifty years, however, alternative explanations or questions have been raised about the source and meaning of this enigmatic symbol. The question that shapes

---

5. See Robin M. Jensen, "Introduction: Early Christian Art," in *Routledge Handbook of Early Christian Art*, ed. Robin M. Jensen and Mark D. Ellison (London: Routledge, 2018), 3.

6. Ostia in the imperial period would become one of the main harbors for supplying Rome.

7. Unless otherwise specified, translations are my own.

8. Castelli, "Symbols of Anchors," 17, esp. n. 18. See also Erin Roberts, "Anchor," in *The Eerdmans Encyclopedia of Early Christian Art and Archaeology*, vol. 1, A–J, ed. Paul Corby Finney (Grand Rapids: Eerdmans, 2017), 58, who calls Heb 6:18–20a the locus classicus for the meaning and origin of the symbol among Christians.

this study is why Christians in Rome chose anchors to decorate their graves. The meaning of visual images is not often precise or monolithic but is often polyvalent. Thus, we must ask what from the viewers' contexts might inform them about the meaning of a symbol or image. This article argues that Heb 6:18–20a still offers the best explanation for the origin and primary meaning of funerary anchors among Christians in Rome.

The argument of this article proceeds in the following manner. First, I survey the use of anchors in iconography and texts as well as symbols for hope from the Greco-Roman context to ascertain what precedents, if any, that context may provide for Christian use of anchors as a symbol of hope similar to the association in Heb 6. Second, I survey the Christian subculture within the Greco-Roman world with regard to the use of anchors in iconography and texts. I particularly note that the catacombs of Rome provide some of the earliest associations of anchor symbols with hope. Third, I make a close analysis of the Heb 6:18–20a, along with the *Wirkungsgeschichte* of Hebrews in Rome in the second century, to assess the likelihood of the influence of Hebrews on the use of funerary anchors by Christians. Finally, I consider the possibility of Rome being the epicenter for Christian funerary anchor iconography.

Greco-Roman Context: Anchors and Hope

Iconography of Anchors and Hope

Anchors are widely found in Greco-Roman iconography. There is an anchor on a coin from Umbria (235 BCE) paired with the image of a frog.[9] The anchor is used with an entwined dolphin in the House of the Trident on Delos (second century BCE). On some Greek vase paintings, shields have anchors, possibly as a symbol for Poseidon or for immovability in fighting.[10] There is also an anchor on part of the frieze from the Porticus Octaviae, which symbolized Augustus's victory at Actium.[11] Anchors appear with Annona, goddess of the grain supply, on imperial coins, signifying the ships that brought the grain from other parts of the

---

9. Friedrich Bischoff, "Spes," *GN* 129 (1989): 15.

10. See George Henry Chase, "The Shield Devices of the Greeks," *HSCP* 13 (1902): 93, catalogue II; and Herodotus, *Hist.* 9.74.

11. Paul Zanker, *The Power of Images in the Age of Augustus*, trans. Alan Shapiro, JL 16 (Ann Arbor: University of Michigan Press, 1988), 126, fig. 102.

empire to Rome (e.g., *RIC* 3.175).¹² During Flavian rule, coins were issued for the Olympian gods, either in response to the eruption of Vesuvius or in celebration of the opening of the Colosseum. The coin that was devoted to Neptune had an anchor.¹³ The anchor with an entwined dolphin is also found on a coin from the reign of Titus (79–81 CE). Supposedly this image represented one of Augustus's favorite mottos, σπεῦδε βραδέως or *festina lente*—"make haste slowly" (fig. 5.1).¹⁴

Fig. 5.1. Golden aureus of Titus, ca. 80 CE. 7.04 g. Reverse: TR P IX IMP XV COS VIII P P. Dolphin coiled around ship's anchor. Wriston Art Galleries, Lawrence University, Appleton, Wisconsin. Ottilia Buerger Coin Collection.

There is also the floor mosaic of an anchor in the House of the Black Anchor in Pompeii (6.10.7). This brief survey of anchor iconography in the Greco-Roman context ranges from a more neutral nuance, to representation of a god, to symbolizing an ideal.¹⁵ The use of the anchor in Greco-Roman iconography, then, is varied, and its meaning determined by the context in which it appears. Many of these images share the common form of anchors that are inscribed in the catacombs of Rome, namely, with two rings, curved arms, and either stock or no stock. If we examine the metaphorical uses of ἄγκυρα in Greco-Roman literature, the anchor is commonly associated with ideas of security (βεβαίως) and safety (ἀσφαλέια; see Appian, *Hist. rom.* 11.56; Plutarch, *Sol.* 19.2; Sophocles, *Frag.* 685; Propertius, *Elegies* 2.22.41; Plato, *Leg.* 12.961c; Euripides, *Frag.* 866; *Hec.* 79–81; Galen, *Syn. libr.* 9.432.10).

With regard to the iconography of hope (ἐλπίς/*spes*), it is noteworthy that, in the Roman imperial context, the goddess Elpis/Spes on coins,

---

12. Sometimes Annona will appear with a ship's prow (e.g., *RIC* 3.231), as well as a cornucopia and possibly a statue of Spes (e.g., *RIC* 3.95).

13. See Harold Mattingly, *Vespasian to Domitian*, vol. 2 of *Coins of the Roman Empire in the British Museum* (London: Trustees of the British Museum, 1923), lxxii–lxxiii.

14. See John Evans, "On Some Rare or Unpublished Roman Gold Coins," *NumC* 8 (1868): 225; Suetonius, *Aug.* 25.4.

15. The searchable Greek inscription site, https://epigraphy.packhum.org/, yields 184 instances/106 texts where ἄγκυρα either is listed as an item or is the city Ancyra.

as statues, and in reliefs is often represented not with an anchor but as a young woman lifting her skirt with one hand and carrying a small flower in the other (fig. 5.2; see, e.g., *RIC* 2.139).¹⁶

Fig. 5.2. Silver denarius of Severus Alexander, 231–232 CE. 3.3 g. Rome. Reverse: SPES PVBLICA. Spes advancing left, right leg forward, holding out a flower and raising the hem of her skirt. *RIC* 4.254d. 18mm. Photograph by Bill Welch. Used with permission.

The goddess Spes in the context of imperial Roman discourse was commonly associated with *victoria*, *salus*, and *opes*.¹⁷ Indeed, the political discourse of Rome in the first century CE was filled with hope. Before the rise of the principate, Romans saw in key political figures the embodiment of hope grounded in divine interest and in the destiny of Rome. According to Livy, Scipio's hope rested on both the fortune of the Roman people and the favor of the gods (*Ab. urb. cond.* 28.44.7). Cicero notes that Rome was founded on the hope of eternal empire (see *Rep.* 2.5). At the time of Augustus, the Temple of Spes in the Forum Holitorium had been dedicated by A. Atilius Calatinus for the victory over the Carthaginians in the first Punic War—a victory that brought national salvation.¹⁸ It had been restored under Augustus in 31 BCE and even became known as *Augusta spes ad forum holitorium* (Tacitus, *Ann.* 2.49; CIL 6.2298).¹⁹ Augustus himself was declared to fulfill and exceed all hopes (OGI 458; SEG 4.490). Additionally, when Augustus chose Tiberius as an heir, Tiberius became the hope of "perpetual security and the eternity of Roman imperium" (Velleius Paterculus, *Hist. rom.* 2.103). After the power vacuum that followed Nero's death, coins were issued under the Flavians with the common representation of Spes as a young woman bestowing her flower on Vespasian.²⁰

---

16. See also "Spes," *LIMC* 8.1:804–6; 8.2:574–74; and "Elpis," *LIMC* 3.1:722–25; 3.2:550–51.

17. Mark Edward Clark, "*Spes* in the Early Imperial Cult: 'The Hope of Augustus,'" *Numen* 30 (1983): 81–82; Claudia Perassi, *Spes: Iconographia, simbologia, ideologia nella moneta romana (I–III sec.)* (Milan: Vita E Pensiero, 1991).

18. Plutarch mentions an altar of Τύχης εὐέλπιδος in the Angiportus Longus (see *Fort. Rom.* 323a).

19. Cited in Clark, "*Spes* in the Early Imperial Cult," 81.

20. On one coin-type issued in 71 CE, see J. Rufus Fears, "Theology of Victory at Rome: Approaches and Problems," *ANRW* 17.2:799.

Vespasian embodied hope for the empire. Domitian was even called the *spes hominum* upon his ascension to emperor (see Statius, *Silvae* 4.2.15).

The significance of ἐλπίς or *spes* outside Roman imperial discourse, however, was ambiguous—ranging from negative, to neutral, to positive characterizations.[21] Ἐλπίς can be a friend—even a doctor or a defender—but also an empty jar, a fetter, or a companion who deceives. In a more neutral sense, ἐλπίς can be a helmsman, a metaphor that moves into the realm of nautical imagery.[22] Romans could also portray *spes* as an evil or delusive force.[23] Some funerary inscriptions contain *spes* and *fortuna*, not so much to express hope in life after death but to declare that the dead have been freed from their delusive influences.[24] Optimism was not typically expressed on pagan epitaphs.[25] One epitaph reads, "I was nothing, I am nothing;/and you who [now] live, eat, drink, play, come!"[26] Indeed, Paul seems to demonstrate awareness of this popular skepticism when he writes, "If only in this life we have hope in Christ, then we are to be more pitied than all people.... If the dead are not raised, let us eat and drink, for tomorrow we die" (1 Cor 15:19, 32).

Ἄγκυρα with Ἐλπίς in the Greco-Roman Context

Our interest is whether ἄγκυρα and its association with safety and security also shares an association with the more positive aspects of ἐλπίς in iconography or literature in the Greco-Roman context. The Letter to the Hebrews relates, as I have noted, the safety and security of an ἄγκυρα with ἐλπίς in the latter part of the first century CE.

---

21. See Douglas Cairns, "Metaphors for Hope in Archaic and Classical Greek Poetry," in *Hope, Joy, and Affection in the Classical World*, ed. Ruth R. Caston and Robert A. Kaster (Oxford: Oxford University Press, 2015), 13–44; and Laurel Fulkerson, "'Torn between Hope and Despair': Narrative Foreshadowing and Suspense in the Greek Novel," in Caston and Kaster, *Hope, Joy, and Affection*, 75–94.
22. Cairns, "Metaphors for Hope," 27, 30, 32–33, 36–37.
23. See Clark, "*Spes* in the Early Imperial Cult," 120 n. 20, for references.
24. See Clark, "*Spes* in the Early Imperial Cult," 102 n. 23, for references.
25. See Hans-Josef Klauck, *The Religious Context of Early Christianity: A Guide to Graeco-Roman Religions*, trans. Brian McNeil (Minneapolis: Fortress, 2003), 79–81; and Franz Cumont, *Afterlife in Roman Paganism* (New York: Dover, 1959), 18.
26. See Klauck, *Religious Context*, 80, for quote and reference. Klauck also cites the inscribed abbreviation n.f.n.s.n.c. (*Non fui, non sum, non curo*—"I did not exist, I do not exist, I do not care").

The association of ἄγκυρα with ἐλπίς does not appear to have any strong precedents in the Greco-Roman world at the time that Hebrews was written or at the beginning of the Christian use of the catacombs in Rome. Before the fourth century CE, there is hardly any other association of ἐλπίς or *spes* with ἄγκυρα or *ancora*. If we examine the occurrence of ἄγκυρα with ἐλπίς among extant Greek texts, almost no Greek text (pagan, Christian, or Jewish) associates ἄγκυρα with ἐλπίς prior to the fourth century CE.[27] In fact, the earliest occurrence of ἄγκυρα and ἐλπίς within fifty words of each other found in a search in Thesaurus Linguae Graecae is Heb 6:18–19.[28] Certainly Castelli is correct, then, to note that among literary sources, hope is not associated with an anchor, making Hebrews a unicum even among early Christian texts.[29]

There is one potentially early Greco-Roman association of these terms in the second century CE by Epictetus. One of the extant fragments of his discourses collected by Arrian reads, "We ought neither to fasten our ship to one small anchor [ἀγκύρια] nor life to a single hope [ἐλπίς]" (*Frag.* 30 [Oldfather]).[30] Here Epictetus uses the less-frequent diminutive form, ἀγκύριον. The second-earliest textual source to bring these terms syntactically together is Heliodorus's fourth century romance *Aethiopica*, citing a proverb (λόγος): "every cable, as the proverb goes, is broken, every anchor of hope [ἐλπίδος ἄγκυρα] is completely torn loose" (7.25; see *Aeth.* 4.19). Later Christian texts from the fourth century and after associate these terms together more frequently. The use of anchor in these Christian texts as a metaphor for hope, even in hope in life after death, likely indicates the

---

27. There is potentially one indirect association. The metaphor of a sacred anchor (ἱερά ἄγκυρα) or one anchor, i.e., a last resort, however, implicitly conveys the metaphor of an "only hope" in modern idiom. See Galen, *Ven.* 11.182.13; Lucian, *Jupp. trag.* 51; *Apol.* 10; Silius Italicus, *Punica* 7.24; Euripides, *Hel.* 277–279.

28. The *TLG* search is taken as representative. It searches a large corpus of Greek texts over an extensive time frame (eighth century BCE to fifteenth century CE), such that broad conclusions can be reached over the frequency of words and idioms over periods of time.

29. Castelli, "Symbols of Anchors," 17.

30. Also recorded in Sent. Pyth. 14; Joannes Stobaeus, *Anth.* 3.1, 4.46. There is one other pithy statement of interest that uses the diminutive form ἀγκύριον with ἐλπίς cited in Sent. Pyth. 135; Joannes Stobaeus, *Anth.* 3.2 (Ταὐτὸν ἐξ ἀσθενοῦς ἀγκυρίου σκάφος ὁρμίζειν καὶ ἐκ φαύλης γνώμης ἐλπίδα—"To bring this ship to safe harbor by a weak small anchor and to bring hope from a base purpose").

growing influence and developing canonicity of Hebrews among Christian communities, especially in the East.[31]

Christian Use: Anchors and Hope

Paucity of Anchor Imagery in the Earliest Christian Texts

When we turn to the early Christian subculture in the Greco-Roman world before the fourth century CE, even more puzzling is the lack of references to just ἄγκυρα/*ancora* to explain the use of ἄγκυρα with ἐλπίς in Hebrews. The Jewish context out of which early Jesus-followers emerged does not appear to explain the association in Hebrews. The LXX, which significantly shaped early Christian discourse, never mentions ἄγκυρα. It should also be noted that ἄγκυρα is rarely used by Josephus, and only literally (*B.J.* 3.469, *A.J.* 15.333, *Vita* 1.167). Philo of Alexandria uses the term only twice (*Post.* 142, 163), of which one is a metaphor for the roots of a plant, not hope. Philo, however, employs other metaphorical nautical imagery for the soul finding safe harbor or stability in virtue and in the vision of God (see *Sacr.* 90, *Her.* 305, *Somn.* 2.225).[32] Here security and safety in these references are related to the harbor and not to an anchor or ἐλπίς. With regard to Jewish iconography, in his multivolume study of Jewish symbols in the Greco-Roman world, Erwin R. Goodenough notes that Jews never adopted the anchor as an important symbol.[33]

Among the New Testament texts, ἄγκυρα only occurs three times apart from Heb 6:19. The three occurrences are all in Acts 27 (vv. 29, 30,

---

31. E.g., Athanasius, *Ep. Marcell.* 22 (promise of God's deliverance = anchor of hope); John Chrysostom, *Hom. Heb.* 11.3; *Theod. laps.* 1.2 (hope in God for salvation = secure anchor [τὴν ἄγκυραν τὴν ἀσφαλῆ]); *Stat.* 16.2 (hope in God = anchor), 21.2 (hope = anchor of salvation; the use of κατεφύγομεν creates a strong echo of Hebrews); *Laz.* 1.10 (hope of resurrection = anchor [that endures afflictions]); *Hom. Gen.* 25.22 (hope = anchor, ἀσφαλῆ καὶ βεβαίαν creates a strong echo of Hebrews); *Hom. 2 Thess.* 1.1 (hope = anchor); Eusebius, *Praep. Ev.* 1.5.8 (good hope = anchor of salvation); Gregory of Nyssa, *Virg.* 23.6 (the use of ἐλπίδος, ἀσφαλοῦς, and ἐβεβαίωσαν with ἀγκύρας creates as strong echo of Hebrews); Theodoret, *Comm. Isa.* 14.577 (hope = anchor).

32. See also Harold W. Attridge, *The Epistle to the Hebrews: A Commentary on the Epistle to the Hebrews*, Hermeneia (Philadelphia: Fortress, 1989), 183 n. 70.

33. See Erwin R. Goodenough, *Jewish Symbols in the Greco-Roman Period*, BollS 37 (New York: Pantheon, 1956), 1:272.

40), and all are references to literal anchors. Additionally, ἄγκυρα is not used in the early Christian texts known as the Apostolic Fathers, texts of varying provenances from the end of the first to the middle of the second centuries. At the end of the second century and beginning of the third, ἄγκυρα or *ancora* is not mentioned among the extant texts of Tertullian or Origen.[34]

There are, however, two early Eastern Christians who provide some comment on anchors—Hippolytus and Clement of Alexandria, at the beginning of the third century.[35] Clement writes explicitly of the anchor as a symbol in his instructions about Christian decorum (clothes, jewelry, hair, signet rings, and more):

> Let our signets be a dove or a fish or a ship running before a favorable wind or a musical lyre, which Polycrates used, or an anchor, which Seleucus[36] had engraved on his signet, and a fisherman will remember the apostles and the children drawn from the water. For it is forbidden for us that the image of a god be impressed (on our signets) or the sword or bow for us pursuers of peace or the goblet for us temperate people. (*Paed.* 3.11.59)[37]

Hippolytus, in *Antichr.* 59, compares the church to a ship whose iron anchors are the commands of Christ (ἄγκυραι σιδηραῖ, αὐτοῦ τοῦ Χριστοῦ αἱ αἵγιαι ἐντολαί). Neither Clement nor Hippolytus connects the anchor with Christian burials. Clement shows awareness of some symbols or images that Christians also use in their funerary art, but, removed from

---

34. Both a PL and a *TLG* search do not list any usage of *ancora*/ἄγκυρα by Tertullian or Origen.

35. For the Asian origins of the Hippolytus referenced here, see John A. Cerrato, *Hippolytus between East and West: The Commentaries and the Provenance of the Corpus*, OTM (Oxford: Oxford University Press, 2002). See also Allen Brent, *Hippolytus and the Roman Church in the Third Century: Communities in Tension before the Emergence of a Monarch-Bishop*, VCSup 31 (Leiden: Brill, 1995); and Castelli, "Symbols of Anchors," 17 n. 20.

36. The reference to Seleucus can be found in Roman histories of the second-century Alexandrian historian Appian (*His. rom.* 11.56). In Appian's recounting, Seleucus was given a ring with an engraved anchor by his mother, which he later lost at the Euphrates—a portent of his kingship over that region. When he became king, he had an anchor engraved on his signet ring.

37. Translation follows Charles Kennedy, "Early Christians and the Anchor," *BA* 38 (1975): 119.

the funerary context, these symbols are no longer anchored to that context for meaning. Instead, Clement seems to indicate the anchor symbol as neutral by linking its use on a ring to the story of Seleucus.[38] Certainly visual stock images such as anchors, as noted before, have fluid meanings depending on the viewer and the viewer's social context. One still must ask what the nautical image of an anchor meant to Christians in Rome that led them to inscribe these symbols on their graves. Certainly, the symbol was not chosen for its neutral connotations.

Previous Explanations of Christian Funerary Anchors

Apart from Heb 6:18–20a, there have been some proposals put forward to explain the presence of anchor icons among Christian burials in Rome. Some have proposed that the anchor is a disguised cross in order to avoid the shame of being a worshiper of a crucified man. The entry "Archaeology of the Cross and Crucifix" from the *Catholic Encyclopedia* states:

> The truculent sarcasms of the heathens prevented the faithful from openly displaying this sign of salvation. When the early Christians did represent the sign of the cross on their monuments, nearly all sepulchral in character, they felt obliged to disguise it in some artistic and symbolical way. One of the oldest of the symbols of the cross is the anchor. … The anchor, originally a symbol of hope in general, takes on in this way a much higher meaning: that of hope based on the Cross of Christ. The similarity of the anchor to the cross made the former an admirable Christian symbol.[39]

There are several difficulties with this proposal. A search of the Epigraphic Database Bari contains one hundred images of complete anchors in the catacombs. There are fifty-four images that have no stock. Thus, over half the images do not evoke the image of the cross.[40] Of those images with stocks, seventeen are lying on their side (ICUR 1.1872; 2.6540; 4.9453,

---

38. See Castelli, "Symbols of Anchors," 18.
39. See Orazio Marucchi, "Cross and Crucifix, The. 1. Archaeology of the Cross," in *The Catholic Encyclopedia*, ed. Charles G. Herbermann et al., 15 vols. (New York: Appleton, 1907–1912), 4:521, https://tinyurl.com/SBL4830p1.
40. ICUR 1.705, 1778, 2233, 2680, 2745, 2898; 2.4246; 3.6556, 6576, 6568, 6581, 6673, 6680, 7223, 7230, 7260, 7314, 7315; 4.9644b, 10714; 5.13971, 14187, 14284, 14525, 14751, 14845, 14982, 15221, 15223, 15246a, 15246b; 6.17138, 17232; 7.18794,

9484; 5.12891, 15146, 15360; 8.20998, 21072, 21553, 22429, 22792, 23243; 9.25005, 25145, 25515; 10.26545b), four are inverted (ICUR 3.6718, 6875; 9.25428, 25465), two have slanted stocks (ICUR 5.12892, 13269b), two have stocks that are bowed (ICUR 5.12900; 9.26038 [lying]), and one is integrated into the *chi-rho* (ICUR 5.15246a). In these instances the association with the cross would be more obscure. This leaves twenty upright anchors with stocks, which very likely evoke the image of a cross for Christians (ICUR 5.13528 [whole image slanted]; 9.24072).[41] The anchor icons without stocks, however, likely communicated a distinctive message not tied to the cross. Additionally, Christians were not trying to disguise the cross. There are three prefourth century crosses among the Christian burials in Rome. There are two *T*-shaped crosses and one equilateral cross that are not hidden by being integrated into other images (ICUR 4.999b; 5.12889).[42] Moreover, these symbols were in dark, underground burial spaces and not regularly exposed to the public gaze. The tombs initially were visited only by family members and only on special occasions. It seems unnecessary, then, to mask the image of the cross in these spaces out of a sense of shame.

One of the more fascinating proposals during the last forty-five years has been put forward by Charles Kennedy. He proposes that the anchor is a symbolic representation of a wordplay on ἐν κυρίῳ.

ἐν – κυρ – ί – ῳ
ἄγ – κυρ – α

The symbol of the anchor (which Clement recommends for signet rings) in the catacombs then serves as a seal to indicate that the one who has died has died ἐν κυρίῳ ("in the Lord").[43] Revelation 14:13 provides an interesting correlation that reads, "Blessed are the dead in the Lord.... They will rest from their labors." The strength of Kennedy's proposal in light of Rev

---

19260, 20622; 8.21026, 21077, 21084, 22817, 22865, 23308; 9.23780, 24417, 24931, 25068, 25119, 26041, 26027, 26300f, 26303; 10.26497, 26541, 27057.

41. For the tendency of Christians to see the cross in other objects see Justin Martyr, *1 Apol.* 55; Tertullian, *Nat.* 1.12, cited in Bruce W. Longenecker, *The Cross before Constantine: The Early Life of a Christian Symbol* (Minneapolis: Fortress, 2015), 85.

42. For the *tau* being taken as a symbol of the cross, see Barn. 9.8.

43. Kennedy, "Early Christians and the Anchor," 121–22.

14:13 is that the meaning of the anchor is fitting to the context of Christian burial. Additionally, such symbolic representations of wordplays, Kennedy notes, can be found on coins where symbols represent cities. For example, Τραπεζοῦς in Turkey employed a table (τράπεζα); the island of Ῥόδος, a rose (ῥόδον); the Greek city of Αἰγαί, a goat (αἴξ; αἴγα); and Σελινοῦς in Sicily the wild celery (σέλινος).[44]

There are three potential difficulties with these observations. First, ἄγκυρα / ἐν κυρίῳ do not share as close of similarity in spelling or potentially in sound as the other examples Kennedy cites. The less-frequent diminutive form, however, comes closer, with at least the same number of syllables, and the middle two syllables potentially sounding the same.[45]

ἐν – κυρ – ί – ῳ
ἀγ – κύρ – ι – ον

Second, in the catacombs, anchors are found with the phrase ἐν θεῷ. For example, the inscription from the Crypt of Pope Cornelius on the Via Appia reads:[46]

	Χ ΗΤ Η	
(anchor)	ΖΗCΗC	(anchor)
	ΕΝΘΕW	

We might expect that the symbol of the anchor, if it stood for ἐν κυρίῳ, would exert pressure over the inscribed words so that it would read ἐν κυρίῳ. Third, another inscription from the Catacomb of Callixtus is also telling. It reads:[47]

CEYΔIC EK (anchor) EN ΘEW

---

44. Kennedy, "Early Christians and the Anchor," 123.

45. Of course, the dative singular form of the diminutive comes even closer, with only the beginning sound of the declined word and the phrase being potentially different. One wonders, however, why the symbol of the anchor would suggest the less frequently used diminutive form in the dative singular case. *TLG* lists twenty-five occurrences of ἀγκύριον compared to 1,124 occurrences of ἄγκυρα.

46. "Chete, you will live in God" (ICUR 4.9506; ca. 200–299).

47. The proposed inscription is Σευδὶς ἐκ(οιμήθη) [anchor] ἐν θεῷ (ICUR 3.9290; ca. 290–325).

"Seudis has fallen asleep in God." The anchor in its intervening location between EK and EN ΘEW, if it stood for ἐν κυρίῳ, would have seemed redundant, reading, "Seudis has fallen asleep (in the Lord) in God." At the very least, we would again imagine that the anchor as a wordplay for ἐν κυρίῳ would put pressure on the inscription to read ἐν κυρίῳ and not ἐν θεῷ. If the anchor is treated as a pictogram for "hope," as we will discuss below, the inscription then reads, "Seudis has fallen asleep (with hope) in God." Moreover, of thirteen recorded instances of ἐν κυρίῳ in the Roman catacombs, none occur with an anchor symbol—a potential oddity if ἄγκυρα is a wordplay for ἐν κυρίῳ (ICUR 1.2569, 4027; 2.4435; 3.7167, 8039, 8068; 4.10698a, 10698b; 5.15108; 7.19875a; 9.24615; 10.26515, 26519).

Finally, Castelli offers a more guarded proposal. Castelli does not find the exegesis of Heb 6:18–20a to be fully convincing for the origins of the meaning of funerary anchors. He believes the unstable meanings of the anchor among the very limited early Christian textual evidence (Hippolytus, Clement, and Hebrews) problematize the relationship between the iconographic images and the written sources. Thus, the meaning or meanings of the anchor icon are indeterminant.[48] Castelli, however, issues a summons to examine this issue further.

Anchors of Hope in the Catacombs of Rome

The catacombs provide clues concerning how early Christians understood the meanings of the anchor symbol in their burials. Furthermore, one of the primary meanings corresponds to use of the anchor simile in Hebrews. Indeed, some evidence points to the association of anchor iconography with the idea of hope. As we will see from our examination of Heb 6:18–19a in the next section, the association of an anchor and its stability and security with hope is fitting to the context of Christian burial.

There are three examples from catacombs that associate the anchor icon with hope (ἐλπίς or *spes*). As with most anchor iconography, these examples occur prior to the fourth century. The most telling example comes from the Catacomb of Priscilla on the Via Salaria Nova and of Praetextatus on the Via Appia.[49] Potentially dating from the beginning of the

---

48. Castelli, "Anchor and Fish," 17–18.
49. See Carlo Carletti, "'Epigrafia cristiana,' 'epigrafia dei cristiana': Alle origini della terza età dell'epigrafia," in *La terza età dell'epigrafia: Colloquio AIEGL–Borghesi 86, Bologna 1986*, ed. Donati Angela, EpigA 9 (Faenza: Lega, 1988), 115–35. Carletti

third century, one of the most interesting inscriptions from the Catacomb of Priscilla in the northern area of Rome reads (fig. 5.3):

ΕΥΕΛΠΙΣΤΟΣ   EVELPISTVS   (anchor)

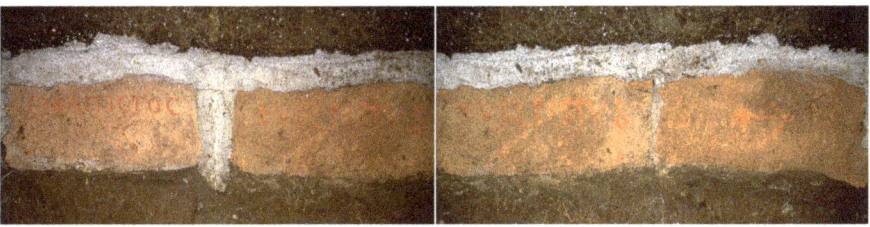

Fig. 5.3. Funerary painted inscription, 200–299 CE. Opus latericium. Catacomb of Priscilla. ICUR 9.26038. Photograph by Antonio E. Felle. Used by permission of the Pontificia Commissione di Archeologia Sacra.

The name of the Christian buried in the loculus is "Good Hope." His name is spelled in Greek, then transcribed in Latin, and then signified with an ideograph of an anchor.[50] This inscription, then, provides the clearest association of ἐλπίς with the symbol of the anchor.

Next, from the Catacomb of Praetextatus on the Via Appia in the southern area of Rome, there is an *E* linked with an anchor laying on its side. The *E* with the anchor possibly stands for "E(lpis)" (ICUR 5.15246c). The anchor occurs elsewhere with names derived from ἐλπίς: ELPIS (ICUR 8.22429 [ca. 276–300; in Coemeterium Maius on the Via Nomentana]), ELPIZ[usa] (ICUR 9.25118 [ca. 200–299; in Coemeterium Priscillae on the Via Salaria Nova]), ELPI[D]I (ICUR 9.25116 [ca. 200–299; in Coemeterium Priscillae on the Via Salaria Nova] and ICUR 1.1592 [in Vatican Museum]), and HELPIS (ICUR 7.20429 [ca. 200–299; in Coemeterium Novatiani on the Via Tuburtina]). The association of the anchor with

---

notes that the Catacomb of Priscilla preserves the most consistent and homogenous Christian epigraphic complex (119).

50. Giovanni Battiste de Rossi, "L'epigrafia primitiva priscilliana, ossia le iscrizioni incise sul marmo e dipinte sulle tegole della regione primordiale del cimitero di Priscilla," *BAC* (1886): 73. See ICUR 9.26038 (ca. 200–299). Also among Justin's companions in the account of their martyrdoms in Rome is a Euelpistus. See *The Martyrdom of the Holy Martyrs Justin, Charito, Euelpistus, Hierax, Paeon, and Liberian* (Recension B), 4.3.

names derived from ἐλπίς in the catacombs strengthens the identification of *E* + anchor with ἐλπίς (Elpis) or a named derived from ἐλπίς.

There is one other example of interest, though not as clear as the previous two. Again, from the Catacomb of Priscilla, there is a loculus with the following inscription (ca. 290–325; ICUR 8.23285), which uses the Latin word for hope (*spes*):

(anchor) (2 palm branches)   SPES   PAX TIB

In this inscription the palm branches, possibly signifying victory, might be associated with PAX TIB.[51] Victory and peace were commonly associated in the Roman imperial world.[52] Here the suggestion might be victory over death, or, if these are palms of martyrdom, then victory through martyrdom has led to a declaration of peace for the one buried in the loculus.[53] The anchor then would be associated with SPES following the order of the symbols.

In light of this funerary context, we should interpret figural images, and indeed all iconography in the catacombs, as representing Christian hope in life after death.[54] Further, Robin M. Jensen notes that some historians believe that the persecutions of Christians in the third century had a formative influence on Christian iconography. The imagery tends to emphasize safety, security, or deliverance from danger.[55] Certainly the hope in life after death would provide a sense of security and stability,

---

51. Palm leaves were regularly associated with victory in the ancient world. See Aulus Gellius, *Noct. att.* 3.6.1–3; Philo, *Leg.* 3.74; Suetonius, *Cal.* 32.2; 1 Macc 13:51; 2 Macc 10:6–7.

52. See Jason A. Whitlark, "The God of Peace and His Victorious King: Hebrews 13:20–21 in Its Roman Imperial Context," in *Hebrews in Context*, ed. Gabriella Gelardini and Harold W. Attridge, AJEC 91 (Leiden: Brill, 2016), 155–78.

53. See Rev. 7:9–14, where those who have come through the great affliction are given palms. Later Christian iconography and art depict martyrs holding palm leaves. For the use of palms in a more general sense of victory over death, see Irenaeus, *Haer.* 5.21.1. Thus the palm branch might signify victory over death no matter the manner of dying or signify a hope in an afterlife of abundance, i.e., peace as abundance. For the relationship between peace/*pax* and abundance, see Whitlark, "God of Peace," 157–59.

54. Jean Guyon, "Catacomb: Early Christian (Rome)," in *Eerdmans Encyclopedia of Early Christian Art*, 1:283. See also Carlos Galvao-Sobrinho, "Funerary Epigraphy and the Spread of Christianity in the West," *Athenaeum* 83 (1995): 453–58.

55. Robin M. Jensen, *Understanding Early Christian Art* (New York: Routledge, 2000), 27.

ideas also associated with an anchor, in a context of Christian suffering with its insecurity and instability in the second and third centuries. As we will see, such a context is addressed by Hebrews. It is also of interest that Christians chose not to borrow and adapt the common representation of hope as a young woman lifting her skirt and holding out a flower. The earliest Christian art and symbols were adaptation of prior pagan stock images, such as the popular image of the Good Shepherd based on the depiction of Hermes Kriophoros, or Christ Helios in the tomb of the Julii (Mausoleum M) in the Vatican necropolis. As Bisconti notes, early catacomb art was derived from stock images in artisan shops and points to an "economy of reuse" by the Christians; Christians either strengthened or changed the initial meaning of the iconographical themes adopted from the Greco-Roman tradition.[56] With regard to hope, Christians instead chose the uncommon association of hope with an anchor.

Additionally, Paul Corby Finney asserts that the items including anchors listed by Clement, cited earlier, were second-century intaglios that were "garden-variety devices" and the stonecutter's "stock-in-trade."[57] As mentioned above, the representation of anchors in catacombs shared a common iconography with anchors elsewhere in the Greco-Roman world. Thus, if Christians were going into artisan shops where these images might be displayed, whether one picked an anchor for a ring or an inscription in a tomb, they would be influenced by the context in which the anchor icon was used.[58] Again, Bisconti notes that images such as anchors move

---

56. In Vincenzo Fiocchi Nicolai, Fabrizio Bisconti, and Danilo Mazzoleni, *The Christian Catacombs of Rome: History, Decoration, Inscriptions*, trans. Cristina Carlo Stella and Lori-Ann Touchette (Regensburg: Schnell & Steiner, 1999), 100–101. See Fabrizio Bisconti, "La cristianizzazione delle immagini in Italia tra tarda antichità e alto medioevo," in *Lacristianizzazione in Italia tra tardoantico ed altomedioevo, Atti del IX Congresso Nazionale di Archeologia Cristiana (Agrigento,20–25 novembre 2004)*, ed. Rosa Maria Bonacasa Carra and Emma Vitale (Palermo: Saladino, 2007), 151–61.

57. Finney, *Invisible God*, 111.

58. Jeffrey Spier provides an extensive collection of early Christian rings in *Late Antique and Early Christian Gems*, SFCBKEJ 20 (Wiesbaden: Reichert, 2013). Ring gems from the third–fourth centuries with anchors are indeed interesting. Many rings have two fish with an anchor (nos. 198–210). Some are more elaborate, with an upper register of the good shepherd and of Jonah in repose under his vine with a dove. In the lower register is Jonah being tossed from a ship and swallowed by a sea monster, a dove on the ark, a fish, and an anchor (no. 429). Possibly, the earliest of these rings used by a Christian comes from the Catacomb of Domitilla in Rome, on which there

from a more neutral context to take on Christian significance because these symbols are judged salient and accommodate polyvalent meaning.[59] Interpretation of Hebrews indicates why a Christian, then, might choose an anchor (even if a garden-variety device of a stonecutter's or painter's workshop) for display on a loculus as a representation of hope in a safe and secure life after death.

Hebrews, Anchors, and Hope

The anchor simile in Hebrews is explicitly associated with hope, like the association of some anchor icons in the catacombs: "we who have fled to take hold of the hope [ἐλπίδος] set before us, which is as an anchor [ὡς ἄγκυραν] for the soul, secure and reliable." In the Greek text, the feminine relative pronoun ἥν immediately follows the feminine noun ἐλπίδος, making ἐλπίς the nearest and most likely referent to the adjectival relative clause.

Hebrews 6:18–20a comes at the end of the third major deliberative section beginning in 5:11. The focus of this section is a call to perseverance, namely, to undergo the same educational curriculum of suffering that Jesus underwent on his way to becoming the exalted high priest in the heavenly realm. Jesus's educational suffering and exaltation were described in the previous epideictic section in 5:1–10: "who in the days of his flesh offered up, with strong cries and tears, prayers and supplications to the one who is able to save him from death, and he was heard because of reverent submission, even though a son. He learned obedience from suffering, and

---

are the *kriophoros*, a tree with birds, sheep, a dolphin, and an anchor (no. 409, p. 63). Without inscriptions, the combination of these symbols is what primarily identifies these rings as Christian. Indeed, many of these symbols are found in the catacombs of Rome, though, unlike the catacombs, the anchor does not appear as the sole symbol on a ring gem or with inscriptions of words or names derived from ἐλπίς or *spes*. It is worth noting that these rings with anchors are found across the Roman Empire (e.g., Rome, Ravenna, Italy, Asia Minor, Egypt, Syria, Bulgaria, Israel). Spier, as well, notes that almost no gem with a fish and anchor can be dated earlier than the third century (46). Most of the earliest Christian engraved gems cannot be dated before the second half of the third century. The anchor does appear on pagan gems and rings and is not one of the primary images used on gems by Christians. At times it is not clear whether an engraved gem with an anchor always belonged to a Christian (45). Further studies are needed to assess what kind of relationship might exist between Christian gem iconography and that in the catacombs of Rome and elsewhere.

59. Nicolai et al., *Christian Catacombs*, 125.

after he was perfected, he became the source of eternal salvation to all who obey him" (5:7–8). Thus, the audience is exhorted in the following deliberative section to "imitate those who through faith(fulness) and patience inherit the promise" (6:12). Abraham is next brought forth as part of a comparative argument to encourage such patient endurance.

The comparative argument is built on Jesus's education of suffering in 5:6–10. When Heb 11:17–19 is taken into consideration, interesting parallels emerge between Jesus's education and Abraham's education, which are the focus of 6:13–17. There are five such points of contact: (1) both Jesus and Abraham are tested by the prospect of death (Jesus, his own [5:7], and Abraham, his son's [11:17]); (2) both Jesus and Abraham are given promises with confirming oaths by God (5:6, 6:13–14 [see 11:17]); (3) both Jesus and Abraham are given the assurance of resurrection on the basis of the promise (Jesus, his own resurrection [5:5–7; see 7:11–25], and Abraham, his son's [11:19]); (4) both Jesus and Abraham respond obediently to God's command on the basis of this hope (Jesus, a command to die [5:6–10; see 12:2], and Abraham, a command to sacrifice Isaac [11:17–19; see 6:13–15a]); and (5) both Jesus and Abraham's son are delivered from death via resurrection (Jesus actually [5:6–10; see 13:20] and Isaac figuratively [11:17–19; see 6:15b]).[60] These parallels emphasize the need for faithful endurance, even in the face of the threat of death. Moreover, faithful endurance is enabled by hope in God's promise, a promise that brings deliverance from death via resurrection. Indeed, the audience has greater reasons than Abraham for such endurance. The author has already presented Jesus as one who has received his joy and entered the world to come or the heavenly realm, that is, into the very presence of God (see Heb 1:5–14). Jesus has realized the hope of the audience of Hebrews and has become their forerunner into God's eschatological presence (see Heb 2:5–9). The concluding simile in Heb 6, then, likens the audience's hope in God's promise to an anchor. This hope is "secure and reliable" amid the trials of suffering, even death, that the audience must face. Thus, the use of *anchor* in Hebrews to convey the idea of security and safety belongs to

---

60. For a fuller discussion of these points, see Michael W. Martin and Jason A. Whitlark, *Inventing Hebrews: Design and Purpose in Ancient Rhetoric*, SNTSMS 171 (Cambridge: Cambridge University Press, 2018). See also David M. Moffitt, *Atonement and the Logic of Resurrection in the Epistle to the Hebrews*, NovTSup 141 (Leiden: Brill, 2011), 192–93.

the broader cultural milieu of the author, though the relationship to hope is an uncommon association.

The anchor in Hebrews is then a symbol of hope in God's secure promise amid persecution. It is a promise of eschatological, immortal life after death, namely, resurrection from the dead into the presence of God in the world to come. This association of the anchor with Christian hope in life after death amid suffering is certainly fitting for the primary meaning of anchors in the context of Christian burial prior to the fourth century CE.

Associating ἐλπίς with ἄγκυρα as a symbol of stability and security in Hebrews may have had a particular Christian attraction in light of the prominence that eschatological hope (ἐλπίς) had among early Christ-followers (e.g., Rom 8:24–25, 1 Cor 13:13) and especially for the author of Hebrews (see Heb 3:6; 6:11, 18; 7:19; 10:23; 11:1). Hope for Christians was not a delusional sort of hope but one that was secure and stable like an anchor, especially for Christians living in a hostile culture of lethal prejudice and not in a context that could be described as a safe harbor.

The context of burial in the catacombs actually strengthens a connection to the influence of Hebrews, because *only* Hebrews among extant Christian, Jewish, or pagan discourse prior to the fourth century links the anchor to hope in life after death.[61] A Christian living in Rome who had heard Hebrews, or better yet, who had heard the anchor simile (even if unaware that it had come from Hebrews), might, upon seeing this symbol, be drawn to have it put on a loculus as an expression of hope amid suffering in life after death. As noted above, at key places in the catacombs of Rome, the unique connection between anchor and hope that is made in Hebrews emerges. It is this literary unicum in Hebrews that strongly suggests Hebrews as the origin of the anchor symbol in the catacombs. Moreover, the connection moves beyond general ideas of security and safety, common to anchor metaphors in the Greco-Roman context, to one of Christian hope in life after death—the same hope as is expressed in Hebrews. Again, Euelpistos ("Good Hope") in the Catacomb of Priscilla is represented solely by an anchor.

---

61. See Carletti, "Epigrafia cristiana," 122. Carletti refers to the anchor symbol as a figurative-symbolic version of eschatological concepts.

Wirkungsgeschichte of Hebrews in Rome

This connection between Hebrews and funerary anchors in Rome is further strengthened if both share a common provenance, namely, Rome. Thus, we next need to consider the presence of Hebrews in Rome prior to the second century CE. This would place Hebrews in Rome almost a century before the appearance of anchor icons in the catacombs at the end of second and beginning of the third centuries.[62] Hebrews, then, is potentially a legitimate source of influence on the anchor iconography, since both share a common location, and Hebrews precedes the appearance of the funerary anchors in the Roman catacombs.

Hebrews may have originally addressed a Christian community residing in Rome in the latter half of the first century.[63] Even if we were to set aside the issue of the location of the original audience of Hebrews, there is evidence that points to an effective, persistent influence of Hebrews in Rome at the end of the first century to the end of the second century.[64] First, the earliest citation of Hebrews comes at the end of the first century from 1 Clement (ca. 96 CE), a document of Roman provenance.[65] Because

---

62. Hebrews is commonly dated by scholars between 60 and 90 CE. See Craig R. Koester, *Hebrews: A New Translation with Introduction and Commentary*, AB 36 (New York: Doubleday, 2001), 50–54.

63. See Raymond E. Brown and John P. Meier, *Antioch and Rome: New Testament Cradles of Catholic Christianity* (New York: Paulist, 1983), 146. Another potential piece of textual evidence in Hebrews for a Roman destination is if "here we do not have a city that remains" in Heb 13:14 is understood as a figured critique of Rome and its eternity. See Jason A. Whitlark, "'Here We Do Not Have a City That Remains': A Figured Critique of Roman Imperial Propaganda in Hebrews 13:14," *JBL* 131 (2012): 161–79. For further discussion see Whitlark, *Resisting Empire: Rethinking the Purpose of the "Letter to the Hebrews,"* LNTS (London: Bloomsbury, 2014), 4–16.

64. Detecting allusive references or influence can be methodologically challenging. See the discussion by Andrew F. Gregory and Christopher M. Tuckett, "Reflections on Method: What Constitutes the Use of the Writings That Later Formed the New Testament in the Apostolic Fathers," in *The Reception of the New Testament in the Apostolic Fathers*, ed. Andrew Gregory and Christopher Tuckett (Oxford: Oxford University Press, 2007), 61–82. I am mainly considering language and ideas that are peculiarly associated with Hebrews while proceeding with the understanding that Hebrews precedes all these texts.

65. When both external and internal evidence are considered, the traditional dating of 1 Clement in the 90s remains the most likely option, as opposed to early or late dates. The witness of Hegesippus (Eusebius, *Hist. eccl.* 3.16; 4.22), Irenaeus

of the frequently recognized citation, 1 Clement typically serves as the *terminus ad quem* for dating Hebrews. While there are several parallels,[66] 1 Clem. 36:1–5 is most striking:

> This is the path, loved ones, in which we have found our salvation—Jesus Christ, the high priest of our offerings, the benefactor and who helps us in our weakness [τὸν ἀρχιερέα ... βοηθὸν τῆς ἀσθενείας ἡμῶν // ἀρχιερέα ... ἀσθενείαις ἡμῶν ... εἰς εὔκαιρον βοήθειαν (Heb 4:15–16)].
>
> Through this one we gaze into the heights of the heavens; through this one we see the reflection of his perfect and superior countenance; through this one the eyes of our hearts have been opened; through this one our foolish and darkened understanding springs up into the light; through this one the Master has wished us to taste the knowledge of immortality. He is the radiance of his magnificence, as superior to angels as he has inherited a more excellent name [ὃς ὢν ἀπαύγασμα τῆς μεγαλωσύνης αὐτοῦ, τοσούτῳ μείζων ἐστὶν ἀγγέλων, ὅσῳ διαφορώτερον ὄνομα κεκληρονόμηκεν // ὃς ὢν ἀπαύγασμα τῆς δόξης ... μεγαλωσύνης ... τοσούτῳ κρείττων γενόμενος τῶν ἀγγέλων ὅσῳ διαφορώτερον παρ' αὐτοὺς κεκληρονόμηκεν ὄνομα (Heb 1:3–4)].

(*Haer.* 3.3.3), Clement of Alexandria (*Strom.* 4.17), and Eusebius (*Hist. eccl.* 3.15–16, 5.6.2–3) all point to 1 Clement being written under the reign of Domitian and during the episcopacy of Clement. Additionally, Polycarp in his *Letter to the Philippians* (ca. 110–130 CE) appears to reference 1 Clement (see Polycarp, *Phil* 3.2//1 Clem. 21.1; Polycarp, *Phil* 5.3//1 Clem. 1.3; Polycarp, *Phil* 9.2//1 Clem. 5.4; Polycarp, *Phil* 11.4//1 Clem. 37.5). See Michael Holmes, "Polycarp of Smyrna, Letter to the Philippians," *ExpTim* 118 (2006): 60–62; and Paul Hartog, *Polycarp and the New Testament*, WUNT 2/134 (Tübingen: Mohr Siebeck, 2002), 176. The internal evidence also fits this dating regarding 1 Clem. 5 (martyrdoms of Peter and Paul occurred in "our own generation"), 42–44 (still-living leaders appointed by apostles with possibly others appointed by these former leaders), 47 (Corinthian believers are part of an ancient church), and 63 (the letter carriers have been believers from youth to old age).

66. Other potential connections between Hebrews and 1 Clement are 1 Clem. 17.1 = Heb 11:37, 39; 1 Clem. 17.5 = Heb 3:5; 1 Clem. 21.9 = Heb 4:12; 1 Clem. 27.2 = Heb 6:8; and 1 Clem. 31.3 = Heb 11:20. Eusebius notes, as well, Clement's dependence on Hebrews (see *Hist. eccl.* 3.38.1–3). See also Koester, *Hebrews*, 22 nn. 7, 9; and Andrew F. Gregory, "1 Clement and the Writings That Later Formed the New Testament," in Gregory and Tuckett, *Reception of the New Testament*, 152–57. Additionally, Gregory also concludes that Clement's knowledge of Hebrews (along with Romans and 1 Corinthians) does not necessarily indicate familiarity through a Pauline letter collection. The presence of these three letters can be explained by Clement's location in Rome.

For so it is written, "The one who makes his angels spirits and ministers flames of fire." But the Master says this about his Son: "You are my Son, today I have given you birth. Ask from me, and I will give you the nations as your inheritance, and the ends of the earth as your possession." And again he says to him, "Sit at my right hand until I make your enemies a footstool for your feet" [ὁ ποιῶν τοὺς ἀγγέλους αὐτοῦ πνεύματα καὶ τοὺς λειτουργοὺς αὐτοῦ πυρὸς φλόγα // ὁ ποιῶν τοὺς ἀγγέλους αὐτοῦ πνεύματα καὶ τοὺς λειτουργοὺς αὐτοῦ πυρὸς φλόγα (Heb 1:7). ἐπὶ δὲ τῷ υἱῷ αὐτοῦ οὕτως εἶπεν ὁ δεσπότης· υἱός μου εἶ σύ, ἐγὼ σήμερον γεγέννηκά σε· αἴτησαι παρ' ἐμοῦ, καὶ δώσω σοι ἔθνη τὴν κληρονομίαν σου καὶ τὴν κατάσχεσίν σου τὰ πέρατα τῆς γῆς // Τίνι γὰρ εἶπέν ποτε τῶν ἀγγέλων υἱός μου εἶ σύ, ἐγὼ σήμερον γεγέννηκά σε (Heb 1:5). καὶ πάλιν λέγει πρὸς αὐτόν· κάθου ἐκ δεξιῶν μου, ἕως ἂν θῶ τοὺς ἐχθρούς σου ὑποπόδιον τῶν ποδῶν σου // πρὸς τίνα δὲ τῶν ἀγγέλων εἴρηκέν ποτε· κάθου ἐκ δεξιῶν μου, ἕως ἂν θῶ τοὺς ἐχθρούς σου ὑποπόδιον τῶν ποδῶν σου (Heb 1:13)]. (Ehrman)

While the influence of the language and claims of Hebrews can be discerned in this passage by Clement, the content of Hebrews is taken up by Clement and synthesized to fit Clement's own purposes.

Hebrews also seems to have influenced the issue of a second repentance discussed in the Shepherd of Hermas (ca. 120–140 CE). Hermas reflects conflicting viewpoints or tensions on this issue. In Mand. 31.1–7, Hermas states that he has heard from some teachers "that there is no repentance apart from that which came when we descended into the water and received forgiveness for the sins we formerly committed." Such a position appears to echo Heb 6:4–6 (see 10:26), especially if "those who have once been enlightened" in Hebrews was understood as a reference to baptism. The angel then informs Hermas that this position is correct, but because of the Lord's compassion there is only one opportunity for repentance open after baptism. Hermas, however, in Vis. 6.4–5 (see 25.7) learns that repentance is available to believers for sins committed prior to the giving of the revelation but is not accepted afterwards. Finally, these rigorist positions appear to be modified in Sim. 103.5–6, where repentance is possible for those who have "denied the Lord" before final judgment but not afterwards. Again, this denial recalls the stern warning in Heb 6:6 and 10:29–31 of subjecting the son of God to public disgrace by falling away. Like Clement, Hermas does not directly mention Hebrews, though one wonders whether the mention of "teachers" who hold the rigorist position might be an allusion to Hebrews or to those who adapted its instructions.⁶⁷ Both the author of Hebrews and Hermas not only address the issue of suffering for allegiance to Christ and his community but also wrestle with the consequences of defection to avoid suffering (see Sim. 98.3).⁶⁸

Justin Martyr (d. ca. 165 CE) demonstrates the influence of Hebrews, though, like Clement, he never explicitly identifies Hebrews in his writings and adapts Hebrews to his own ends.⁶⁹ There are four references of interest. First, in *Dial.* 11.2, Justin speaks about the Mosaic covenant as old or obsolete (παλαιός) and then quotes the Jeremiah prophecy of a new covenant in 11.3.⁷⁰ The logic and language are certainly reminiscent of Hebrews 8, where, after quoting the Jeremiah prophecy of the new covenant, the author declares that "by calling it 'new' he has made old/obsolete [πεπαλαίωκεν] the first. And whatever is becoming obsolete and growing old will soon disappear" (v. 13).⁷¹ Second, in *Dial.* 13.1, Justin states that the repentant "are no longer cleansed [καθαριζομένοις] by the blood of goats and [αἵμασι τράγων καὶ] sheep or by the ashes of a heifer [σποδῷ δαμάλεως] or by the offerings of fine flour but by faith through the blood of Christ [τοῦ αἵματος τοῦ Χριστοῦ]." The language is reminiscent of Heb 9:13–14, where a comparison is offered, namely,

> if the blood of goats and [τὸ αἷμα τράγων καὶ] bulls and the ashes of a heifer [σποδὸς δαμάλεως] which were sprinkled on those who were defiled so that their flesh is purified [καθαρότητα] how much more will the blood of Christ [τὸ αἷμα τοῦ Χριστοῦ] ... cleanse [καθαριεῖ] our conscience from dead works to serve the living God.

---

67. See Patrick Gray, "The Early Reception of Hebrews 6:4–6," in *Scripture and Traditions: Essays on Early Judaism and Christianity in Honor of Carl R. Holladay*, ed. Patrick Gray and Gail R. O'Day, NovTSup 129 (Leiden: Brill, 2008), 327–33. Gray argues that Hermas appropriates Heb 6:4–6.

68. See Joseph Verheyden, "The *Shepherd of Hermas* and the Writings That Later Formed the New Testament," in Gregory and Tuckett, *Reception of the New Testament*, 293–329. Indeed, Verheyden states that the opportunity for repentance after baptism is the "book's core message" (295 and n. 7).

69. See Oskar Skarsaune, *The Proof from Prophecy: A Study in Justin Martyr's Proof-Text Tradition: Text-Type, Provenance, Theological Profile*, NovTSup 56 (Leiden: Brill, 1987), 108: "it is practically certain that he knew [Hebrews] and made use of it. This can only be said of the *Dialogue*, however."

70. See Skarsaune, *Proof from Prophecy*, 73.

71. See Knut Backhaus, *Der neue Bund und das Werden der Kirche* (Münster: Aschendorff, 1996), 315–24, esp. 320.

Third, in *Dial.* 19.4, Justin recounts the story of Melchizedek from Gen 14, emphasizing that Melchizedek was priest of God Most High, received tithes from Abraham, and blessed Abraham. Justin then quotes Ps 110:4, where God makes the exalted Lord a priest forever, according to the order of Melchizedek. In *Dial.* 33.1–2, Justin returns to Ps 110:4 to reemphasize that Jesus is indeed this eternal high priest in the order of Melchizedek about whom God swore. Here again, Justin emphasizes two events in Gen 14, where Melchizedek, as priest of God Most High, received tithes from Abraham and blessed him. Like Melchizedek, Justin will refer elsewhere to Jesus as the eternal king and priest (*Dial.* 36.1) or simply the eternal priest (*Dial.* 42.1). These points are all emphasized in Hebrews, where Christ is uniquely (at least in the NT) portrayed as the heavenly enthroned king and the Melchizedekian priest, with an indestructible life based on the oath God swore in Ps 110:4 (Heb 6:20; 7:16, 20–21). Hebrews also highlights from Gen 14 that Melchizedek was priest of God Most High, one who received tithes from Abraham and blessed him (Heb 7:1, 4–10). Justin, like Hebrews, leaves out the very attractive eucharistic elements of bread and wine in the encounter—an aspect of the narrative that found its way into Christian liturgy and art. Finally, in *Apol.* 1.63, Justin refers to Christ as the apostle, a designation Hebrews gives to Christ in 3:1. All of these echoes cumulatively point to the influence of Hebrews in Justin's writings.

There emerged at the end of the second century in Rome an adoptionistic sect of Christians who were labeled by later heresiologists as Melchizedekians. These so-called Melchizedekians are identified as such by Epiphanius in *Pan.* 55.1.1–5. Epiphanius notes they are an offshoot of the Theodotians. Theodotus the Byzantine had been excommunicated from Rome in 190 CE by Victor for his adoptionist Christology. Theodotus the Banker accepted the Byzantine's adoptionism but added to it a theory about Melchizedek. Theodotus yielded to Pope Zephyrinus in 217 CE, thus effectively ending the history of this adoptionist sect.[72] The earlier *Refutatio omnium haeresium* (ca. 222 CE) traditionally attributed to Hippolytus confirms such an offshoot discussed by Epiphanius (see 7.36.1).[73] Also, in the first half of the third century Pseudo-Tertullian's *Refutatio*

---

72. See Fred L. Horton, *The Melchizedek Tradition: A Critical Examination of the Sources to the Fifth Century A.D. and in the Epistle to the Hebrews*, SNTSMS 30 (Cambridge: Cambridge University Press, 1976), 90–101.

73. Hippolytus, *Refutation of All Heresies*, trans. M. David Litwa, WGRW 40 (Atlanta: SBL Press, 2016), xli.

omnium haeresium states again that Theodotus the Banker started a new sect in Rome that held Melchizedek was intercessor for angels and Christ was an intercessor for humans. Moreover, Melchizedek is greater because according to Heb 7:3, he has no father, no mother, and no genealogy (PL 2:91–92). This sect then witnesses to the presence and influence of Hebrews in Rome at the end of the second century.[74]

All this evidence from Christians in Rome and its environs points to the influence of Hebrews from the end of the first to the beginning of the third century. Such an early and persistent presence of the ideas and language of Hebrews among Christians for over a century in Rome not only makes Hebrews eligible as the source of influence on the funerary anchors in the catacombs but also increases the likelihood of that influence. Anchors in the catacombs emerged in a context where Hebrews had been circulating and influencing Christians for over a century. In fact, Christian symbols and art emerged in a context where Christian literature was already flourishing.[75]

Rome as the Epicenter of the Christian Funerary Anchor Phenomenon?

Not only were funerary anchors prominent early among Christians in Rome, but Rome also appears to have been the epicenter of this phenomenon. There are potentially two conditions that point to Rome as the epicenter:

---

74. We could also consider Irenaeus (d. ca. 200 CE), who at the end of the second century demonstrates knowledge of Hebrews. Irenaeus was familiar with Roman Christianity. He had been a letter carrier from Gaul to Rome during the episcopacy of Eleutherus (174–189 CE) and possibly had been in Rome earlier during Polycarp's visit in 154/5 CE in the episcopacy of Anicetus (155–166 CE). Irenaeus may have gained his knowledge of Hebrews through these visits. Eusebius acknowledges that Irenaeus mentions and makes use of Hebrews in a text no longer extant (see *Hist. eccl.* 5.26.1). Irenaeus shows familiarity with Hebrews in *Adversus haereses*, though never explicitly identifying Hebrews in this treatise (see *Haer.* 3.3.4; Eusebius, *Hist. eccl.* 5.4.1–3). The Moscow manuscript of the Martyrdom of Polycarp (22.2–4) places Irenaeus in Rome at the time of Polycarp's martyrdom. For further discussion, see Charles E. Hill, *From the Lost Teaching of Polycarp: Identifying Irenaeus' Apostolic Presbyter and the Author of "Ad Diognetum,"* WUNT 186 (Tübingen: Mohr Siebeck, 2006), 73–75. See also D. Jeffrey Bingham, "Irenaeus and Hebrews," in *Christology, Hermeneutics, and Hebrews: Profiles from the History of Interpretation*, ed. Jon C. Laansma and Daniel J. Treier, LNTS 423 (London: T&T Clark, 2012), 48–73.

75. Vincenzo Fiocchi Nicolai, *Strutture funerarie ed edifici di culto paleocristiani di Roma dal II al VI secolo* (Vatican City: IGER, 2001).

(1) the earliest funerary anchors used by Christians appear in Rome, and (2) the more frequent occurrence of this symbol in Roman Christian burials is much higher than elsewhere among early Christians. There were several Christian underground burial complexes of varying size on the Italian peninsula and one in Melos, Greece, that emerged at or after the time of the emergence of the catacomb complexes in Rome.[76] Early Christian burials in North Africa, however, might provide our best available comparative data with Christian burials in Rome and the use of funerary anchors.

First, funerary anchors as Christian iconography have their earliest occurrence in the catacombs of Rome in comparison to North Africa. They began to appear around the beginning of the third century, possibly even earlier.[77] In North Africa and Egypt, however, much Christian material culture does not predate the late third century.[78] There is an exception—the catacomb complex in Hadrumetum (Sousse, Tunisia).[79] Augustin Leynaud believes the Hadrumetum catacombs could date to the early third century (if not earlier), thus making them contemporaneous with some of the earliest catacombs in Rome.[80] One Christian inscription

---

76. For a survey of these sites see Vincenzo Fiocchi Nicolai, "The Catacombs," in *The Oxford Handbook of Early Christian Archeology*, ed. William R. Caraher, Thomas W. Davies, and David K. Pettegrew (Oxford: Oxford University Press, 2018), 77–84.

77. See note 2. The earliest date range for the appearance of anchors from the EDB is 150–225. Castelli states, "The most ancient funerary inscriptions of which we can be certain that they were commissioned by Christians date back to the last years of the 2nd and the first half of the 3rd centuries. These have all been found *in situ*, in the primitive parts of the Catacombs of Priscilla, Callistus, Calepodius, Praetextatus and so on" ("Symbols of Anchors," 12). Nicolai notes, "From the second half of the second century Christians were inserted into pagan cemeteries ... beneath the Basilica of S. Sebastiano"—in which cemetery anchor icons have been found (Nicolai, Bisconti, and Mazzoleni, *Christian Catacombs of Rome*, 14).

78. See the general assessments of the lack of archaeological remains of Christian activity for this period by J. Patout Burns Jr. and Robin M. Jensen, *Christianity in Roman Africa: The Development of Its Practices and Beliefs* (Grand Rapids: Eerdmans, 2014), 40–41, 113; Maureen A. Tilley, "North Africa," in *Origins to Constantine*, ed. Margaret M. Mitchell and Frances M. Young, CHC (Cambridge: Cambridge University Press, 2006), 1:381–82; and Birger A. Pearson, "Egypt," in Mitchell and Young, *Origins to Constantine*, 1:331.

79. Tilley lists other North African catacombs, but these have yet to be dated reliably at the time of the publication of her essay ("North Africa," 382).

80. Augustin Fernand Leynaud, *Les catacombes africaines, Sousse-Hadrumète*, 2nd ed. (Alger: Carbonel, 1922), 8–15. The dating depends on which consular named

with anchors potentially comes from an early period of Hadrumetum in the Catacomb of the Good Shepherd. It reads:[81]

(anchor) FLAVIAE DOMITITAE IN PACE (anchor)
(bird with olive branch)

In the same complex of catacombs, there is also an elaborate fourth-century floor mosaic of an anchor with an entwined dolphin that appears in the catacomb of Hermes (fig. 5.4).[82]

Fig. 5.4. Fourth-century tomb mosaic for Hermes. Cubiculum of Hermes at Hadrumetum. Sousse Archaeological Museum. Photograph by Robin M. Jensen.

Lupus that one chooses and also on the dating of the burial of the centurion Quintus Papius Saturninus Julianus from the catacomb of Severus. Christians may not have been the only ones buried in these catacomb complexes or even started them (so Tilley, "North Africa," 382).

81. See no. 98 in Leynaud, *Les catacombes africaines*, 181; see also 80–81.

82. See Stephen E. Potthoff, *The Afterlife in Early Christian Carthage: Near-Death Experience, Ancestor Cult, and the Archeology of Paradise*, RSECW (New York: Routledge, 2017), 195–209. See also discussion of the dolphin as symbol in Goodenough, *Jewish Symbols* 5:22–27.

In Carthage, the cemetery basilica of Mcidfa (Basilica Maiorum) contains seven potential anchor inscriptions. The clearest of these inscriptions reported by Liliane Ennabli reads:[83]

RESTUTA
IN PACE (anchor)

The earliest inscriptions from this site date from the early fourth century.[84] This Christian basilica still remains one of the oldest in North Africa.[85] These instances of anchors in North African Christian burials would still postdate their first occurrence in Rome, except possibly for an early third-century date for the inscription in the Catacomb of the Good Shepherd. The presence of anchors in Christian burials in North Africa potentially points to Roman influence.[86]

Second, there is a greater number and higher relative percentage of anchors in the places of Christian burials in Rome as compared to the catacombs in Hadrumetum. Among all the inscriptions in Rome, anchors (551) occur in 1.35 percent of the epitaphs.[87] In Hadrumetum, anchors (two) occur in 0.723 percent of the epitaphs.[88] In fact, anchors are among the more common earliest Christian symbols in Rome, concentrating in the earliest areas of the catacombs.[89] I have been able to find only ten potential Christian funerary inscriptions with anchors from the North

---

83. See no. 11 in Liliane Ennabli, *Les Inscriptions funéraires chrétiennes de Carthage: La Basilique de Mcidfa* (Paris: Publications de l'Ecole Française de Rome, 1982), 2:46.

84. Ennabli, *Les Inscriptions funéraires*, 20.

85. Burns and Jensen, *Christianity in Roman Africa*, 118.

86. There is also one interesting epitaph with two anchors of uncertain date from an Alexandrian necropolis reported by Giuseppe Botti. See Botti, "Le iscrizioni cristiane: Di Alessandria d'Egitto," *Bessarione* 7 (1900): 280.

87. See note 1.

88. This percentage is based on two anchor inscriptions among 275 total inscriptions recorded by Leynaud (*Les catacombes africaines*, 133–98 [139-Catacomb of the Good Shepherd], 281–308 [70-Catacomb of Hermes], 337–40 [8-Catacomb of Agrippa], 393–428 [58-Catacomb of Severus]). These are rough calculations and possibly could be refined to compare relative dates of inscriptions in the earliest part of the catacombs with the appearance of anchors. In Rome, since anchors occur early and not later, this modification would most likely increase percent of occurrence of anchors among inscriptions.

89. See note 2.

African region of the empire.⁹⁰ As previously mentioned, Ennabli lists seven potential anchors among the funerary inscriptions of the cemetery basilica of Mcidfa in Carthage (nos. 11, 36, 48, 53, 98, 332, and 743) and one undated inscription taken from the publication of Delattre at the other Carthaginian cemetery basilica of Sainte-Monique (no. 278).⁹¹ Among the thousands of burials in the Hadrumetum catacombs, there is one anchor mosaic and one inscription. From this evidence, we may conclude that the anchor as a symbol of Christian hope in life after death, even a symbol of security and safety in the midst of persecution, apparently did not take hold pervasively in the North African context.⁹² The present state of the evidence suggests that the phenomenon of funerary anchor inscriptions has its epicenter or origins in Rome.

Conclusion

In sum, there are three broad reasons to see the influence of the anchor simile from Heb 6:18–20a in the use of the anchor symbol in the catacombs of Rome. (1) Hebrews was written in the latter half of the first century. Though possibly sent to a community in Rome, Hebrews at least was known among Christian communities in Rome predating the emergence of the funerary anchors. Moreover, the influence of Hebrews in Rome can be discerned for more than a century. Consequently, Hebrews is eligible to serve as a potential source of influence for the symbol among Christian burials in the catacombs of Rome. (2) The meaning of the ἄγκυρα-ἐλπίς association in Hebrews as a reference to hope in life after death is fitting

---

90. An examination of *cupulae* in North Africa shows these barrel-shaped grave markers to be rare in the fourth century CE and afterwards. Some of these later *cupulae* contain Christian symbols, but none of these symbols is an anchor. See Lea M. Stirling, "The Koine of the Cupula in Roman North Africa and the Transition from Cremation to Inhumation," in *Mortuary Landscapes of North Africa*, ed. David L. Stone and Lea M. Stirling (Toronto: Toronto University Press, 2007), 121–22.

91. Liliane Ennabli, *Les Inscriptions funéraires chrétiennes de la Basilique dite de Sainte-Monique à Carthage* (Paris: Publications de l'Ecole Française de Rome, 1975), 28, 313. The inscription reads: "VIVAS […] / PASTOR […] / FELIX […] / (inclined anchor)." The oldest funerary inscriptions examined by Ennabli at this site date to the late fourth or early fifth century (33–35).

92. If we were able to do isotopic analysis of bones in the graves, we might be able to indicate whether those buried were migrants to North Africa. Such data could indicate that the anchor funerary iconography was distinctive to these migrants.

for the use of the anchor symbol in the context of Christian burial, namely, the catacombs of Rome. Moreover, as symbol of security and safety amid the threat of persecution and suffering presupposed by Hebrews, such an association fits the use of funerary anchors that primarily occur prior to Constantine. (3) In the larger Greco-Roman context prior to fourth century, the association of ἄγκυρα and ἐλπίς is both distinct and peculiar to Hebrews. Also, the anchor was not chosen as a representation of ἐλπίς or *spes* in the Greco-Roman context. More common in the imperial context was a woman with a lifted dress holding forth a flower. Even extant Christian texts prior to the fourth century do not use the simile. Hebrews is the only extant early text that takes a central tenet of Christian preaching, hope in God's promise through Jesus Christ for life after death, and associates it with the stability and safety of an anchor. The only other place this connection manifests itself before the fourth century is in the Roman catacombs. Thus, the later Christian burials in Rome, which associate the anchor with ἐλπίς or *spes*, suggest a connection with the phenomenon in Heb 6:18–20a.

Works Cited

Attridge, Harold W. *The Epistle to the Hebrews: A Commentary on the Epistle to the Hebrews*. Hermeneia. Philadelphia: Fortress, 1989.

Backhaus, Knut. *Der neue Bund und das Werden der Kirche*. Münster: Aschendorff, 1996.

Bingham, D. Jeffrey. "Irenaeus and Hebrews." Pages 48–73 in *Christology, Hermeneutics, and Hebrews: Profiles from the History of Interpretation*. Edited by Jon C. Laansma and Daniel J. Treier. LNTS 423. London: T&T Clark, 2012.

Bischoff, Friedrich. "Spes." *GN* 129 (1989): 14–19.

Bisconti, Fabrizio. "La cristianizzazione delle immagini in Italia tra tarda antichità e alto medioevo." Pages 151–67 in *La cristianizzazione in Italia tra tardoantico ed altomedioevo: Atti del IX Congresso Nazionale di Archeologia Cristiana (Agrigento,20–25 novembre 2004)*. Edited by Rosa Maria Bonacasa Carra and Emma Vitale. Palermo: Saladino, 2007.

Botti, Giuseppe. "Le iscrizioni cristiane: Di Alessandria d'Egitto." *Bessarione* 7 (1900): 270–81.

Brent, Allen. *Hippolytus and the Roman Church in the Third Century: Communities in Tension before the Emergence of a Monarch-Bishop.* VCSup 31. Leiden: Brill, 1995.

Brown, Raymond E., and John P. Meier. *Antioch and Rome: New Testament Cradles of Catholic Christianity.* New York: Paulist, 1983.

Burns, J. Patout, Jr., and Robin M. Jensen. *Christianity in Roman Africa: The Development of Its Practices and Beliefs.* Grand Rapids: Eerdmans, 2014.

Cairns, Douglas. "Metaphors for Hope in Archaic and Classical Greek Poetry." Pages 13–44 in *Hope, Joy, and Affection in the Classical World.* Edited by Ruth R. Caston and Robert A. Kaster. Oxford: Oxford University Press, 2015.

Carletti, Carlo. "'Epigrafia cristiana,' 'epigrafia dei cristiana': Alle origini della terza età dell'epigrafia." Pages 115–35 in *La terza età dell'epigrafia: colloquio AIEGL–Borghesi 86, Bologna 1986.* Edited by Donati Angela. EpigA 9. Faenza: Lega, 1988.

Castelli, Emanuele. "The Symbols of Anchor and Fish in the Most Ancient Parts of the Catacomb of Priscilla: Evidence and Questions." StPatr 59 (2011): 11–20.

Cerrato, John A. *Hippolytus between East and West: The Commentaries and the Provenance of the Corpus.* OTM. Oxford: Oxford University Press, 2002.

Chase, George Henry. "The Shield Devices of the Greeks." *HSCP* 13 (1902): 61–127.

Clark, Mark Edward. "*Spes* in the Early Imperial Cult: 'The Hope of Augustus.'" *Numen* 30 (1983): 80–105.

Cumont, Franz. *Afterlife in Roman Paganism.* New York: Dover, 1959.

Ehrman, Bart D., ed. and trans. *The Apostolic Fathers.* Vol. 1, *1 Clement; 2 Clement; Ignatius; Polycarp; Didache.* LCL. Cambridge: Harvard University Press, 2003.

Ennabli, Liliane. *Les Inscriptions funéraires chrétiennes de Carthage.* Vol. 2, *La Basilique de Mcidfa.* Paris: Publications de l'Ecole Française de Rome, 1982.

———. *Les Inscriptions funéraires chrétiennes de la Basilique dite de Sainte-Monique à Carthage.* Paris: Publications de l'Ecole Française de Rome, 1975.

Epictetus. *Discourses, Books 3–4; Fragments; The Encheiridion.* Translated by William A. Oldfather. LCL. Cambridge: Harvard University Press, 1928

Evans, John. "On Some Rare or Unpublished Roman Gold Coins." *NumC* 8 (1868): 223–34.
Fears, J. Rufus. "Theology of Victory at Rome: Approaches and Problems." *ANRW* 17.2:736–826.
Finney, Paul Corby. *The Invisible God: The Earliest Christians on Art.* New York: Oxford University Press, 1994.
Fulkerson, Laurel. "'Torn between Hope and Despair': Narrative Foreshadowing and Suspense in the Greek Novel." Pages 75–94 in *Hope, Joy, and Affection in the Classical World*. Edited by Ruth R. Caston and Robert A. Kaster. Oxford: Oxford University Press, 2015.
Galvao-Sobrinho, Carlos. "Funerary Epigraphy and the Spread of Christianity in the West." *Athenaeum* 83 (1995): 432–62.
Goodenough, Erwin R. *Jewish Symbols in the Greco-Roman Period.* Vol. 1. BollS 37. New York: Pantheon, 1956.
Gray, Patrick. "The Early Reception of Hebrews 6:4–6." Pages 321–39 in *Scripture and Traditions: Essays on Early Judaism and Christianity in Honor of Carl R. Holladay*. Edited by Patrick Gray and Gail R. O'Day. NovTSup 129. Leiden: Brill, 2008.
Gregory, Andrew F. "1 Clement and the Writings That Later Formed the New Testament." Pages 129–57 in *The Reception of the New Testament in the Apostolic Fathers*. Edited by Andrew Gregory and Christopher Tuckett. Oxford: Oxford University Press, 2007.
Gregory, Andrew F., and Christopher M. Tuckett. "Reflections on Method: What Constitutes the Use of the Writings That Later Formed the New Testament in the Apostolic Fathers." Pages 61–82 in *The Reception of the New Testament in the Apostolic Fathers*. Edited by Gregory and Tuckett. Oxford: Oxford University Press, 2007.
Guyon, Jean. "Catacomb: Early Christian (Rome)." Pages 279–85 in *The Eerdmans Encyclopedia of Early Christian Art and Archeology*. Vol. 1, A–J. Edited by Paul Corby Finney. Grand Rapids: Eerdmans, 2017.
Hartog, Paul. *Polycarp and the New Testament.* WUNT 2/134. Tübingen: Mohr Siebeck, 2002.
Hill, Charles E. *From the Lost Teaching of Polycarp: Identifying Irenaeus' Apostolic Presbyter and the Author of "Ad Diognetum."* WUNT 186. Tübingen: Mohr Siebeck, 2006.
Hippolytus. *Refutation of All Heresies.* Translated by M. David Litwa. WGRW 40. Atlanta: SBL Press, 2016.
Holmes, Michael. "Polycarp of Smyrna, *Letter to the Philippians*." *ExpTim* 118 (2006): 53–63.

Horton, Fred L. *The Melchizedek Tradition: A Critical Examination of the Sources to the Fifth Century A.D. and in the Epistle to the Hebrews.* SNTSMS 30. Cambridge: Cambridge University Press, 1976.

Jensen, Robin M. "Introduction: Early Christian Art." Pages 1–12 in *Routledge Handbook of Early Christian Art.* Edited by Robin M. Jensen and Mark D. Ellison. London: Routledge, 2018.

———. *Understanding Early Christian Art.* New York: Routledge, 2000.

Kennedy, Charles. "Early Christians and the Anchor." *BA* 38 (1975): 115–24.

Klauck, Hans-Josef. *The Religious Context of Early Christianity: A Guide to Graeco-Roman Religions.* Translated by Brian McNeil. Minneapolis: Fortress, 2003.

Koester, Craig R. *Hebrews: A New Translation with Introduction and Commentary.* AB 36. New York: Doubleday, 200.

Leynaud, Augustin Fernand. *Les catacombes africaines, Sousse-Hadrumète.* 2nd ed. Alger: Carbonel, 1922.

Longenecker, Bruce W. *The Cross before Constantine: The Early Life of a Christian Symbol.* Minneapolis: Fortress, 2015.

Martin, Michael W., and Jason A. Whitlark. *Inventing Hebrews: Design and Purpose in Ancient Rhetoric.* SNTSMS 171. Cambridge: Cambridge University Press, 2018.

Marucchi, Orazio. "Cross and Crucifix, The. 1. Archaeology of the Cross." Pages 517–29 in vol. 4 of *The Catholic Encyclopedia.* Edited by Charles G. Herbermann et al. 15 vols. New York: Appleton, 1907–1912. https://tinyurl.com/SBL4830p1.

Mattingly, Harold. *Vespasian to Domitian.* Vol. 2 of *Coins of the Roman Empire in the British Museum.* London: Trustees of the British Museum, 1923.

Moffitt, David M. *Atonement and the Logic of Resurrection in the Epistle to the Hebrews.* NovTSup 141. Leiden: Brill, 2011.

Nicolai, Vincenzo Fiocchi. "The Catacombs." Pages 68–88 in *The Oxford Handbook of Early Christian Archeology.* Edited by William R. Caraher, Thomas W. Davis, and David K. Pettegrew. Oxford: Oxford University Press, 2018.

———. *Strutture funerarie ed edifici di culto paleocristiani di Roma dal II al VI secolo.* Vatican City: IGER, 2001.

Nicolai, Vincenzo Fiocchi, Fabrizio Bisconti, and Danilo Mazzoleni. *The Christian Catacombs of Rome: History, Decoration, Inscriptions.* Translated by Cristina Carlo Stella and Lori-Ann Touchette. Regensburg: Schnell & Steiner, 1999.

Nicolai, Vincenzo Fiocchi, and Jean Guyon, eds. *Origine delle catacombe romane: Atti della giornata tematica dei Seminari di Archeologia Cristiana (Roma, 21 marzo 2005)*. Vatican City: Pontificio Istituto di Archeologia Cristiana, 2006.

Pearson, Birger A. "Egypt." Pages 331–50 in *Origins to Constantine*. Edited by Margaret M. Mitchell and Frances M. Young. CHC 1. Cambridge: Cambridge University Press, 2006.

Perassi, Claudia. *Spes: Iconographia, simbologia, ideologia nella moneta romana (I–III sec.)*. Milan: Vita E Pensiero, 1991.

Potthoff, Stephen E. *The Afterlife in Early Christian Carthage: Near-Death Experience, Ancestor Cult, and the Archeology of Paradise*. RSECW. New York: Routledge, 2017.

Roberts, Erin. "Anchor." Pages 58–59 in *The Eerdmans Encyclopedia of Early Christian Art and Archaeology*. Vol. 1, *A–J*. Edited by Paul Corby Finney. Grand Rapids: Eerdmans, 2017.

Rossi, Giovanni Battista de. "L'epigrafia primitiva priscilliana, ossia le iscrizioni incise sul marmo e dipinte sulle tegole della regione primordiale del cimitero di Priscilla." *BAC* (1886): 34–165.

Rutgers, Leonard V., Klaas van der Borg, Arie F. M. de Jong, Constance van der Linde, and Jelle Prins. "Further Radiocarbon Dates from the Catacombs of St. Callixtus in Rome." *Radiocarbon* 49 (2007): 1221–29.

Skarsaune, Oskar. *The Proof from Prophecy: A Study in Justin Martyr's Proof-Text Tradition: Text-Type, Provenance, Theological Profile*. NovTSup 56. Leiden: Brill, 1987.

Spier, Jeffrey. *Late Antique and Early Christian Gems*. SFCBKEJ 20. Wiesbaden: Reichert, 2013.

Stirling, Lea M. "The Koine of the Cupula in Roman North Africa and the Transition from Cremation to Inhumation." Pages 164–203 in *Mortuary Landscapes of North Africa*. Edited by David L. Stone and Lea M. Stirling. Toronto: Toronto University Press, 2007.

Tilley, Maureen A. "North Africa." Pages 381–96 in *Origins to Constantine*. Edited by Margaret M. Mitchell and Frances M. Young. CHC 1. Cambridge: Cambridge University Press, 2006.

Verheyden, Joseph. "The *Shepherd of Hermas* and the Writings That Later Formed the New Testament." Pages 293–329 in *The Reception of the New Testament in the Apostolic Fathers*. Edited by Andrew Gregory and Christopher Tuckett. Oxford: Oxford University Press, 2007.

Whitlark, Jason A. "Funerary Anchors of Hope and Hebrews: A Reappraisal of the Origins of the Anchor Iconography in the Catacombs of Rome." *PRSt* 48 (2021): 219–41.

———. "The God of Peace and His Victorious King: Hebrews 13:20–21 in its Roman Imperial Context." Pages 155–78 in *Hebrews in Context*. Edited by Gabriella Gelardini and Harold W. Attridge. AJEC 91. Leiden: Brill, 2016.

———. "'Here We Do Not Have a City That Remains': A Figured Critique of Roman Imperial Propaganda in Hebrews 13:14." *JBL* 131 (2012): 161–79.

———. *Resisting Empire: Rethinking the Purpose of the "Letter to the Hebrews."* LNTS. London: Bloomsburg, 2014.

Zanker, Paul. *The Power of Images in the Age of Augustus*. Translated by Alan Shapiro. JL 16. Ann Arbor: University of Michigan Press, 1988.

Who Is the Good Shepherd?
Answers from Early African Sources

David E. Wilhite

In his exchange with Trypho, Justin's argument takes a strange twist. Justin has laboriously reviewed the Hebrew prophets to demonstrate that the Messiah must suffer and die. After Trypho and his other Jewish friends—allegedly—concede this point, they ask Justin to prove that Jesus was this Messiah.[1] Justin, somewhat surprisingly, refuses to do so but instead insists that he must first explain how the Scriptures do more than speak of Jesus prophetically. They speak of Jesus in various ways, especially by speaking of him as God and Lord: "I will supply the proofs you wish, but for the present permit me to quote the following prophecies to show that the Holy Spirit by parable called Christ *God*, and *Lord of hosts* and (*Lord*) *of Jacob*" (*Dial.* 36.2).[2] The apologist then proceeds to review passages from the Septuagint, claiming that the theophanies therein are in fact the Word of the Lord, who was later revealed in the flesh as Jesus. In other words, for Justin and his Christian community, when they read about the Lord appearing to Abraham, Moses, and other people in the Old Testament, Christians understood that to be Jesus preincarnate.

---

1. *Dial.* 36.1: "But prove to us that Jesus Christ is the one about whom these prophecies were spoken." Translations follow Michael Slusser, ed., *Justin Martyr: Dialogue with Trypho*, trans. Thomas B. Falls and Thomas P. Halton, FC 3 (Washington, DC: Catholic University of America Press, 2003), 56. See also Philippe Bobichon, trans., *Justin Martyr, Dialogue avec le Tryphon: édition critique*, Paradosis 47 (Fribourg: Département de patristique et d'histoire de l'Église de l'Université de Fribourg, 2003), 272: εἰ οὗτος δέ ἐστι περὶ οὗ ταῦτα προεφητεύξη, ἀπόδειξον.

2. Bobichon, *Dialogue avec le Tryphon*, 272: ἐλεύσομαι πρὸς ἃς βούλει ταύτας ἀποδείξεις ἐν τῷ ἁρμόζοντι τόπῳ ἔφην. τὰ νῦν δὲ συγχωρήσεις μοι πρῶτον ἐπιμνησθῆναι ὧνπερ βούλομαι προφητειῶν, εἰς ἐπίδειξιν ὅτι καὶ Θεὸς καὶ κύριος τῶν δυνάμενων ὁ Κριστὸς καὶ Ἰακὼβ καλεῖται ἐν παραβολῇ ὑπὸ τοῦ ἁγίου πνεύματος.

Justin's view of Jesus preexisting as the Lord of Israel is not news to scholars of early Christian history. In fact, it was a very widespread and widely accepted view among early Christians,[3] one that arguably is even evidenced in early Christian art. However, outside the field traditionally known as patristics, many modern Christians—whether scholars or practitioners—tend to think of the Lord encountered in the Old Testament as God the Father, while Jesus as God's Son is not revealed until the New. This is the opposite of how most early Christians read their Scriptures.

Where this belief originated and how it developed will be the subject of a separate forthcoming research project.[4] In the present essay, however, I limit the scope of studying this phenomenon to one image, the motif of the Good Shepherd as it can be detected in early African sources (both material and literary) in order to find out whether any unique features can be detected there.[5] In particular, I argue that much of the symbolism of the Good Shepherd, at least for ancient African writers, derives from Jewish Scriptures as much as, if not more than, New Testament sources. In other words, when Christians from this context saw the Good Shepherd in early Christian art, they believed they were seeing the Lord of Israel.

One material item in particular serves as the focal point of this discussion: the Good Shepherd discovered in what is modern day Sousse, Tunisia (fig. 6.1). The catacombs from what was the ancient city of Hadrumetum were excavated in 1903, and they consist of 105 tunnels and nearly

---

3. For a recent study, see Bogdan Gabriel Bucur, *Scripture Re-envisioned: Christophanic Exegesis and the Making of a Christian Bible* (Leiden: Brill, 2019).

4. To be coauthored with Adam Winn (under contract with Fortress).

5. For bibliography on this image in early Christian art, see Felicity Harley-McGowan and Laurence Vieillefon, "Shepherd," in *The Eerdmans Encyclopedia of Early Christian Art and Archaeology*, ed. Paul Corby Finney (Grand Rapids: Eerdmans, 2017), 2:498–99. Also see the recent study by Jennifer Awes-Freeman, "The Good Shepherd and the Enthroned Ruler: A Reconsideration of Imperial Iconography in the Early Church," in *The Art of the Empire: Christian Art in Its Imperial Context*, ed. Lee Jefferson and Robin M. Jensen (Minneapolis: Fortress, 2015), 159–95; and Awes-Freeman, *The Good Shepherd: Image, Meaning, and Power* (Waco, TX: Baylor University Press, 2021), esp. 3 n. 3. For North African Christianity as a unique tradition, see J. Patout Burns Jr. and Robin M. Jensen, *Christianity in Roman Africa: The Development of Its Practices and Beliefs* (Grand Rapids: Eerdmans, 2014); and David E. Wilhite, *Ancient African Christianity* (London: Routledge, 2017).

five thousand burial sites.⁶ The names from the inscriptions are mostly "native," according to Paul L. MacKendrick, which is to say Punic, including names such as Felix, Saturninus, Restitutus, Dativa, and Donata.⁷ The oldest of these catacombs is the Bon Pasteur, which takes its name from the depiction of a Kriophoros, a ram bearer, who is unanimously agreed to be an image of Jesus as "the Good Shepherd."⁸ The tombs and this image may date as early as the mid-third century. The scholar who unearthed this image notes how dissimilar it is compared to the depictions of the Good Shepherd found in Roman catacombs, finding it to contain unique African imagery.⁹ I take this dissimilarity and uniqueness as my starting point of inquiry, but first I need to address other, later images of the Good Shepherd from North Africa.

African and Non-African Sources

At this point, three stipulations need to be made. The first relates to later images from North Africa that must be set aside for this discussion. Four other Good Shepherd images have recently been unearthed in the cata-

---

6. See Augustin-Ferdinand Leynaud, *Les catacombes africaines: Sousse-Hadrumète* (Alger: Carbonel, 1922); and Burns and Jensen, *Christianity in Roman Africa*, 121.

7. Paul L. MacKendrick, *The North African Stones Speak* (Chapel Hill: University of North Carolina Press, 1980), 102.

8. While there has been some dispute that the "Good Shepherd" in general might not be Jesus—e.g., Klauser—the overwhelming majority of scholars accept the identification. See Harley-McGowan and Vieillefon, "Shepherd," 2:498; cf. Theodor Klauser, "Studien zur Entstehungsgeschichte der christlichen Kunst I," *JAC* 1 (1958): 20–51; Klauser, "Studien zur Entstehungsgeschichte der christlichen Kunst III," *JAC* 3 (1960): 112–33; Klauser, "Studien zur Entstehungsgeschichte der christlichen Kunst IX," *JAC* 10 (1967): 82–120. To my knowledge, no one has questioned the identity of the Good Shepherd from Sousse as being Jesus.

9. Leynaud writes, "In Africa, the Good Shepherd does not normally bear the sheep on his shoulders.... In the Christian material remains in Rome, the Good Shepherd is normally a handsome, beardless youth. Here he is wearing long hair and a beard, in a rustic fashion" (*Les catacombes africaines*, 206–7, my trans.). Leynaud earlier noted that the sheep itself is a unique local species: "this was the Good Shepherd bearing on his shoulders a sheep of the African race [*de race africaine*], a large breed with a long tail" (*Les Catacombes africaines*, 61–62, my trans.). He goes on to point out that the shepherd's bare feet reflect the "nomad shepherds" he has witnessed in the area.

Fig. 6.1. *The Good Shepherd*, early to mid-third century CE. Bon Pasteur Catacomb, Sousse, Tunisia. Engraving, 9.5 x 14.5 in. Sousse Museum, Sousse, Tunisia. Photograph by Album / Art Resource.

combs discovered in Leptiminus/Lamta, Tunisia, in 1999, 2000, and 2006.[10] This site consists of tombs dating from the second through the fourth centuries, but the Christian complex was added later and mostly consists of burials from a later period.[11] One Kriophoros on the tomb of a Christian named Afrodite is beardless, wearing a white tunic and a red mantle, and has on sandals. He carries a ram on his shoulders and has two lambs at his feet. Two other shepherd figures can be found in the same room on different burial inscriptions: one to Fortucius and one to Pascassus. The other Good Shepherd is found on a tomb mosaic dedicated to a certain Tripolius, and this one is a hybrid image of a shepherd and Orpheus.[12] These images from Lamta certainly show influence from the Greek mythology of the underworld, such as that associated with Hermes. However, I contend that the Lamta images fall outside of the scope of the present argument for the following reasons. First, these are dated to at least the fourth century and show Byzantine influences. Likewise, seven out of the twelve names from this one room alone are of Greek origin. Therefore, these images and the community that produced them represent later and foreign influence not known to Perpetua, Tertullian, Cyprian, and their peers.

The second stipulation is the relation of the Good Shepherd image in North Africa to those found elsewhere. When Christians in various regions in late antiquity looked at an image like this, they likely attributed meaning to it from an amalgamation of sources.[13] For one thing, the name, "the Good Shepherd," is taken from John 10:11, where Jesus says, "I am the good shepherd" (ἐγώ εἰμι ὁ ποιμὴν ὁ καλός).[14] However, Tertullian may be the first example of a source applying this title to such an image, as

---

10. See Nejib Ben Lazreg, "Roman and Early Christian Burial Complex at Leptiminus (Lamta): First Notice," *JRA* 15 (2002): 336–45; Lazreg et al., "Roman and Early Christian Burial Complex at Leptiminus (Lamta): Second Notice," *JRA* 19 (2006): 347–68; David L. Stone, David J. Mattingly, and Nejib Ben Lazreg, *Leptiminus (Lamta) Report No. 3: The Field Survey*, JRASup 87 (Portsmouth, RI: Journal of Roman Archaeology, 2011).

11. Lazreg et al. note how in one group of markers, seven out of twelve inscriptions from the site include names that are of Greek origin ("Roman and Early Christian Burial," 365).

12. See Lazreg, "Roman and Early Christian Burial."

13. See Mary Charles-Murray, "The Emergence of Christian Art," in *Picturing the Bible: The Earliest Christian Art*, ed. Jeffrey Spier (New Haven: Yale University Press, 2007), 58, on how early Christians explained their art as *graphe siopōsa*, visual writing.

14. Unless otherwise noted, biblical translations follow the NRSV.

we will see momentarily.[15] In John, there is no mention of Christ carrying the lamb on this shoulders, so scholars should not assume that the image derives primarily from the Fourth Gospel.[16] The description of the shepherd placing the lamb "on his shoulders" (ἐπὶ τοὺς ὤμους αὐτοῦ) comes from Luke 15:5 in the parable of the lost sheep. Even so, there is no certainty that these images are directly derived from the Lukan parable, and there are a few curiosities about this passage in Luke that are pertinent to our discussion.

For one thing, this parable does not appear in Mark, but it is found in Matthew (18:12–13), which—according to the two-source hypothesis—suggests that the story belonged to Q or oral tradition.[17] Another item to note is that the Matthean version makes no mention of the shepherd placing the sheep on his shoulders, so the discrepancy suggests an intentional redaction on the part of either Matthew or Luke. Greg Forbes finds the phrase in Luke to be an intentional reference to Isa 40:11.[18] I would add that in Isaiah, the Shepherd is none other than the Lord. One should also note

---

15. Aside from the Shepherd of Hermas, which is discussed below, there may also be a reference to Christ as a/the Shepherd in Justin: "One day, as I approached that place with the intention of being alone, a respectable old man, of meek and venerable appearance [παλαιός τις πρεσβύτης, ἰδέσθαι οὐκ εὐκαταφρόνητος], followed me at a short distance" (*Dial.* 3.1 [PG 6:480]). While this does not explicitly use pastoral imagery, the old man is looking for "some missing members of my household" (3.1)—almost as if they were lost sheep. On the identity of this old man as Christ, see Andrew Hofer, "The Old Man as Christ in Justin's Dialogue with Trypho," *VC* 57 (2003): 1–21.

16. E.g., Leynaud, *Catacombes Africaines*, 203, 476. Laynaud also cites Luke 15:5 for this detail.

17. Also see Gos. Thom. 107, which, like Matthew, makes no mention of carrying the sheep.

18. Greg Forbes, *The God of Old: The Role of the Lukan Parables in the Purpose of Luke's Gospel* (London: Bloomsbury, 2000), 116. Forbes also provides discussion and bibliography on the possible references to Ezek 34:13–14, 23–25 in the Lukan version. We would add how in Ezek 34:4, "the Lord" faults the "shepherds of Israel," for they have not "sought the lost." In the place of these wicked shepherds, the Lord himself becomes the Shepherd; "For thus says the Lord God: I myself will search for my sheep, and will seek them out" (Ezek 34:11). Furthermore, the Lord adds, "I will seek the lost, and I will bring back the strayed" (34:16). Verses 23–24 are also important: "I will set up over them one shepherd, my servant David, and he shall feed them: he shall feed them and be their shepherd. And I, the Lord, will be their God, and my servant David shall be prince among them; I, the Lord, have spoken." In Hermas, the Shepherd (see Vis. 5.1–4) echoes the concern from Ezekiel in Herm. 104/Sim. 9.27. See Carolyn Osiek, *Shepherd of Hermas: A Commentary*, Hermeneia (Minneapolis: Fortress, 1999),

how the verbal parallels between Luke's passage and the LXX translation of Isaiah—while not an exact quote, since different terms are used—are nonetheless striking, for both specify the shoulders in particular, not the arms in general, on which the sheep is placed.[19] Finally, it is worth noting that in Luke (as well as in Matthew and the Gospel of Thomas) Jesus is nowhere explicitly identified as the shepherd in the parable.

Whereas archaeologists are confident that Good Shepherd imagery was widespread among early Christians, they nevertheless insist that the image did not originally depict Christ.[20] The specific imagery may derive from the pre-Christian Hermes Kriophoros, that is, Hermes the Ram Bearer, who was often depicted as carrying a ram on his shoulders and who was thought to guide souls into the underworld.[21] Even if the earliest Christian images were indebted to prior depictions of Hermes, we can explore how Christians would have interpreted this image in light of their own Scriptures.

100, for additional discussion and bibliography. Also, Clement of Alexandria explicitly reads this passage from Ezekiel as the preincarnate Word speaking (*Paed.* 1.9).

19. See Isa 40:11 LXX: τῷ βραχίονι αὐτοῦ; and Luke 15:5: ἐπὶ τοὺς ὤμους αὐτοῦ.

20. On Good Shepherd imagery being widespread among early Christians, see Henri Leclercq and Fernand Cabrol, "Pasteur (Bon)," in vol. 13.2 of *Dictionnaire d'archéologie Chrétienne et de Liturgie*, ed. Fernand Cabrol and Henri Leclerq (Paris: Librarie Letouzey et Ané, 1937–1938), 2272–2390, who list 337 examples. Many more have been discovered since their study. I am indebted to Robin Jensen for reminding me that these images are symbolic and nothing like modern pictures. In what follows, I accept this premise and explore the array of meanings found in the sources rather than assume that the Good Shepherd (and other images) are meant to depict Jesus per se. For further discussion, see Robin M. Jensen, "Early Christian Images and Exegesis," in Spier, *Picturing the Bible*, 67. For this image in particular, see Awes-Freeman, *Good Shepherd*, 5, who states, "the shepherd figure ... need not *necessarily* signify Jesus as the Good Shepherd but could simply be an image of philanthropy."

21. See Snyder, *Ante Pacem*; and Robin M. Jensen, *Baptismal Imagery in Early Christianity: Ritual, Visual, and Theological Dimensions* (Grand Rapids: Baker Academic, 2012), 79 n. 95, for bibliography and discussion. Because the shepherd in these images carries a "ram" (κριός) instead of a "lamb" or "sheep" mentioned in the Gospels (Luke 15:6, τὸ πρόβατόν; John 10:11, τῶν προβάτων), the image is often thought by modern scholars to be indebted to Hermes Kriophoros. See Graydon F. Snyder, *Ante Pacem: Archaeological Evidence of Church Life before Constantine* (Macon, GA: Mercer University Press, 2003), 44–45. However, while I do not contest the possible influence, this detail is itself insufficient evidence of such influence: many sheep species display horns on both the rams and the ewes. Therefore, the presence of horns in Good Shepherd images is simply inconclusive.

For example, Michael Peppard, in his study of the Dura Europos house-church, has shown how the Good Shepherd image there likely has Ps 23 (LXX 22) in view.[22] To be sure, Christ is also in view, for Jesus is the Lord and Shepherd of the Psalm in most early Christian interpretation, as was demonstrated above with Justin in particular. My point is simply to note how early Christians would have been as likely, if not more likely, to associate the Good Shepherd image with details found in their Old Testament as they would have been to do so with the Gospel of John.[23] That being said, one other text also needs to be considered, and that is the Shepherd of Hermas. However, I will show that this text's absence in North Africa is important in that the African depictions of the Good Shepherd develop along different lines from those in Rome.

The Shepherd of Hermas

Hermas (as I will call the text for the sake of convenience) was written in Rome sometime in the first half of the second century. In the last of five visions, Hermas is visited by a shepherd: "There came a man, glorious in appearance, dressed like a shepherd, with a white skin wrapped around him and with a bag on his shoulders and a staff in his hand" (Herm. 25.1/ Vis. 5.1.1).[24] While in this essay I am looking for possible amalgamations of images, it should be stipulated here that the shepherd figure in Hermas should be distinguished from two figures in particular.

First, we can acknowledge the possible syncretism of Hermas's shepherd and the Hermes Kriophoros figure in general, mentioned above. However, as Carolyn Osiek notes in her commentary, nothing in the text itself suggests influence of the Hermes Kriophoros motif for this text in particular.[25] Second, we should also notice how the shepherd in Hermas

---

22. Michael Peppard, *The World's Oldest Church: Bible, Art, and Ritual at Dura-Europos, Syria* (New Haven: Yale University Press, 2016), 87, 102–4.

23. Jutta Dresken-Weiland notes that most early Christian art depicted scenes from the OT, not the life of Jesus; Christian sarcophagi were the exception to this pattern. See Dresken-Weiland, "Christian Sarcophagi from Rome," in *The Routledge Handbook of Early Christian Art*, ed. Robin M. Jensen and Mark D. Ellison (London: Routledge, 2018), 47.

24. Text and translation follow Michael W. Holmes, ed., *The Apostolic Fathers: Greek Texts and English Translations*, 3rd ed. (Grand Rapids: Baker Academic, 2008), 500–501.

25. Osiek, *Shepherd of Hermas*, 100. Osiek notes prior attempts to identify Her-

is in fact not Jesus himself. While modern readers might anticipate this heavenly visitor to be an appearance of Christ, that is, *the* Good Shepherd, there is nothing in Hermas that identifies this shepherd with Jesus. Of course, we must admit that the Christology in Hermas is notoriously difficult to categorize: the text makes no mention of Jesus or Christ or the cross or the resurrection.[26] However, the Son of God and the Holy Spirit (who at times seems to be synonymous with the Son in a binitarian framework) are mentioned throughout as examples of holiness.[27] This shepherd who appears to Hermas, however, is "sent by the most holy angel" (25.2). Also, this shepherd is himself "the angel of repentance" (25.7). In other words, this character is not *the* Shepherd, but *a* shepherd, an angelic figure sent to guide Hermas.

To quote the text again, he is "the shepherd to whom you [Hermas] were entrusted" (25.3). The "most holy angel" (25.2) sent this shepherd, and so it is readily apparent that Hermas's shepherd is a lower angel of some sort, not Christ himself, the Good Shepherd. Even so, there is one detail where the shepherd of Hermas might inform later images: the shepherd is not only said to be "dressed like a shepherd" (σχήματι ποιμενικῷ) (25.1.1);[28] he also carries a shepherd's "bag" or "wallet" (πήραν) (25.1.1). This detail may be important in helping to trace this text's influence on later Good Shepherd imagery. To see its importance, we now must turn briefly to this text's reception.

From Eusebius, we learn that Hermas was widely but not universally accepted as canonical (*Hist. eccl.* 3.3.6, 3.25.4, 5.8.7). It is no surprise that this text is known to be received and influential in Rome and the surrounding area, given that it was written there. In the Catacomb of San Gennaro, there is an image of three women building a tower, an image

---

mas's shepherd with Hermes Kriophorus but then adds, "The model may be partially Hermes, but the image has surely been given greater christological import."

26. For discussion and bibliography of scholars who attempted to categorize this text's Christology (often with diametrically opposed and mutually exclusive forms of Christology), see Robert John Hauck, "The Great Fast: Christology in the Shepherd of Hermas," *AThR* 75.2 (1993): 187–98.

27. Bogdan Gabriel Bucur shows that this category is insufficient for Hermas on the whole. See Bucur, "Early Christian Binitarianism: From Religious Phenomenon to Polemical Insult to Scholarly Concept," *ModTheol* 27 (2011): 102–20, esp. 112.

28. See Pass. Perp. 4.8, "in shepherd's clothes" (*in habitu pastoris*). Text and translations of the Passion of Perpetua and Felicity follow Thomas J. Heffernan, *The Passion of Perpetua and Felicity* (Oxford: Oxford University Press, 2012).

taken from the third vision and the ninth parable of Hermas. Osiek documents this and other paintings from catacombs in and around Rome, and from this evidence concludes that Christians held "high authority for [Hermas] in central Italy at the time."[29] In light of this clear literary influence on the material remains, it is very likely that the images known as the Good Shepherd, such as the one found in the Catacomb of Priscilla, are influenced by Hermas. This image is on the ceiling of the Cubiculum of the Veil, and there one can clearly see the shepherd's bag (fig. 6.2).[30] In fact, based on my initial survey, most, if not all, of the Good Shepherd images found in and around Rome have this bag (e.g., figs. 6.2–7).[31]

When we turn from Rome to Africa, we find no mention of this shepherd's bag. It is not depicted in the image from Sousse, nor is it mentioned in any description of a shepherd in the North African Christian sources. This missing detail from the Shepherd of Hermas should prompt us to see what positive evidence can be found, if any, for the reception of this text in Africa.

The Reception, or Lack Thereof, of Hermas in Africa

One North African text that shows a possible awareness of Hermas is the Passion of Perpetua and Felicity, recording events from 203 CE and written possibly as early as 209.[32] In her first vision, Perpetua reports, "And I saw an

---

29. Osiek, *Shepherd of Hermas*, 8.

30. It is also worth noting that the cubiculum also contains images of a dove carrying an olive branch, which refers to the story of Noah, and to three men in the furnace, which refers to the story from Daniel. Therefore, this is another image that likely invoked Old Testament imagery for the Good Shepherd as much as, if not more so than, the Gospel of John.

31. Even the late third-century Good Shepherd marble statue from Asia Minor has a bag, but it is on the figure's back (see figs. 6.6–7). See further details in Heidi J. Hornik, "Freestanding Sculpture," in Jensen and Ellison, *Routledge Handbook of Early Christian Art*, 76–79. While inconclusive because of the image's poor quality, the shepherd at Dura Europos in Syria also appears to lack any such bag or wallet (see fig. 3.6).

32. For debate regarding this date, see Éric Rebillard, *Greek and Latin Narratives about the Ancient Martyrs* (Oxford: Oxford University Press, 2017), 296. William Farina claims Hermas "clearly left a strong impression on the writings of Perpetua and Saturus." See Farina, *Perpetua of Carthage: Portrait of a Third-Century Martyr* (Jefferson, NC: McFarland, 2009), 138. I, however, have not found the impression to be so clear. Similarly, Rex D. Butler finds parallels between Hermas and the Passion of Perpetua and Felicity, but none of his examples show direct citation of any kind. See

Who Is the Good Shepherd?   153

Fig. 6.2. *The Good Shepherd*, mid- to late third century CE. Catacombs of Saint Priscilla, Rome. Fresco. Photograph by Erich Lessing / Art Resource, NY.

Fig. 6.3. *The Good Shepherd*, late third century. Restored in the eighteenth century. Marble, 100 cm restored height; as preserved, height, 55 cm, head 15.5 cm. Museo Pio Cristiano, Vatican Museums, Vatican State. Photograph by Album / Art Resource, New York.

Fig. 6.4. Sarcophagus with the Good Shepherd, third century CE. Museo Lateranense, Vatican Museums. Photograph by Alinari Archives / Art Resource, NY.

enormous garden and a white-haired man sitting in the middle of it dressed in shepherd's clothes, a big man, milking sheep" (Pass. Perp. 4.8). There are a few details to note with this statement. First, the man is dressed *in habitu pastoris*, "in shepherd's clothes," which may be a direct quotation/translation of the statement in Hermas where the angel is "dressed like a shepherd" (σχήματι ποιμενικῷ) (Herm. 25.1.1). If this detail about the shepherd's clothes found in the Passion of Perpetua is indebted directly to Hermas, then it is the only extant instance where any dependence can be shown, for other descriptions of Perpetua's shepherd draw from other sources. For example, the description of his hair as *canum*, usually translated as "white" or "gray," is a word used to emphasize old age. This describes, in classical sources, old, stiff hair, with no real commitment to hair color, so that the word is usually translated as "hoary." This detail is not found in Hermas but instead likely alludes to the image of Christ in Rev 1:14, where his hair is λευκός, or "white," like snow. This is further corroborated by the fact that Perpetua next notices a number of people dressed in white robes (Pass. Perp. 4.8), which is a description found several times in Revelation (3:4–5, 6:11, 7:9). I am tempted to think that the curious spiked hair found in the image

---

Butler, *The New Prophecy and "New Visions": Evidence of Montanism in the Passion of Perpetua and Felicitas*, PMS 18 (Washington, DC: Catholic University of America Press, 2006), *passim*.

from Sousse (fig. 6.1) is attempting to depict this "hoary" or "white" hair from the Passion of Perpetua, since it differs so markedly from the brown, wavy hair found in the images from Rome.[33]

The other detail from Perpetua's vision is that this Shepherd calls her "daughter" (τέκνον; Pass. Perp. 4.9).[34] This curious switch to a Greek word, Thomas Heffernan suggests, is additional evidence that Christ himself is speaking, since he would stand out among the Latin-speaking North Africans.[35] Later in this martyrdom, Saturus has a vision in which he describes a room filled with people wearing white robes. Then he states, "And we saw sitting in the same place what appeared to be an aged man. He had white hair and a youthful face" (*et vidimus in eodem loco sedentem quasi hominem canum, niveos habentem capillos et vultu iuvenili*).[36] Again, the agedness is emphasized since his hair is once again described as "hoary" (*canum*), but the added specification is given that the hairs are "white" or "snowy" (*niveos*). The people's white robes and Christ's white hair further confirm that this imagery is primarily drawn from Revelation. In short, there is no reason to think that this text is indebted to or even knows Hermas, except for the detail about being "dressed like a shepherd," which is said about an angel in Hermas but about Christ in the Passion of Perpetua. Such a small detail leaves much to be desired when trying to establish the reception of Hermas in North Africa.

The next source to speak to this question is Tertullian, but he offers only evidence that Hermas was rejected. In his work *On Prayer*, written in 198, Tertullian criticizes those who sit after the ritual prayer. The only justification his opponents could possibly offer for such a novel practice is to cite Hermas:

---

33. E.g., fig. 6.2. Other examples include the Good Shepherds in the Catacomb of Callixtus (Rome, mid-third century; see fig. 1.5) and in the Catacomb of Marcellinus and Peter (Rome, ca. fourth century).

34. Note the curious switch to Greek for this word.

35. Heffernan, *Passion of Perpetua*, 180–83. One might also consider Mark 10:24–25, where Jesus says to his disciples, "Children [τέκνα], how hard it is to enter the kingdom of God! It is easier for a camel to go through the eye of a needle than for someone who is rich to enter the kingdom of God." The description is apt for Perpetua, since she belongs to the nobility (see Pass. Perp. 2.1), and throughout the text she forsakes her family, which also fits nicely with Jesus's next statement in Mark 10:29–30. Thanks to Robin Jensen for asking about alternative explanations for this word choice, which pointed me to find this passage.

36. Heffernan, *Passion of Perpetua*, 131.

Fig. 6.5. Sarcophagus with Jonah, seated man, the Good Shepherd, and the baptism of Christ, late third century CE. Santa Maria Antiqua, Rome. Photograph by Alinari Archives / Art Resource, NY.

> If that Hermas, whose writing is entitled *The Shepherd* or something of the sort, had not sat down upon his bed when he had finished his prayer, but had done you know what, should we claim that that also must be made an observance? Surely not. For even as it is it is stated without any afterthought, *When I had prayed and had sat down on the bed,* for the order of the narrative, not with the import of an instruction. (*Or.* 16.2 [*ANF* 3])[37]

The quote is from Shepherd of Hermas (25.1/Vis. 5.1), the section where the shepherd first appears to Hermas. This quote from Tertullian demon-

---

37. "Si Hermas ille, cuius scriptura fere 'Pastor' inscribitur, transacta oratione non super lectum assedisset verum aliud quid fecisset, id quoque ad observationem vindicaremus? utique non. Simpliciter enim et nunc positum est, cum adorassem et assedissem super lectum, ad ordinem narrationis non ad instar disciplinae." See Elgius Dekkers et al., *Quinti Septimi Florentis Tertulliani Opera*, 2 vols., CCSL 1–2 (Turnholt: Brepols, 1954). All additional citations will be taken from this edition unless otherwise noted.

Fig. 6.6. *Good Shepherd*, 280–290 CE, late Roman–early Christian. Asia Minor. Marble, 49.5 x 26 x 16.2 cm. Cleveland Museum of Art, John L. Severance Fund 1965.241.

strates that Hermas is seen as Scripture by some. But, we should ask, by whom? Tertullian certainly does not here (or elsewhere) affirm it. In fact, Tertullian hardly knows the title: note his description of it as a "writing entitled *The Shepherd* or something of the sort" (*cuius scriptura fere Pastor inscribitur*). He does not think it authoritative, but for the sake of argument assumes that it could be and still shows that the statement is descriptive, not prescriptive. His statement aims to demonstrate the absurdity of his opponents' conclusion, even if he were to accept the opponents' premise—a tactic Tertullian employs frequently. In short, this passage, rather than showing approval of Hermas, shows that Tertullian (and his audience) is unfamiliar with the work.[38]

Much later in his career (ca. 210), Tertullian counters another ecclesiastical practice, which he considers to be a novel error. A certain bishop, whose identity I will return to shortly, publicly pardoned the sin of adultery. Part of Tertullian's response in *On Modesty* is to show that no Scripture permits such laxity, but Tertullian has to address Hermas as a possible exception, since it grants a single opportunity for penance from a postbaptismal mortal sin. And yet this text, Tertullian happily reports, is apocryphal. The passage is worth citing in full:

> I would surrender to you, if the scripture entitled "The Shepherd," the only one that delights in adulterers, had happened to have earned the status of an inspired document, (I would surrender to you) if not for the fact that every council—even your own—judges this text to be among the apocryphal and false scriptures. (Being) adulterous itself, this text is the Patron of (adulterous) allies; (and so) from it you also initiated other things; it just so happens that that shepherd does serve as patron: you paint that prostitutor on chalices, even the Christian sacramental chalice itself. Following after this chalice are the merits of drunkenness, idolatry, and sanctuary for adultery. From him (i.e., this shepherd painted on your chalice) you drink nothing but the eagerness for (granting) a second repentance to a sheep. I, however, drink from the writings of the Shepherd who cannot be shattered (i.e., like a glass chalice[39]). This Shepherd John concretely presents to me when speaking of the bath and service of repentance, "Bear fruit worthy of repentance. Do not say, 'We

---

38. Alistair Stewart-Sykes notes that the practice of sitting down after prayer is a non-Christian practice known in Africa, citing Apuleius, *Flor.* 1.1. See Stewart-Sykes, *Tertullian, Cyprian: On the Lord's Prayer*, PPS 29 (Crestwood, NY: Saint Vladimir's Seminary Press, 2004), 52–53. However, the passage does not so much speak of sitting after a ritual prayer but instead describes practice of offering a votive whenever coming upon a place to rest when traveling.

39. This leads Paul Corby Finney to conclude that the chalice was made of glass. See Finney, *The Invisible God: The Earliest Christians on Art* (Oxford: Oxford University Press, 1994), 144 n. 89.

have Abraham as our ancestor'—for on the contrary, it is evident that they should not claim the grace of the ancestors as flattery of faults. 'For God is able from these stones to raise up children of Abraham.'" (*Pud.* 10.12–13)⁴⁰

After this distinction between the two shepherds, Tertullian returns to his primary topic: the proper stance on repentance. A few observations can be made at this point about Tertullian's statement on the shepherd from Hermas. First, Tertullian confidently asserts that "every ecclesiastical council" (*ab omni concilio ecclesiarum*) has deemed Hermas to be "apocryphal" (*inter apocrypha*) (*Pud.* 10.12). Tertullian even claims that his opponents' council rejected the text, that is, "even your own council" (*etiam vestrarum*), which implies a regional gathering of bishops. What is contested among scholars is where this regional council was located: the traditional reading is that this is aimed at the bishop of Rome and his supporters, whereas in the last century many scholars believed Tertullian was speaking about an African gathering in Carthage. Tertullian does not place himself within this communion any longer, according to proponents of the African hypothesis, because of his joining the sect of the New Prophecy. However, as I have argued elsewhere, this creates problems since scholars today are almost unanimous in their view that Tertullian never understood himself to be in schism from his local Christian community.⁴¹ Furthermore, this view leaves much unexplained in

---

40. My translation of this quote from John the Baptist follows closely the NRSV. See Vulg. Matt 3:8–9: "Facite ergo fructum dignum paenitentiae. Et ne velitis dicere intra vos: Patrem habemus Abraham. Dico enim vobis quoniam potens est Deus de lapidibus istis suscitare filios Abrahae"; and Vulg. Luke 3:8: "Facite ergo fructus dignos paenitentiae, et ne caeperitis dicere: Patrem habemus Abraham. Dico enim vobis quia potens est Deus de lapidibus istis suscitare filios Abrahae."

41. See argument and bibliography in David E. Wilhite, *Tertullian the African: An Anthropological Reading of Tertullian's Context and Identities* (Berlin: de Gruyter, 2007), 174–76; Wilhite, "Identity, Psychology, and the Psychici: Tertullian's 'Bishop of Bishops,'" *IJRR* (2009): 1–26. Recent scholars who support the Roman provenance of Tertullian's bishop include Karlmann Beyschlag, "Kallist Und Hippolyt," *TZ* 20 (1964): 103–24; Ernest Evans, *Tertullian's Treatise on the Resurrection: The Text Edited with an Introduction, Translation, and Commentary* (Eugene, OR: Wipf & Stock, 2016), 32; Allen Brent, *Hippolytus and the Roman Church in the Third Century* (Leiden: Brill, 1995), 503–35; Eric Osborn, *Tertullian, First Theologian of the West* (Cambridge: Cambridge University Press, 1997), 175 n. 31; Jane E. Merdinger, *Rome and the African Church in the Time of Augustine* (New Haven: Yale University Press, 1997), 32–33;

160   David E. Wilhite

Tertullian's writings at this time against the *psychici*, namely, the many indicators that his opponents are in Rome.⁴² If this interpretation is correct, and Tertullian's laxist bishop is the bishop of Rome, then Tertullian's statement is further evidence that Hermas was largely unknown in Africa and instead belonged—from his perspective—to the provenance of Rome.⁴³

Another observation to be made about Tertullian's statement here is that he knows his opponents depict what he believes is the Shepherd of Hermas on their Communion chalices, as he says, "those paintings on your chalices" (*ipsae picturae calicum vestrorum*), and then later he adds, "[shepherd] whom you paint on your chalices" (*quem in calice depingis*; *Pud*. 7.1, 10.12). It is noteworthy that Tertullian speaks of Communion chalices in the plural, so he clearly has a group or even a region of churches in mind, which, as said above, was probably the area around Rome. It is also curious that he knows this is the shepherd from Hermas and not Christ himself. Was there some visual clue on these chalice images? How would Tertul-

---

Ronald E. Heine, "Hippolytus, Ps.-Hippolytus, and the Early Canons," in *The Cambridge History of Early Christian Literature*, ed. Francis Young (Cambridge: Cambridge University Press, 2004), 142–51; Hermann Tränkle, "Q. Septimius Florens Tertullianus," in *Die Literatur des Umbruchs. Von der Römischen zur Christlichen Literatur 117 Bis 284 n. Chr.*, ed. Klaus Sallmann, HDLLA 4 (Munich: Beck, 1997), 499; Butler, *New Prophecy*, 23.

42. See details in Wilhite, *Tertullian the African*, 174–76; Wilhite, "Identity, Psychology," 17–20.

43. This can be further scene in his only other reference to Hermas: "And, of course, the Epistle of Barnabas is more generally received among the churches than that apocryphal 'Shepherd' of adulterers" (*Pud*. 20.2: *Et utique receptior apud ecclesias epistola Barnabae illo apocrypho Pastore moechorum*). In other words, Tertullian admits that it is accepted by some, but "the Epistle of Barnabas" (= Hebrews) is more widely accepted, and that text supports Tertullian's stance (see Heb 6:1–8). For the present argument, it is important to note that Tertullian's mention of "churches [*ecclesias*]" in the plural likely refers to Christian communities in different cities, since this is how he tends to speak elsewhere: e.g., *Praescr*. 20.5, "churches in every individual city [*ecclesias apud unamquamque civitatem*]"; 32.1–2; 32.6; 36.4, "and even with churches in Africa [*cum Africanis quoque ecclesiis contesseratis*]," which clearly refers to churches across the province, not simply in Carthage. In *De pudicitia* Tertullian continues this usage: e.g., Paul founded "churches [*ecclesiarum*]" in different cities (14.27). Furthermore, since he refers to his opponents' sacramental chalices in the plural ("your chalices [*calicum vestrorum*]" in 7.1; see also 10.12), he likely is imagining several house-churches in Rome.

lian know? He has either seen his opponents' liturgy in person or he has a report. Either way, this statement demonstrates that Tertullian believes there is a clear difference between the angel-shepherd from Hermas and

Fig. 6.7. *Good Shepherd*, back view, 280–290 CE, late Roman–early Christian. Asia Minor. Marble, 49.5 x 26 x 16.2 cm. Cleveland Museum of Art, John L. Severance Fund 1965.241.

the Good Shepherd, Christ himself. It is not clear that the distinction was made by his opponents. Did Christians in Rome amalgamate the shepherd from Hermas into their images of Christ as the Good Shepherd? Tertullian's statement would suggest such a conclusion—especially when compared to material evidence that survives, wherein the Roman Good Shepherd imagery always includes the shepherd's bag or wallet mentioned by Hermas (discussed above).

A fourth and final observation about Tertullian's statement in this paragraph is to note the Scriptures he cites. The quote about repentance is from John the Baptist, recorded in Matt 3:8–9 // Luke 3:8, not Jesus. Furthermore, this is not a reference to the Gospel of John's title for Jesus as the Good Shepherd (see John 10:11). Despite historians' category for this motif as the Good Shepherd, Tertullian's reference to Jesus as a shepherd does not turn to the Johannine description, as one might expect. This, as we will see below, is true throughout all North African Christian sources that speak of Jesus as a shepherd. As we will see shortly, when Tertullian speaks of Jesus as the Shepherd, he (1) rejects Hermas—either explicitly or implicitly, (2) ignores John, and (3) almost always uses Old Testament imagery about the Lord God, the Shepherd of Israel, to supplement the Synoptic material.

In sum, Tertullian's statements about the Shepherd of Hermas serve as evidence that his North African communion rejected the text, and he believes that every other communion of churches did the same—although he simultaneously betrays that in popular practice some Christians (probably those in Rome) still used this text to inform their liturgy and practice.

To recap, our earliest African sources, namely, the Passion of Perpetua and the writings of Tertullian, show no positive reception of Hermas. Instead, they largely ignore or are ignorant of the work, and Tertullian at two points even shows a clear rejection of that text. This raises the question: Is there any evidence that Hermas was received or even known in Africa? We can quickly answer this question with the following review of the remaining sources. First, Cyprian never cites or mentions this text,[44] which further confirms my claim that Tertullian's statements about Christians who do use this text refers to Rome, not to

---

44. For possible references to Hermas in Cyprian, see Theodor Zahn, *Geschichte Des Neutestamentlichen Kanons* (Erlangen: Deichert, 1888), 181 n. 2, who finds them questionable.

the so-called Catholics or opponents of the New Prophecy in Carthage. Second, one could point to the pseudo-Cyprianic text known as *Adversus Aleatores*, since this text cites Hermas several times and so seems to affirm it. However, this text is not attributed to Cyprian until the fourteenth century, and modern scholars, such as Adolf von Harnack, believe it derives from Rome.[45] Third, to the best of my knowledge, Augustine never cited nor approved of the Shepherd of Hermas, and none of the evidence from the Donatist controversy makes any mention of this text.[46] The fourth and final source that could address our question is Commodian. In his *Instructions* (30), there is a probable allusion to the parable about the vine and the elm tree from Hermas (51/Sim. 2). But Commodian nowhere names this source, and the allusion is made in passing and offers no clear affirmation. Furthermore, Commodian cannot be reliably dated, and while scholars once placed him in the third century (which I think is plausible), many now place him in the fifth. It must also be noted that his provenance is not known with certainty (although he was probably writing from Africa).[47] Thus, there is no evidence that this text was positively received by African Christians; and, subsequently, there is no evidence to suggest that the Good Shepherd motif in Africa was influenced by the account of Hermas.

The Good Shepherd Motif in Africa

Now that we have set aside the text of Hermas, we can look to the literary depictions of the Good Shepherd from North Africa to see how African Christians understood this motif. We will briefly review three literary sources: the Passion of Perpetua, Tertullian, and Cyprian.

---

45. Adolf von Harnack, *Der Pseudocyprianische Tractat de Aleatoribus*, TU 5.1 (Leipzig: Hinrichs, 1889). Others still posit an African provenance, but the evidence is slim. See discussion in Geoffrey Mark Hahneman, *The Muratorian Fragment and the Development of the Canon* (Oxford: Clarendon, 1992), 64.

46. See Christian Tornau and Paolo Cecconi, *The Shepherd of Hermas in Latin: Critical Edition of the Oldest Translation Vulgata*, TUGAL 173 (Berlin: de Gruyter, 2014).

47. See discussion and bibliography in Wilhite, *Ancient African Christianity*, 151–52.

Perpetua's Shepherd

First, as discussed above, Perpetua shows little to no sign of any contact with Hermas. Instead, to recap, the Shepherd in this text is Christ himself, and the only additional details to be gleaned are from Revelation, where Jesus has white hair. It should be noted, however, that this detail could also come from the Old Testament book of Daniel, where the Ancient of Days is described as wearing white and having hair like wool (7:9).[48] The Shepherd also gives Perpetua "milk" or "cheese" (*caseo*), which is coagulated, perhaps even heavily creamed milk. This mouthful is then said to be "sweet" (*dulce*) to the taste (4.9). The sweet cheese or milk is a detail that has somewhat confused modern interpreters.[49] But if the Old Testament Lord is in view in this text, then suddenly the gift of "milk and honey" in Perpetua's vision of the land of rest makes perfect sense.[50] We can add a further detail that emerges when seeing the Good Shepherd in the Passion of Perpetua as the Lord described in Old Testament passages: the Shepherd gives Perpetua "milk/cheese" (*canum*) to "chew" (*mandicavi*), which likely reflects part of Ezek 34, where the "milk" (γάλα) of Israel's flock "is eaten" (κατέσθετε) (LXX 34:3). Jesus is the Shepherd of Israel who now welcomes the new Israel into the promised land.

Another example of understanding the christological image as informed by Old Testament theophanies is found in Saturus's vision (Pass. Perp. 11): once again the martyrs see a man with white hair, this time enthroned, but "we could not see his feet" (11.3). This oddity perplexes Heffernan, who in his commentary stipulates, "I have been unable to find an earlier analogue of this motif."[51] If, however, Jesus is understood to be

---

48. It is also worth noting that in the earliest Greek version of Daniel there is an identification of the Son of Man (7:13) with the Ancient of Days (7:9): instead of saying "the Son of Man came *to* the Ancient of Days," it reads "the Son of Man came *as* [ὡς] the Ancient of Days." See discussion in Benjamin E. Reynolds, *The Apocalyptic Son of Man in the Gospel of John* (Tubingen: Mohr Siebeck, 2008), 35–37.

49. See discussion in Heffernan, *Passion of Perpetua*, 169.

50. For other early Christian sources that reference milk and honey as part of the liturgy, see Teresa Berger, *Gender Differences and the Making of Liturgical History: Lifting a Veil on Liturgy's Past* (Farnham, Surrey, UK: Ashgate, 2011), 80–88. Also, Tertullian reports that the newly baptized are given a "union of milk and honey [*lactis et mellis concordiam*]" (*Cor.* 3.3). This most likely would have been served in some form of a cup, which explains how "milk" (or even soft cheese) could be placed in her hands.

51. Heffernan, *Perpetua and Felicity*, 288.

the Lord who appeared in the Old Testament theophanies (as Justin and most other early Christians assumed), then the allusion becomes salient.[52] When the Lord descended on Mount Sinai before Moses and the seventy elders, the text (at least in the LXX) indicates that God was not actually seen, not even his "feet" (Exod 24:10; see John 1:17–18). Likewise, in Saturus's vision, the martyrs now see the Lord incarnate, and his hidden feet (Pass. Perp. 11.3) illustrate the continuity between this vision and that of Moses and the elders of Israel. In sum, while the details are sparse and open to various interpretations, I think it can be affirmed with reasonable assurance that the Passion of Perpetua describes Jesus as a shepherd using Old Testament symbolism, which is a pattern that is certainly found in later North African writers.

Tertullian's Good Shepherd

The notion of Christ as the Good Shepherd is prevalent in Tertullian's works, and he too has a penchant for drawing from Old Testament imagery when discussing this motif. One prominent example is when Tertullian attacks those who flee from persecution: he singles out the clergy in particular who would hide from arrest and trials (*Fug.* 11.1). These clergy function as shepherds, which leads Tertullian to apply Jesus's teaching from John 10:11 as a criterion for pastoring: "the good shepherd lays down his life for his sheep" (*bonus pastor animam pro pecoribus point*) (*Fug.* 11.2). Tertullian, however, finishes this sentence not by giving credit to John, or even to Jesus as recorded in John, but to Moses: "At the time when the Lord had not yet been revealed as the Christ, he already spoke figuratively as Moses himself to say, 'If you condemn this people,' he said, 'then you should even destroy me equally with this people'" (*Moyses non domino adhuc Christo revelato et iam in se figurato ait: Si perdis hunc populum, inquit, et me pariter cum eo disperde*) (*Fug.* 11.2). The reference is to Exod 32:32, where God threatens to destroy the Israelites for their idolatry. Moses, however, stands in solidarity with the people and offers to die with them, as should all good shepherds. Tertullian next returns to Jesus's statement from John 10, which is now about "the bad shepherd" who abandons his flock (*Fug.* 11.2, citing John 10:12). While Tertullian does think of Christ as the example of a Good Shepherd, it is nevertheless curious that his quotation of the Good

---

52. See Jeffrey Hubbard's essay in this volume.

Shepherd statement from John is supplemented with a reference to Moses and the exodus. Tertullian continues to supplement John by next citing Jer 23 and Ezek 34, both of which attack bad shepherds. As we will see in his other reference to Christ as a shepherd, Tertullian especially looks to God's statements in Ezek 34. But in all cases, he uses the persona found in the Lord of the Old Testament in order to describe the character of Jesus as a shepherd.

To return to his work *On Modesty*, when Tertullian discusses the shepherd depicted on the Communion chalice (or "cups";[53] *Pud.* 7.1, 10.12, referenced above), he does mention the parable from Luke with the sheep on Christ's "shoulders" (*Pud.* 7.1). His reference, however, is in the context of a debate over how to interpret the particular parable of the lost sheep from Luke 15:3–7 (see *Pud.* 7.1, 13.7). His opponents, who are granting absolution to an adulterer, believe that the sheep in the parable represents a wayward Christian, while the flock symbolizes the church, and the "Good Shepherd is Christ" (*pastor bonus Christus*; *Pud.* 7.4). At this point we should reiterate that in Luke (as well as in Matthew and the Gospel of Thomas) Jesus is nowhere explicitly identified as the shepherd in the parable. The title "Good Shepherd" has been taken from John 10:11 and applied to the Lukan parable by Tertullian's opponents, not by Tertullian himself.

Tertullian agrees with this part of the interpretation, but he disputes the interpretation of the lost sheep as a Christian sinner. For him, the parable is given by Jesus in answer to the Pharisees' question about accepting gentiles (*ethnicos*)—a point that we should admit may be special pleading on Tertullian's part, for he only bases this claim on the mention of "tax collectors" (οἱ τελῶναι) in Luke 15:1, who could easily have been local Jews, not foreign gentiles.[54] Tertullian continues to contrast his interpretation, so that just as the sheep is a non-Christian, not a wayward Christian, the flock likewise is not the church but the whole human race (*Pud.* 7.6).[55] In

---

53. *Pud.* 7.1: "those paintings on your chalices" (*ipsae picturae calicum vestrorum*).

54. *Pud.* 7.2: *publicanos et peccatores ethnicos admittentem*.

55. In his earlier work, *De paenitentia*, Tertullian's language implies or at least allows for the interpretation that the lamb is a wayward Christian and the flock is the church (*Paen.* 8). Furthermore, there he seems to permit a "second repentance" (*Paen.* 7) and so contradict himself here (*Pud.* 3). There are three ways of resolving the tension between these two texts. First, Tertullian can be said to have developed in his view, especially if he converted to "Montanism." Second, Tertullian may be speaking of forgiveness for mortal sins only in the early part of *Paen.* (see 4–5) and then for venial

this way, the shepherd is not merely a patron of one community or church, which is a point that Tertullian's opponents would not dispute, but in shifting to this cosmic level Tertullian now speaks of Christ as "the same God who is both the Lord and Shepherd of all the nations" (*universarum gentium idem Deus et Dominus et pastor est*) (*Pud.* 7.6 [my trans.]).

Once Tertullian shifts from his opponents' interpretation of this particular parable[56] to Christ as Lord and Shepherd more generally, he then invokes the passage from Ezek 34:1–4 (*Pud.* 7.18). In Ezekiel (34:1–10) the prophet records the Lord's anger against the shepherds of Israel who have neglected the sheep. Then, the Lord declares, "I myself will be the shepherd of my sheep" (34:15).[57] The obvious rhetorical opportunity at this point is for Tertullian to deem his laxist opponents as negligent shepherds. However, he uncharacteristically misses this opportunity to denigrate his opponents and instead focuses on the right interpretation of the parable,[58] which for him is in large part guided by the character of God. For Tertullian, the "Lord" who claims to be the shepherd in Ezekiel is the same Lord who told the parable in Luke. In other words, even when explicitly debating the Lukan parable, and even when using the title of Good Shepherd, which his opponents explicitly imported from the Gospel of John, Tertullian fills those parables and titles with the character and persona found in Old Testament passages about the Lord of Israel. This is further underscored by the fact that Tertullian even prefers to call Jesus "Lord" (*Dominus*) in this section.[59]

---

sins only later in the work (*Paen.* 7). Third, Tertullian may sincerely believe in second repentance and forgiveness in both works, but not permit forgiveness and readmittance into the church's communion in *De pudicitia*. I find the first option unconvincing for reasons I have articulated elsewhere (cited above), while the second and third would require much more exegetical work in his treatises before they could be persuasive answers to the apparent contradictions. These two later options, however, do offer valid possibilities.

56. Tertullian does have several asides before moving to this argument in *Pud.* 7.8–17, but he returns to his main line of argument in 7.18.

57. See Ezek 34:15–31 for the lengthier explanation of YHWH's personal role in restoring Israel.

58. Or better, parables, including the lost coin and the prodigal son, which are also found in Luke 15.

59. *Dominus* is used to describe Jesus twenty-one times in the rest of his argument about how to interpret these parables (*Pud.* 7–10).

That Tertullian sees the Good Shepherd as more than the human Jesus and as the incarnation of the one who was revealed to Moses and the prophets is not surprising given what I said earlier about how widespread this view is among early Christians. What is noteworthy is that Tertullian, who happily amalgamates various Scriptures in making this interpretation, does not allow any amalgamation of the biblical Good Shepherd with the shepherd described in Hermas. As we have said above, this is likely in large part because the Shepherd of Hermas was largely unknown, if not intentionally rejected, by African Christians. Furthermore, Tertullian does not seem to know that Hermas's shepherd is described as an emissary "sent by the most holy angel" (Herm. 25.2). While this alone would have been sufficient theological grounds for excluding Hermas's angel when depicting Christ, Tertullian instead insists that Hermas's shepherd is excluded on the grounds of his moral character. That is, Hermas's shepherd absolves the mortal sin of adultery, whereas Tertullian belongs to a unique African tradition that is strictly rigorist.[60] The details of this unique African tradition can be found in the seventh chapter of the extensive study of Christian practices as known in Roman Africa carried out by Patout Burns, Robin Jensen, and their collaborators in their book *Christianity in Roman Africa*.[61] Even though they hold the view that Tertullian's opponent was the local bishop of Carthage (i.e., not the bishop of Rome, as I have argued), they still conclude that this bishop's practice of offering forgiveness to adultery is novel in North Africa and Tertullian represents the prior local tradition.[62]

In addition to this unique tradition, which Burns and Jensen trace for the practice of repentance, we can also now identify a unique pattern in African Christianity of describing Christ as a shepherd. When Tertullian thinks about a godly shepherd, such as that seen in the parable from Luke, he is informed by passages from the Old Testament about the "Lord." I think it is safe to surmise that if Tertullian, or those in his community, ever did see a Good Shepherd portrait in a catacomb or elsewhere, they likely did the same. Perhaps they used titles from the Gospel of John, where it is the title claimed by Jesus, but they also added layers of meaning about this Good Shepherd from the Old Testament so that they saw in the human

---

60. See Charles-Murray on Good Shepherd images in Rome as having to do with forgiveness ("Emergence of Christian Art," 61).
61. Burns and Jensen, *Christianity in Roman Africa*, 295–312.
62. Burns and Jensen, *Christianity in Roman Africa*, 311–12.

carrying a sheep on his shoulders the Lord God of Israel who had promised to be a shepherd for the chosen people.

Cyprian

A generation later, Cyprian continued the pattern seen thus far in African sources: when describing Jesus as a shepherd, he primarily turns to the Old Testament. At the beginning of his episcopacy, when Cyprian went into hiding during the Decian persecution, the Roman clergy implied that he was the negligent shepherd (*Ep.* 8.1.1, citing Ezek 34:3–4).[63] Alternatively, Simon Peter was like Jesus, "the good shepherd" (*Ep.* 8.1.2, citing John 10:11–12). Therefore, Peter (and, by implication, his successors in Rome) was one of "the good shepherds," but the flock in Carthage had been left vulnerable (*Ep.* 8.2.1). In his response, Cyprian returns this letter to the Roman clergy, but he does not address the charge of poor shepherding. Instead, in a not-so-thinly veiled retort, Cyprian alerts the Roman authors that their letter must have been falsified because it contains statements (which ones he does not say) that he believes could not have been written by them, so he sends his copy to them for inspection. The debate over who is a good shepherd does not arise again in the early letters of Cyprian until Cornelius becomes bishop of Rome in 251.[64]

In *Ep.* 51 to Cornelius, Cyprian does reference the result of returning a lost sheep, which is "the greatest rejoicing in heaven over a sinner who does penance" (*summum gaudium in caelo super peccatore paenitentiam agente*)—a citation of Luke 15:7—but Cyprian nowhere mentions shepherds explicitly in this letter (*Ep.* 51.2.1).[65] Later, however, in *Ep.* 55, also written in 251 but to a fellow African bishop, Cyprian recalls how "the Lord left the ninety-nine sheep" (*dominus relictis nonaginta*) to pursue the

---

63. From the Roman clergy to the Christians in Carthage. Graeme W. Clarke comments on this passage to say, "It is worth remembering on this passage of pastoral analogy that this document comes from the Church of the Shepherd of Hermas (cf. *Simil.* 9.31.5f. on negligent pastors)." See Clarke, trans., *Letters 55–66*, vol. 3 of *The Letters of St. Cyprian of Carthage*, ACW 46 (New York: Newman, 1986), 210. Translations of this work follow Clarke unless otherwise noted.

64. In his *Eleem.* 23, Cyprian cites a lengthy passage from Matt 25 on the separation of sheep and goats, and therein he calls Jesus the "Shepherd."

65. See also *Ep.* 43.5.1, where Jer 23:16–17 about false prophets is cited. While Jeremiah's chapter begins with a condemnation of false shepherds, the title or role of shepherd is not explicitly mentioned in the letter.

one, but then he contrasts Jesus's shepherding with the "false prophets" (*pseudoprophetae*) who are in the flock of Christ (*Ep.* 55.15.1).[66] The passage is a clear linking of the parable of the lost sheep from Luke 15 with the contrast found in Ezek 34 between the false shepherds and the Lord who is himself the Shepherd of Israel.[67]

Finally, Cyprian calls God a shepherd in a letter to Stephen of Rome, probably dating to around 255.[68] In one of the last references to a divine shepherd in Cyprian, the bishop of Carthage cites at length Ezek 34 (*Ep.* 68.4.1, citing Ezek 34:4–6, 10, 16).[69] His citation attacks the "shepherds" (*pastores*) who have neglected the flock of the "Lord" (*dominus*) (i.e., the Novatianists; *Ep.* 68.4.2). This Lord, for Cyprian, is undoubtedly the Lord Jesus Christ. Yet it is worth noting that Cyprian does not use material from John or other New Testament passages to elaborate on how Christ is a Good Shepherd. Instead, when Cyprian thinks of the Lord as a shepherd, he repeatedly turns to Ezekiel, where it is the LORD God of Israel who says, "I myself will search for my sheep, and will seek them out" (34:11). In short, Cyprian speaks of the Lord as a Shepherd primarily in Old Testament terms.

Conclusion

At this point, it must be stipulated that Augustine and other later writers from Africa cannot be considered here because not only do they represent a later period, in which there would have been even more cross-pollination of texts and ideas from other regions, but also because Augustine in particular represents the Christianity of Rome and Milan as much as, if not more so, than the Christianity of Carthage and Africa.

---

66. The line about rejoicing in heaven over one repentant sinner is repeated later in the letter (55.22.1).

67. See Michael A. Fahey, *Cyprian and the Bible: A Study in Third-Century Exegesis* (Tübingen: Mohr Siebeck, 1971), 231–32, 353. Also, see the same kind of link in *Test.* 2.30, between Christ as one who "shepherds" the people (citing Rev 19:11–16 and then Matt 25:31–46) and the Lord God, who is judge and king in Ps 71 LXX.

68. Clarke, *Letters of St. Cyprian* 4:158–59.

69. Cyprian's reference to a "shepherd" welcoming back the abducted and strayed sheep (in *Ep.* 71.2.2) may refer to the bishop and not to God (as is clearly the case elsewhere; see *Laps.* 4; *Unit. eccl.* 8; *Hab. virg.* 1; *Test.* 1.14; *Ep.* 69.5.1, 74.12). The passage in *Ep.* 71 does not cite any Scripture.

To summarize my findings in this brief exploration of the Good Shepherd motif in early North Africa, I will restate my two main points. First, unlike Rome and its surrounding area, there is no evidence that Christians in Africa used the Shepherd of Hermas when describing Christ as the Good Shepherd, and therefore it is likely that when seeing images such as the one found in Sousse, these ancient African Christians did not import any of the information from that text to understand the image. Second, despite the frequent descriptions of Jesus as a shepherd, the Christians of North Africa did not leave a record of focusing on the Gospel of John when doing so in order to invoke the title "Good Shepherd." Instead, when the early African Christians did describe Jesus as a shepherd, they frequently invoked Old Testament passages about the Lord of Israel, who promised to be a shepherd to the people. Therefore, the surviving evidence leads us to conclude that in North Africa, when Christians envisaged the Good Shepherd, they were not simply envisioning the human Jesus but were primarily envisioning him as the God of Israel incarnate, or put differently, the Lord in shepherd's clothing.

Works Cited

Awes-Freeman, Jennifer. "The Good Shepherd and the Enthroned Ruler: A Reconsideration of Imperial Iconography in the Early Church." Pages 159–95 in *The Art of the Empire: Christian Art in Its Imperial Context*. Edited by Lee Jefferson and Robin M. Jensen. Minneapolis: Fortress, 2015.

———. *The Good Shepherd: Image, Meaning, and Power*. Waco, TX: Baylor University Press, 2021.

Berger, Teresa. *Gender Differences and the Making of Liturgical History: Lifting a Veil on Liturgy's Past*. Farnham, Surrey, UK: Ashgate, 2011.

Beyschlag, Karlmann. "Kallist Und Hippolyt." *TZ* 20 (1964): 103–24.

Bobichon, Philippe. *Justin Martyr, Dialogue avec le Tryphon: edition critique*. Paradosis 47. Fribourg: Département de patristique et d'histoire de l'Eglise de l'Université de Fribourg, 2003.

Brent, Allen. *Hippolytus and the Roman Church in the Third Century*. Leiden: Brill, 1995.

Bucur, Bogdan Gabriel. "Early Christian Binitarianism: From Religious Phenomenon to Polemical Insult to Scholarly Concept." *ModTheol* 27 (2011): 102–20.

———. *Scripture Re-envisioned: Christophanic Exegesis and the Making of a Christian Bible*. Leiden: Brill, 2019.

Burns, J. Patout, Jr., and Robin M. Jensen. *Christianity in Roman Africa: The Development of Its Practices and Beliefs*. Grand Rapids: Eerdmans, 2014.

Butler, Rex D. *The New Prophecy and "New Visions": Evidence of Montanism in the Passion of Perpetua and Felicitas*. PMS 18. Washington, DC: Catholic University of America Press, 2006.

Charles-Murray, Mary. "The Emergence of Christian Art." Pages 51–63 in *Picturing the Bible: The Earliest Christian Art*. Edited by Jeffrey Spier. New Haven: Yale University Press, 2007.

Clarke, Graeme W., trans. *Letters 55–66*. Vol. 3 of *The Letters of St. Cyprian of Carthage*. ACW 46. New York: Newman, 1986.

———, trans. *Letters 67–82*. Vol. 4 of *The Letters of St. Cyprian of Carthage*. ACW 47. New York: Newman, 1989.

Dekkers, Elgius, Jan W. P. Borleffs, Radbodus Willems, François Refoulé, Gerardus F. Diercks, and Emil Kroymann. *Quinti Septimi Florentis Tertulliani Opera*. 2 vols. CCSL 1–2. Turnholt: Brepols, 1954.

Dresken-Weiland, Jutta. "Christian Sarcophagi from Rome." Pages 39–55 in *The Routledge Handbook of Early Christian Art*. Edited by Robin M. Jensen and Mark D. Ellison. London: Routledge, 2018.

Evans, Ernest. *Tertullian's Treatise on the Resurrection: The Text Edited with an Introduction, Translation, and Commentary*. Eugene, OR: Wipf & Stock, 2016.

Fahey, Michael A. *Cyprian and the Bible: A Study in Third-Century Exegesis*. Tübingen: Mohr Siebeck, 1971.

Farina, William. *Perpetua of Carthage: Portrait of a Third-Century Martyr*. Jefferson, NC: McFarland, 2009.

Finney, Paul Corby. *The Invisible God: The Earliest Christians on Art*. Oxford: Oxford University Press, 1994.

Forbes, Greg. *The God of Old: The Role of the Lukan Parables in the Purpose of Luke's Gospel*. London: Bloomsbury, 2000.

Hahneman, Geoffrey Mark. *The Muratorian Fragment and the Development of the Canon*. Oxford: Clarendon, 1992.

Harley-McGowan, Felicity, and Laurence Vieillefon. "Shepherd." Pages 498–99 in *The Eerdmans Encyclopedia of Early Christian Art and Archaeology*. Edited by Paul Corby Finney. Grand Rapids: Eerdmans, 2017.

Harnack, Adolf von. *Der Pseudocyprianische Tractat de Aleatoribus*. TU 5.1. Leipzig: Hinrichs, 1889.
Hauck, Robert John. "The Great Fast: Christology in the Shepherd of Hermas." *AThR* 75.2 (1993): 187–98.
Heffernan, Thomas J. *The Passion of Perpetua and Felicity*. Oxford: Oxford University Press, 2012.
Heine, Ronald E. "Hippolytus, Ps.-Hippolytus, and the Early Canons." Pages 142–51 in *The Cambridge History of Early Christian Literature*. Edited by Francis Young. Cambridge: Cambridge University Press, 2004.
Hofer, Andrew. "The Old Man as Christ in Justin's Dialogue with Trypho." *VC* 57 (2003): 1–21.
Holmes, Michael W., ed. *The Apostolic Fathers: Greek Texts and English Translations*. 3rd ed. Grand Rapids: Baker Academic, 2008.
Hornik, Heidi J. "Freestanding Sculpture." Pages 73–85 in *The Routledge Handbook of Early Christian Art*. Edited by Robin M. Jensen and Mark D. Ellison. London: Routledge, 2018.
Jensen, Robin M. *Baptismal Imagery in Early Christianity: Ritual, Visual, and Theological Dimensions*. Grand Rapids: Baker Academic, 2012.
———. "Early Christian Images and Exegesis." Pages 65–85 in *Picturing the Bible: The Earliest Christian Art*. Edited by Jeffrey Spier. New Haven: Yale University Press, 2007.
Klauser, Theodor. "Studien zur Entstehungsgeschichte der christlichen Kunst I." *JAC* 1 (1958): 20–51.
———. "Studien zur Entstehungsgeschichte der christlichen Kunst III." *JAC* 3 (1960): 112–33.
———. "Studien zur Entstehungsgeschichte der christlichen Kunst IX." *JAC* 10 (1967): 82–120.
Lazreg, Nejib Ben. "Roman and Early Christian Burial Complex at Leptiminus (Lamta): First Notice." *JRA* 15 (2002): 336–45.
Lazreg, Nejib Ben, Susan Stevens, Lea Stirling, and Jennifer Moore. "Roman and Early Christian Burial Complex at Leptiminus (Lamta): Second Notice." *JRA* 19 (2006): 347–68.
Leclercq, Henri, and Fernand Cabrol. "Pasteur (Bon)." Pages 2272–2390 in *Dictionnaire d'archéologie Chrétienne et de Liturgie*. Vol. 13.2. Edited by Fernand Cabrol and Henri Leclerq. Paris: Librarie Letouzey et Ané, 1937–1938.
Leynaud, Augustin-Ferdinand. *Les Catacombes Africaines: Sousse-Hadrumète*. Alger: Carbonel, 1922.

MacKendrick, Paul L. *The North African Stones Speak*. Chapel Hill: University of North Carolina Press, 1980.
Merdinger, Jane E. *Rome and the African Church in the Time of Augustine*. New Haven: Yale University Press, 1997.
Osborn, Eric. *Tertullian, First Theologian of the West*. Cambridge: Cambridge University Press, 1997.
Osiek, Carolyn. *Shepherd of Hermas: A Commentary*. Hermeneia. Minneapolis: Fortress, 1999.
Peppard, Michael. *The World's Oldest Church: Bible, Art, and Ritual at Dura-Europos, Syria*. New Haven: Yale University Press, 2016.
Rebillard, Éric. *Greek and Latin Narratives about the Ancient Martyrs*. Oxford: Oxford University Press, 2017.
Reynolds, Benjamin E. *The Apocalyptic Son of Man in the Gospel of John*. Tübingen: Mohr Siebeck, 2008.
Slusser, Michael, ed. *Justin Martyr: Dialogue with Trypho*. Translated by Thomas B. Falls and Thomas P. Halton. FC 3. Washington, DC: Catholic University of America Press, 2003.
Snyder, Graydon F. *Ante Pacem: Archaeological Evidence of Church Life before Constantine*. Macon, GA: Mercer University Press, 2003.
Stewart-Sykes, Alistair. *Tertullian, Cyprian: On the Lord's Prayer*. PPS 29. Crestwood, NY: Saint Vladimir's Seminary Press, 2004.
Stone, David L., David J. Mattingly, and Nejib Ben Lazreg. *Leptiminus (Lamta) Report No. 3: The Field Survey*. JRASup 87. Portsmouth, RI: Journal of Roman Archaeology, 2011.
Tornau, Christian, and Paolo Cecconi. *The Shepherd of Hermas in Latin: Critical Edition of the Oldest Translation Vulgata*. TUGAL 173. Berlin: de Gruyter, 2014.
Tränkle, Hermann. "Q. Septimius Florens Tertullianus." Pages 438–511 in *Die Literatur des Umbruchs. Von der Römischen zur Christlichen Literatur 117 Bis 284 n. Chr*. Edited by Klaus Sallmann. HDLLA 4. Munich: Beck, 1997.
Wilhite, David E. *Ancient African Christianity*. London: Routledge, 2017.
———. "Identity, Psychology, and the Psychici: Tertullian's 'Bishop of Bishops.'" *IJRR* 9 (2009): 1–26.
———. *Tertullian the African: An Anthropological Reading of Tertullian's Context and Identities*. Berlin: de Gruyter, 2007.
Zahn, Theodor. *Geschichte des Neutestamentlichen Kanons*. Erlangen: Deichert, 1888.

Christian Children's Sarcophagi: Testaments to Grief and Hope

Eric J. Brewer

> I send to you a letter which I wrote to Marullus when he lost his young son and was said to be behaving weakly.... "Do you expect comfort? Accept censure! You take your son's death like a weakling."[1]
> —Seneca, *Epistle* 99.1–2

> When, therefore, you lose a child at an untimely age, who was not yet able to do anything, why do you lament? Why do you seek after it?
> —John Chrysostom, *Homilies on 1 Thessalonians* 6.2

The death of children was frightfully common in the ancient world. Estimates vary widely, but perhaps only half, and certainly no more than two-thirds, of children born in the Roman world lived to see their fifth birthday.[2] At that rate, most parents would have experienced the loss of a young child. This, combined with the seemingly callous attitudes expressed in quotes such as those above, led a generation of scholars to theorize that Roman parents intentionally avoided affective bonds with their children as a way to protect themselves from emotional trauma in the event of their child's (not unlikely) death.[3] Recent studies in Roman burial practices, not

---

1. Unless otherwise noted, all translations are mine.
2. See discussion in Tim Parkin, "The Demography of Infancy and Early Childhood in the Ancient World," in *The Oxford Handbook of Childhood and Education in the Classical World*, ed. Judith Evan Grubbs, Tim Parkin, and Roslynne Bell (Oxford: Oxford University Press, 2013), 40–61.
3. See, for example, Keith R. Bradley, "Wet-Nursing at Rome: A Study in Social Relations," in *The Family in Ancient Rome: New Perspectives*, ed. Beryl Rawson (Ithaca, NY: Cornell University Press, 1986), 201–29. For an influential rejoinder, see Mark Golden, "Did the Ancients Care When Their Children Died?," *GR* 35 (1988): 152–63.

to mention opposing voices from the ancient world,[4] paint a very different picture, however, of parental grief and attachment to children. For many Roman parents, the loss of a child appears to have aroused genuine grief for someone who was dearly loved.

In this essay, I use Christian children's sarcophagi to explore early Christian attitudes toward childhood and the expression of grief. After addressing some preliminary methodological considerations, I compare pagan and Christian children's sarcophagi, focusing especially on a representative example of each. This comparison highlights both the lack of mourning scenes on Christian children's sarcophagi and their strong resemblance to those of Christian adults, raising questions regarding Christian views of mourning and the relationship between childhood and adulthood. I then address those questions in conversation with key texts from the New Testament and other early Christian literature.

Methodological Considerations

Before one can seriously study Christian children's sarcophagi, the subject of such a study must be defined. There is little debate about what constitutes a sarcophagus, but questions arise when it comes to identifying sarcophagi as Christian and used for children. In the case of children's sarcophagi, there is first the question of who ought to be regarded as a child. In modern English usage, people can be children in terms of their age (i.e., younger than the legal age of majority) or in terms of their relationships to other people, namely, their parents. This essay considers only children in the first sense, though even here there is some ambiguity, as the age of majority was not clearly defined in the Roman world.[5] As for

---

4. Margaret King, "Commemoration of Infants on Roman Funerary Inscriptions," in *The Epigraphy of Death: Studies in the History and Society of Greece and Rome*, ed. Graham J. Oliver (Liverpool: Liverpool University Press, 2000); Maureen Carroll, "'No Part in Earthly Things': The Death, Burial, and Commemoration of Newborn Children and Infants in Roman Italy," in *Families in the Roman and Late Antique World*, ed. Mary Harlow and Lena Larsson Lovén (London: Continuum, 2012). See, for example, Plutarch's characterization of the uncontrollable grief of "most mothers" in his *Cons. ux.* 6, though this must be read in light of Plutarch's own rhetorical program of exhorting his wife to temper her grief at the death of their infant daughter. See discussion in Jo-Marie Claassen, "Plutarch's Little Girl," *ActaCl* 47 (2004): 27–50.

5. Beryl Rawson, *Children and Childhood in Roman Italy* (Oxford: Oxford University Press, 2003), 134–45.

identifying sarcophagi as belonging to children, inscriptions stating the age of the deceased or portraits can provide clear indicators that a sarcophagus was intended for a child, but these are often lacking. Even size is not an entirely reliable indicator since children could be interred in full-sized sarcophagi, while smaller sarcophagi could have been used for the secondary burial of bones or ashes.[6] For this study, I have avoided ambiguous cases and instead focused on sarcophagi that can clearly be identified as used for children.

For Christian sarcophagi, the use of clear Christian imagery (e.g., the *chi-rho*, biblical scenes), use of Christian terminology in inscriptions (e.g., *dormit in pace*), and location near other indisputably Christian sarcophagi all allow a sarcophagus to be identified as Christian with a high degree of confidence.[7] At the same time, numerous sarcophagi whose inscriptions identify them as Christian lack any specifically Christian imagery (Rep. 1.87, 172, 238, 475). The sarcophagus of Curtia Catiana provides an excellent example of this among Christian children's sarcophagi (fig. 7.1).[8] Mythological sea creatures cover most of the face of the sarcophagus, with the two most central figures holding a circular frame (*clipeus*) featuring a bust of the deceased. On the lid are depictions of scenes from daily life, such as a servant carrying food and two boys boxing. The only indication that this is a Christian sarcophagus comes in the inscription, which reads, "Curtiae/ Catianae/ c(larissima) p(uella) in pace."[9] The final two words, *in pace*, appear exclusively on Christian sarcophagi, allowing this sarcophagus to be identified as Christian in spite of the lack of distinctly Christian iconography. Based on this example and others like it, one can reasonably conclude that at

---

6. Janet Huskinson, *Roman Children's Sarcophagi: Their Decoration and Its Social Significance* (Oxford: Clarendon, 1996), 2.

7. Betty I. Knott, "The Christian 'Special Language' in the Inscriptions," VC 10 (1956): 65–79. See also the discussion of the difficulties with classifying an artifact as "Christian" in Robert Couzin, "'Early' 'Christian' 'Art,'" in *The Routledge Handbook of Early Christian Art*, ed. Robin M. Jensen and Mark D. Ellison (London: Routledge, 2018), 384–89.

8. For additional examples of Christian children's sarcophagi without distinctively Christian iconography, see the table in Manuela Studer-Karlen, *Verstorbenendarstellungen auf frühchristlichen Sarkophagen* (Turnhout: Brepols, 2012), 41–42.

9. The use of the conventional *clarissima puella* is the strongest evidence that this is a child's sarcophagus, though its small size and the childlike features found on the bust of the deceased also cohere with this.

Fig. 7.1. Sarcophagus of Curtia Catiana, 300–325 CE. Marble, 1 ft x 3 ft 8 in x 1 ft 2 in. In situ, Catacomb of Praetextatus, Rome. Photograph by Pontifical Commission for Sacred Archaeology.

least some sarcophagi with neither Christian imagery nor inscriptions did in fact belong to Christians, especially when Christians were just beginning to use sarcophagi and distinctively Christian iconography remained undeveloped. The impossibility of identifying such sarcophagi with any degree of confidence precludes their inclusion in the study of Christian sarcophagi.

Even after sarcophagi have been identified as Christian and as used for children, significant questions remain regarding how properly to interpret their iconography. The main difficulties arise from the social location of sarcophagi and the influence of both clients and craftspeople in their production. First, the high costs associated with both the marble itself and with transporting and sculpting that marble ensured that only people with significant wealth could afford to inter their dead in this way.[10] As a result, sarcophagi do not provide a representative sample of burial practices in the ancient world. One cannot assume, therefore, that the iconography of Christian children's sarcophagi reflects the beliefs of a wide swath of Christians in the Roman world. Instead, reference to a variety of roughly contemporary Christians texts can help to situate these sarcophagi in a broader context and identify areas in which they reflect Christian belief more generally.[11]

---

10. Robert Couzin, "The Christian Sarcophagus Population of Rome," *JRA* 27 (2014): 275–303.

11. Even here it must be acknowledged that many of the texts considered in the

Second, both clients and sculptors appear to have contributed to the iconographic programs of sarcophagi.[12] In addition to having a repertoire of images from which clients could choose, workshops would also produce nearly finished sarcophagi, complete apart from the face on the central portrait, which would then be carved in the likeness of that of the deceased.[13] This means that sculptors themselves played a significant role in the design of the sarcophagi that they produced. At the same time, the wide variety among sarcophagi indicates that clients could request varying degrees of personalization, likely depending on the amount they were willing to pay and the skill of the sculptor they employed. It is therefore exceedingly difficult to determine the degree to which the iconographic program of a given sarcophagus reflects the beliefs of the client or those of the sculptor. One could easily imagine a situation in which a pagan sculptor crafted sarcophagi with iconographic programs intended to appeal to Christian clients. The iconography would likely reflect the beliefs of the clients more than those of the producer, but perhaps it would reflect those beliefs only imperfectly. Once again, incorporating roughly contemporary Christian texts into this study will enable interpretation of these sarcophagi in the context of broader Christian belief and avoid potential distortions arising from their production process.

Pagan Children's Sarcophagi

Pagan children's sarcophagi display many of the same motifs found on those of their adult counterparts. Many feature scenes from myths, most notably those of Selene and Endymion (*RS* 144), Meleager (*RS* 187), Ceres and Proserpina,[14] and Cupid and Psyche (*BMCat* no. 30). Seasonal themes

---

present study were produced and preserved by relative social elites. In the case of sermons, however, at least their audiences would have included the nonelite.

12. Ben Russell, "The Sarcophagus Trade," in *The Economics of the Roman Stone Trade* (Oxford: Oxford University Press, 2013), 256–310.

13. The main evidence for this comes from the many sarcophagi, especially children's sarcophagi, with portraits that have been left unfinished (e.g., *ASR* 1.2, no. 60; 4.3, no. 214; Rep. 1.364). Huskinson offers a brief but informative survey of possible explanations for this phenomenon in *Roman Children's Sarcophagi*, 82.

14. "Sarcophagus Panel," Saint Petersburg, Hermitage Museum, no. ГР-3087, https://tinyurl.com/SBL4830q.

are also common,[15] as were scenes taken from everyday life. The latter include scenes from the life of the deceased, chariot rides (*RS* 113), and chariot races (*BMCat* no. 11).[16]

One such scene from the life, or rather the death, of the deceased appears exclusively on children's sarcophagi. This depicts the *conclamatio*, a ritual performed shortly after death. After a close relative had given the deceased a last kiss and closed her eyes, there would be loud shouting of the name of the deceased.[17] This calling of the name of the deceased would be continued intermittently until the funeral. Janet Huskinson suggests that this procedure was intended to provide mutual reassurance, "to confirm for the living that death had really taken place, and to comfort the departed soul."[18] The scene appears only rarely on sarcophagi, with children's sarcophagi providing all of the surviving examples. In most cases, it appears along with other scenes from the life of the deceased, typically in the central position.[19] Occasionally, as in the example presented below, the *conclamatio* scene occupies the entire front face of the sarcophagus.[20]

A child's sarcophagus currently housed at the British Museum provides a representative example of this scene (fig. 7.2).[21] In the middle of the front face of the sarcophagus, a deceased girl lies on a *klinē*, propped up

---

15. Oxford, Ashmolean Museum, no. ANMichaelis.144, https://tinyurl.com/SBL4830r.

16. Paris, Louvre, Ma 659, https://tinyurl.com/SBL4830s; Guntram Koch and Hellmut Sichtermann, *Römische Sarkophage*, HdA (Munich: Beck, 1982), 90–126; Huskinson, *Roman Children's Sarcophagi*, 9–24.

17. Jocelyn M. C. Toynbee, *Death and Burial in the Roman World* (Ithaca, NY: Cornell University Press, 1971), 44. Toynbee suggests that "all the near relatives called upon the dead by name," which might lead one to question the scholarly convention of calling the images on these sarcophagi "*conclamatio* scenes," given that they uniformly depict both parents mourning silently (Koch and Sichtermann, *Römische Sarkophage*, 112–13). A careful examination of Toynbee's sources, however, reveals that the apparent silence of the parents represents no obstacle to identifying this scene as a depiction of the *conclamatio*. His sources mention that the name of the deceased was called but do not specify who did the calling (Servius, *Comm. Aen.* 6.218; Lucan, *Bell. civ.* 2.23).

18. Huskinson, *Roman Children's Sarcophagi*, 13.

19. RS 115; Paris, Louvre, Ma 319, https://tinyurl.com/SBL4830t.

20. For more on sarcophagi depicting the *conclamatio*, see Koch and Sichtermann, *Römische Sarkophage*, 112–13; Huskinson, *Roman Children's Sarcophagi*, 13–15.

21. Susan Walker, *Catalogue of Roman Sarcophagi in the British Museum* (London:

Fig. 7.2. Child's sarcophagus with *conclamatio* scene, 200–220 CE. Marble, 3 ft 5 in x 1 ft 2 in. British Museum, London. Photograph by British Museum Images.

by pillows. A garland has slipped from her hand and is now entertaining a pet dog, who lies on the ground beneath the *klinē*, next to the girl's slippers. Her father sits at her head, wearing a veil and grieving as he holds his head in his right hand. The girl's mother is similarly depicted at her feet. A young man, perhaps the girl's brother, stands next to the mother. Behind the mother stand two women mourning, just as two men stand mourning behind the father. Three female mourners with hands raised stand around the *klinē*. While the figures flanking the mother and father most likely represent household servants, the three women around the *klinē* appear to be professional mourners (*praeficae*), a phenomenon well-known in the Greco-Roman world.[22]

The scene well conveys the sorrow of this family in the face of a life cut short. The fallen garland, much like the spilled baskets that appear throughout Roman funerary art, may depict death as an interruption

---

British Museum Publications, 1990), 17–18. A high-resolution image can be viewed online at https://www.britishmuseum.org/collection/object/G_1805-0703-144.

22. See discussion in Anthony Corbeill, *Nature Embodied: Gesture in Ancient Rome* (Princeton: Princeton University Press, 2004), 77; Amy Richlin, "Emotional Work: Lamenting the Roman Dead," in *Essays in Honor of Gordon Williams: Twenty-Five Years at Yale*, ed. Elizabeth Ivory Tylawsky and Charles Gray Weiss (New Haven: Schwab, 2001), 229–48, esp. 243–45. Historically, it is unclear whether such professional mourners would have been present for the *conclamatio*, but their presence in the *conclamatio* scenes in Roman relief sculpture adds to the theme of mourning that these convey.

of life's expected course.²³ The slippers help to recall her daily life in the home but also evoke sorrow when the viewer realizes that those slippers will never again be worn. All of the living figures are visibly grieved, supporting their heads with a hand, pulling out hair, or beating their chests. Viewing this sarcophagus, it is difficult not to sense some of the grief of this family at the loss of their little girl.

Christian Children's Sarcophagi

Christian children's sarcophagi resemble those of their pagan peers in terms of size and certain inscriptional conventions (e.g., *filio dulcissimo*, *clarissima puella*), but in their iconography the sarcophagi of Christian adults correspond to them much more closely. As in the example of the sarcophagus of Curtia Catiana mentioned above, some sarcophagi, whether of adults or children, can be identified as Christian only on the basis of their inscriptions. Most Christian children's sarcophagi, however, depict the same specifically Christian symbols and biblical scenes as those of Christian adults.²⁴ As Huskinson summarizes, "The conclusion from this sample is that Christian child sarcophagi made minimal adaptation of the compositions which regularly adorned [Christian] adult pieces. Most of the adjustment that they did make was for size; alteration of content seems incidental."²⁵

One can compare, for example, two sarcophagi from the collection of the Vatican's Museo Pio Cristiano. The first, the famous "Dogmatic Sarcophagus," displays a variety of biblical and traditional scenes in two registers, with an unfinished portrait of the deceased, in this case a married couple, within a *clipeus* in the middle of the upper register (fig. 7.3).²⁶ From the left, the scenes in the upper register consist of the creation of Adam and Eve, Christ with the first couple in the garden of Eden, the mar-

---

23. Franz Cumont, *Recherches sur le symbolisme funéraire des Romains* (New York: Arno, 1975), 400 n. 2.

24. See table in Studer-Karlen, *Verstorbenendarstellungen auf frühchristlichen Sarkophagen*, 41–42.

25. Huskinson, *Roman Children's Sarcophagi*, 69.

26. See the analysis and extensive bibliography for this sarcophagus in Friedrich Wilhelm Deichmann, ed., *Repertorium der christlich-antiken Sarkophage* (Wiesbaden: Steiner, 1967–2018), 1:39–41. A high-resolution photo can be viewed at https://tinyurl.com/SBL4830u.

riage at Cana, the multiplication of the loaves, and the raising of Lazarus. The lower register, again from left to right, portrays the adoration of the magi, Christ healing a blind man, Daniel in the lion's den, the *Hahnszene* with Christ and Peter,[27] the arrest of Peter, and Peter providing water from the rock. In the portrait of the couple, the male figure holds a scroll, a symbol of learning, in his left hand and makes a gesture indicative of oratory with his right.

Fig. 7.3. Large sarcophagus, including creation of Adam and Eve, adoration of the magi, 325–350 CE, early Christian. 8 ft 9 in x 4 ft 9 in x 4 ft 4 in. Museo Pio Cristiano, Vatican Museums, Vatican State. Photograph by Scala / Art Resource, New York.

27. The most thorough analysis of this scene available can be found in Paulus Gijsbertus Johannes Post, *De haanscène in de vroeg-christelijke kunst: een iconografische en iconologische analyse* (Voerendaal: Schrijen-Lippertz, 1984). For non-Dutch speakers, Peter C. J. van Dael provides a thorough review in *VC* 45 (1991): 96–101. The scene most likely depicts Christ's prediction of Peter's denial, Christ's commissioning of Peter, or both.

The second sarcophagus is a less well known Christian child's sarcophagus (fig. 7.4).[28] It also displays a variety of biblical and traditional scenes in two registers, with a portrait of the deceased, in this case a young boy, within a *clipeus* in the middle of the upper register. From the left, the scenes in the upper register consist of Jesus's entry into Jerusalem,[29] the multiplication of the loaves, and the crossing of the Red Sea. The lower register is best read out from the center. Directly below the portrait one finds the adoration of the magi, followed by Daniel in the lion's den, Adam and Eve in the garden of Eden, the sacrifice of Isaac, and Noah in the ark to its right. Moving left from the adoration of the magi, one encounters the *Hahnszene* with Christ and Peter, the arrest of Peter, and Peter providing water from the rock. As with the man in the portrait of the Dogmatic Sarcophagus, the boy in the portrait of this sarcophagus holds a scroll in his left hand and makes a gesture indicative of oratory with his right.[30]

Fig. 7.4. Front of a child sarcophagus, with scenes from the Old and New Testaments, 325–350 CE, early Christian. Marble high relief, 3 ft 9 in x 1 ft 4 in. Museo Pio Cristiano, Vatican Museums, Vatican State. Photograph by Vanni Archive / Art Resource, New York.

---

28. For analysis and bibliography, see Deichmann, *Repertorium der christlich-antiken Sarkophage*, 1:36–37. A high-resolution photo can be viewed at https://tinyurl.com/SBL4830v.

29. The man in the tree may recall the story of Zacchaeus for some viewers, though in that story Jesus appears to be walking rather than riding on a donkey (Luke 19:1–10), as he is portrayed here.

30. Deichmann describes the boy as "mit beiden Händen Buchrolle haltend" (*Repertorium der christlich-antiken Sarkophage* 1:36), but comparison with the Dogmatic Sarcophagus makes clear that the boy is making the same "Redegestus" that Deichmann himself identifies in that portrait (40).

It would be difficult to overstate the similarities between these two sarcophagi. Apart from the similarities in their overall format, they both portray their deceased as learned and skilled in oratory. In the case of the child's sarcophagus, this likely indicates the hopes that the parents had held for their now-deceased son rather than his actual oratorial accomplishments at the time of his passing.[31] This is a common phenomenon in the portraits found on children's sarcophagi and will be treated more fully below. Turning to biblical and traditional scenes, they both include the multiplication of the loaves, Daniel in the lion's den, Adam and Eve in the garden of Eden, the adoration of the magi, and the cycle of three Petrine scenes. While the Dogmatic Sarcophagus lacks the depictions of Noah in the ark, the crossing of the Red Sea, and Jesus's entry into Jerusalem that one finds on the child's sarcophagus, none of these scenes seem especially related to children, and all of them appear on other Christian adult sarcophagi.[32]

One might expect biblical scenes with special resonances for children to appear with increased frequency on Christian children's sarcophagi, but this does not appear to be the case.[33] For example, the Christian child's sarcophagus in our comparison portrays the sacrifice of Isaac, while the Dogmatic Sarcophagus does not. The presence of this scene, in which Abraham receives his son back from the dead (Heb 11:17–19), is perhaps especially poignant on a child's sarcophagus, but it occurs with no greater frequency or prominence in Christian children's sarcophagi generally than in Christian adults' sarcophagi.[34] It does not appear to have held any special meaning for bereaved parents beyond its usual use as a type for Jesus's crucifixion and resurrection.[35] The situation is similar with another

---

31. Huskinson, *Roman Children's Sarcophagi*, 93.

32. Guntram Koch, *Frühchristliche Sarkophage*, HdA (Munich: Beck, 2000), 138–39, 142–43, 173–74. For Noah: Rep. 1.35, 46, 269, 750, 987. For the Red Sea: Rep. 1.714, 899; Rep. 2.12. For Jesus entering Jerusalem: Rep. 1.14, 21, 28, 38, 40, 63, 680, 692, 772, 946.

33. This has already been pointed out in Janet Huskinson, "The Decoration of Early Christian Children's Sarcophagi," StPatr 24 (1993): 114–18.

34. The scene is far too common to allow for even a representative sample to be provided here, but examples of adult sarcophagi with the scene include Rep. 1.7, 39, 40, 42, 44, 45, 144, 625, 677, 680, 771, 772, 991.

35. For this interpretation of the sacrifice of Isaac in early Christian art, see Robin M. Jensen, "The Offering of Isaac in Jewish and Christian Tradition: Image and Text," BibInt 2 (1994): 85–110; Jensen, "Early Christian Images and Exegesis," in *Picturing the*

biblical scene, the adoration of the magi. This scene, in which an infant or child Jesus receives gifts from the magi, might remind parents that Christ himself came as a child to save children, but they do not appear to have chosen it with any greater frequency for children's sarcophagi than for those of adults.[36] The adoration of the magi is indeed popular on children's sarcophagi (e.g., Rep. 1.5, 16, 41, 526, 662; 2.32, 34), but it also appears quite frequently on adult sarcophagi (e.g., Rep. 1.28, 43, 241, 692, 735, 949; 2.20, 148, 149, 150), as it does on the Dogmatic Sarcophagus. When it comes to their iconography, there is very little separating Christian children's sarcophagi from those of their adult coreligionists.

Grief and Mourning

The two children's sarcophagi analyzed above, those of a pagan girl and a Christian boy, differ remarkably. In particular, the *conclamatio* scene that occupies the entire front face of the pagan girl's sarcophagus finds no counterparts on any Christian sarcophagi. This can be partially explained by simple chronology. Most surviving *conclamatio* sarcophagi date from the mid- to late second century, with a couple of outliers likely belonging to the early third century.[37] This is earlier than any surviving Christian children's sarcophagi, which all date from the late third century or later.[38] Based on this, one could argue that the lack of *conclamatio* on Christian children's sarcophagi merely reflects ever-changing fashions and has little if anything to do with underlying ideology.

This may be true to a certain degree, but it does not fully explain why Christian children's sarcophagi did not employ this scene. As Jutta Dresken-Weiland explains, more members of the upper class appear among early Christian sarcophagi buyers than they do among pagan

---

Bible: The Earliest Christian Art, ed. Jeffrey Spier (New Haven: Yale University Press, 2007), 65–85, esp. 78–82. Jensen also connects Christian depictions of the sacrifice of Isaac with the sacraments of baptism and the Eucharist.

36. For more on the interpretation of these scene in early Christian art, especially as it pertains to Mary, see Felicity Harley, "Visual Apocrypha: The Case of Mary and the Magi in Early Christian Rome," in *Apocryphal and Esoteric Sources in the Development of Christianity and Judaism*, ed. Igor Dorfmann-Lazarev (Leiden: Brill, 2021), 383–410.

37. Huskinson, *Roman Children's Sarcophagi*, 13–14.

38. Studer-Karlen, *Verstorbenendarstellungen auf frühchristlichen Sarkophagen*, 41–42.

sarcophagi buyers from the second and third centuries, likely indicating that "social climbers" elevated by Constantine sought sarcophagi as a traditional form of burial to display their newfound status.[39] Even while they adopted the general form of the sarcophagus, however, they did not adopt the specific imagery of the *conclamatio* scene.

This may have been due in part to Christian teaching regarding grief and mourning, with numerous Christian leaders from this period counseling against what they considered excessive public displays of grief (Gregory of Nazianzus, *Or.* 7.1; John Chrysostom; *Hom. Matt.* 31.5; *Hom. 1 Thess.* 6; Augustine, *Hom.* 172, 173).[40] Such admonitions often referenced Paul's words to the Thessalonians expressing his desire that they not grieve their dead "as others do who have no hope" (1 Thess 4:13; see Ambrose, *Exc.* 1.9; *Ob. Val.* 45, 48; Jerome, *Ep.* 39.3; Augustine, *Ep.* 92.1). Jerome, for example, clearly recalls this verse in his letter to Paula, a mother grieving the death of her adult daughter, Blaesilla. Paraphrasing the verse as a prohibition given by Jesus through Paul, Jerome writes, "This is what I have commanded you through my apostle, that you not grieve in the manner of the heathen for those who sleep" (*Ep.* 39.3 [PL 22:469]). In addition to rephrasing Paul's purpose clause as a command, Jerome also translates Paul's very general οἱ λοιποί ("the others") with the more specific *gentes* ("heathen").[41] Jerome thus clarifies the identity of those "who do not have hope" and characterizes non-Christians as lacking such hope for an afterlife.[42]

Evidence indicates that many non-Christians in the Roman world did in fact lack any expectation of a continued existence following death. After

---

39. Jutta Dresken-Weiland, "Christian Sarcophagi from Rome," in Jensen and Ellison, *Routledge Handbook of Early Christian Art*, 41; Jutta Dresken-Weiland, *Sarkophagbestattungen des 4.–6. Jahrhunderts im Westen des römischen Reiches* (Rome: Herder, 2003), 33–34, 42–43, 46–47.

40. Note, however, that such opposition to excessive displays of grief was by no means unique to Christians, as clearly indicated by the quote from Seneca at the beginning of this essay.

41. Augustine does the same in *Ep.* 92.1. The grammatical shift from a purpose clause to a command may be slight, but the difference in pastoral perspective is far greater. It is one thing to say to bereaved parents, "I am telling you this in order to assuage your grief," and quite another to tell them, "Jesus commands you not to grieve for your child!"

42. Later in the letter he also places a comparison between Paula and "heathen" mothers in the mouths of an unbelieving crowd that witnessed her faint at her daughter's funeral, arguing that her behavior reflected poorly on the faith (39.6 [PL 22:473]).

all, a common Roman epitaph reads, "I was not; I was; I am not; I don't care."[43] At the same time, such denial of an afterlife was far from universal. Plutarch, consoling his wife upon learning of the death of their young daughter, reminded her of the soul's ascent to more divine regions (*Cons. ux.* 10–11). Belief in an afterlife was a feature of several mystery religions, especially the popular cult of Isis.[44] Such hope for continued existence after death also found expression on pagan sarcophagi. Many feature Bacchic themes of feasting and depictions of agricultural abundance that may represent attempts to portray the idyllic existence now enjoyed by the deceased (*RS* 221–36).[45] Portrayals of the deceased among the Muses, as one finds on several pagan children's sarcophagi, likely also attest to a hope for some form of communion with or inclusion among divine beings in the afterlife (fig. 7.5).[46] When Jerome claimed that non-Christians lacked a hope for the afterlife, that represented a Christian interpretation of their situation rather than the beliefs of all non-Christians in the Roman world.[47] Christian may have possessed distinctive conceptions of the afterlife and the basis for participation in it, but many of their non-Christians neighbors shared their belief that death was not the end.[48]

---

43. In Latin, *non fui, fui, non sum, non curo*, often abbreviated NFFNSNC. See the examples in Richmond Lattimore, *Themes in Greek and Latin Epitaphs* (Urbana: University of Illinois Press, 1962), 84–85; Valerie M. Hope, *Death in Ancient Rome: A Sourcebook* (London: Routledge, 2007), 230–31. Similar sentiments also appear in Lucretius, *Rerum nat.* 3.830–1094.

44. Walter Burkert, *Ancient Mystery Cults* (Cambridge: Harvard University Press, 1987), 21–27.

45. See discussion in Koch and Sichtermann, *Römische Sarkophage*, 191–95.

46. Huskinson, *Roman Children's Sarcophagi*, 38–40, 97–99.

47. Jerome himself acknowledges this in the same letter mentioned above, immediately following his quotation of 1 Thess 4:13, by writing, "Blush, for you are bested by the compassion of a heathen. The devil's maid is better than mine. She imagines that her unbelieving husband has been translated to heaven, but you either do not believe that your daughter is at rest with me, or do not want her to be" (39.3 [PL 22:469]). He recognizes that some non-Christians believed in a pleasant afterlife for their deceased but characterizes such hope as false.

48. For a brief introduction to some of the many different understandings of the afterlife in the Roman world, see Valerie M. Hope, *Roman Death: Dying and the Dead in Ancient Rome* (London: Continuum, 2009), 97–120. One can also gain a greater appreciation for this diversity by surveying the essays in Katherina Waldner, Richard Gordon, and Wolfgang Spickermann, eds., *Burial Rituals, Ideas of Afterlife, and the Individual in the Hellenistic World and the Roman Empire* (Stuttgart: Steiner, 2016).

Fig. 7.5. Kline sarcophagus of a young boy with Muses, 270–290 CE. Marble, 2 ft 11 in x 3 ft 10 in x 1 ft 6 in. Vatican Museum, Rome. Photograph by Deutschen Archäologischen Institut, D-DAI-ROM-41.935.

Nor were Christian prohibitions against grief by any means absolute.[49] Even elsewhere in his letter to Paula, Jerome describes his own great grief at the death of her daughter, Blaesilla, writing of his tears and groanings (*Ep.* 39.1–2). He is careful to make clear that his grief is not for Blaesilla, who "now reigns with Christ" (39.5), but rather for those, including himself, who will no longer see her (39.1). Jerome accepts some grief in the face of the death of a beloved Christian, provided it does not flow from a lack of faith in God's saving power and is directed

---

49. The same is true for Stoics such as Seneca, whom I also quoted at the beginning of this essay (*Marc.* 7; *Ad Polybium de consolatione*). See discussion in David Konstan, "The Grieving Self: Reflections on Lucian's *On Mourning* and the Consolatory Tradition," in *Greek and Roman Consolations: Eight Studies of a Tradition and Its Afterlife*, ed. Han Baltussen (Swansea: Classical Press of Wales, 2013), 139–52; Jon Davies, *Death, Burial, and Rebirth in the Religions of Antiquity* (London: Routledge, 1999), 130–38. Expressions of grief were acceptable so long as they did not breach decorum.

toward one's own loss rather than a sense of pity for the deceased, who ought rather to be envied. His letter generally, however, allows little scope for grief.[50]

One encounters a similar mix of acceptance but also discouragement of expressions of grief in John Chrysostom.[51] In one sermon addressing the death of children, he tells his congregation, "Weep; I do not forbid you" (*Hom. Col.* 8.5 [PG 62:360]).[52] In a different sermon on the same topic, however, he commands them not to weep if they truly believe in the resurrection, not even making allowance for human nature (*Hom. Matt.* 31.5 [PG 57:375]). This second sermon seems to have more intense expressions of grief in mind, mentioning both lamenting (θρηνέω) and wailing (ὀλολύζω), but it does not even allow for milder expressions such as weeping (δακρύω).[53] Perhaps more importantly, however, it specifically targets the bringing in of "Greek [i.e., non-Christian] women" to lead mourning (*Hom. Matt.* 31.5 [PG 57:374]). This likely refers to the same class of professional mourners portrayed on the pagan girl's sarcophagus discussed above. Regardless of Chrysostom's views of grief in general, he clearly considers the employment of such professional mourners unacceptable.[54]

Augustine, perhaps reflecting his own experience of grief after the deaths of his mother and his son, allows considerably more room for

---

50. Much of Jerome's letter to Paula would likely strike many modern readers as excessively harsh and even manipulative. He rebukes her for fainting during her daughter's funeral procession, implying that this testified against the truth of the gospel (39.6), and even imagines Blaesilla's own rebukes of Paula, making her say, "If you wish to be my mother, you must please Christ. I do not know a mother who displeases my Lord" (39.7).

51. For a fuller treatment of John Chrysostom's response to grieving parents, see Xueying Wang, "John Chrysostom on the Premature Death of Children and Parental Grief," *JECS* 27 (2019): 443–63. For more on John Chrysostom's treatment of mourning, see Jesse Siragan Arlen, "'Let Us Mourn Continuously': John Chrysostom and the Early Christian Transformation of Mourning," StPatr 83 (2017): 289–312.

52. John Chrysostom likewise gives permission for moderate expressions of grief in *Hom. Jo.* 62.4.

53. John Chrysostom similarly targets intense expressions of grief in *Hom. 1 Thess.* 6 (PG 62:429–34), which also mentions mourning (πενθέω) and lamentation (θρηνέω).

54. For more on John Chysostom's condemnation of the use of professional mourners, see Éric Rebillard, *The Care of the Dead in Late Antiquity* (Ithaca, NY: Cornell University Press, 2010), 132–33.

grief than does either Jerome or John Chrysostom (*Conf.* 9.14, 27–37 [PL 32:769, 775–80]).[55] Funeral rites, though of no benefit to the deceased, are acceptable as means to "soothe their natural grief" (*Hom.* 172.3 [PL 38:937]). At the same time, Augustine considers the shouting of the *conclamatio* to be inappropriate for Christians, as can be seen especially in his description of the rites performed for his mother, Monica, upon her death (*Conf.* 9.29–32 [PL 32:776–77]). Augustine closed her eyes, just as in the *conclamatio*, but he never mentions a last kiss and, more importantly, states, "We judged it unfitting to mark this death by plaintive protests and laments, since these are customarily employed to mourn the misery of the dying, or death as complete extinction. But she neither died in misery nor died altogether" (*Conf.* 9.29 [Boulding]). There does not appear to have been any repeated shouting of her name. Instead, Augustine writes, "Evodius took up the psalter and began to sing a psalm. All of us in the house joined in: *I will sing to you of your mercy and justice, O Lord*" (*Conf.* 9.31 [Boulding]). The scene around Monica's deathbed, at least as Augustine portrays it in his *Confessions*, differed significantly from the *conclamatio* scenes found on the sarcophagi of pagan children. Even Augustine, who seems to have granted more room for expressions of grief than did many of his peers, did not consider the *conclamatio* an appropriate rite of mourning for Christians.

This evidence from Christian leaders in the fourth and fifth centuries does much to explain the lack of *conclamatio* scenes on Christian children's sarcophagi. It would be too much to say that these leaders forbade Christians from any expression of grief at the death of a child. Augustine in particular allows for and even encourages the expression of natural grief. At the same time, both Jerome and John Chrysostom sought to limit expressions of grief by the Christians whom they addressed. Additionally, John Chrysostom's condemnation of the use of professional mourners and Augustine's portrayal of the rites performed upon his mother's death both indicate opposition to the *conclamatio* or at least to elements of its portrayal on pagan children's sarcophagi.

---

55. For Augustine's open attitude toward moderate expressions of grief, see especially his two sermons on 1 Thess 4:13, *Hom.* 172 and 173. See also Joseph Grabau, "The Limits of Grief in Augustine of Hippo's *Sermones* 172–173 and *Sermo* 396," *Vox Patrum* 78 (2021): 293–309.

Children as Adults, Adults as Children

Christian children's sarcophagi may not have adopted the use of the *conclamatio* scene from their pagan counterparts, but they did tend to follow the broader practice of frequently portraying children with adult attributes. This often took the form of portraying the child as an orator, as seen in figures 7.4–5 above, but additional examples abound among both pagan and Christian sarcophagi. The deceased child could be portrayed as a soldier (Rep. 1.663) or perhaps fulfill the role of the great hunter Meleager (*ASR* 12.6, no. 26). By comparison, depictions of children doing childish things such as playing are relatively rare.[56] This depiction of children as adults is often explained on the basis of the Roman understanding of childhood primarily as a period of preparation for being an adult.[57] Hence scenes of learning or portrayals of boys as orators testify to the lost hopes of parents that their sons would attain the standard of the ideal adult male in elite Roman society.[58] As Stine Birk writes, "The representations of the child as a small adult were a way for the bereaved relatives to show the world the potential virtues which had been lost when death took a child."[59] By depicting their children in the guise of adults, bereaved parents, whether pagan or Christian, expressed their grief over the loss of a future.

The portraits of the deceased are not the only area in which the sarcophagi of children resemble those of adults. In the case of Christian sarcophagi, children's sarcophagi feature the same repertoire of biblical scenes as do those of their adult coreligionists, as seen in the comparison of figures 7.3 and 7.4 above.[60] Where adaptations are made, they appear

---

56. For a Christian example, see Rep. 1.766. For the main pagan examples, see the list provided in Huskinson, *Roman Children's Sarcophagi*, 16.

57. Huskinson, *Roman Children's Sarcophagi*, 93; Stephanie Dimas, *Untersuchungen zur Themenwahl und Bildgestaltung auf römischen Kindersarkophagen* (Münster: Scriptorium, 1998), 205–6; Stine Birk, *Depicting the Dead: Self-Representation and Commemoration on Roman Sarcophagi with Portraits* (Aarhus: Aarhus University Press, 2013), 157–80.

58. Huskinson, *Roman Children's Sarcophagi*, 93. Huskinson also discusses the more subtle ways in which ideals of womanhood stand behind the portrayal of deceased girls on their sarcophagi.

59. Birk, *Depicting the Dead*, 180.

60. Pagan children's sarcophagi also employ many of the same scenes that are found on the sarcophagi of pagan adults, but, unlike Christian sarcophagi, there are

to be practical responses to the smaller size of the sarcophagi rather than conscious attempts to reflect the deceased's status as a child.[61] Thus the front of a child's frieze sarcophagus might include only two scenes, whereas an adult sarcophagus would likely feature more (e.g., Rep. 1.5, 12), or the number of magi presenting gifts to Jesus might be reduced to two from the typical three (e.g., Rep. 2.20, 32). Whether intentionally or not, this use of the same repertoire of biblical scenes with very little adaptation testifies to the hope that Christian parents held for their children. Many of the most popular scenes, such as the Jonah cycle, the sacrifice of Isaac, and the raising of Lazarus, recall God's saving power to bring about life on the other side of death. Just as these scenes were the same on adult and child sarcophagi, so Christian hope that God would ultimately deliver from death was the same for both children and adults.[62]

In addition to depicting children as adults, Christian sarcophagi also demonstrate the opposite practice of depicting certain adults in a childlike manner. Though some examples of this appear in figure 7.3, most notably in Christ's healing of the blind man in the lower register, it is especially striking in another Christian adult sarcophagus (fig. 7.6).[63] This frieze sarcophagus features the sacrifice of Isaac, Christ healing a blind man, Christ healing a paralytic, Christ multiplying the loaves, a

---

several scenes that appear exclusively or predominantly on pagan children's sarcophagi. These include the *conclamatio* scenes discussed above as well as depictions of children playing and cupids racing chariots.

61. Huskinson, "Early Christian Children's Sarcophagi," 117. Here Huskinson also notes that this is not exactly the case with pagan children's sarcophagi, which "had evolved different ways of acknowledging the child, whether by developing specially suitable compositions or by making some regular, if predictable, adaptations to existing 'adult' decorative themes."

62. This paper has not addressed Christian belief related to the fate of unbaptized children. Most of the children buried in Christian sarcophagi were no longer infants and therefore had probably already been baptized, either as infants or shortly before their deaths, making the issue largely moot with respect to this essay. On the development of infant baptism, see David F. Wright, *Infant Baptism in Historical Perspective: Collected Studies* (Milton Keynes: Paternoster, 2007). For more on Christian discussion of the fate of unbaptized infants, see Maria Doerfler's chapter, including the notes, on early Christian reflection on the Holy Innocents (Matt 2:16–18) in her *Jephthah's Daughter, Sarah's Son: The Death of Children in Late Antiquity* (Berkeley: University of California Press, 2020), 175–203.

63. For examples on Christian children's sarcophagi, see Rep. 1.9, 15, 20, 364, 662, 991; 2.31.

Fig. 7.6. Frieze sarcophagus with scenes from the Old and New Testaments, 300–330 CE. Marble, 1 ft 11 in x 6 ft 3 in. Vatican Museum, Rome. Photograph by Art Resource.

kneeling woman whose identity is uncertain, Adam and Eve, and Ezekiel's vision.[64] The appearance of Isaac as a child is unremarkable, but it draws attention to the figures of the blind man, the paralytic, the kneeling woman, and the people being raised in Ezekiel's vision, all of whom share Isaac's childlike appearance. This is typical of the depictions of recipients of healing on Christian sarcophagi.[65] It may mirror the broader Roman practice of symbolic sizing, in which relatively low-status figures appear child-sized.[66] On Christian sarcophagi, the small size of these healed figures relative to Jesus, the apostles, patriarchs, and prophets would speak to their relative status within the community of faith.[67]

The childlike portrayal of these characters also coheres remarkably well, however, with early Christian use of childhood as a metaphor for the Christian life. Already in the New Testament, this theme appears ubiquitously in the form of references to God as Father (e.g., Matt

---

64. See discussion in Deichmann, *Repertorium der christlich-antiken Sarkophage* 1:11. Possibilities for the identity of the kneeling woman include the woman with the flow of blood, faith personified, the Canaanite woman, and the blind widow healed by Peter (Acts Pet. 20).

65. Figures receiving baptism also typically appear as children. See Robin M. Jensen, *Living Water: Images, Symbols, and Settings of Early Christian Baptism* (Leiden: Brill, 2011), 43–83.

66. Janet Huskinson, "Constructing Childhood on Roman Funerary Memorials," *Constructions of Childhood in Ancient Greece and Italy*, ed. Ada Cohen and Jeremy B. Rutter, HespSup 41 (Princeton: American School of Classical Studies at Athens, 2007), 323–38.

67. Lee M. Jefferson, *Christ the Miracle Worker in Early Christian Art* (Minneapolis: Fortress, 2014), 93.

6:9, Luke 6:36, John 1:12, Rom 1:7, Eph 1:2, Heb 12:7).[68] Regardless of their age, Christians relate to God the Father as his children. This can take the form of asking from God in faith (Luke 11:9–13), expecting an inheritance (Rom 8:14–17), or accepting discipline from him (Heb 12:7). Childhood as a metaphor for the Christian life also appears prominently in Jesus's teaching that one must becoming like a child in order to enter the kingdom of God (Matt 18:1–5, 19:13–15, Mark 10:13–16, Luke 18:15–17). Addressing his adult disciples, Jesus says, "Unless you change and become like the children, you will certainly not enter into the kingdom of the heavens" (Matt 18:3), and, "Let the children come to me and do not hinder them, for the kingdom of the heavens belongs to such as these" (Matt 19:14). Here, children are held up as an ideal that adults ought to imitate, though, apart from Matthew's mention of humbling oneself in 18:4, the exact sense in which children embody this ideal remains undeveloped.[69]

In subsequent centuries, numerous Christian writers picked up the idea of childhood as a metaphor for the Christian life, but it appears especially frequently and positively in the writings of Clement of Alexandria (e.g., Irenaeus, *Epid.* 36; 96; Ambrose, *Off.* 21; Augustine, *Ep.* 140.9–11; *Hom.* 340A.1; *Ver. rel.* 49; John Chrysostom, *Hom. Matt.* 62.4; Jerome, *Comm. Matt.* 18.3–4).[70] In one example, Clement seeks to clarify the meaning of Matt 18:3–4, writing,

---

68. On the development of the idea of God as Father and its theological significance in the New Testament, see Reinhard Feldmeier and Hermann Spieckermann, *God of the Living: A Biblical Theology* (Waco, TX: Baylor University Press, 2011), 17–91.

69. For more on children in the gospels, see Judith M. Gundry-Volf, "The Least and the Greatest: Children in the New Testament," in *The Child in Christian Thought*, ed. Marcia J. Bunge (Grand Rapids: Eerdmans, 2001), 29–60, esp. 36–48. For children in the New Testament and early Christianity, see Marcia J. Bunge, Terence E. Fretheim, and Beverly Roberts Gaventa, eds., *The Child in the Bible* (Grand Rapids: Eerdmans, 2008); Cornelia B. Horn and John W. Martens, *"Let the Little Children Come to Me": Childhood and Children in Early Christianity* (Washington, DC: Catholic University of America Press, 2009); Margaret Y. MacDonald, *The Power of Children: The Construction of Christian Families in the Greco-Roman World* (Waco, TX: Baylor University Press, 2014).

70. See also the review of patristic sources in Odd M. Bakke, *When Children Became People: The Birth of Childhood in Early Christianity* (Minneapolis: Fortress, 2005), 56–109.

> He does not mean by "little child" one who has not yet reached the use of reason because of his immaturity, as some have thought. When He says: "Unless you become as these children, you shall not enter the kingdom of heaven," we must not foolishly mistake His meaning. We are not little ones in the sense that we roll on the floor or crawl on the ground as snakes do. That is to grovel in unreasoning desires with our whole body prostrate.... Really, then, children are those who look upon God alone as their father, who are simple, little ones, uncontaminated, who are lovers of the horn of the unicorn. (*Paed.* 1.5.16–17 [Wood])[71]

Here Clement elaborates the sense in which children provide an ideal toward which adults can strive. It is not the rolling and crawling of infants that Christians are to imitate, nor their inability to reason, but rather their simplicity, purity, and faith.[72] Furthermore, they are defined as children with respect to God, to whom they relate as children to their father. This text typifies the characterization of Christian discipleship in terms of childhood found throughout Clement's writings.[73]

When, therefore, recipients of Jesus's healing are portrayed as children on Christian sarcophagi, this echoes the broader use of childhood as a metaphor for the Christian life. Many of these characters were healed on the basis of their faith (e.g., Matt 9:2, 22, 29 and parallels), thus becoming paradigms for later Christians who hoped that their faith in Christ would lead to deliverance for them as well. Their requests for healing demonstrated honesty and simplicity, the same virtues Christian writers recognized in children (Matt 7:9–13, Luke 11:9–13; Clement, *Paed.* 1.5.17; John Chrysostom, *Hom. Matt.* 62.4). Their healings marked the beginning of new life for them, analogous to the resurrected life for which Christians hoped, which could be visually represented in a childlike appearance, just as baptized figures were also often portrayed as children in early Christian art.[74] As Christians identified themselves and their deceased coreligionists

---

71. Greek text available in PG 8:268–69.

72. This, at least, is the interpretation that Wood suggests for the difficult phrase οἱ κεράτων μονοκεράτων ἐρασταί. See Clement, *Christ the Educator*, trans. Simon P. Wood, FC 23 (Washington, DC: Catholic University of America Press, 1954), 18 n. 25.

73. For more on children as models in Clement, see Henny Fiskå Hägg, "Aspects of Childhood in Second- and Third-Century Christianity: The Case of Clement of Alexandria," in *Childhood in History: Perceptions of Children in the Ancient and Medieval Worlds*, ed. Reidar Aasgaard and Cornelia Horn (London: Routledge, 2017), 127–41.

74. Jensen, *Living Water*, 43–83, 166–67, 177.

with these figures, hoping that they would receive Christ's saving power just as the characters in these stories had, they recognized the childlikeness of these figures whom they hoped to emulate and even the childlikeness of resurrected life.

Conclusion

In both their omission of the *conclamatio* scene found on pagan children's sarcophagi and their close resemblance to Christian adults' sarcophagi, Christian children's sarcophagi attest to Christian hope in an afterlife. Such a hope transformed death, tempering its bitterness by making it only temporary and partial. The Christian leaders who prohibited excessive displays of grief, including those depicted in *conclamatio* scenes, may appear callous or at least tone-deaf to modern audiences, but they did so on the basis of belief that deceased Christians, including children, were alive with Christ.

This is not to say that Christian children's sarcophagi banished all signs of parental grief at the loss of a child. Most notably, the depiction of children in the guise of adults bears witness to the unfulfilled, and now unfulfillable, hopes that these parents held for the adult lives of their deceased children. At the same time, however, they adorned their children's sarcophagi with biblical scenes that testified to Christ's power over death and the hope that death would be followed by life. Many of those same scenes would be carved into their own sarcophagi, showing that they held the same hopes for themselves, believing that their children had preceded them into the life that they too would one day enjoy.[75]

Works Cited

Augustine. *The Confessions*. Translated by Maria Boulding. WSA. Edited by John E. Rotelle. Hyde Park, NY: New City, 1997.

Bakke, Odd M. *When Children Became People: The Birth of Childhood in Early Christianity*. Minneapolis: Fortress, 2005.

---

75. I wrote these words months before the tragic death of my friend and colleague Jeff Dale but now dedicate them to his family. May our Lord sustain you in this hope until you meet again.

Birk, Stine. *Depicting the Dead: Self-Representation and Commemoration on Roman Sarcophagi with Portraits*. Aarhus: Aarhus University Press, 2013.

Bradley, Keith R. "Wet-Nursing at Rome: A Study in Social Relations." Pages 201–29 in *The Family in Ancient Rome: New Perspectives*. Edited by Beryl Rawson. Ithaca, NY: Cornell University Press, 1986.

Bunge, Marcia J., Terence E. Fretheim, and Beverly Roberts Gaventa, eds. *The Child in the Bible*. Grand Rapids: Eerdmans, 2008.

Burkert, Walter. *Ancient Mystery Cults*. Cambridge: Harvard University Press, 1987.

Carroll, Maureen. "'No Part in Earthly Things': The Death, Burial, and Commemoration of Newborn Children and Infants in Roman Italy." Pages 41–63 in *Families in the Roman and Late Antique World*. Edited by Mary Harlow and Lena Larsson Lovén. London: Continuum, 2012.

Claassen, Jo-Marie. "Plutarch's Little Girl." *ActaCl* 47 (2004): 27–50.

Clement. *Christ the Educator*. Translated by Simon P. Wood. FC 23. Washington, DC: Catholic University of America Press, 1954.

Corbeill, Anthony. *Nature Embodied: Gesture in Ancient Rome*. Princeton: Princeton University Press, 2004.

Couzin, Robert. "The Christian Sarcophagus Population of Rome." *JRA* 27 (2014): 275–303.

———. "'Early' 'Christian' 'Art.'" Pages 380–92 in *The Routledge Handbook of Early Christian Art*. Edited by Robin M. Jensen and Mark D. Ellison. London: Routledge, 2018.

Cumont, Franz. *Recherches sur le symbolisme funéraire des Romains*. New York: Arno, 1975.

Dael, Peter C. J. van. Review of *De Haanscène in de Vroeg-Christelijke Kunst: Een Iconografische En Iconologische Analyse*, by Paulus G. J. Post. *VC* 45 (1991): 96–101.

Davies, Jon. *Death, Burial, and Rebirth in the Religions of Antiquity*. London: Routledge, 1999.

Deichmann, Friedrich Wilhelm, ed. *Repertorium der christlich-antiken Sarkophage*. 5 vols. Wiesbaden: Steiner, 1967–2018.

Dimas, Stephanie. *Untersuchungen zur Themenwahl und Bildgestaltung auf römischen Kindersarkophagen*. Münster: Scriptorium, 1998.

Doerfler, Maria E. *Jephthah's Daughter, Sarah's Son: The Death of Children in Late Antiquity*. Berkeley: University of California Press, 2020.

Dresken-Weiland, Jutta. "Christian Sarcophagi from Rome." Pages 39–55 in *The Routledge Handbook of Early Christian Art*. Edited by Robin M. Jensen and Mark D. Ellison. London: Routledge, 2018.

———. *Sarkophagbestattungen des 4.-6. Jahrhunderts im Westen des römischen Reiches*. Rome: Herder, 2003.

Feldmeier, Reinhard, and Hermann Spieckermann. *God of the Living: A Biblical Theology*. Waco, TX: Baylor University Press, 2011.

Golden, Mark. "Did the Ancients Care When Their Children Died?" *GR* 35 (1988): 152–63.

Grabau, Joseph. "The Limits of Grief in Augustine of Hippo's *Sermones* 172–173 and *Sermo* 396." *Vox Patrum* 78 (2021): 293–309.

Gundry-Volf, Judith M. "The Least and the Greatest: Children in the New Testament." Pages 29–60 in *The Child in Christian Thought*. Edited by Marcia J. Bunge. Grand Rapids: Eerdmans, 2001.

Hägg, Henny Fiskå. "Aspects of Childhood in Second- and Third-Century Christianity: The Case of Clement of Alexandria." Pages 127–41 in *Childhood in History: Perceptions of Children in the Ancient and Medieval Worlds*. Edited by Reidar Aasgaard and Cornelia Horn. London: Routledge, 2017.

Harley, Felicity. "Visual Apocrypha: The Case of Mary and the Magi in Early Christian Rome." Pages 383–410 in *Apocryphal and Esoteric Sources in the Development of Christianity and Judaism*. Edited by Igor Dorfmann-Lazarev. Leiden: Brill, 2021.

Hope, Valerie M. *Death in Ancient Rome: A Sourcebook*. London: Routledge, 2007.

———. *Roman Death: Dying and the Dead in Ancient Rome*. London: Continuum, 2009.

Horn, Cornelia B., and John W. Martens. *"Let the Little Children Come to Me": Childhood and Children in Early Christianity*. Washington, DC: Catholic University of America Press, 2009.

Huskinson, Janet. "Constructing Childhood on Roman Funerary Memorials." Pages 323–38 in *Constructions of Childhood in Ancient Greece and Italy*. Edited by Ada Cohen and Jeremy B. Rutter. HespSup 41. Princeton: American School of Classical Studies at Athens, 2007.

———. "The Decoration of Early Christian Children's Sarcophagi." StPatr 24 (1993): 114–18.

———. *Roman Children's Sarcophagi: Their Decoration and Its Social Significance*. Oxford: Clarendon, 1996.

Jefferson, Lee M. *Christ the Miracle Worker in Early Christian Art*. Minneapolis: Fortress, 2014.

Jensen, Robin M. "Early Christian Images and Exegesis." Pages 65–85 in *Picturing the Bible: The Earliest Christian Art*. Edited by Jeffrey Spier. New Haven: Yale University Press, 2007.

———. *Living Water: Images, Symbols, and Settings of Early Christian Baptism*. Leiden: Brill, 2011.

———. "The Offering of Isaac in Jewish and Christian Tradition: Image and Text." *BibInt* 2 (1994): 85–110.

King, Margaret. "Commemoration of Infants on Roman Funerary Inscriptions." Pages 117–54 in *The Epigraphy of Death: Studies in the History and Society of Greece and Rome*. Edited by Graham J. Oliver. Liverpool: Liverpool University Press, 2000.

Knott, Betty I. "The Christian 'Special Language' in the Inscriptions." *VC* 10.2 (1956): 65–79.

Koch, Guntram. *Frühchristliche Sarkophage*. HdA. Munich: Beck, 2000.

Koch, Guntram, and Hellmut Sichtermann. *Römische Sarkophage*. HdA. Munich: Beck, 1982.

Konstan, David. "The Grieving Self: Reflections on Lucian's *On Mourning* and the Consolatory Tradition." Pages 139–52 in *Greek and Roman Consolations: Eight Studies of a Tradition and Its Afterlife*. Edited by Han Baltussen. Swansea: Classical Press of Wales, 2013.

Lattimore, Richmond. *Themes in Greek and Latin Epitaphs*. Urbana: University of Illinois Press, 1962.

MacDonald, Margaret Y. *The Power of Children: The Construction of Christian Families in the Greco-Roman World*. Waco, TX: Baylor University Press, 2014.

Parkin, Tim. "The Demography of Infancy and Early Childhood in the Ancient World." Pages 40–61 in *The Oxford Handbook of Childhood and Education in the Classical World*. Edited by Judith Evan Grubbs, Tim Parkin, and Roslynne Bell. Oxford: Oxford University Press, 2013.

Post, Paulus Gijsbertus Johannes. *De haanscène in de vroeg-christelijke kunst: een iconografische en iconologische analyse*. Voerendaal: Schrijen-Lippertz, 1984.

Rawson, Beryl. *Children and Childhood in Roman Italy*. Oxford: Oxford University Press, 2003.

Rebillard, Éric. *The Care of the Dead in Late Antiquity*. Ithaca, NY: Cornell University Press, 2010.

Richlin, Amy. "Emotional Work: Lamenting the Roman Dead." Pages 229–48 in *Essays in Honor of Gordon Williams: Twenty-Five Years at Yale*. Edited by Elizabeth Ivory Tylawsky and Charles Gray Weiss. New Haven: Schwab, 2001.

Russell, Ben. "The Sarcophagus Trade." Pages 256–310 in *The Economics of the Roman Stone Trade*. Oxford: Oxford University Press, 2013.

Siragan Arlen, Jesse. "'Let Us Mourn Continuously': John Chrysostom and the Early Christian Transformation of Mourning." StPatr 83 (2017): 289–312.

Studer-Karlen, Manuela. *Verstorbenendarstellungen auf frühchristlichen Sarkophagen*. Turnhout: Brepols, 2012.

Toynbee, Jocelyn M. C. *Death and Burial in the Roman World*. Ithaca, NY: Cornell University Press, 1971.

Waldner, Katherina, Richard Gordon, and Wolfgang Spickermann, eds. *Burial Rituals, Ideas of Afterlife, and the Individual in the Hellenistic World and the Roman Empire*. Stuttgart: Steiner, 2016.

Walker, Susan. *Catalogue of Roman Sarcophagi in the British Museum*. London: British Museum Publications, 1990.

Wang, Xueying. "John Chrysostom on the Premature Death of Children and Parental Grief." *JECS* 27 (2019): 443–63.

Wright, David F. *Infant Baptism in Historical Perspective: Collected Studies*. Milton Keynes: Paternoster, 2007.

Reimagining the Silver Casket of San Nazaro

Zen Hess

In 1578, the silver casket of San Nazaro was discovered functioning as a reliquary beneath the high altar of Ambrose's Basilica Apostolorum. In this essay I ask whether the silver casket was *always* a reliquary (fig. 8.1). Based on the condition of the casket and its iconography, I argue that it was not. Instead, I propose that the silver casket served for some time as a eucharistic vessel, one that was later repurposed for housing relics. Fur-

Fig. 8.1. Silver casket of San Nazaro, mid- to late fourth century CE. Silver with gilding, 20.5 x 20.5 x 20.6 cm. Diocesan Museum of Milan. Photograph by Archivio fotografico Museo Diocesano.

ther, I suggest that a letter written by Athanasius that urges Christians to participate in the eucharistic feast served as a literary inspiration for the casket's iconographic theme.

The Silver Casket of San Nazaro: A Brief Introduction

The silver casket of San Nazaro was created in the fourth century, likely in Rome or Milan.[1] At some unknown time, the casket was buried beneath the high altar of the Basilica Apostolorum. The Basilica Apostolorum (now San Nazaro Maggiore) was completed under the supervision of Ambrose of Milan in 382 and dedicated to the apostles. After being destroyed in the eleventh century, the basilica was rebuilt in the sixteenth. During this process Carlo Borromeo had the area beneath the original high altar excavated, leading to the first discovery of the silver casket.[2] The casket was found among reliquaries and contained a small, round reliquary bearing pieces of fabric traditionally believed to belong to some of the apostles. The smaller reliquary is inscribed with the phrase DEDALIA VIVAS IN CHRISTO ("Dedalia, may you live in Christ"). Apparently, Manlia Dedalia, an aristocratic woman who was socially connected with Ambrose himself, donated this personal reliquary for the church's use.[3] Unfortunately, the silver casket bears no such inscription to help us determine who commissioned it or its location of manufacture.

---

1. For a more comprehensive bibliography up to 2009, see Elisabetta Gagetti, "Bibliografia Storica. La Fortuna Nei Secoli di un Oggetto Tra Devozione e Arte," in *Il Tesoro di San Nazaro: Antichi Argenti Liturgici della Basilica di San Nazaro al Museo Diocesano di Milano*, ed. Gemma Sena Chiesa (Milan: Silvana, 2009), 63–71. Throughout the twentieth century, scholars vigorously debated the dating of this object. C. R. Morey wrote an essay that argued the silver casket of San Navaro was not from the early Christian period but rather the work of a Renaissance artist attempting to practice classical skills. Theories like Morey's persisted until the turn of the century, when more technical studies enabled us to date the object quite firmly to the mid-fourth century. For an overview of the dating debate and further bibliography, see Gemma Sena Chiesa and Fabrizio Slavazzi, "La capsella argentea di San Nazaro. Primi risultati di una nuova indagine," *AT* 7 (2000): 192–93.

2. Ruth E. Leader-Newby, *Silver and Society in Late Antiquity: Functions and Meanings of Silver Plate in the Fourth to Seventh Centuries* (Burlington, VT: Ashgate, 2003), 121.

3. "Treasure of Saint Nazarus," Chiostri Di Sant'Eustorgio, https://tinyurl.com/SBL4830w. For more on the smaller reliquary and Manlia Dedalia, see Elisabetta Gagetti, "La Teca Di Manlia Dedalia," in Sena Chiesa, *Il Tesoro Di San Nazaro*, 73–95.

Borromeo then had the casket interred beneath the reconstructed basilica's high altar, which is where it was discovered once more, this time in the late nineteenth century. The casket became an object of great interest in the early twentieth century after, in 1898, a facsimile of it appeared in Turin at an art exhibition, accompanied with the provocative (but unproven) description: "facsimile of the silver box in which Pope Damasus sent to St. Ambrose the relics of the Holy Apostles, which were later deposited in the sarcophagus of S. Nazaro."[4] The casket is now on display at the Carlo Maria Martini Diocesan Museum.

All four sides and the lid of this rather small box (20.5 x 20.5 x 20.6 cm) are expertly decorated with Christian imagery.[5] The general scenes depicted on the casket are more or less agreed on:[6]

- the lid: Jesus seated between twelve disciples with baskets of bread and water basins (fig. 8.2)[7]
- side A: Mary seated with child with two figures offering gifts (fig. 8.3)
- side B: the judgment of Solomon (fig. 8.4)
- side C: the judgment of Joseph or the judgment of Daniel (fig. 8.5)
- side D: the three youths in the fiery furnace (fig. 8.6)

The iconography of the casket is notable for several reasons. First, both the judgment of Solomon and the judgment of Joseph (or Daniel, for that

---

4. Charles R. Morey, "The Silver Casket of San Nazaro in Milan," *AJA* 23 (1919): 101.

5. For a brief and accessible introduction to the iconography (as well as other issues and a small bibliography), see Gemma Sena Chiesa, "Reliquary with Old and New Testament Scenes," in *Picturing the Bible: The Earliest Christian Art*, ed. Jeffrey Spier (New Haven: Yale University Press, 2007), 259–64.

6. The only side about which there is significant disagreement regarding the scene it depicts is side C, which is why I have included both options in the description above. For more detailed overview of the scenes and bibliography, see Sena Chiesa and Slavazzi, "La capsella," 188–90. Most scholars agree that side D depicts the three youths, though some claim it is the magi. See Verena Alborino, *Das Silberkästchen von San Nazaro in Mailand*, HabD 13 (Bonn: Habelt, 1981), 94.

7. Koch misrepresents the casket, indicating that there are only eleven disciples. The mistake is quite understandable, since the twelfth figure (in the upper left-hand corner) is so faintly etched that is nearly undetectable in photographs. See Guntram Koch, "Reliquary: Silver," in *The Eerdmans Encyclopedia of Early Christian Art and Archaeology*, ed. Paul Corby Finney (Grand Rapids: Eerdmans, 2017), 2:409–11.

matter) are not common scenes in early Christian art. Second, even the more common scenes are presented in peculiar ways. As Ruth Leader-Newby points out, the scene of Jesus with the apostles is most like Christ the philosopher teaching, but it is unique for its inclusion of the breadbaskets and wine jars, which Leader-Newby assumes is a "eucharistic allusion."[8] The scene of Mary with the Christ child is unique, Leader-Newby continues, because the figures who bring gifts to Mary and the child do not follow earlier conventions for the magi or the shepherds. This leads to another notable feature of the iconography. As Gemma Sena Chiesa observes, every scene on the casket was composed using imperial styles and motifs.[9] For this reason, the iconographic style is a very early example of what would become Theodosian style. Finally, the iconography is notable because, as is often noted, the iconographic program is quite unclear, leaving interpreters often to suggest that the imagery is meant to convey a general theological theme such as power or salvation.

In all, the silver casket of San Nazaro is an important piece of early Christian art. It encapsulates an important shift in artistic style while also offering unique expressions of common scenes and significant examples of rarer scenes. The likelihood of the casket coming from an imperial workshop and employing imperial themes also represents a significant visualization of the increasing integration of the political with the ecclesial. The debates about dating, style, and iconography have inspired a significant body of literature on this piece. That it is a reliquary, however, has largely been assumed.

Reasons for Rethinking the Original Function of the Silver Casket

Since its rediscovery in 1894, the silver casket has been cited as a textbook example of early silver reliquaries. Of course, it *was* discovered among reliquaries and contained a reliquary with relics itself. It *is* a reliquary. But this does not necessitate that it was *always* a reliquary. Commenting on ivory reliquaries, Guntram Koch writes, "It is clear that ivory boxes carved in late antiquity were used as reliquaries in a later secondary context, but how they were used in their original contexts is largely a matter

---

8. Leader-Newby, *Silver and Society*, 104; similarly, Sena Chiesa and Slavazzi, "La capsella," 197.

9. Sena Chiesa, "Reliquary." Along with the imperial style, it is worth commenting on the expert quality of the work itself, especially the gilding.

for speculation."[10] This same insight bears on silver boxes from the same period. Unless it is unmistakably clear that it was made to be a reliquary, it may just as well have been used as something else first. The casket does not have any feature that confirms its original function as a reliquary. Not only does the casket not have anything unmistakably confirming that it was made to be a reliquary, but observation of the casket's components encourages some doubt.

While earlier studies remarked on unusual wear and tear for a casket made to serve as a reliquary in the Basilica Apostolorum, Lucia Miazzo's technical study indicates that the apparent damage is due more to age and material than to actual wear and tear.[11] The casket is in remarkable shape. Nonetheless, it appears that the casket was modified at some point after its initial creation. Drawing on Miazzo's analysis, Sena Chiesa remarks that the cross beneath the lid is a later addition and that the closing system also appears to have been added at some other point.[12] These interventions, Sena Chiesa hypothesizes, could well have come when the casket was transitioned from private devotional use to its function as a reliquary in the Basilica Apostolorum.[13]

---

10. Koch, "Reliquary: Silver," 2:409.

11. In 1999, Gemma Sena Chiesa wrote, "The heavy wear on the box cannot be explained by the brief use that the piece would have had if it had been specifically created (in Milan or Rome) to contain the relics destined for the Basilica Apostolorum" (Chiesa and Slavazzi, "La capsella," 194, my trans.). A decade later, Sena Chiesa's mind changed due to Miazzio's study. Sena Chiesa said in 2009, "For her part, Lucia Miazzo has demonstrated that the box—contrary to what everyone has suggested up to now—has no traces of wear, while the small round pyx does" (Sena Chiesa, *Il Tesoro Di San Nazaro*, 47, my trans.). For the technical analysis of the casket's condition, see Lucia Miazzo, "Indagini Tecniche e Conservative Sul Tesoro Di San Nazaro," in Sena Chiesa, *Il Tesoro Di San Nazaro*, 133–53.

12. Sena Chiesa, *Il Tesoro Di San Nazaro*, 30.

13. Sena Chiesa writes, "Concerning the problems posed by the addition of the cross and the possibility of an 'adaptation' after the object's closing mechanism was created, perhaps added precisely at the moment of the insertion of the sacred relics, I refer once again to the observations of Fabrizio Slavazzi and Lucia Miazzo in this volume. It is possible that the box was, like other containers, made for personal devotional use—as we will probably see in a court setting—and was only later used by Ambrose in his new basilica for a solemn deposition of the sacred cloth considered relics of the apostles" (Sena Chiesa, *Il Tesoro Di San Nazaro*, 30, my trans.).

Turning to a more comparative analysis, the silver casket differs from other silver reliquaries in its design.[14] In comparison to the fourteen other reliquaries surveyed by Koch, one of the most obvious differences is that the silver casket is twice the size of the next largest silver reliquary and four times larger than several others. Reliquaries in this period often held fabrics or small bones, such as fingers.[15] While many reliquaries appear sized to fit the object they were created to hold, the silver casket is oversized. The size could be meant to signify the importance of the object, especially if the intended contents were apostolic remains. However, the size could also indicate that the casket was made to contain something more voluminous than were most relics, especially contact relics.

The secondary interventions and unusual size of the casket do not rule out the possibility that it was made to be a reliquary. These observations, however, compel us to reconsider the original function of the casket. Is there another function that squares with the casket's condition and size, while accounting for its unique eucharistic imagery?

The Silver Casket of San Nazaro as a Eucharistic Vessel

The iconography is the best place to begin imagining an alternative original function. On the lid scene, Jesus is seated in the center with twelve disciples surrounding him, divided into six groups on either side. Peter and Paul stand at the front of each group. This scene is somewhat common in early Christian art, though other silver reliquaries generally depict only Peter and Paul.[16] What is especially peculiar about the scene on the silver casket of San Nazaro, as mentioned earlier, is that it includes five baskets of bread and six wine jars. These symbols are foregrounded at the bottom of the scene, and they are the only inanimate objects that the artist depicts independent of a human figure.[17] Echoing the multiplication mir-

---

14. See Koch, "Reliquary: Silver." The fifteen silver reliquaries overviewed in Koch's entry are not an exhaustive list but give a representative sample of the extant evidence.

15. Indeed, the contents of the casket included bits of fabric thought to be associated with the apostles (Sena Chiesa and Slavazzi, "La capsella," 191). For a recent engagement on the rise of relic veneration, see Robert Wiśniewski, *The Beginnings of the Cult of Relics* (Oxford: Oxford University Press, 2019).

16. See the following caskets: Chersonesos, Jabalkovo, Nea Herakleia, Novalia on Pag in Croatia. The Ballana casket has seven disciples.

17. So, in Solomon's judgment scene, there are shields and swords, but they are being held by human figures.

acles (John 6) and the miracle at Cana (John 2), these two miracle scenes together represent the Eucharist.[18] It appears that, in this image, Christ is

Fig. 8.2. Silver casket of San Nazaro, Christ with apostles, mid- to late fourth century CE. Silver with gilding. Diocesan Museum of Milan. Photograph by Archivio fotografico Museo Diocesano.

---

18. Ulrich Kuder challenges earlier arguments that rejected a eucharistic interpretation of depictions of the multiplication of loaves and fishes or the wedding at Cana in early Christian art. (Morey echoes that claim in his 1919 essay, suggesting the silver casket of San Navaro is eucharistic but that such a meaning cannot be claimed for earlier pieces; see Morey, "Silver Casket of San Navaro," 108). Kuder notes that already in the NT, the stories in John 2 and 6 have eucharistic connections. He then argues that several other instances of both scenes independently represent the Eucharist. See

presented as a teacher with imagery that suggests the topic about which he is teaching.[19]

The eucharistic image potentially intimates an alternative original function for the casket: holding the bread of Communion. Boxes for keeping the consecrated host were already in use in the third century. In the mid-fourth century, these boxes functioned in various contexts, both at home and in ecclesiastical settings.

In the third century, Cyprian tells the following story: "And when a certain woman tried with unclean hands to open her box (*arcana*), in which was the holy [body] of the Lord, thereupon she was deterred by rising fire from daring to touch it" (Deferrari). In this story, Cyprian describes a woman participating in home Communion, a common practice in the West through to the fifth century and in the East even longer.[20] Around the time the silver casket was made, Basil wrote, "It is good and beneficial to communicate every day, and to partake of the holy body and blood of Christ" (*Ep.* 93 [*NPNF* 2/8:179]). He goes on to acknowledge that in Alexandria and Egypt, "each one of the laity, for the most part, keeps the communion at his house." Likewise, in one letter, Jerome acknowledges daily Communion in "the churches of Rome and Spain" and, in another letter, urges people receiving Communion at home to practice the ritual with the same

---

Ulrich Kuder, "Die Eucharistie in Bildwerken vom frühen 3. bis zum 7. Jahrhundert," in *The Eucharist: Its Origins and Contexts* (Tübingen: Mohr Siebeck, 2017), 2:1327–31.

19. Quite like Morey, "Silver Casket of San Nazaro," 108. Another interpretation is more provocative, though less likely. The object sitting on Christ's lap, on which he rests his hand, does not fit the standard scroll or open codex of Jesus as teacher/philosopher. Rather, the small square object appears as though it could be a box-like casket. It is approximately analogous in scaled size and appears to have beveled edges like the casket. If Christ here holds a eucharistic box, this scene could provide a christological interpretation of the box's function. That is, the image reminds the person who receives Communion from this box that it is Christ who feeds them. This is not unlike the sixth-century silver Stuma and Riha patens, used to distribute Communion, which depict Christ distributing Communion to the disciples. The difficulty with this reading is that Christ's hand gesture follows the standard presentation of someone speaking, not distributing.

20. For more on home Communion and eulogia bread, see Nathan Mitchell, OSB, *Cult and Controversy: The Worship of the Eucharist outside Mass* (Collegeville, MN: Liturgical Press, 1990), 10–43; Robert Taft Jr., "Home-Communion in the Late Antique East," in *Ars Liturgiae: Worship, Aesthetics, and Praxis; Essays in Honor of Nathan D. Mitchell*, ed. Clare Veronica Johnson and Nathan Mitchell (Chicago: Liturgy Training, 2003), 1–25; Godefridus J. C. Snoek, *Medieval Piety from Relics to the Eucharist: A Process of Mutual Interaction*, SHCT 63 (New York: Brill, 1995), 69–81.

mind for holiness they have when receiving in congregational worship (*Ep.* 71, 48). Cyprian's story makes clear that the consecrated host reserved for home Communion was kept in a special box. It is reasonable to assume that those practicing home Communion in the fourth century would have kept their eucharistic bread in a similar kind of vessel.

At the conclusion of worship, congregants would receive a portion of the consecrated bread to take home for daily Communion. It seems that the typical practice was to receive daily Communion in the morning before consuming any food. In her survey of ancient Christian private religious rituals, Kimberly Bowes shows that private chapels were common in urban and rural homes alike, not least among aristocratic Christians in northern Italy (such as, say, Manlia Dedalia, who gifted her small, personalized reliquary to Ambrose's church in Milan).[21] Bowes includes a brief comment on the kinds of boxes possibly used to house reserved Communion:

> In aristocratic homes, the containers used to guard the bread ... may have taken on a newly elaborate form reflective of the eucharist's perceived power: some of the fourth- through sixth-century ivory *pyxides* manufactured in Rome may have been used for the purpose.... These diminutive containers would have been too small to hold the communion bread for a large community mass, yet frequent depiction of scenes like Multiplication of the Loaves and Fishes or the Wedding at Cana strongly point to eucharistic use.[22]

Bowes's comment applies equally well to the silver casket. The casket would have been well suited to serve as a eucharistic box for home Communion. Not only does this kind of function resonate with the unique eucharistic imagery included on the lid's image, but the need to hold enough bread for the family for a week might explain the casket's size in comparison to many other silver reliquaries.[23] It is not at all difficult to imagine a well-to-

---

21. Kimberly Diane Bowes, *Private Worship, Public Values, and Religious Change in Late Antiquity* (Cambridge: Cambridge University Press, 2008). Her review of estate and villa churches in the countryside is especially illuminating. It is a reminder that the church was not always so fully institutionalized, such that private estates might have rather complex accommodations for domestic worship and devotions.

22. Bowes, *Private Worship, Public Values*, 77. Bowes also mentions that people kept Communion at home for apotropaic and curative purposes as well (76–78).

23. McLachlan discusses the size of ivory pyxes in relation to communion. The largest ivory pyxis she notes is the great Berlin pyxis, which is 14.6 cm in diameter,

do figure from Ambrose's church commissioning the casket for personal use in their private chapel.

A second context for eucharistic vessels would be fitting for the casket. Beginning in the second century, it was custom to bring the Eucharist to those who could not be present for worship, especially the sick.[24] "From this practice," writes Joanne M. Pierce, "the small portable *arca*, *pyx*, or *theca* ('box') developed."[25] Though the textual evidence is rather slim, it appears that the eucharistic box would hold the bread in a sacristy within the church, but that deacons would take the box to those in need.[26] Given the lack of wear and tear on the casket, it is unlikely that the casket was used as a transport vessel. However, it would have served very well as a vessel for storing bread in the sacristy, which would be retrieved for distribution throughout the week.

Home Communion and Communion taken to the sick provide two fourth-century practices for which a box like the silver casket would have been very useful. These eucharistic practices were already firmly established in the third century, with good evidence for their ongoing practice in the fourth. The same is not true for relic veneration, which was in its first generation of popular practice in the mid- or even late fourth century.[27] And while Ambrose was an ambitious advocate for relic veneration, he was also concerned with increasing the laity's participation in eucharistic devotion. In a teaching on the sacraments, Ambrose urges

---

making it even smaller than the silver casket of San Navaro. See McLachlan, "Liturgical Vessels and Implements," in *The Liturgy of the Medieval Church*, ed. Thomas J. Heffernan and E. Ann Matter (Kalamazoo, MI: Western Michigan University Press, 2001), 396.

24. A similar practice involved taking blessed but not consecrated bread to those who were spiritually unable to receive Communion. See George Galavaris, *Bread and the Liturgy* (Madison: University of Wisconsin Press, 1970), 109–66.

25. Joanne M. Pierce, "Vestments and Objects," in *The Oxford History of Christian Worship*, ed. Geoffrey Wainwright and Karen B. Westerfield Tucker (Oxford: Oxford University Press, 2006), 852.

26. Frank L. Cross, "Reservation," in *The Oxford Dictionary of the Christian Church*, ed. Elizabeth A. Livingstone (Oxford: Oxford University Press, 2009), 1155–56; Stephen J. P. van Dijk and Hazelden Walker, *The Myth of the Aumbry: Notes on Medieval Reservation Practice and Eucharistic Devotion* (London: Burns & Oates, 1957), 25–27.

27. Wiśniewski, *Beginnings of the Cult of Relics*, 8–26.

his readers to receive Communion daily (*Sacr.* 4.24–25).[28] We are certain that one of his congregants took his plea to heart. Augustine describes his mother, Monica, as having one wish before her death in 387: "She desired only to be remembered at your altar where she had served you with never a day's absence. From that altar, as she knew, the holy Victim is made available to us, he through whom the record of debt that stood against us was annulled" (*Conf.* 9.13.36).[29] Monica's daily service, of course, would have taken place in Milan.[30] All of this to say that there is very good reason to think that the silver casket—more than likely made in Rome or Milan, where daily Communion practices were promoted by the clergy and enacted by the laity in the fourth century—started its life not as a reliquary but as a eucharistic vessel.

A Eucharistic Textual Background: Athanasius's *Festal Letter* 10

Up to this point, we have focused on the lid scene and its eucharistic imagery. But if we want to argue that the box was created to be a eucharistic vessel, how do we account for the other four scenes, which do not have any obvious relevance to celebrating the Eucharist? Or do the other images not relate to the function in the same way the lid does? The iconographic program has remained enigmatic since the casket's discovery. Erik Thunø sums up my first impression of the casket's imagery when he suggests that the scenes appear, at first glance, randomly chosen.[31] But, as Thunø indicates, they are surely not random. In this section, I will argue that the scenes of the silver casket serve to visualize an important letter sent from Athanasius to his churches, urging them to participate in the eucharistic celebration on Easter day.

---

28. Specifically, from 4.25, "Si quotidianus est panis, cur post annum illum sumis, quemadmodum Graeci in Oriente facere consuerunt. Accipe quotidie, quod quotidie tibi prosit. Sic vive, ut quotidie merearis accipere."

29. Augustine, *The Confessions*, trans. Maria Boulding (New York: Vintage Books, 1998), 195. Unless otherwise noted, translations follow Boulding's work.

30. Though, Bowes's survey of private devotions and estate villas raises questions about whether the "altar" we imagine Monica serving at daily is in one of the official church buildings or a more domestic setting.

31. Erik Thunø, "Reliquaries and the Cult of Relics in Late Antiquity," in *The Routledge Handbook of Early Christian Art*, ed. Robin M. Jensen and Mark D. Ellison (London: Routledge, 2018), 151.

For most years during his tenure as bishop of Alexandria (328–373), Athanasius wrote a letter to the Egyptian churches under his care, encouraging them to gather for the Easter feast.[32] *Festal Letter* 10 is one of these letters, sent for Easter 338. In this relatively brief letter, there are textual parallels to all five scenes depicted on the silver casket.[33] In addition to Athanasius's popularity in the fourth century, this particular Athanasian letter is noteworthy because of its style and its content. Moreover, the letter is not very long, and its tone is warm, pastoral, even beautiful.[34] One can imagine that a beautiful and important letter from a profoundly important figure could grip someone's imagination, providing an inspiration for the imagery of a work of art.

Though the letter's exact date and location of writing are debated, the year is not.[35] Athanasius wrote this letter in a turbulent season of his career. In 335, Athanasius was exiled from Alexandria because of accusations brought forward by Arian leaders, though he remained bishop in his absence. In the fall of 337, after the death of Constantine, Athanasius

---

32. The festal letters of Alexandrian bishops are an area of growing interest, especially Athanasius's festal letters. Generally, see Doru Costache, Philip Kariatlis, and Mario Baghos, eds., *Alexandrian Legacy: A Critical Appraisal* (Newcastle upon Tyne: Cambridge Scholars, 2015), 164–79. For Athanasius specifically, see Johan Leemans, "Thirteen Years of Athanasius Research (1985–1998). A Survey and Bibliography," *SacEr* 39 (2000): 163–67; Rudolf Lorenz, *Der zehnte Osterfestbrief des Athanasius von Alexandrien: Text, Übersetzung, Erläuterungen* (Berlin: de Gruyter, 1986); Alberto Camplani, *Lettere Festali: Atanasio Di Alessandria. Indice Delle Lettere Festali*, LCPM 34 (Milan: Paoline, 2003); Timothy David Barnes, *Athanasius and Constantius: Theology and Politics in the Constantinian Empire* (Cambridge: Harvard University Press, 1993), 183–91; Camplani, "Festal Letters," in *Encyclopedia of Ancient Christianity* (Downers Grove, IL: InterVarsity Press, 2014), 2:230–33.

33. So long as side C is the judgment of Joseph rather than the judgment of Daniel. Side C *could* be Daniel judging the elders who wronged Susanna (Dan 13). However, scenes of Daniel judging the elders on early sarcophagi typically include Susanna in the image. She does not appear among the other figures here. Also, the depiction on the casket is strikingly comparable to the sixth-century throne of Maximianus, which includes the same scene but in a Joseph-narrative cycle. The similarity may indicate the development of a typical way of depicting Joseph and his brothers, perhaps beginning in the fourth century and continuing into the sixth.

34. "The Tenth Festal Letter of Athanasius deserves the attention of historians because of the information it contains and its warm personal tone as well as because of its intellectual content" (Lorenz, *Der zehnte Osterfestbrief*, 1, my trans.).

35. I agree with Barnes, who argues that Athanasius wrote the entire letter from Alexandria (*Athanasius and Constantius*, 33–35).

returned to Alexandria.[36] Sometime between the end of his exile in Gaul and the spring of 338, Athanasius wrote *Festal Letter* 10. Upon his return to Alexandria in late 337, the same opponents who had Athanasius exiled in 335 may have already been taking steps to depose him and install a new bishop sympathetic to the Arian constituency in Alexandria. Although Athanasius quickly earned a reputation as one who "laughs at danger," the threat of another separation, of suffering for himself and for his congregations, certainly lingered as he wrote this letter, as the content of the letter reveals.[37] Indeed, he was forced to flee Alexandria again only a year later, in 339, and this time he was fully deposed. He fled immediately to Rome, where he found refuge and support with Pope Julius.[38]

Festal Letter 10 is significant both among the Athanasian festal letters and within Athanasius's literary corpus more generally. Among his festal letters, *Festal Letter* 10 stands out as the longest letter.[39] It is also of theological significance, because it is the "earliest open refutation of Arianism from the pen of Athanasius, which has been little appreciated until now."[40] No doubt his exile in Gaul and the looming threat of another emboldened him to write explicitly against the Arians. Given Athanasius's lifelong and celebrated struggle for what would become orthodox Christology, ratified at the first Council of Constantinople in 381 and enforced by Theodosius thereafter, this letter is highly significant, both for Athanasius's biography and for the church's theological history.

The letter's structure is not complicated.[41] It is outlined as follows:

---

36. For details about this period, see Barnes, *Athanasius and Constantius*, 34–46.

37. This is how Emperor Constantius describes Athanasius in 355 in a discourse with Pope Liberius. See Hugo Rahner, *Church and State in Early Christianity* (San Francisco: Ignatius, 1992), 86.

38. Pope Julius warmly received Athanasius, even suggesting Athanasius came to Rome in response to his personal invitation. For introductory and primary source material on Julius's advocacy for Athanasius from this period and slightly later, see Glen L. Thompson, *The Correspondence of Pope Julius I* (Washington, DC: Catholic University of America Press, 2015).

39. David M. Gwynn, *Athanasius of Alexandria: Bishop, Theologian, Ascetic, Father*, CTC (Oxford: Oxford University Press, 2012), 31.

40. Lorenz, *Der zehnte Osterfestbrief*, 82. Gwynn notes that this is the only "detailed theological attack on 'Arianism' to be found anywhere in his *Festal Letters*" (*Athanasius of Alexandria*, 31).

41. Festal letters usually followed a customary structure. This letter both follows

1. Introduction (*Ep. fest.* 10:1–2): The significance of the Easter Feast and Christ as the "Giver of the Feast," who unites believers both to God and to one another.
2. Framing persecution positively (*Ep. fest.* 10.3–4): Persecution increases our thankfulness for God's presence; Christ meets us in persecution and enables each of us to live faithfully in ways fitting to our capacity.
3. Responding to persecution philanthropically (*Ep. fest.* 10.4–8): Christ wisely enables us to meet misanthropy with philanthropy, just as Christ himself did; points to ways that prophets hardships indicated God's nearness.
4. Defining and resisting the Arian enemies (*Ep. fest.* 10.9–11): The problem of Arianism, its theology and its schismatic effect; Christ is the answer and will save the church; the church needs, then, to praise, especially through the Easter Feast.
5. Conclusion (*Ep. fest.* 10.12).

By way of summary, the letter appears to have three primary concerns. First, Athanasius is concerned to articulate the significance of the Easter Feast, and he embeds its significance within his theology of the Eucharist. Celebrating Eucharist on Easter serves to *unify* the church, wherever they may be. The unifying effect of Eucharist is the foil to the schismatic Arians, whom Athanasius addresses at the end of the letter. Second, Athanasius is concerned to comfort his congregants pastorally during a trying season but also to prepare them to respond faithfully to persecution. Athanasius employs biblical stories and sayings to underscore the presence and protection of God and to inspire faithful living. Third, Athanasius seeks to undermine Arian Christology and reaffirm his own. This is really the climax of the letter. It is here that Athanasius brings into view the purpose of his theological and ethical meditations in the first sections of the letter.

The question before us now is how the silver casket visualizes Athanasius's letter. In what follows, I will compare the visual scenes to their textual parallels in the letter itself.

---

and diverges from the structure outlined in Costache, Kariatlis, and Baghos, *Alexandrian Legacy*, 178–79.

The Lid: Christ, the Apostles, Baskets of Bread, and Jars of Wine (Fig. 8.2)

Having noted his own hardship and the wearying experience of separation from his beloved congregations in Egypt, Athanasius writes:

> For although place separates us, yet the Lord the Giver of the feast, and Who is Himself our feast, Who is also the Bestower of the Spirit, brings us together in mind, in harmony, and in the bond of peace. For when we mind and think the same things, and offer up the same prayers on behalf of each other, no place can separate us, but the Lord gathers and unites us together. (*Ep. fest.* 10.2)[42]

This is the first substantial theological statement of the letter. It serves to ground one of the primary pastoral themes, that is, reminding the believers that no matter what kind of separation they might experience, now or in the future, Christ unites them through the Spirit, especially through breaking the bread of Eucharist together.[43] The eucharistic theme is a natural one to occur in a festal letter, and it threads throughout the various sections of *Festal Letter* 10. After assuring the congregations that the presence of enemies does not indicate God's abandonment, Athanasius calls God "the one who *multiplied* his lovingkindness toward us" by granting us common salvation through the Word. However, the multiplication is not just "common" salvation but the unique way that God "works in divers manners for our salvation by means of His Word." One way of doing so, Athanasius suggests, is by meeting Christians in the Communion meal, where they have "the Word for bread, and flesh for food." In paragraph 6, Athanasius refers directly to John 6 by indicating that the bread Lazarus received was Christ, "the bread of heaven" (6:33, 51), when Lazarus rested from his earthly toil.[44] In the final paragraphs, the Easter Feast and the

---

42. Unless otherwise noted, all Athanasius citations and quotes follow the translation of Archibald Robertson in *NPNF* 2/3.

43. The theme is preempted by his quotation of Rom 8:35 in *Ep. fest.* 10.1.

44. The theme of multiplication is picked up after several verses when people from the crowd who received multiplied bread came again to Jesus (see John 6:25–59). Lorenz notes that Athanasius is not always referring to the physical Communion meal. Sometimes he refers instead to spiritual communion. This distinction is helpful to an extent but does not detract from my claim that the eucharistic motif runs throughout the letter (Lorenz, *Der zehnte Osterfestbrief*, 88–89).

unifying effect of the Eucharist are associated with the "apostolic customs" as opposed to the schismatic effects of the Arians, who are by Athanasius's reckoning antiapostolic (esp. *Ep. fest.* 10.11).[45] Thus, we have in *Festal Letter* 10 the eucharistic meal as a frame, a thread, and as an act in unity with the apostolic customs.

On the lid of the silver casket, Christ sits centered with the twelve apostles surrounding him. At their feet, the artist has included five baskets of bread and six jars. As noted above, these are the only inanimate objects that appear on the casket independent from any human figure, inviting us to pay specific attention to them. The baskets and jars allude to the multiplication of the loaves in John 6:1–14 (see Matt 15:32–39, Mark 8:1–13) and the miracle at Cana in John 2:1–11. These Johannine stories are more than appropriate to visualize Jesus as "the Giver of the feast" (*Ep. fest.* 10.2). By the mid-fourth century, wine and bread symbols had already taken on eucharistic meaning.[46] Here, the multiplication story is alluded to, without fish, increasing the certainty that the images have been paired on purpose, as a eucharistic allusion. Additionally, the inclusion of all twelve disciples is somewhat unusual in comparison with other silver caskets.[47] The combination of a fuller representation of the apostolic community with the eucharistic imagery creates an interesting parallel to Athanasius's eucharistic theme and its association with apostolic tradition and unity.

Side A: Mary, Christ, and Others (Fig. 8.3)

Athanasius accuses the Arians of seeking to reimpose the divisions of the devil (*Ep. fest.* 10.8). In response to this, Athanasius advances an ethic of humility and meekness that follows Christ's example. This meekness is characteristic of the God who became human in the incarnation. Moving from a pastoral exhortation, Athanasius transitions in paragraph 9 to a

---

45. Athanasius frames the letter with apostolic concerns as well (*Ep. fest.* 10.1).

46. Kuder, "Die Eucharistie in Bildwerken Vom Frühen 3," 1327–31.

47. For an introduction to the major silver caskets available for comparison, see Koch, "Reliquary: Silver." I count four other silver caskets with *tradition legis* imagery: Chersonesos, Jabalkovo, Nea Herekleia, and Novalja. These include only Jesus, Peter, and Paul. The Ballana casket includes seven disciples. From photographs, it is difficult to count all twelve disciples. The twelfth is barely visible in the top left corner, faded into the background as a very faint etching.

Fig. 8.3. Silver casket of San Nazaro, Mary, Jesus, and others, mid- to late fourth century CE. Silver with gilding. Diocesan Museum of Milan. Photograph by Archivio fotografico Museo Diocesano.

theological rejection of Arian Christology. Referring to the argument just described from paragraph 8, Athanasius writes:

> Now because they did not thus consider these matters, the Ario-maniacs, being opponents of Christ, and heretics, smite Him who is their Helper with their tongue, and blaspheme Him who set Them free, and hold all manner of different opinions against the Saviour. Because of His coming down, which was on behalf of man, they have denied His essential Godhead; and seeing that *He came forth from the Virgin, they doubt His being truly the Son of God*, and considering Him as become incarnate in time, they deny His eternity. (*Ep. fest.* 10.9)

Athanasius here describes certain reasons why his opponents deny Christ's full divinity, also mentioning just after this quote their embarrassment at Christ's suffering. According to Athanasius, the Arians point to all these "problems" as evidence for believing Jesus is not equally divine with the Father. Naturally, Mary is at the heart of the problem, as the human mother who gave birth to Jesus.

Mary as a stumbling block for the Arians is evidenced by the attention Athanasius gives to Mary throughout his four orations against the Arians. While Athanasius does not develop a Mariology per se, Mary is the *theotokos*, the one from whom Jesus took his flesh, and the one through whom Jesus came "at the end of the ages for the abolition of sin" (Athanasius, *C. Ar.* 3.26).[48] She is the one by whom the Son of God is birthed *so that* the Son of God might transfer our origin into himself (3.33). She is not a stumbling block to Christ's divinity but the necessary collaborator for God's renewing appropriation of humanity.

In *Festal Letter* 10, Athanasius leads into his argument against the Arians by pointing to the efficacy of Christ's incarnation. He writes, "This is the grace of the Lord, and these are the Lord's means of restoration for the children of men.... He descended that He might raise us up, He took on Him the trial of being born, that we might love Him Who is unbegotten" (*Ep. fest.* 10.8). As in his *Orations against the Arians*, Athanasius here suggests that Mary is not a problem for Christ's divinity but is the entryway, and the collaborator, for God to become a human, "that we who die as men might live again" (*Ep. fest.* 10.8).

On side A of the silver casket, an infant Jesus sits on Mary's lap. It is in this scene that one of the casket's stylistic motifs creates its most poignant effect. Sena Chiesa draws out just how indebted the casket's imagery is to imperial iconography. Focusing on the scene of Mary with Christ, Sena Chiesa comments on the cushion on which Mary sits, saying it is "a large ceremonial cushion, which in Roman imperial iconography was used to characterize high status and even divinity," in contrast with earlier Marian iconographic style, in which the chair was typically "a simple wicker chair."[49] Additionally, Mary's dress and the plates being offered to her echo imperial customs and ceremonies. Sena Chiesa concludes that the imag-

---

48. *Theotokos* appears three times in the third discourse and once in the fourth, though Mary is discussed and referenced throughout.

49. Sena Chiesa, "Reliquary," 261.

ery honors Mary as the mother of God.⁵⁰ In this scene, as in Athanasius's letter, the Virgin should not be seen as a stumbling block for accepting Christ's divinity. Rather, the casket visualizes Mary as a royal one, the *theotokos* through whom God came to save the world.

Side B: Judgment of Solomon (Fig. 8.4)

In *Festal Letter* 10, Athanasius invokes Solomon at one of the most pastoral points in the letter, as he seeks to assure his churches that God is aware of both their collective and individual needs. Affirming their "common sal-

Fig. 8.4. Silver casket of San Nazaro, judgment of Solomon, mid- to late fourth century CE. Silver with gilding. Diocesan Museum of Milan. Photograph by Archivio fotografico Museo Diocesano.

50. Sena Chiesa, "Reliquary," 263.

vation" granted "through the Word," Athanasius wants to also ensure them that God's Word will meet each individual in the way they need, in the face of their persecution as well as in light of their spiritual capacity (*Ep. fest.* 10.4). Athanasius writes:

> [The Word] does not then possess one method only of healing, but being rich, He works in divers manners for our salvation by means of His Word, Who is not restricted or hindered in His dealings towards us; but since He is rich and manifold, He varies Himself according to the individual capacity of each soul. For He is the Word and the Power and the Wisdom of God, as Solomon testifies concerning Wisdom, that "being one, it can do all things, and remaining in itself, it makes all things new; and passing upon holy souls, fashions the friends of God and the prophets."[51]

Solomon is a source of contention elsewhere in Athanasius's writings against the Arians, because they lean on him to say that "Wisdom," who is the Word, has a beginning. Here, however, Athanasius lets Solomon speak against the anxieties of the Egyptian Christians: Christ is able to meet them in various ways and according to their needs.

On side B, Solomon is seated, judging the case of the two women (1 Kgs 3:16–28). This is a rare scene in early Christian art. The connection between the way Athanasius uses Solomon and the scene chosen for the casket is not immediately clear. This is not a significant problem, seeing as the scene of Solomon's wisely judging is the predominant way of representing Solomon in early Christian art.[52] The image, then, does not simply convey the specific scene from 1 Kgs 3 but rather evokes the whole of Solomon's wisdom.

A passage from Ambrose, however, shows that the story of Solomon's judgment was interpreted in the fourth century in a way that echoes the theological point Athanasius uses Solomon to make (*Off.* 2.8.40–47). Ambrose focuses on *how* Solomon was able to judge the women's case. He suggests that that "the mind of God was in" Solomon, given Solomon's unexpected ability to discern the "secret heart-thoughts, to draw the truth from hidden springs, and to pierce as it were with the sword of the Spirit

---

51. Solomon's statement comes from Wis 7:27.

52. Solomon is not often represented in early Christian art. Besides the scene of him judging the women's case, he is sometimes depicted on his own with an inscription and, at other times, being visited by the Queen of Sheba.

not only the inward parts of the body" (*Off.* 2.8.46–47 [*NPNF* 2/10]). For Ambrose, then, Solomon's judgment is not just a testimony to the prudence of Solomon but a reflection of the wisdom of God, which meets individuals according to their individual need and capacity.

Ambrose's interpretation of Solomon's judgment follows the grain of Athanasius's point that the Word as Wisdom takes into account the needs of the individual, offering them what they need. So, while Athanasius does not refer directly to Solomon's judgment, one can imagine how that powerful story could be used as an image to visualize the point Athanasius intends to make: the Word is wise and knows your needs and how best to meet them.

Side C: The Judgment of Joseph (Fig. 8.5)

Repaying misanthropy with philanthropy is Athanasius's primary ethical exhortation to his congregations. They are not to return evil for evil but to return evil with good. Athanasius lists several biblical paradigms for this ethic: David refusing to kill Saul, Jacob's meekness to Esau, and, importantly for us, Joseph's mercy to his brothers (*Ep. fest.* 10.4). The example of Joseph gives way to the primary and predominant paradigm: Jesus grieving for those who crucified him (10.5). As such, Joseph functions as a typological character, whose own mercy toward his brothers is in alignment with Christ's mercy, which is ultimately the guiding ethical example Athanasius wishes to give his churches.

The scene depicted on the silver casket is Joseph seated in judgment over his arrested brothers, another rare scene in early Christian art. The scene of the brothers likely depicts Benjamin, who was found with the "stolen" cup, and Judah, who is the only brother who speaks in Joseph's presence (Gen 44). The interrogation scene in Genesis 44, of course, is the catalyst that leads Joseph to reveal himself to his brothers in Genesis 45 and, ultimately, to extend his mercy to them in more abundance than he already had. It is not difficult, then, to see how this particular scene resonates with Athanasius's use of Joseph, the concluding Old Testament exemplar of returning philanthropy for misanthropy.

Side D: The Three Hebrew Youths in the Fiery Furnace (Fig. 8.6)

Early in the letter, Athanasius seeks to encourage his congregations to remember, even in times of peace, that their persecution gave them an

Fig. 8.5. Silver casket of San Nazaro, judgment of Joseph, mid- to late fourth century CE. Silver with gilding. Diocesan Museum of Milan. Photograph by Archivio fotografico Museo Diocesano.

opportunity to experience God's presence and power. "For at no time should a man freely praise God, more than when he has passed through afflictions; nor, again, should he at any time give thanks more than when he finds rest from toil and temptations" (*Ep. fest.* 10.3). To exemplify this, Athanasius again uses multiple biblical scenes: Hezekiah praising God at the fall of the Assyrians and the three youths in the fiery furnace. Athanasius compares his and his communities' situation to these characters' situations, suggesting that even in Athanasius's time God was making impossible things possible. All of this should be an encouragement to his churches. Just as God did not allow the fire of the furnace to swallow the youths, God "does not give us as a prey to those who seek to swallow us

Fig. 8.6. Silver casket of San Nazaro, three youths in fiery furnace, mid- to late fourth century CE. Silver with gilding. Diocesan Museum of Milan. Photograph by Archivio fotografico Museo Diocesano.

up" (10.3). This section introduces a theme that is always close at hand in the letter: God will protect the true church.

Little needs to be said about how the image of the three youths in the furnace might connect with Athanasius's use of the story in *Festal Letter* 10. This image was already well-known from the Christian catacombs, and it is present on other silver caskets from the era. It would have been an obvious candidate for visualizing Athanasius's recurring theme of God's presence in times of trial and power to overcome evil.

In this section, I have demonstrated how the imagery of the silver casket of San Navaro visualizes important points from *Festal Letter* 10. In summary: (1) Jesus and the apostles with eucharistic imagery visualize

Athanasius's central themes of unity through the Eucharist and maintaining apostolic custom, (2) Mary with Jesus visualizes Athanasius's anti-Arian christological arguments, (3) Solomon's judgment visualizes Athanasius's pastoral assurance that the Word meets individuals in ways specific to their needs, (4) Joseph's judgment visualizes Athanasius's ethical exhortation to repay misanthropy with philanthropy, and (5) the three youths in the fiery furnace visualize Athanasius's recurring encouragement that God is present in suffering and powerful to overcome evil.[53]

One question is fairly raised. Athanasius is notorious for flooding his writing with Scripture references. Given the number of biblical quotes and allusions, is it naive to think these five would have stood out? For two reasons, I do not think so. First, despite the substantial number of biblical allusions, there is a rather limited number of allusions that commend themselves to visual depiction. Besides the five on the silver casket, other easy-to-visualize options include the exodus, the Passover lamb, the crucifixion, and, perhaps, Jacob and Esau. Most other allusions are nonnarrative in a way that would make rendering them into images more difficult. The second argument comes from what I identified in the above analysis: it appears that the images connect to broader themes or points within the letter. If the commissioner wished to highlight themes or points, then the number of options for biblical images was restricted to the biblical references employed to support the chosen themes.[54] So, while there are dozens of biblical allusions in *Festal Letter* 10, it is reasonable that the allusions that correspond to the iconography of the silver casket would have been among the most obvious choices for illustrating key points and themes from the letter.

---

53. There are differences in emphasis, but these five themes come close to Lorenz's six themes: (1) unity through Easter and Pentecost, (2) gratitude to God in light of persecution, (3) salvation of the philanthropic God, (4) saints passing through tribulation, (5) Arian controversy and rebuttal, and (6) passage through trial (*Der zehnte Osterfestbrief*, 70).

54. For example, for visualizing God caring for his people in times of trouble, the references Isaiah uses are Hezekiah celebrating the fall of the Assyrians and the three youths in the fiery furnace. From a search of the Index of Medieval Art (https://theindex.princeton.edu), there are no extant images of Hezekiah in early Christian art. The choice, then, is obvious. To illuminate philanthropy toward wrongdoers, Athanasius references Joseph and his brothers, David's refusing to kill Saul, and Jacob's meekness to Esau. Once again, I can find no visualization of David refusing to kill Saul. There are some depictions of Jacob and Esau in the period.

So then, it is quite striking to see how the iconography of the silver casket visualizes key theological and pastoral elements of Athanasius's festal letter. The possibility of the letter having inspired the casket's imagery is only increased by evidence that Athanasius's festal letters, though written for Christians in Egypt, were being read throughout the Mediterranean.[55] That Athanasius could easily send these kinds of letters abroad is obvious, given that he sent numerous festal letters during his various exiles in Gaul and Rome. Jerome provides evidence that major church figures were promoting Athanasius's festal letters. In his *On Illustrious Men*, Jerome includes the festal letters among Athanasius's most important writings (without mentioning *On the Incarnation*!).[56] In a letter to a woman who asked for advice on instructing her child in the Christian faith, Jerome does not hesitate to encourage reading the letters of Athanasius (*Ep.* 107). Jerome does not specify which letters, though his commendation of the festal letters specifically in *On Illustrious Men* gives us a clue. And, as a reminder, *Festal Letter* 10 was Athanasius's first explicit written defense against Arian theology. This makes it of special significance in the mid- to late fourth century, even in Milan, where Ambrose continued to struggle against Arianism. In fact, Augustine remembers the dire situation in Milan during the 380s: "Justina, mother of the boy-emperor Valentinian, had been persecuting your faithful Ambrose, in the interests of the Arian heresy by which she had been led astray. His God-fearing congregation, prepared to die with their bishop, your servant, stayed up all night in the church" (*Conf.* 9.7).[57] The situation that led Athanasius to write his

---

55. For more on the transmission of festal letters generally, see Camplani, "Festal Letters"; Costache, Kariatlis, and Baghos, *Alexandrian Legacy*.

56. Jerome's entry for Athanasius reads: "Athanasius, Bishop of the city of Alexandria, having endured many sufferings as a result of the intrigues of the Arians, sought refuge with Constans, the governor of Gaul, from where he returned with a letter of commendation, and again, after the death of Constans, he was put to flight and stayed in hiding until the reign of Jovian, who restored him to his church; he died under Valens. Two books of his, *Against the Pagans*, are known; and one, *Against Valens and Ursacius*; a work, *On Virginity*; and many *On the Persecutions of the Arians*; *On the Titles of the Psalms*; a history containing *The Life of Antony the Monk*; also Ἑορταστικαί, *Festal Letters*; and many other works which it would take too long to enumerate." Jerome, *On Illustrious Men*, trans. Thomas P. Halton, FC 100 (Washington, DC Catholic University of America Press, 1999), 120–21.

57. It is interesting to note that in this section Augustine acknowledges that the entire congregation took to singing hymns "in the manner customary in religions of

pastoral word of encouragement was to some degree playing itself out in Milan. All of this to say that it is safe to assume that Athanasius's letter was available and of interest to devoted Christians in Rome or Milan at the same time that some devoted Christian in Rome or Milan commissioned a special casket with imagery that parallels Athanasius's letter.

It is quite possible that Athanasius's letter inspired the silver casket's iconography. The centrality of the Eucharist in Athanasius's letter makes it an appropriate literary inspiration for a casket that, as argued above, may have been created to hold the eucharistic bread. In this way, we see that the iconographic program is not singularly eucharistic, but that it visualizes a letter written to inspire weary and frightened Christians to gather to celebrate the Eucharist in keeping with the custom of the apostles, a custom appropriately enshrined on the casket's lid.

Conclusion: Reimagining the Silver Casket of San Nazaro

We have covered a great deal of ground in this essay. Beginning with the observation that the condition of the silver casket raises questions about its original function, I argued that the casket would have served well as a eucharistic vessel (either for home Communion or for taking Communion to the sick) and that its iconographic program might have been inspired by an Athanasian festal letter. Both of these arguments remain speculative in nature, of course. We must remember, however, that no historical evidence exists that verifies the origin story often given to the silver casket, that is, that it was made to be a reliquary in the Basilica Apostolorum. I have attempted to make a compelling case for the casket's backstory, one that accounts for not only its condition but its iconography.

There are a variety of implications if these arguments prove persuasive. How does it add to our knowledge of the way sacred objects were used and reused? What might it mean for understanding the way pastoral letters from figures such as Athanasius reached beyond their target audiences? What might the repurposing of a eucharistic vessel into a reli-

---

the East." The simple but significant reminder here is that Ambrose looked to the East for resources to pastorally encourage his congregation in the West. While Augustine discusses the practice of singing hymns, one might also wonder whether Ambrose or other clergy were looking for useful and accessible literary resources to inspire faith and endurance in their congregations.

quary teach us about the relationship between eucharistic devotion and relic veneration?[58]

Even if the arguments are not accepted in part or full, I hope this essay might lead to further research exploring the space between the object as it was discovered and as it was made. The predominant approach to engaging with the iconography of the silver casket has been to prioritize the casket's function as a reliquary (as it was discovered), asking how the imagery might relate to its function as a reliquary. But objects do not always end their lives as they began them. I have taken a different tack to the iconographic problem by prioritizing the eucharistic imagery given to the casket when it was made, asking how this imagery might intimate the casket's original function. This approach invited further research on relevant eucharistic practices and literature, which reminds us that this object is not simply an artifact with a particular function but a piece of art that belongs to a complex and quickly evolving period in the church's life. That complex history, I suggest, includes the likelihood that this object began its life as a eucharistic vessel but was given a second life as a reliquary.

Works Cited

Alborino, Verena. *Das Silberkästchen von San Nazaro in Mailand*. HabD 13. Bonn: Habelt, 1981.

Augustine. *The Confessions*. Translated by Maria Boulding. New York: Vintage Books, 1998.

Barnes, Timothy David. *Athanasius and Constantius: Theology and Politics in the Constantinian Empire*. Cambridge: Harvard University Press, 1993.

Bowes, Kimberly Diane. *Private Worship, Public Values, and Religious Change in Late Antiquity*. Cambridge: Cambridge University Press, 2008.

Camplani, Alberto. "Festal Letters." Pages 230–33 in *Encyclopedia of Ancient Christianity*. Vol. 2. Downers Grove, IL: InterVarsity Press, 2014.

———. *Lettere Festali: Atanasio Di Alessandria. Indice Delle Lettere Festali*. LCPM 34. Milan: Paoline, 2003.

---

58. For more on this, see Snoek, *Medieval Piety from Relics*.

Costache, Doru, Philip Kariatlis, and Mario Baghos, eds. *Alexandrian Legacy: A Critical Appraisal*. Newcastle upon Tyne: Cambridge Scholars, 2015.

Cross, Frank L. "Reservation." Pages 1155–56 in *The Oxford Dictionary of the Christian Church*. Edited by Elizabeth A. Livingstone. Oxford: Oxford University Press, 2009.

Cyprian. *On the Lapsed*. Translated by Roy J. Deferrari. FC 36. New York: Fathers of the Church, 1958.

Dijk, Stephen J. P. van, and Hazelden Walker. *The Myth of the Aumbry: Notes on Medieval Reservation Practice and Eucharistic Devotion*. London: Burns & Oates, 1957.

Gagetti, Elisabetta. "Bibliografia Storica. La Fortuna Nei Secoli di un Oggetto Tra Devozione e Arte." Pages 63–71 in *Il Tesoro di San Nazaro: Antichi Argenti Liturgici della Basilica di San Nazaro al Museo Diocesano di Milano*. Edited by Gemma Sena Chiesa. Milan: Silvana, 2009.

———. "La Teca Di Manlia Dedalia." Pages 73–95 in *Il Tesoro di San Nazaro: Antichi Argenti Liturgici della Basilica di San Nazaro al Museo Diocesano di Milano*. Edited by Gemma Sena Chiesa. Milan: Silvana, 2009.

Galavaris, George. *Bread and the Liturgy*. Madison: University of Wisconsin Press, 1970.

Gwynn, David M. *Athanasius of Alexandria: Bishop, Theologian, Ascetic, Father*. CTC. Oxford: Oxford University Press, 2012.

Jerome. *On Illustrious Men*. Translated by Thomas P. Halton. FC 100. Washington, DC: Catholic University of America Press, 1999.

Koch, Guntram. "Reliquary: Silver." Pages 409–11 in *The Eerdmans Encyclopedia of Early Christian Art and Archaeology*. Vol. 2. Edited by Paul Corby Finney. Grand Rapids: Eerdmans, 2017.

Kuder, Ulrich. "Die Eucharistie in Bildwerken vom frühen 3. bis zum 7. Jahrhundert." Pages 1297–1374 in vol. 2 of *The Eucharist: Its Origins and Contexts*. Tübingen: Mohr Siebeck, 2017.

Leader-Newby, Ruth E. *Silver and Society in Late Antiquity: Functions and Meanings of Silver Plate in the Fourth to Seventh Centuries*. Burlington, VT: Ashgate, 2003.

Leemans, Johan. "Thirteen Years of Athanasius Research (1985–1998). A Survey and Bibliography." *SacEr* 39 (2000): 105–217.

Lorenz, Rudolf. *Der zehnte Osterfestbrief des Athanasius von Alexandrien: Text, Übersetzung, Erläuterungen*. Berlin: de Gruyter, 1986.

McLachlan, Elizabeth Parker. "Liturgical Vessels and Implements." Pages 333–90 in *The Liturgy of the Medieval Church*. Edited by Thomas J. Heffernan and E. Ann Matter. Kalamazoo, MI: Western Michigan University Press, 2001.

Miazzo, Lucia. "Indagini Tecniche e Conservative Sul Tesoro Di San Nazaro." Pages 135–53 in *Il Tesoro di San Nazaro: Antichi Argenti Liturgici della Basilica di San Nazaro al Museo Diocesano di Milano*. Edited by Gemma Sena Chiesa. Milan: Silvana, 2009.

Mitchell, Nathan, OSB. *Cult and Controversy: The Worship of the Eucharist outside Mass*. Collegeville, MN: Liturgical Press, 1990.

Morey, Charles R. "The Silver Casket of San Nazaro in Milan." *AJA* 23 (1919): 101–25.

Pierce, Joanne M. "Vestments and Objects." Pages 841–57 in *The Oxford History of Christian Worship*. Edited by Geoffrey Wainwright and Karen B. Westerfield Tucker. Oxford: Oxford University Press, 2006.

Rahner, Hugo. *Church and State in Early Christianity*. San Francisco: Ignatius, 1992.

Sena Chiesa, Gemma. "Reliquary with Old and New Testament Scenes." 259–64 in *Picturing the Bible: The Earliest Christian Art*. Edited by Jeffrey Spier. New Haven: Yale University Press, 2007.

Sena Chiesa, Gemma, and Fabrizio Slavazzi. "La capsella argentea di San Nazaro. Primi risultati di una nuova indagine." *AT* 7 (2000): 187–204.

Snoek, Godefridus J. C. *Medieval Piety from Relics to the Eucharist: A Process of Mutual Interaction*. SHCT 63. Leiden: Brill, 1995.

Taft, Robert, Jr. "Home-Communion in the Late Antique East." Pages 1–25 in *Ars Liturgiae: Worship, Aesthetics, and Praxis; Essays in Honor of Nathan D. Mitchell*. Edited by Clare Veronica Johnson and Nathan Mitchell. Chicago: Liturgy Training, 2003.

Thompson, Glen L. *The Correspondence of Pope Julius I*. Washington, DC: Catholic University of America Press, 2015.

Thunø, Eric. "Reliquaries and the Cult of Relics in Late Antiquity." Pages 150–68 in *The Routledge Handbook of Early Christian Art*. Edited by Robin M. Jensen. London: Routledge, 2018.

"Treasure of Saint Nazarus." Chiostri Di Sant'Eustorgio. https://tinyurl.com/SBL4830w.

Wiśniewski, Robert. *The Beginnings of the Cult of Relics*. Oxford: Oxford University Press, 2018.

A Christlike Tree:
Personifying and Christomorphizing the
Cross in Early Christianity

Christian Sanchez

1. Introduction

Inside a small church in Dumfries, Scotland, stands a stone cross, eighteen feet tall and dated to the eighth century (fig. 9.1). Inscribed into its surface are bucolic patterns, images from the gospels, and eighteen verses of the famous Old English poem *The Dream of the Rood* (seventh to eighth century) written in Northumbrian runic script. The poem quite literally adds character to the stone cross by the fact that it is mostly narrated by the cross. What is striking about this poem is how it connects the cross to the experiences of Christ:[1]

> Black nails
> Battered through me, opening wide
> The wounds of wickedness. When they scoffed
> At the Saviour, their spit spattered
> Me. In His blood when it sprang
> From His side, was my splintered surface
> Soaked. (lines 64–70)[2]

---

1. Christopher Irvine, "The Iconography of the Cross as the Green Tree," in *The Edinburgh Companion to the Bible and the Arts*, ed. Stephen Prickett (Edinburgh: Edinburgh University Press, 2014), 200.

2. All translations of *The Dream of the Rood* are taken from Graham Holderness, "The Sign of the Cross: Culture and Belief in 'The Dream of the Rood,'" *LitTh* 11 (1997): 366–75.

The cross elaborates its own suffering as Christ undergoes crucifixion; both experience the passion. More striking is that the cross describes itself as an "uprooted" tree that experiences its own burial, resurrection, ascension, and glorification:

> For a second time
> They savagely felled me, ripped up my roots,
> Cruelly cast me in a deep pit.
> Earth closed coldly over my eyes, eyes
> That had seen God's dying. Days,
> Years passed: and I perceived only
> Comfortless clay, and the darkness of death.
> Then the earth parted, and in pain I was pulled
> From the world's womb, born again to the brightness
> Of light. God's disciples dug me up,
> Heaved me heavenwards, raised me and dressed me
> In raiment of silver, garments. (lines 103–117)[3]

Such personification and christomorphization of this tree may seem strange and unique to modern eyes, but in reality *The Dream of the Rood* participates in an ancient tradition of presenting the cross in a personified and Christlike manner. It is true that much of our earliest extant Christian literature uses the cross as a symbol to evoke Jesus's passion and crucifixion or the Christian way of life. Yet there is also a notable pattern in early Christian literature and iconography wherein the cross acts more like a character than an object and is discussed in ways similar to Christ.

In this essay I intend to exhume early Christian literary and iconographic antecedents for the kind of personification and christomorphization of the cross witnessed in *The Dream of the Rood*.[4] This study will be divided into two parts. First, I will highlight instances in early Christian literature in which the cross is individualized and personified to some extent, sometimes even anthropomorphized. Though

---

3. Holderness, "Sign of the Cross," 361.

4. I limit my evidence to literature and art produced between the first century CE and the seventh century (i.e., roughly prior to *Dream of the Rood*). I will use evidence from a variety of early Christianities, including factions traditionally labeled heterodox (e.g., Valentinian Christians, gnostic Christians, Manichaean Christians). My primary criterion for inclusion of documents is that they participate in remembering the cross of Jesus (heavenly or earthly).

Fig. 9.1. Ruthwell cross, seventh–eighth century CE. Red sandstone, 18 ft. Ruthwell Church, Drumfries, Scotland. Photograph by South West Images Scotland / Alamy Stock Photo.

several examples in this section may not include a christological similitude, they will illustrate how some early Christians could imagine the cross as having some autonomy. More space will be dedicated to the second part of this paper, which will discuss instances in which the cross is not only given personhood but is treated or described in a *Christlike* manner—a process I label christomorphizing for ease of description. This section will be composed of three subsections. The first subsection considers how early Christians used similar hermeneutics to tie both the cross and Christ to Edenic figures to explicate their salvific identities. The second subsection will examine instances where the cross receives Christlike divine attributes: omnipresence, cosmos-structuring power, and eternality. Finally, I will highlight instances where early Christians mapped salvific events and experiences ordinarily associated with Christ (such as, suffering, burial, resurrection, ascension, or enthronement) to the cross. The texts and images discussed in this paper will serve to demonstrate the presence of christomorphizing tendencies in early Christian imaginations as well as demonstrate that the Christlike tree of *The Dream of the Rood* has its thematic roots buried in ancient textual and iconographic soil.

2. Personifying the Cross

Instances of cross personification begin with the Acts of Andrew (possibly second century), which depicts Andrew delivering a moving address to the cross at his martyrdom. He speaks to the cross with reverential praise and with encouragement: "Greetings, O cross! Greetings indeed! I know well that, though you have been weary for a long time, planted and awaiting me, even you now at last can rest. I come to you, whom I have known. I recognize your mystery, why you were planted. So then, cross that is pure, radiant, full of life and light, receive me, I who have been weary for so long" (54[4]).[5] Addressing the cross as if it were a person, the apostle attributes humanlike actions and emotions to the cross (i.e., tiring, waiting, and receiving) and attempts to encourage it.[6] Additionally, the cross is

---

5. Dennis Ronald MacDonald, *The Acts of Andrew and the Acts of Andrew and Matthias in the City of the Cannibals*, SBLTT 33.1 (Atlanta: Scholars Press, 1990), 405.

6. Monika Pesthy, "Cross and Death in the Apocryphal Acts of the Apostles," in *The Apocryphal Acts of Peter: Magic, Miracles and Gnosticism*, ed. Jan N. Bremmer, SAAA 3 (Leuven: Peeters, 1998), 130. On addressing the cross as a living character, see

also characterized as something—or, rather, *someone*—to be revered and praised in speech.[7]

Sometimes the cross would talk back. The conviction that the cross *could* speak is preserved in Origen (third century), who records that some mocked Christians for their belief concerning the "voice from the cross" at Jesus's crucifixion (*Cels.* 2.55, 58).[8] These criticisms may have had some connection to the Gospel of Peter (second century), which does attribute speech to the cross, but at Jesus's resurrection:

> Then those soldiers seeing it awoke the centurion and the elders, for they were present also keeping guard. While they were reporting what they had seen, again they saw coming out from the tomb three men, and the two were supporting the one, and a cross following them. And the head of the two reached as far as heaven, but that of the one being led by them surpassed the heavens. And they were hearing a voice from the heavens saying, "have you preached to those who sleep?" and a response was heard from the cross, "Yes." (10.38–42)[9]

The Gospel of Peter's cross is famously called "the walking, talking cross," for obvious reasons. Not only does it speak, but the cross seems to be able to walk, or at least follow Jesus and the two other figures out of the tomb.

---

also Ephrem the Syrian, *Crucifixion* 9.2. My thanks to Dr. Bruce W. Longenecker for bringing this reference to my attention.

7. See also Peter's address to the cross in Acts Pet. 37–38, where the cross is equated with the cosmic extension of the Logos. See Pesthy, "Cross and Death," 130–31; Jean Daniélou, *The Theology of Jewish Christianity*, ed. and trans. John A. Baker (London: Darton, Longman & Todd, 1964), 282–83.

8. Georgia Frank, "Christ's Descent to the Underworld in Ancient Ritual and Legend," in *Apocalyptic Thought in Early Christianity*, ed. Robert J. Daly, HCSPTH (Grand Rapids: Baker Academic; Holy Cross Orthodox Press, 2009), 215. A similar talking-wood phenomenon can be seen in the Testament of Abraham, a Christianized text that attributes speech to a *tree*: "As they were leaving the field in the direction of [Abraham's] house, beside the road there stood a cypress tree. And by the command of God the tree cried out in a human voice and said, 'Holy, Holy, Holy is the Lord God who is summoning him to those who love him'" (3:1–3 recension A [trans. Ed P. Sanders, *OTP* 1:883]).

9. All translations from the Gospel of Peter follow Paul Foster, *The Gospel of Peter: Introduction, Critical Edition and Commentary*, TENTS 4 (Leiden: Brill, 2010).

One wonders whether the author of Gospel of Peter imagined the cross to have feet.[10]

At least one other writer from roughly the same period could imagine the cross with humanlike limbs. Though its wording is perhaps figurative, the *Paschal Homily* attributed to Pseudo-Hippolytus, dated between the late second and early fourth century, describes the cross as an enormous dendromorphic and anthropomorphic figure who supports the cosmos:

> This tree, high as heaven, rose from the earth into heaven
> > A deathless plant, stationed itself between heaven and earth
> > > Establishment of all things
> > > Fixation of everything
> > > Support of the whole universe
> > > Cosmic entanglement
> > > > Firm holder of being, diverse and human
> > > Nailed together with the invisible bolts of the Spirit
> > So that it is fastened together with God and may never be loosened.

---

10. Mark Goodacre has proposed an emendation to the Greek text that would help us resolve the "almost unbelievably absurd" image of a walking, talking cross. See Goodacre, "A Walking, Talking Cross or the Walking, Talking Crucified One?," NT Blog, 18 October 2010, https://tinyurl.com/SBL4830x. Instead of reading σταυρόν in this resurrection account, we should read σταυρωθέντα, "the crucified one." In support of this proposal, Goodacre notes that the singular manuscript witness we have is late, "unreliable and riddled with errors." The scribe could have mistranslated a *nomen sacrum* στα, which in another document is short for σταυρωθέντα. His suggestion is certainly possible, but its persuasive power weakens when considering the multiple other examples of cross personification and christomorphization in early Christian literature. Indeed, many early Christians probably found it absurd that Jesus's cross was simply an instrument of torture without its own story and career. I wonder whether Goodacre's evaluation of this passage could be unhelpfully influenced by his Western social location. There are non-Western people groups today that, perhaps in a manner similar to some ancients, would not find a personified Christlike cross as unrealistic as Goodacre. For a discussion of vivified inanimate objects in ancient literature, see Dale C. Allison, *Testament of Abraham*, CEJL (Berlin: de Gruyter, 2003), 107–11. A famous modern novel that challenges Western "realistic" perspectives of the world is Gabriel García Márquez, *Cien Años de Soledad*, anniversary ed. (New York: Vintage Español; Penguin Random House, 2017). For a direct response to Goodacre's proposal, see Peter Head's comment on Goodacre, "Walking, Talking Cross," 19 October 2010, at 11:11 am, as well as Paul Foster, "Do Crosses Walk and Talk?: A Reconsideration of Gospel of Peter 10.39–42," *JTS* 64 (2013): 89–104.

A Christlike Tree 239

> Whereas [this cross was] grazing the heavens with its high head(s), [it was] fixing the earth
> with its feet, as well as embracing the great and middling spirit
> on all sides with its massive hands, it was all in everything and everywhere. Filling everything through itself, it stripped itself naked to face the rulers of the air. (51.26–40)[11]

Pseudo-Hippolytus, like others (see below), attributes a structuring role to the cross in the cosmos.[12] Unlike others, though, Pseudo-Hippolytus describes the cross's cosmic work in decidedly somatic terms. Its body, including its head, feet, and massive hands, holds the universe in place. Such language may not have been intended as a literal description of the cross, but it does contribute to a bodily, personified picture of the cross.

Though subtle, one can detect glimpses of the cross's individuality and personification in early Christian iconography as well. Perhaps the earliest iconographic instantiations of the cross, a few early Christian manuscripts (dated to the second century) treat the cross as its own entity separate from Christ. Instead of spelling out crucifixion-related terms, they insert a *tau* with a *rho* superimposed over it (fig. 9.2). The resulting image is what scholars have referred to as a staurogram (⳨). Iconographically, the symbol looks like a figure on a cross.[13] More importantly, however, the staurogram, unlike later *chi-rho* monograms, did not always refer to Christ's crucifixion. Rather, as Matthew Black, Larry Hurtado, and Dieter Roth each demonstrate, the staurogram appears in some of the earliest Christian manuscripts as a *nomen sacrum* for the term *cross* and its cognates.[14] There are narrative contexts where the staurogram takes the place

---

11. All translations of Pseudo-Hippolytus are mine, based on the critical edition of his *Paschal Homily* in Giuseppe Visonà, *Pseudo Ippolito, In Sanctum Pascha: Studio Edizione Commento*, SPMed 15 (Milan: Vita e pensiero, 1988), 302.

12. On the date of the *Paschal Homily*, see Dragoş-Andrei Giulea, "Pseudo-Hippolytus's *In Sanctum Pascha*: A Mystery Apocalypse," in Daly, *Apocalyptic Thought in Early Christianity*, 127–42.

13. Robin M. Jensen, *Understanding Early Christian Art* (London: Routledge, 2000), 138.

14. Matthew Black, "The Chi-Rho Sign: Christogram and/or Staurogram ?," in *Apostolic History and the Gospel: Biblical and Historical Essays Presented to F. F. Bruce on His Sixtieth Birthday*, ed. W. Ward Gasque and Ralph P. Martin (Exeter: Paternoster, 1970), 319–27; Larry W. Hurtado, *The Earliest Christian Artifacts: Manuscripts and Christian Origins* (Grand Rapids: Eerdmans, 2006), 135–54; Dieter T. Roth, "Raising

of a cross-term that does *not* refer to Christ's crucifixion (such as in fig. 9.2), becoming an image simply of the cross.

A mid-fourth-century passion sarcophagus discovered in the catacomb of Domitilla (fig. 9.3) may subtly personify the cross. The cross takes a central position on this sarcophagus and is depicted, in part, as a symbol of victory and immortality (note the eagle and the jeweled laurel wreath). A *chi-rho* monogram lies at its top (within the wreath), and two soldiers flank its base. The image of the two soldiers could allude to the two sleeping guards of the Matthean resurrection story (Matt 27:64; 28:4, 23) or to a conventional image of Roman captives—an image signifying military victory.[15] I see no reason to exclude either possibility, as contemporary Christians could have supplied either context for the image. Symbolically, the cross proclaims victory over death. Yet in some ways, the image also subtly personifies the cross. Given Christ's presence in the scenes surrounding the center, the cross seems to interrupt this sequence and take his place in the scene, evoking both the crucifixion and the resurrection. It receives a wreath on its head and is presented standing, perhaps in a resurrected state, victorious over death, between two sleeping soldiers. Had one recently read or heard the story of the Gospel of Peter, one might be reminded of the cross's exit from the tomb.[16]

The cross on this sarcophagus, subtly positioned as if it were Christ, adopts a specific persona for its personification. This kind of christomorphization of the cross occurred quite often in early Christian literature, often in a likewise subtle manner. Perhaps on account of its involvement in the salvific work of Christ, the cross receives Christlike treatments and features. These phenomena are discussed below.

---

the Bar: An Overlooked Element for Identifying a Staurogram within Nomina Sacra," *NovT* 63 (2021): 112–27.

15. Felicity Harley-McGowen, "Picturing the Passion," in *The Routledge Handbook of Early Christian Art*, ed. Robin M. Jensen and Mark D. Ellison (London: Routledge, 2018), 297; Robin M. Jensen, *The Cross: History, Art, and Controversy* (Cambridge: Harvard University Press, 2017), 68–69.

16. Other visual examples might include the "star and wreath" sarcophagus (stone relief, 350–400 CE, Gallo Roman) from the crypt of the Palermo Cathedral, which depicts the twelve apostles venerating the cross, which stands between the two sleeping/conquered soldiers. See Gertrud Schiller, *The Passion of Jesus Christ*, vol. 2 of *Iconography of Christian Art*, trans. Janet Seligman (Greenwich: New York Graphic Society, 1972), fig. 9.

A Christlike Tree 241

Fig. 9.2. Above: Chester Beatty I (P45), fol. 15 (Luke 13:29–14:10, 14:17–33), 200–250 CE. Egypt. Papyrus, 210 mm x 230 mm. Chester Beatty Museum, Dublin, Ireland. Photograph by Chester Beatty Museum. Below: Highlighted detail of staurogram at Luke 11:24.

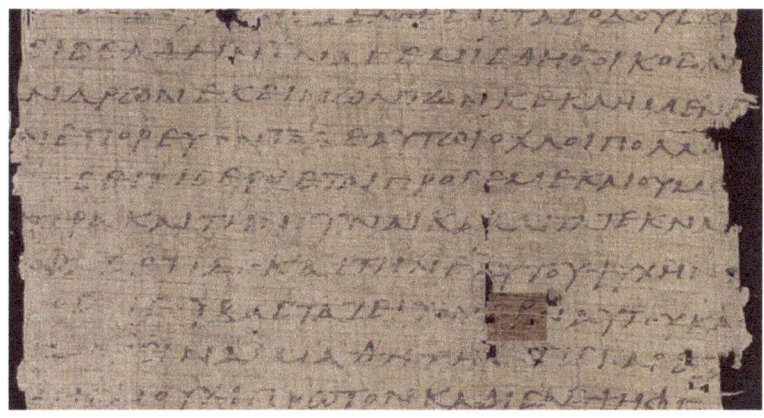

Fig. 9.3. Columnar anastasis sarcophagus with the cross surmounted by a *chi-rho* monogram within a wreath, ca. 340 CE. Marble high relief. Museo Pio Christiano, Vatican Museums, Vatican State. Photograph by Vanni Archive / Art Resource, New York.

3. Christological Hermeneutics

Hermeneutically, early Christians looked to Scripture to understand the significance of the cross in the same manner they did Christ. The Epistle of Barnabas (first to second century), for example, presents several Old Testament typologies of the cross (e.g., the red heifer ceremony [8.1, 5], Abraham's household [9.7–9], the bronze serpent [12.5–7]), excavating the Scriptures to unearth its identity. Perhaps the most prominent relationship explicated in early Christian literature is the link between the cross and Eden's legendary trees. Several of the earliest Christian writers use the term *tree* (ξύλον) as a synecdoche for the cross (e.g., Acts 5:30; 10:39; 13:29; Gal 3:13; 1 Pet 2:22, 24; Polycarp, *Phil.* 8.1; Barn. 5.13). It was not long before this "tree" conjoined typologically with the prominent trees of the Genesis story.[17] The Gospel of Truth (second century), a gospel perhaps written by Valentinus, speaks of the cross as the antithesis to the tree of the knowledge of good and evil:

> He was nailed to a tree and became the fruit of the father's acquaintance. Yet it did not cause ruin because it was eaten. Rather, to those who ate of it, it gave the possibility that whoever he discovered within himself might be joyful in the discovery of him. And as for him, they discovered him within them—the inconceivable uncontained, the father, who is perfect, who created the entirety. (18.24–31)[18]

---

17. For a fuller explication of the typological development between the cross and the tree, see Irvine, "Iconography of the Cross," 195–200.

18. Bentley Layton and David Brakke, *The Gnostic Scriptures*, 2nd ed., AYBRL (New Haven: Yale University Press, 2021), 314.

For the Gospel of Truth, the fruit of the cross provides knowledge but not knowledge that leads to death. This knowledge, or "acquaintance," leads to God (see Gos. Phil. 80). In the proto-orthodox tradition, Irenaeus (second century) expresses a similar theology of the cross in his *Against Heresies*, arguing from Phil 2:8 that Jesus's obedience to the tree of the cross rectified Adam and Eve's disobedience with respect to the tree of knowledge (Irenaeus, *Haer.* 5.16.3; 5.19.1; see Acts Pet. 38 [mid-second century]). Tertullian (third century) specifies that, while the fruit of Eden's tree was death for Adam and Eve, the fruit of the cross was life for many (*Adv. Jud.* 13; see Gos. Phil. 80 [third century]). Other writers, such as Origen (third century), follow this same kind of reasoning but explicitly link the cross to Eden's tree of life (*Cels.* 6.36; see Commodian, *Instr. adv. gent.* 35). Just as Christ was thought of as a new Adam, so the cross could be thought of as a new tree.

There is a kind of recapitulatory atoning significance for the cross alongside Christ. The cross undoes what the tree of knowledge had done, just as Christ undid what Adam had done (see Ephrem the Syrian, *Church* 51.8; *Cross, passim*). Both original entities, Adam and the tree of knowledge, needed a counterpart to rectify them. So as Jesus, the descendent of Adam, undoes original sin, the cross, the descendant of the tree of life, undoes the curse of the tree of knowledge. This tradition of interpreting the cross in light of Eden's trees was quite common in antiquity and continued well into the Middle Ages.[19] The thirteenth-century *Legend of the Holy Rood Tree*, for example, follows the cross's story from being a seed of the tree of life, to a sapling in the Old Testament, to the wood of Jesus's cross.[20]

A Monza pilgrimage ampulla dated the late sixth century exemplifies the scriptural relationship between the cross, Eden, Christ, and salvation

---

19. See e.g., Disc. Sav. 7 (fourth century?); P.Berol. 22220 10:1 (fifth century?); Encom. Mar. 17.3 (fifth to sixth century); John of Damascus, *Fide* 4.11 (seventh to eighth century). A sixth- to seventh-century homily attributed to Evodius of Rome reads: "For when Eve stretched out her hand and ate from the tree, and shut the door to paradise, Jesus, too, stretched out his hands for the nails that pierced them. They became keys and opened the gates of paradise, and humanity entered." See *Hom. Pass. Res.* 55, trans. Dylan M. Burns, *New Testament Apocrypha: More Noncanonical Scriptures*, ed. Tony Burke (Grand Rapids: Eerdmans, 2020), 2:73.

20. The story builds on traditions preserved in the Latin Life of Adam and Eve and the Gospel of Nicodemus (see discussion in Jensen, *Cross*, 140–44).

(fig. 9.4, right ampulla).[21] As an ampulla that was supposed to have carried oil from the true cross, it was no doubt believed to be imbued with divine power, perhaps even salvific power.[22] On its front, it portrays the Holy Sepulchre with women approaching and an angel directing their attention (bottom). Above the Holy Sepulchre and at the center of the ampulla, the cross sprouts upward as a tree between two other crucified individuals. Two pilgrims kneel at the base of the tree-cross. At the top of the scene is a bust of a bearded and, perhaps, risen Jesus encircled with a cross nimbus. The motif of life dominates the entire scene from the Holy Sepulchre to

Fig. 9.4. Reliquary silver ampulla containing oil from holy places, n. 10, late sixth–early seventh century. Recto: crucifixion and figure resurrection. Alloy of lead and tin, silver. Museum and Treasury of Monza Cathedral, Italy. Photograph by Museo e Tesoro del Duomo di Monza / photo Piero Pozzi.

---

21. See Schiller, *The Passion of Jesus Christ*, 2:90, fig. 324.
22. Pilgrimage ampullae contained oil that was supposed to have touched the true cross. For a brief introduction to ampullae and the true cross, see Erik Thunø, "Reliquaries and the Cult of Relics in Late Antiquity," in Jensen and Ellison, *Routledge Handbook of Early Christian Art*, 162.

(the risen) Jesus in the sky. Situated in the middle of the scene, the cross too is alive and life-giving, like the tree of life.

4. Christlike Divine Attributes

Early Christians also infused the cross with Christlike divine attributes.[23] We may begin with the cross's *omnipresence*.[24] The text of Pseudo-Hippolytus (quoted above) includes one of strongest examples of this staurological omnipresence: "on all sides with its massive hands, [the cross] was all in *everything* and *everywhere*. Filling *everything* through itself" (51.38–39). The cross, like Christ, or perhaps even like Wisdom in Jewish traditions, pervades the entire cosmos.[25] Certain manuscripts of the Acts of Andrew (M and L) and the Acts of John (99) contain parallel forms of staurological omnipresence.[26] Less ontologically bold in their articulation but no less noteworthy, the apologists frequently spoke of the sign of the cross as if it were everywhere. For Justin Martyr (mid-second century), the sign of the cross not only appeared almost everywhere, but it empowered things such as ships to sail or the earth to be plowed, and distinguished humans from other creatures (*1 Apol.* 55). Tertullian (*Apol.* 12.3, 16.7; *Nat.* 1.12; *Marc.* 4.20.2–4; *Or.* 29), Hippolytus of Rome (*Antichr.* 59), and Minucius Feix (*Oct.* 29.7–8), in their defenses of Christianity, likewise speak of the sign of the cross permeating all creation, even other cults. The cross seems to

---

23. Here I am not arguing for a one-to-one correspondence with Christ's divine attributes. I am simply noting a resemblance. Moreover, though the evidence would certainly add to my thesis, the apotropaic and healing qualities of the cross and its veneration before and after Constantine will not be discussed in this essay. On these topics, see especially Jensen, *Cross*, 49–149; Bruce W. Longenecker, *The Cross before Constantine: The Early Life of a Christian Symbol* (Minneapolis: Fortress, 2015); Jean Daniélou, *The Bible and the Liturgy*, LiSt (Notre Dame: University of Notre Dame Press, 1956), 54–69.

24. On the omnipresence of Christ in early Christianity, see Irenaeus, *Epid.* 34; Origen, *Princ.* 2.11.6; Athanasius, *Inc.* 17. Here I use a flexible notion of staurological omnipresence, attempting to capture early Christian claims concerning the *presence* of the cross everywhere and the *visibility* of the cross/sign of the cross in the world.

25. I owe the insightful comparison with Wisdom to Dr. Bruce Longenecker.

26. The texts M, L, and Armenian Passion provide expansions on Andrew's speech to the cross (see above). Though later, they may preserve early material—perhaps even original material (see MacDonald, *Acts of Andrew*, 409).

be integral to the fabric of creation.[27] Comparably, Manichaean literature from the Roman period treats "the cross of light" as shards of divine life scattered throughout earth's vegetation.[28]

Similarly, just as early Christians attributed a structuring and organizing role to Christ (or the Word) in the cosmos, so this was also the case with the cross (noted in Pseudo-Hippolytus above).[29] One recension of the Acts of Andrew records the apostle praising the cross for its stabilizing function in the cosmos: "For you were planted in the cosmos in order to stabilize what is unstable, extending with your right and your left in order to drive out the jealous and oppressive power and to gather the cosmos into one. Your other [part] has been planted into the earth in order to unite the things on the earth and the subterranean things with the heavenly things" (M 14; see L 46).[30] The cross serves as reality's skeleton, extending in all directions to "stabilize what is unstable" and connect all things to one another. The notion that the cross delimits the cosmos was particularly popular among Christian gnostic sects and Valentinian Christians, who viewed the earthly cross as an image of a heavenly cross that separated the *plēroma* (the divine reality) from earthly reality (see, e.g., Gos. Phil. 105; see also Irenaeus, *Haer.* 1.2.4, 1.3.5; Clement of Alexandria, *Exc.* 22.4, 42.1–43.1).[31] The Acts of John provides the clearest example of this structuring heavenly cross. Unable to bear the Messiah's crucifixion, John flees to the Mount of Olives, where the heavenly Christ reveals himself and shows him the heavenly cross of light:

---

27. See fuller discussion in Jensen, *Cross*, 32–34.

28. Iain Gardner and Samuel N. C. Lieu describe the Manichaean "cross of light" as the "divinity of the living soul in matter, particularly as crucified in vegetation and plant life, where the divine hangs on every tree or bush or herb; it was a particular concern of the elect to reverence and never to harm the Cross." See Gardner and Lieu, *Manichaean Texts from the Roman Empire* (Cambridge: Cambridge University Press, 2004), 291.

29. On the Word providing structure and organization to the cosmos, see, e.g., Act Pet. 38–39, Pseudo-Hippolytus, *IsP* 29. See also Russell Bradner Norris Jr., "Logos Christology as Cosmological Paradigm," *ProEccl* 5 (1996): 196; Jean-Marc Prieur, *Das Kreuz in der christlichen Literatur der Antike*, trans. Ellen Pagnamenta, TC 14 (Bern: Lang, 2006), xxiv.

30. My translation is based on the critical edition of Acts of Andrew in Jean-Marc Prieur, *Acta Andreae*, 2 vols., CCSA 5–6 (Turnhout: Brepols, 1989), 738–40.

31. See Layton and Brakke, *Gnostic Scriptures*; Pieter J. Lalleman, *The Acts of John: A Two-Stage Initiation into Johannine Gnosticism*, SAAA 4 (Leuven: Peeters, 1998), 189; Prieur, *Kreuz in der christlichen Literatur*, xx–xxi.

But what [the cross of light] is, truly, is this (known by itself and spoken to you): it is the division of all things and the strong leading-up of what is fixed things out of unstable things, and the harmony of wisdom. When wisdom is in harmony, the right things and the left things, powers, authorities, principalities [and] demons, energies, threats, passions, accusations, Satan and the inferior root (from which the nature of created things proceeds) come into existence. (98)[32]

Like the cross in the expansions of Acts of Andrew, this cross stabilizes and organizes the cosmos.[33] Distinctively, however, the Acts of John describes the cross as participating in the origination of all things. It is as if the cross precedes creation and broaches the time of divinity.

A few other writers also gesture toward the *eternality* of the cross. Pseudo-Hippolytus's *Paschal Homily* includes a section where the narrator magnifies the cross, or tree, in such a manner: "This [tree] with its blooming flowers, I rejoice fully with its fruits, and without hindrance I gather these fruits reserved for me from the beginning" (51.10–12). The participial phrase "reserved from the beginning" (ἐξ ἀρχῆς μοι τετηρημένους) seems to situate the cross at the origination of all things, an ancient tree indeed. More explicitly, the Dance of the Savior (fourth to seventh century) records Jesus hymning to the cross prior to his crucifixion. At one point in his singing, Jesus states: "What is the Cross? Where is it from? It is from the Spirit—Amen. It is forever, from all time, from the foundation of the world—Amen" (4.18–19). Like Pseudo-Hippolytus, the Dance of the Savior treats the cross as if it were present at the "beginning," but strengthens this notion with eternal statements: "it is forever, from all time."

In the literature discussed above, the cross participates in the divine sphere, adopting as its own attributes ordinarily attributed to Christ.[34] There are a few iconographic complements to this literary phenomenon.

---

32. All translations of the Acts of John are mine based on the critical edition of the text in Éric Junod and Jean-Daniel Kaestli, *Acta Johannis*, 2 vols., CCSA 1–2 (Turnhout: Brepols, 1983), 209–11.

33. On this function of the cross in other apocryphal acts, see János Bolyki, "'Head Downwards': The Cross of Peter in the Lights of Apocryphal Acts, of the New Testament and of the Society-Transforming Claim of Early Christianity," in Bremmer, *Apocryphal Acts of Peter*, 116.

34. The cross for at least one writer stands so close to the divinity that it takes on divine names ordinarily associated with Christ (Acts John 98). Pseudo-Hippolytus, likewise, may blur the lines between the cross and Christ: "O extension of the divine

The apse mosaic in Ravenna's Sant' Apollinare depicts a large, bejeweled cross with Christ's face at its heart, situated in a starry sky with divine labels at every arm (fig. 9.5). Above the cross is written the Greek acrostic ΙΧΘΥΣ (Jesus Christ God's Son Savior); beneath is written SALVSMUNDI (Salvation of the World); and flanking its right and left are the letters A (*alpha*) and Ω (*omega*). The scene provides an interpretation of the transfiguration: Moses and Elijah flank the starry sky, and three distinguished sheep, representing Peter, James, and John, stare up at the cross. The mosaic places the cross in divine space, in the heavens among the stars and divine labels, harking back to traditions of the cross's second coming or perhaps its ascension (see below) as well as its structuring role in the cosmos. The placement of Jesus's face in the middle of the cross resonates

Fig. 9.5. Apse mosaic with cross in a starry sky, ca. 540 CE. Basilica of Sant' Apollinare. Mosaic. Ravenna, Italy. Photograph by Alfredo Dagli Orti / Art Resource, New York.

in all things and every place! O crucifixion unfolding in all things! O unique one, [you are] truly all in all things!" (*IsP* 56). See Visonà, *Pseudo Ippolito*, 310.

with Justin's interpretation of Plato's *Timaeus*, wherein he claims that the Son is stationed in the cosmos crosswise (Justin Martyr, *1 Apol.* 60.1–7; see Irenaeus, *Epid.* 34).[35]

5. The Cross Event

The cross's similarities to Christ are heightened in disparate texts that apply events and experiences ordinarily belonging to Christ to the cross. Though these christomorphizing tendencies may not have occupied much space in early Christianity discourses concerning the cross, they were nevertheless present and should be noted.

Mournful and Docetic Crucifixion

As some early Christians looked to the Old Testament Scriptures to elucidate both Christ and the cross, others provided docetic understandings of the crucifixion for them both as well.[36] Some writers not only envisioned two Christs, a heavenly Christ and an earthly crucified Christ, but also two crosses, a heavenly cross and an earthly, wooden cross.[37] An example of this phenomenon can be seen in the Acts of John: "This cross, then, which has established all things by the Logos and delimited what is created and inferior, and then has extended itself into all things—this is not the wooden cross which you are about to see when you go down from here. Neither am I the one who is on the cross—I whom you currently do not see, rather, you only hear my voice" (99; see Gos. Phil. 84). For the Acts of John, the earthly wooden cross on which Christ was crucified was simply a facsimile of a truer heavenly cross of light. One wonders whether the theological issues that docetic Christologies aimed to resolve had any applicability also to the cross, thus requiring docetic staurologies as well.

Like the Acts of Andrew, hymns to the cross that arose after Constantine regularly attributed actions and emotions to the cross. These hymns portray Jesus speaking to the cross, encouraging it, praising it, and giving

---

35. Justin uses the term χιάζω, "to mark with two lines crossing like a X" (LSJ, 1991), to describe the position of the Son in the cosmos (see PG 6:287a–b).

36. On the docetic understanding of Christ's crucifixion see, e.g., Coptic Apoc. Pet. 81–83.

37. On this phenomenon, see also Irenaeus's description of Ptolemy's gnostic myth in *Haer.* 1.3.5, 1.4.1.

it commands. Most relevant to the present purposes are instances where the cross fears and mourns prior to the crucifixion. The Berlin-Strasbourg Apocryphon (fifth century?) records Jesus addressing the cross:

> O Cross, do not be afraid. I am rich. I shall fill you with my wealth. (8.31 [Sucio])

> [Do not] weep, O [Cross], but rejoice instead and know that [your] Lord who is coming [to] you is [gentle] and [humble], Amen! (8.35 [Sucio]; see Dance Sav. 1.11)[38]

Like Christ who grieves his cup (B-S Ap. 5.1–14), the cross experiences its own grief for the crucifixion that is coming—as if the cross experiences the passion, suffering with Christ. Moreover, the Berlin-Strasbourg Apocryphon unites the cross to Christ so closely that it treats attitudes toward the cross as attitudes toward Christ: "[me and you], O Cross, truly, [the one who is] far from [you] is far [from me]" (9.10).

Burial, Descent into Hell, and Resurrection

Contra those who boasted docetic interpretations of the cross (see above), a few texts presume that the cross fully experienced Jesus's suffering, death, and even burial. Perhaps the most striking example of this tradition occurs in the Gospel of Peter (discussed above), wherein the cross follows Jesus out of the grave and even speaks, responding to a voice from heaven. Presupposed in this story is the notion that the now-living cross had died with Christ and been buried with him as well. Sibylline Oracle 6 (third century) preserves this cross-burial tradition. In its prophecy addressed to the tree "upon which God was outstretched," it promises the cross that it will not remain buried but ascend to heaven (see below).

In the Gospel of Peter, the cross also appears to have joined Christ in his ministry to the dead, proclaiming the gospel to them. When a voice from heaven asks, "Have you preached to those who sleep [i.e., the dead]?," it is the *cross* who responds, "Yes" (10.41–42). This postmortem ministry of the cross is partly preserved in the Latin A recension of the Descent into Hell portion of the Gospel of Nicodemus (fifth to sixth century): "O

---

38. Tony Burke and Brent Landau, *New Testament Apocrypha: More Noncanonical Scriptures* (Grand Rapids: Eerdmans, 2016), 1:180–81.

Lord, set the sign of the victory of your cross in Hades that death may no more have dominion" (8[24].1 [Elliott]).[39] Though it is the *sign* of the cross descending into Hades in the Descent and not necessarily the cross itself, the text preserves memory of the cross's presence in Hades.

What is more, the cross does not stay in Hades, according to the Gospel of Peter. It walks out of the grave behind Christ: "While they were reporting what they had seen, again they saw coming out of the tomb three men, and two were supporting the one, and a cross following them" (10:39 [Foster]). The cross is resurrected with Christ. Jean Daniélou suggests that Barnabas 12.1 could provide the earliest antecedent to the tradition of the cross's death and resurrection: "And when will these things be accomplished? The Lord says: When a tree be bends and rises back up [ἀναστῇ] and when blood drips from a tree" (12.1).[40] The verb ἀνίστημι ("to rise up [from the dead]") was one of the most common terms used for resurrection among early Christians. The Martyrdom of Pionius (third to early fifth century) has Pionius present an apologetic speech against Christians visiting synagogues. In it he alludes to a rumor among Jews that Jesus and the cross had been raised through necromancy: "They [the Jews] say that they did necromancy to raise Christ with the cross" (13.8 [Rebillard]).[41] Presupposed in this reference is the idea that the cross was buried with Christ.

Ascension

Some early Christians even attribute an ascension to the cross. Sibylline Oracle 6 preserves a prophecy of the cross ascending to heaven: "O blessed

---

39. See Foster, *Gospel of Peter*, 429. On dating of the written form of the Descent, see Bart Ehrman and Pleše Zlatko, eds. and trans., *The Apocryphal Gospels: Texts and Translations* (Oxford: Oxford University Press, 2011), 465.

40. My translation, based on Michael Holmes's edition of the text, *The Apostolic Fathers: Greek Texts and English Translations* (Grand Rapids: Baker Books, 1999). See Daniélou, *Theology of Jewish Christianity*, 266. One should also note that the typological relationship between the cross and the tree of life also lends itself toward the connection between the cross and resurrection.

41. Éric Rebillard, ed., *Greek and Latin Narratives about the Ancient Martyrs*, OECT (Oxford: Oxford University Press, 2017), 69. The phrase "with the cross" (μετὰ τοῦ σταυροῦ) should not be taken instrumentally but as a marker of placement/accompaniment. See Antoon Hilhorst, "The Wounds of the Risen Jesus," *EstBib* 41 (1983): 165–67; Jan den Boeft and Jan N. Bremmer, "Notiunculae Martyrologicae III: Some Observations on the Martyria of Polycarp and Pionius," *VC* 39 (1985): 118.

tree, upon which God was outstretched, the earth will not hold you, rather heaven will be your home, you will look upon heaven as a house at the time when your fiery eye, O God, flashes like lightning" (Sib. Or. 6.26–28).[42] Referring to the cross as "tree," the speaker prophesies its resurrection ("the earth will not hold you") and ascension to heavenly abode.[43] Dated to the end of the fourth century, the Discourse of the Savior on the Mystery of the Cross preserves this ascending cross tradition as well: "After I [Christ] judge the entirety of the just and the sinners, again the cross will rise and go up to the heavens" (8 [Dilley]).[44] The word *again* is noteworthy. In the story of Discourse of the Savior, the cross ascends *twice*: once prior to its return, and again to lead the righteous up to heaven. The two papyri, Papyrus Berolinensis 22220 and Strasbourg Copte 6 + 7,7, which together comprise the Berlin-Strasbourg Apocryphon, also record an ascension for the cross.[45] Following the Papyrus Berolinensis 22220 version, Berlin-Strasbourg Apocryphon 8.30 reads, "Rise up, [rise], O [Cross. Lift] yourself [up] [and] lift up to the [heaven] if this is your wish" (see Strasbourg Copte 7,2.6.4.3 recto 8.8).[46] Important to note is that the cross is not raptured up into heaven (like, e.g., an apocalyptic seer) in the last two examples. Rather, the cross is assumed to have some agency in raising *itself* to heaven.

Enthronement

Though I have not come across any texts discussing the cross's enthronement, a few early Christian mosaics seem to depict it. What scholarship refers to as *hetoimasia* in apse mosaics are often said to be depictions of the empty throne. But, as Robin Jensen notes, the throne is "not actually

---

42. Translation mine, based on the critical edition of the Greek text in Joh Geffcken, *Die Oracula Sibyllina*, GCS 8 (Leipzig: Hinrichs, 1902), 132. On dating, see John J. Collins, "The Sibylline Oracles," OTP 1:406.

43. M. D. Usher argues that the term *tree* here refers to Christ, but the text does not necessitate this conclusion. Later tradition corroborates the cross interpretation. See Usher, "The Sixth Sibylline Oracle as a Literary Hymn," GRBS 36 (1995): 38–39.

44. Burke and Landau, *New Testament Apocrypha*, 1:194. Paul Dilley has amended the text in his translation from the perfect tense to the present tense.

45. Though Alin Sucio dates this text to the fifth century (on account of genre), he notes others have dated it earlier (Burke and Landau, *New Testament Apocrypha*, 1:172–74).

46. Burke and Landau, *New Testament Apocrypha*, 1:180.

'empty'" in these depictions.[47] In the *hetoimasia* apse of Ravenna's Arian baptistry, the cross sits on the throne studded with jewels, with a garment or a towel around its nape, perhaps waiting for Christ to come back from baptism (fig. 9.6). The imagery resonates with the description of God on the throne in Rev 4–5, once again placing the cross in a position one would expect to see Christ. From above, the cross sits enthroned in this apse, overseeing the baptism of Christians.

Fig. 9.6. The cross on the throne, late fifth century CE. Mosaic. Arian baptistry, Ravenna, Italy. Photograph by Alfredo Dagli Orti / Art Resource, New York.

Parousia or Second Coming

The Apocalypse of Pseudo-Methodius preserves the rationale for the cross's ascension: "And the cross will be taken up to heaven … because

---

47. Jensen, *Cross*, 108.

the cross, on which Our Lord Jesus Christ was hanged for the sake of the common salvation of all, itself is destined to appear in front of him at his coming as a refutation of unbelievers" (14.4 [Garstad]).[48] The cross had to have an ascension into heaven because it was supposed to have a second coming. After prophesying the "abomination of desolation" (Matt 24:15–28), Matthew's Jesus states, "The sun will be darkened, the moon will not give its illumination, the stars will fall from heaven, and the powers of the heavens will be shaken. And then *the sign of the Son of Man* will be revealed in heaven, and all the tribes of the earth will mourn, and they will see the Son of Man coming on the clouds of heaven with power and great glory" (24:29–30).[49] Many early interpreters understood the "sign of the Son of Man" to be the cross of Jesus. The cross was expected to go before Jesus at his parousia. For example, the Ethiopic text of the Epistle to the Apostles (mid- to late second century), like the Apocalypse of Peter (1), records Jesus stating that the cross will return with and before him at the parousia: "Truly I say to you, I will come as the sun which bursts forth; thus will I, shining seven times brighter than it in glory, while I am carried on the wings of the clouds in splendour with my cross going on before me, come to the earth to judge the living and the dead" (16 [Elliott]). While other witnesses read "the sign of the cross" (e.g., Coptic Ep. Apost. 16; Apoc. El. 3.2–4; Sib. Or. 8.244–246), the idea remains the same: the cross (sign) has a second coming. The Discourse of the Savior makes much of the cross's parousia, labeling it "the mystery of the cross" (5). Elucidating this "mystery" to his disciples, Jesus states, "I will bring the cross with me so that I might reveal [to the Jews who crucified him] their shame; and I will place their lawlessness upon their head" (6). The cross, in other words, joins Jesus in his second coming and participates in divine judgment.[50]

Some early Christians applied similar theological readings and descriptions to the cross as they did Christ, envisioning the cross as a participant in salvific events beyond simply the crucifixion. While the above examples may not all have had a direct relation to one another (like the connection between ascension and second coming), they are nevertheless significant for identifying a pattern in early Christianity that aligned the

---

48. Benjamin Garstad, *Apocalypse of Pseudo-Methodius: An Alexandrian World Chronicle*, DOML 14 (Cambridge: Harvard University Press, 2012), 65.
49. My translation.
50. See also the *Invest. Abbat.* 10:3.

cross's story with Christ's. Moreover, these christomorphizing traditions or tendencies in Christian discourses concerning the cross persisted into the Middle Ages, eventually being grafted into the story of *The Dream of the Rood*.

6. Conclusion

I have shown that some early Christians could imagine the cross not as some*thing* but some*one*. It was a personified figure that could be spoken to and occasionally respond. What is more, some early Christians engaged in a process that I have labeled christomorphizing, wherein they would apply interpretive strategies, attributes, and stories normally reserved for Christ to the cross. With Christ, the cross typifies Edenic figures and resolves the curse of original sin. With Christ, the cross takes on divine powers, spaces, and characteristics such as omnipresence and eternality. With Christ, the cross suffers, is buried, preaches to the dead, resurrects, ascends into heaven, sits on the throne, and comes again in glory. While there were probably multiple purposes and causes for the practice of christomorphizing the cross in early Christian imagination, we may venture to name one theological cause with much explanatory power. The cross was a *necessary* feature of Christ's saving work (see, e.g., 1 Cor 1), and by its God-ordained necessity, mystery, and involvement in the work of Christ, it easily adopted his features. The cross's proximity to Christ and participation in his mission affects its appearance. The cross, for some Christians, though not identical with Christ, looked like him.

As creative as *The Dream of the Rood* is, this poem did not wholly invent its content. It draws on and participates in ancient imaginings that christomorphized the cross, mapping christological features onto his instrument of death. Later, others would also participate in this activity. In the late medieval period and starting in northern Italy, some artists began to depict what scholars today have labeled the "Living Cross." In these works, the cross is ordinarily depicted with Christ's body still on it and with hands extending out of its extremities.[51] In figure 9.7 below,

---

51. See the studies by Robert L. Füglister, *Das Lebende Kreuz: Ikonographisch-ikonologische und Untersuchung der Herkunft und Entwicklung einer spätmittelalterlichen Bildidee und ihrer Verwurzelung im Wort* (Zürich: Benziger, 1964), 111–220; and Achim Timmermann, "The Avenging Crucifix: Some Observations on the Iconography of the Living Cross," *Gesta* 40 (2001): 141–60. Füglister's study of backgrounds for

the right wing of a Westphalian diptych dating to the early fifteenth century portrays a Living Cross.[52] This Living Cross, like others, is lamentably very anti-Jewish.[53] Through its symmetry of opposites, it weaves hostility toward Jews into its portrayal of the doctrine of salvation. The hand at the top holds the key to heaven's gates, while the hand at the bottom holds a hammer ready to smash hell, death, or Satan. The hand extending out of the right end of the crossbeam holds a sword, symbolizing defeat of the Jewish religion, while the hand on the left blesses the Christian church. The entire scene follows this schema of judgment on the right and blessing on the left. Atop the crossbeam on the right side, Eve offers death to Adam. At the base of the cross, a blindfolded old man, symbolizing Judaism, lies down with his flag broken. Atop the left side, the Virgin Mary offers the pope the Eucharist. At the bottom, the church (presented as a woman) holds the eucharistic chalice in one hand and an unbroken flag in the other as the *Agnus Dei* lies down next to a sealed book in the grass. Out of the very top of the cross, vine branches of the tree of good and evil sprout and bear fruit; the branch that goes to the right holds death, whereas the branch on the left cradles the church.[54] Piecing the many images together, the Living Cross appears to be executing the last judgment for Christ.

The Christlike cross of early Christian imagination, though marginal, persisted—or better yet, *lived*—well into the Middle Ages. While I do not want to pass over as insignificant the detestable instances where Christians have weaponized it against Jews, I wonder whether there is something ecologically and theologically important about this Christlike cross phenomenon that *should* be recovered. Carving Christ's likeness onto their recollections of it, some early Christians attributed to this tree a venerable place in the Christian story. It was given a similar Edenic and salvific backstory, was imbued with divine power, and participated in the gospel

---

this image was unnecessarily narrow. The present study has attempted to widen the range of possible precursors.

52. Timmermann, "Avenging Crucifix," 153–43; Achim Timmerman, "Diptych with Symbols of the Virgin and Redeeming Christ: Christ with the Cross as Redemptor Mundi (Right Wing)," Museo Nacional Thyssen-Bornemisza, 2022, https://tinyurl.com/SBLPress4830a1.

53. Timmermann, "Avenging Crucifix." The Living Cross is not the only time Christians have weaponized the cross against Jews; see, e.g., Disc. Sav. 6. As I use Living Cross to discuss the phenomenon of christomorphizing, I hope not to promote such grotesque prejudice.

54. For a fuller description of the diptych, see Füglister, *Lebende Kreuz*, 17–19.

A Christlike Tree 257

Fig. 9.7. The living cross as *redemptor mundi*, ca. 1410 CE. Painting on the right wing of a diptych. Panel, 28.5 x 18.5 cm. Museo Nacional Thyssen-Bornemisza, Madrid, Spain. Photograph by Museo Nacional Thyssen-Bornemisza, Madrid.

journey from the crucifixion to the resurrection, ascension, and second coming. This holy tree, in other words, participated in Christ's history and activities. That a plant is so involved with the salvation of humanity may seem like foolishness to many. That a tree in many early Christian memories looked more like Christ than many humans will certainly be a stumbling block to some. What are we to make of this plant that has been (literally) caught up into the work of the Son in the imaginations of these early Christians? At the very least, this Christlike tree deserves to have some light shed onto it.

Works Cited

Allison, Dale C. *Testament of Abraham*. CEJL. Berlin: de Gruyter, 2003.
Black, Matthew. "The Chi-Rho Sign: Christogram and/or Staurogram?" Pages 319–27 in *Apostolic History and the Gospel: Biblical and Historical Essays Presented to F. F. Bruce on His Sixtieth Birthday*. Edited by W. Ward Gasque and Ralph P. Martin. Exeter: Paternoster, 1970.
Boeft, Jan den, and Jan N. Bremmer. "Notiunculae Martyrologicae III: Some Observations on the Martyria of Polycarp and Pionius." *VC* 39 (1985): 110–30.
Bolyki, János. "'Head Downwards': The Cross of Peter in the Lights of Apocryphal Acts, of the New Testament and of the Society-Transforming Claim of Early Christianity." Pages 111–22 in *The Apocryphal Acts of Peter: Magic, Miracles and Gnosticism*. Edited by Jan N. Bremmer. SAAA 3. Leuven: Peeters, 1998.
Burns, Dylan M., trans. *A Homily on the Passion and Resurrection*. Pages 41–86 in *New Testament Apocrypha: More Noncanonical Scriptures*. Vol. 2. Edited by Tony Burke. Grand Rapids: Eerdmans, 2020.
Burke, Tony, and Brent Landau, eds. *New Testament Apocrypha: More Noncanonical Scriptures*. Vol. 1. Grand Rapids: Eerdmans, 2016.
Collins, John J. "The Sibylline Oracles." *OTP* 1:317–472.
Daniélou, Jean. *The Bible and the Liturgy*. LiSt. Notre Dame: University of Notre Dame Press, 1956.
———. *The Theology of Jewish Christianity*. Edited and translated by John A. Baker. London: Darton, Longman & Todd, 1964.
"Diptych with Symbols of the Virgin and Redeeming Christ: Christ with the Cross as Redemptor Mundi (Right Wing)." Museo Nacional Thyssen-Bornemisza, 2022. https://tinyurl.com/SBLPress4830a1.

Ehrman, Bart, and Zlatko Pleše, eds. and trans. *The Apocryphal Gospels: Texts and Translations*. Oxford: Oxford University Press, 2011.

Elliott, J. Keith, ed. *The Apocryphal New Testament: A Collection of Apocryphal Christian Literature in an English Translation*. Oxford: Clarendon, 1993.

Foster, Paul. "Do Crosses Walk and Talk?: A Reconsideration of Gospel of Peter 10.39–42." *JTS* 64 (2013): 89–104.

———. *The Gospel of Peter: Introduction, Critical Edition and Commentary*. TENTS 4. Leiden: Brill, 2010.

Frank, Georgia. "Christ's Descent to the Underworld in Ancient Ritual and Legend." Pages 211–26 in *Apocalyptic Thought in Early Christianity*. Edited by Robert J. Daly. HCSPTH. Grand Rapids: Baker Academic; Holy Cross Orthodox Press, 2009.

Füglister, Robert L. *Das Lebende Kreuz: Ikonographisch-ikonologische und Untersuchung der Herkunft und Entwicklung einer spätmittelalterlichen Bildidee und ihrer Verwurzelung im Wort*. Zürich: Benziger, 1964.

García Márquez, Gabriel. *Cien Años de Soledad*. Anniversary ed. New York: Vintage Español; Penguin Random House, 2017.

Gardner, Iain, and Samuel N. C. Lieu. *Manichaean Texts from the Roman Empire*. Cambridge: Cambridge University Press, 2004.

Garstad, Benjamin. *Apocalypse of Pseudo-Methodius: An Alexandrian World Chronicle*. DOML 14. Cambridge: Harvard University Press, 2012.

Geffcken, Joh. *Die Oracula Sibyllina*. GCS 8. Leipzig: Hinrichs, 1902.

Giulea, Dragoș-Andrei. "Pseudo-Hippolytus's *In Sanctum Pascha*: A Mystery Apocalypse." Pages 127–42 in *Apocalyptic Thought in Early Christianity*. Edited by Robert J. Daly. HCSPTH. Grand Rapids: Baker Academic; Holy Cross Orthodox Press, 2009.

Goodacre, Mark. "NT Blog: A Walking, Talking Cross or the Walking, Talking Crucified One?" NT Blog. 18 October 2010. https://tinyurl.com/SBL4830x.

Harley-McGowen, Felicity. "Picturing the Passion." Pages 290–307 in *The Routledge Handbook of Early Christian Art*. Edited by Robin M. Jensen and Mark D. Ellison. London: Routledge, 2018.

Hilhorst, Antoon. "The Wounds of the Risen Jesus." *EstBib* 41 (1983): 165–67.

Holderness, Graham. "The Sign of the Cross: Culture and Belief in 'The Dream of the Rood.'" *LitTh* 11 (1997): 347–75.

Holmes, Michael W. *The Apostolic Fathers: Greek Texts and English Translations*. Grand Rapids: Baker Books, 1999.

Hurtado, Larry W. *The Earliest Christian Artifacts: Manuscripts and Christian Origins*. Grand Rapids: Eerdmans, 2006.

Irvine, Christopher. "The Iconography of the Cross as the Green Tree." Pages 195–207 in *The Edinburgh Companion to the Bible and the Arts*. Edited by Stephen Prickett. Edinburgh: Edinburgh University Press, 2014.

Jensen, Robin M. *The Cross: History, Art, and Controversy*. Cambridge: Harvard University Press, 2017.

———. *Understanding Early Christian Art*. London: Routledge, 2000.

Junod, Éric, and Jean-Daniel Kaestli. *Acta Johannis*. 2 vols. CCSA 1–2. Turnhout: Brepols, 1983.

Lalleman, Pieter J. *The Acts of John: A Two-Stage Initiation into Johannine Gnosticism*. SAAA 4. Leuven: Peeters, 1998.

Layton, Bentley, and David Brakke. *The Gnostic Scriptures*. 2nd ed. AYBRL. New Haven: Yale University Press, 2021.

Longenecker, Bruce W. *The Cross before Constantine: The Early Life of a Christian Symbol*. Minneapolis: Fortress, 2015.

MacDonald, Dennis Ronald. *The Acts of Andrew and the Acts of Andrew and Matthias in the City of the Cannibals*. SBLTT 33.1. Atlanta: Scholars Press, 1990.

Norris, Russell Bradner, Jr. "Logos Christology as Cosmological Paradigm." *ProEccl* 5 (1996): 183–201.

Pesthy, Monika. "Cross and Death in the Apocryphal Acts of the Apostles." Pages 123–33 in *The Apocryphal Acts of Peter: Magic, Miracles and Gnosticism*. Edited by Jan N. Bremmer. SAAA 3. Leuven: Peeters, 1998.

Prieur, Jean-Marc. *Acta Andreae*. 2 vols. CCSA 5–6. Turnhout: Brepols, 1989.

———. *Das Kreuz in der christlichen Literatur der Antike*. Translated by Ellen Pagnamenta. TC 14. Bern: Lang, 2006.

Rebillard, Éric, ed. *Greek and Latin Narratives about the Ancient Martyrs*. OECT. Oxford: Oxford University Press, 2017.

Roth, Dieter T. "Raising the Bar: An Overlooked Element for Identifying a Staurogram within Nomina Sacra." *NovT* 63 (2021): 112–27.

Schiller, Gertrud. *The Passion of Jesus Christ*. Vol. 2 of *Iconography of Christian Art*. Translated by Janet Seligman. Greenwich: New York Graphic Society, 1972.

Thunø, Erik. "Reliquaries and the Cult of Relics in Late Antiquity." Pages 150–68 in *The Routledge Handbook of Early Christian Art*. Edited by Robin M. Jensen and Mark D. Ellison. London: Routledge, 2018.

Timmermann, Achim. "The Avenging Crucifix: Some Observations on the Iconography of the Living Cross." *Gesta* 40 (2001): 141–60.

Usher, Mark D. "The Sixth Sibylline Oracle as a Literary Hymn." *GRBS* 36 (1995): 25–49.

Visonà, Giuseppe. *Pseudo Ippolito, In Sanctum Pascha: Studio Edizione Commento*. SPMed 15. Milan: Vita e pensiero, 1988.

Visualizing the *Adversus Judaeos* Tradition: Understanding Ἰσραήλ as a *Nomen Sacrum* in Early Christian Manuscripts

Mikeal Parsons, Gregory M. Barnhill, and Natalie Webb

1. Introduction

In this essay, we propose that the *nomen sacrum* for Israel was used to visualize the *adversus Judaeos* tradition that emerged in early Christianity in the second century CE. One would not normally turn to Christian manuscripts of the second to fifth centuries for evidence of the emerging visual culture of early Christianity. Typically, only illuminated manuscripts of the sixth century (and later, but not before) are recognized as contributing to the visual vocabulary of Christianity. On the other hand, Larry Hurtado argues that the metadata in certain early Christian papyrus manuscripts "have 'iconographic' significance. As such, they form perhaps our earliest extant expressions of an emergent Christian 'visual culture.'"[1] Part of

---

Initial research into this topic took place during the fall of 2015, when Barnhill and Webb were students in a New Testament Colloquium at Baylor University on the topic of the *Adversus Judaeos* tradition led by Professor Beverly Gaventa; at the same time, they were enrolled in a seminar on New Testament textual criticism with Mikeal Parsons. Subsequent and sporadic work on the intersection of these areas over the next half dozen years or so has resulted in this essay. We are grateful to Professors Beverly Gaventa and Bruce Longenecker for comments on earlier drafts.

1. Larry W. Hurtado, "The 'Meta-Data' of Earliest Christian Manuscripts," in *Identity and Interaction in the Ancient Mediterranean: Jews, Christians and Others; Essays in Honour of Stephen G. Wilson*, ed. Zeba A. Crook and Philip A. Harland (Sheffield: Sheffield Phoenix, 2007), 158.

Hurtado's argument rests on the presence of the staurogram in Christian papyri, and part centers on the use of *nomina sacra*.[2]

The *nomina sacra* are a collection of words written in abbreviated form with a supralinear stroke in early Christian manuscripts to indicate their "sacred character."[3] A group of words has been identified as composing the *nomina sacra* (a term coined by Ludwig Traube, who published the first major study over a century ago).[4] Most attention has focused on the origins and purpose of the four core *nomina sacra*—θεός, χριστός, Ἰησοῦς, κύριος—and there seems to be a general consensus that these terms were singled out for special treatment for reverential and devotional reasons.[5] The other *nomina sacra* include πνεῦμα, σταυρός, ἄνθρωπος, πατήρ, υἱός, σωτήρ, μήτηρ, οὐρανός, Ἰσραήλ, Δαυίδ, and Ἰερουσαλήμ and are not so easily explained. In fact, Bruce Metzger concludes, "The question why it was

---

2. Larry W. Hurtado, "The Staurogram in Early Christian Manuscripts: The Earliest Visual Reference to the Crucified Jesus?," in *New Testament Manuscripts: Their Texts and Their World*, ed. Thomas J. Kraus and Tobias Nicklas (Leiden: Brill, 2006), 207–26; Hurtado, "Meta-Data," 156–60.

3. Larry W. Hurtado, "The Origin of the *Nomina Sacra*: A Proposal," *JBL* 117 (1998): 655.

4. Ludwig Traube, *Nomina sacra: Versuch einer Geschichte der christlichen Kürzung* (Munich: Beck'sche Verlagsbuchhandlung, 1907); other major early studies include Anton H. R. E. Paap, *Nomina sacra in the Greek Paypyri of the First Five Centuries A.D.: The Sources and Some Deductions* (Leiden: Brill, 1959); Colin H. Roberts, "Nomina Sacra Origins and Significance," in *Manuscript, Society and Belief in Early Christian Egypt* (Oxford: Oxford University Press, 1979), 26–48. Additional bibliography can be found in Hurtado, "Origin of the *Nomina Sacra*," 655–57. There are a few other words with a supralinear stroke in a few random manuscripts that suggest that they were also treated as sacred terms in those instances; for a list, see Hurtado, "Origin of the *Nomina Sacra*," 656 n. 3.

5. The reverential function of the core *nomina sacra* is most usually associated with the various writings of Larry Hurtado, who in turn credits Erich Dinkler for this emphasis. See Dinkler, "Älteste christliche Denkmäler: Bestand und Chronologie," in *Signum Crucis* (Tübingen: Mohr Siebeck, 1967), 176–78. The challenge to the view that the *nomina sacra* have theological significance was registered by Christopher M. Tuckett, who saw them as aids for public reading. See Tuckett, "'Nomina Sacra': Yes and No?," in *The Biblical Canons*, ed. Jean-Marie Auwers and Henk J. de Jonge (Leuven: Leuven University Press, 2003), 431–58. Tuckett's objections have been persuasively answered by, *inter alia*, Larry Hurtado, *The Earliest Christian Artifacts: Manuscripts and Christian Origins* (Grand Rapids: Eerdmans, 2006), 122–34; and Jane Heath, "*Nomina Sacra* and *Sacra Memoria* before the Monastic Age," *JTS* 61 (2010): 518–23.

these fifteen names, and only these, that came to be so regarded has not been answered satisfactorily."[6]

Tomas Bokedal has attempted to account for (most of) the collection, suggesting that this second group of terms appears "to have been introduced to the list by association with one or more previously included words" and/or, as in the case of οὐρανός and μήτηρ (also associated with the rise of Marian devotion), within the context of emerging early Christian creeds, such as the *regula fidei*.[7] He associates πνεῦμα, υἱός, and πατήρ with Ἰησοῦς, χριστός and θεός "within an emerging triadic/Trinitarian framing." The terms σταυρός, ἄνθρωπος, and Δαυίδ he associates with Jesus, the latter two presumably as parts of titles, Son of Man and Son of David.

It is instructive that the one term that Bokedal does not account for as a *nomen sacrum* is Ἰσραήλ.[8] It is the place of Ἰσραήλ as a *nomen sacrum* that we seek to explore in this essay. We propose (1) to describe the function of Ἰσραήλ in some key texts of the *adversus Judaeos* tradition (defined below), especially in the pre-Constantinian period, and (2) to argue that this tradition gives a reasonable explanation for the emergence of Ἰσραήλ as a *nomen sacrum*—the visual phenomenon, which to this point has either defied explanation or been neglected altogether.[9]

---

6. Bruce M. Metzger, *Manuscripts of the Greek Bible: An Introduction to Paelaeography* (New York: Oxford University Press, 1981), 37 n. 85.

7. Tomas Bokedal, "Notes on the *Nomina Sacra* and Biblical Interpretation," in *Beyond Biblical Theologies*, ed. Heinrich Assel, Stefan Beyerle, and Christfried Böttrich (Tübingen: Mohr Siebeck, 2012), 281–82; Bokedal, *The Formation and Significance of the Christian Biblical Canon: A Study in Text, Ritual and Interpretation* (London: Bloomsbury, 2014), 113–16.

8. Bokedal does suggest Ἰσραήλ is reflected in the third article of Irenaeus's *Proof of Apostolic Preaching*, but he places it (and Ἰερουσαλήμ) in parentheses, since neither is actually referenced there (*Formation and Significance*, 115).

9. Given our interest in the *nomina sacra* as they appear in texts extant from the second through fifth centuries, we are not pursuing the complex and contested question of the nature and extent of supersessionism in the New Testament texts themselves. Bruce Longenecker has explored supersessionism, especially in Paul. See Longenecker, "On Israel's God and God's Israel: Assessing Supersessionism in Paul," *JTS* 58 (2007): 27–44; on this issue, see also Samuel Sandmel, *Anti-Semitism in the New Testament?* (Philadelphia: Fortress, 1978); John G. Gager, *The Origins of Anti-Semitism* (Oxford: Oxford University Press, 1983); Terence L. Donaldson, *Jews and Anti-Judaism in the New Testament: Decision Points and Divergent Interpretations* (Waco, TX: Baylor University Press, 2010).

2. The *Adversus Judaeos* Tradition

In the early centuries of Christianity, one major aspect of the church's burgeoning theology and identity formation was represented by authors writing antagonistically about and/or toward Jews. Judith Lieu notes, "By the third century we find the systematized collection of arguments and proof texts *Against the Jews*, in Tertullian, Cyprian, Hippolytus and their successors," but "most of the foundations for these arguments were laid in the second century, particularly in Justin's *Dialogue with Trypho* ... or in the *Epistle of (Ps.) Barnabas*."[10] While there is certainly variation in these documents' purposes, uses, and backgrounds (and in scholarly hypotheses concerning these issues in each individual document), the common thread of an apparent hostility toward Jews links the writings known as the *adversus Judaeos* literature.

The hallmark of the *adversus Judaeos* tradition was the claim the church had "replaced Israel in the divine purposes and has inherited all that was positive in Israel's tradition."[11] This struggle over identity often played itself out in the authority and interpretation of Scripture, the Tanak for Jews and the Old Testament for Christians—a common text that divided the two communities. In the *adversus Judaeos* tradition, early Christian writers were concerned to preserve both distinctiveness from the Jews and continuity with Jewish Scripture. These manifestations of replacement theology were rooted in various expressions of early Christian self-definition.[12] We explore the contours of this tradition in several examples below.

Epistle of Barnabas

Written sometime in the late first or early second century, the Epistle of Barnabas plays an early and influential role in the developing *adversus*

---

10. Judith M. Lieu, *Image and Reality: The Jews in the World of the Christians in the Second Century* (Edinburgh: T&T Clark, 1996), 4.

11. Terence Donaldson, "Supersessionism and Early Christian Self-Definition," *JJMJS* 3 (2016): 1. This view is often described as supersessionism, but, as Donaldson points out, there are various strands of supersessionism that do not necessitate a full-blown replacement theology.

12. Donaldson has proposed a complex typology of early Christian self-definition, out of which various supersessionist tendencies emerged. His definition of supersessionism above, perhaps misleadingly, specifies "replacement" as a central feature, despite the nuances he offers in his typology (Donaldson, "Supersessionism and Early Christian Self-Definition," 1–32).

Judaeos tradition. While there is much to be said about scholarly debates regarding author and audience, this project will set these concerns aside and focus on the letter's use of 'Ισραήλ and related terms.[13] The Epistle of Barnabas contains no reference to "Jews" ('Ιουδαῖοι),[14] although it does use the term 'Ισραήλ on twelve occasions (Barn. 4.14; 5.2, 8; 6.7; 8.1, 3; 9.2; 11.1; 12.2 [2x], 5; 16.5). Most of these references are historically oriented (e.g., remembering past wonders among Israel [4.14, 5.8], the prophets' words to Israel [6.7], the abandonment of Israel [16.5], or scriptural quotations or allusions [9.2; 11.1]). In Barn. 5.2, however, the author makes his most explicit hermeneutical statement: "For some of the things written about him [the Lord] concern Israel; others concern us."[15] The multiple referents are presumably demonstrated in the quote from Isa 53 that follows. Here, the author of the Epistle of Barnabas keeps Israel and "us" carefully separated in what Peter Richardson calls "one of his cardinal rules of interpretation."[16] The explicit transposition by which the church became Israel that can be seen in later literature is not found in the Epistle of Barnabas.

Even so, a closer look at the historically oriented references to Israel reveals a tendency in Barnabas for a typological reading that takes the significance of Israel's Scripture and practice and claims not just an analogous meaning for the church, but that the true and right interpretation always had to do with Jesus and his people (or the "us" of Barnabas). For example, Barn. 8.1–3 takes up the command to Israel regarding burnt sacrifice:

---

13. For information on these concerns see Reidar Hvalvik, *The Struggle for Scripture and Covenant: A Purpose of the Epistle of Barnabas and Jewish-Christian Competition in the Second Century*, WUNT 2/82 (Tübingen: Mohr Siebeck, 1996), esp. 6–56; James Carleton Paget, *The Epistle of Barnabas: Outlook and Background*, WUNT 2/64 (Tübingen: Mohr Siebeck, 1994), esp. 3–70; A. Lukyn Williams, *Adversus Judaeos: A Bird's-Eye View of Christian Apologiae until the Renaissance* (Cambridge: Cambridge University Press, 1935), 14–27.

14. Although the Latin translation does include the phrase *populum Judaeorum*. See Robert A. Kraft, "The Epistle of Barnabas: Its Quotations and Their Sources" (PhD diss., Harvard University, 1961), 53.

15. All translations of the Epistle of Barnabas follow Bart D. Ehrman, ed. and trans., *The Apostolic Fathers*, vol. 2, *Epistle of Barnabas, Papias and Quadratus, Epistle to Diognetus, The Shepherd of Hermas*, LCL (Cambridge: Harvard University Press, 2003).

16. Peter Richardson, *Israel in the Apostolic Church* (Cambridge: Cambridge University Press, 1969), 16.

> And what do you suppose is the type found in his command to Israel, that men who are full of sin should offer up a heifer, and after slaughtering it burn it, and that children should then take the ashes and cast them into vessels, and then tie scarlet wool around a piece of wood (see again the type of the cross and the scarlet wool!), along with the hyssop, and that the children should thus sprinkle the people one by one, that they might be purified from their sins? Understand how he speaks to you simply. The calf is Jesus; the sinful men who make the offering are those who offered him up for slaughter. Then they are no longer men and the glory of sinners is no more. The children who sprinkle are those who proclaimed to us the forgiveness of sins and the purification of our hearts. To them he has given the authority to preach the gospel. There are twelve of them as a witness to the tribes, for there were twelve tribes in Israel.

The letter goes on to interpret more details of the scriptural imagery in terms that apply to the church before claiming, "And thus the things that have happened in this way are clear to us, but they are obscure to them, because they have not heard the voice of the Lord" (Barn. 8.7).

Later in the letter, another episode taken from the history of Israel is interpreted by the author as having always been in reference to Jesus and prompted by the Spirit:

> And he again tells Moses, when Israel was attacked by a foreign people, to remind those under assault that they were being handed over to death because of their sins. The Spirit speaks to the heart of Moses that he should make a type of the cross and of the one who was about to suffer, that they might realize, he says, that if they refused to hope in him, they would be attacked forever. And so Moses stacked weapons one on the other in the midst of the battle, and standing high above all the people he began stretching out his hands; and so Israel again gained the victory. But then, when he lowered his hands, they began to be killed. (Barn. 12.2)

Just after this retelling, the author goes on to claim, "Again Moses makes a type of Jesus, showing that he had to suffer and that he will again give life—this one whom they will think they have destroyed. This type came in a sign given when Israel was falling" (Barn. 12.5). The disjunction between Moses the ancestor (who here is a type of Jesus) and Israel-at-large (who here were "falling") is one that peppers this text and other *adversus Judaeos* literature.[17]

---

17. Another example is in the position of the prophets over against Israel, prophesying of Israel's connection to Jesus's death (Barn. 6.7).

While Israel is set in clear opposition to "us" in Barn. 5.2, there are many links between Israelite history and Christ and his followers. Reidar Hvalvik notes that in the scheme of the Epistle of Barnabas, "The patriarchs and the prophets were—so to speak—representatives of Christ in the past."[18] Israel is not explicitly named until later in the chapter, but Barn. 4.6–8 alludes to Israelite history when it claims that the covenant is "ours" since "they" lost it just after Moses had received it, because they turned to idols. Moses then destroyed the tablets, according to Barn. 4.8.[19]

Barnabas stops short of the explicit claim that the church is the new Israel; there are two ways of reading Scripture, for example, the "Jewish-fleshly" way and the "Christian-spiritual" way. But for Barnabas, Christ-followers (the "us" and "we" of the letter) hold the true meaning of Scripture (8.7), are the sole inheritors of God's covenant (4.6–7), and are the location of the spiritual temple of God (16.5–9). The line of argumentation found in Barnabas is influential in subsequent literature that takes these claims even further.[20] Hvalvik argues that "one of [Barnabas's] main strategies is to capture the treasures of Judaism: their Scripture and their covenant."[21] Israel remains a distinct entity, but its ancestors, writings, and promises belong to the church. This coopting of Israel's goods, even while denigrating the people of Israel, may hint at the theological importance of the term Ἰσραήλ for early Christianity.

Justin Martyr's *Dialogue with Trypho*

The *Dialogue with Trypho* by Justin Martyr (ca. 100–165 CE) is thought to have been written in the mid-second century and looks back on a supposed

---

18. Hvalvik, *Purpose of Barnabas*, 146–47. He references Barn. 5.6, 9.7, 10.10, 12.2, 13.5, 14.1–4.

19. Michael Kok cites Barn. 4.6–7 to demonstrate that "in attempting to formulate a distinct Christian ethnic identity and place in the world, *Barnabas* has the Christians replace Israel as the true covenant people." See Michael Kok, "The True Covenant People: Ethnic Reasoning in the Epistle of Barnabas," *ScRel* 40 (2011): 89.

20. Some modern scholars, such as Parkes, go so far as to argue, "The whole of the epistle of Barnabas is an exposition of the Church as the true Israel." See James Parkes, *The Conflict of the Church and the Synagogue: A Study in the Origins of Antisemitism* (Philadelphia: Meridian Books, 1961), 84.

21. Hvalvik, *Struggle for Scripture*, 329.

conversation between Justin and a particular Jew named Trypho.[22] Whether the conversation actually took place is debated (along with questions of its intended purpose and audience).[23] We must set these issues aside for the moment. Regardless of original audience, purpose, and historical veracity, this document provides invaluable information about the early church's understanding of its relationship to Israel.

In *Dialogue with Trypho*, Christ believers are "the true priestly family of God" (*Dial.* 116.3).[24] Christ-believing gentiles "shall receive the inheritance, along with the patriarchs" (26.1). The Jewish Scriptures belong to the church (Justin tells Trypho that they are "not yours but ours" [29.2]) and should be read typologically ("if I were to enumerate all the other Mosaic precepts, gentlemen, I could show that they are types, symbols, and prophecies of what would happen to Christ and those who were foreknown as those who would believe in him" [42.4]). Justin goes beyond previous extant literature, however, by explicitly and repeatedly arguing that the church is the true Israel.

Near the beginning of the text, Justin asserts, "We have been led to God through this crucified Christ, and we are the true spiritual Israel, and the descendants of Judah, Jacob, Isaac, and Abraham, who, though uncircumcised, was approved and blessed by God because of his faith" (*Dial.* 11.5). In *Dial.* 135, Justin connects Christ with Jacob and argues that "we, hewn out of the side of Christ, are the true people of Israel" (135.3). In the same line of argument, Justin tells Trypho, "as your whole people was called after that one Jacob, surnamed Israel, so we who obey the precepts

---

22. Craig D. Allert argues the text was written soon after 155 CE. See Craig D. Allert, *Revelation, Truth, Canon and Intepretation: Studies in Justin Martyr's Dialogue with Trypho*, VCSup 64 (Leiden: Brill, 2002), 32–34.

23. Views range from attributing it to the imagination of Justin, e.g., Michael Mach, to affirming some basis in historical conversation(s), e.g., Lieu, Stanton. See Michael Mach, "Justin Martyr's *Dialogus cum Tryphone Iudaeo* and the Development of Christian Anti-Judaism," in *Contra Iudaeos: Ancient and Medieval Polemics between Christians and Jews*, ed. Ora Limor and Guy G. Stroumsa (Tübingen: Mohr Siebeck, 1996), 34–35; Lieu, *Image and Reality*, 104; Graham N. Stanton, "Justin Martyr's Dialogue with Trypho: Group Boundaries, 'Proselytes' and 'God-Fearers,'" in *Tolerance and Intolerance in Early Judaism and Christianity*, ed. Graham N. Stanton and Guy G. Stroumsa (New York: Cambridge University Press, 1998), 263–64.

24. Translations of Justin Martyr follow Thomas B. Falls, trans., *Dialogue with Trypho*, ed. Michael Slusser, SFC 3 (Washington, DC: Catholic University of America Press, 2003).

of Christ, are, through Christ who begot us to God, both called and in reality are, Jacob and Israel and Judah and Joseph and David and true children of God" (123.9). Justin thus claims both the title of Israel and Israel's ancestors for the church.[25]

While Justin transfers Israel's name, Scriptures, ancestors, and inheritance to the gentile church explicitly, he may not do so exclusively. In some passages, Justin seems to acknowledge a shared future for at least parts of ethnic Israel and the gentile church. For example, Justin denies Trypho's inference that, according to his argument, no Jews will take part in the inheritance (25.6–26.1). In another instance, Justin interprets Jacob's marriages to Leah and Rachel as analogues for Christ's relationship to Jews and Christians:

> It was not lawful for Jacob to marry two sisters at the same time. So he worked in the service of Laban for [one of] his daughters, and, when he was deceived about the younger, he worked another seven years. Now Leah represented your people and the Synagogue, while Rachel was a figure of our Church. And Christ still serves for them and for his servants that are in both. (*Dial.* 34.3)

As the analogy continues, Leah's weak eyes represent the weak souls of the Jews, and Rachel's theft and hiding of Laban's gods represents the stripping of the ancestral gods from the gentile church (134.5). Even if this is a disparaging portrait of Jews, Christ is nevertheless portrayed as serving for both.

In addition to calling the church the true Israel, Justin equates Christ himself with Israel. One move toward this development (seen in examples above) is the connection of Christ with Jacob: "Jacob was surnamed Israel, and it has been shown that Israel is also Christ, who is, and is called, Jesus" (*Dial.* 134.6). Justin also points to the supposed etymology of the term, which he believes means "a man who overcomes power" (125.3). The logic of Justin's argument is a bit convoluted, but according to Justin, Christ accomplishes this overcoming of power, which is foretold in Jacob's wrestling. At the same time, Christ predates Jacob: "His name from of old was Israel—a name which he conferred on the blessed Jacob when he blessed

---

25. See also *Dial.* 82.1, where "the gifts of prophecy" are said to be transferred to "us," and 119.5, in which Justin asserts that gentile Christ-believers will inherit the Holy Land with Abraham.

him with his own name, announcing thereby that all who come to the Father through him are part of the blessed Israel" (125.5).

In Justin's *Dialogue with Trypho*, the term Ἰσραήλ is used not in opposition to the church but as the church's own designation. Kendall Soulen writes that in the *Dialogue with Trypho*, "the Hebrew Scriptures point beyond themselves at every point to Christ and the church, the new spiritual Israel."[26] The Scripture, inheritance, gifts, ancestors, and name of historical Israel are therefore said to belong to the church. This conception of the church as the true Israel (and of the equation of Israel/Jacob and Christ) both is garnered from a specific reading of Scripture and pushes forward a view of Scripture as in continuity with Christian literature and belief. The appropriations of Israel's name and sacred texts are mutually reinforcing. It would be an understatement to say that the term carries Christian theological freight in this text.

On the other hand, Justin does suggest that "Israel itself comprised two different types of people from the very beginning."[27] He writes in *Dial.* 135.6: "So, we must here conclude that there were two seeds of Judah, and two races, as there are two houses of Jacob: the one born of flesh and blood, the other of faith and the Spirit." Here, for Justin, "the church is not so much a new entity that replaces Israel as it is a fuller manifestation of a portion of Israel that was represented by the saints of old. Israel always contained within itself a 'true' and a 'false' Israel."[28]

While Justin writes *Adversus Judaeos*, and speaks disparagingly of Trypho and his fellow Jews, he does *not* write *against Israel*. Instead, he carefully explicates the Scriptures, albeit sometimes with torturous logic, in such a way that the appellation Ἰσραήλ is taken up and assumed by the church. Oskar Skarsaune writes,

> Justin set a precedent for Christian hermeneutics with regard to the Jews and the Church that was to dominate for centuries to come: every negative and critical remark about Israel in the Bible was taken to describe in a timeless, almost ontological way, the very nature of the Jewish people.

---

26. R. Kendall Soulen, *The God of Israel and Christian Theology* (Minneapolis: Fortress, 1996), 37.

27. Donaldson, "Supersessionism and Early Christian Self-Definition," 8.

28. Donaldson, "Supersessionism and Early Christian Self-Definition," 15–16. One could also cite Barn. 9.7, in which Abraham "was looking ahead in the spirit to Jesus" (see also Moses in Barn. 12.2–3).

On the other hand, every positive saying about Israel was transferred to the Church, and the Gentiles were found to be believers almost by nature as well.[29]

There is much more that could be said about this hermeneutical maneuver and its origins and goals; however, it is enough for our purposes to demonstrate its pervasiveness in such a prominent text.[30]

5 Ezra

Composed around the same time as Justin's *Dialogue*, 5 Ezra is a "short, early Christian writing … that is a thinly veiled successionist tract."[31] Fifth Ezra argues that ethnic Israel has been succeeded by gentile Christians. "What shall I do to you, O Jacob? You, Judah, would not obey me. I will turn to other nations and will give them my name, so that they may keep my statutes" (5 Ezra 1:24). Later, the author writes:

> I will give your houses to a people that will come, who without having heard me will believe. Those to whom I have shown no signs will do

---

29. Oskar Skarsaune, "Scriptural Interpretation in the Second and Third Centuries—Except Clement and Origen," in *Hebrew Bible / Old Testament: The History of Its Interpretation*, ed. Magne Sæbø (Göttingen: Vandenhoeck & Ruprecht, 1996), 1:404.

30. Pressures from the Roman world and its emphasis on antiquity surely had an impact on Justin's determination to lay claim to Israel's history. Richardson notes a possible philosophical motivation from Justin, whose logic leads to the conclusion that "the Church has superseded Israel and taken over its status as a respectable philosophy" (*Israel in the Apostolic Church*, 14).

31. Theodore A. Bergren, "Gentile Christians, Exile, and Return in 5 Ezra 1:35–40," *JBL* 130 (2011): 593. Fifth Ezra is typically printed as the first two chapters of 2 Esdras (as in the NRSV). Bergren gives a range of second to third century CE for its date of composition (593), but Graham Stanton offers a convincing argument for dating the document to the middle of the second century, "perhaps shortly after the Bar Kochba rebellion." See Graham Stanton, *A Gospel for a New People: Studies in Matthew* (Louisville, KY: Westminster John Knox, 1992), 260. The text is extant in Latin (probably also its original language) and preserved in two manuscript traditions, the French (S A) and the Spanish (CM [N V L]). On the text, see Thomas A. Bergren, *Fifth Ezra: The Text, Origin and Early History*, SCS 2 (Atlanta: Scholars Press, 1990). All translations follow the NRSV unless otherwise noted.

Arguments that 5 Ezra was a Jewish text overlaid with Christian interpolations (e.g., Steck) have failed to persuade. See Odil H. Steck, *Israel und das gewaltsame Geschick der Propheten* (Neukirchen-Vluyn: Neukirchener Verlag, 1967).

what I have commanded. They have seen no prophets, yet will recall their former state. I call to witness the gratitude of the people that is to come, whose children rejoice with gladness; though they do not see me with bodily eyes, yet with the spirit they will believe the things I have said. (1:35–37)

In these passages, 5 Ezra emphasizes the discontinuity between Israel and the church. Because of its disobedience, Israel has been replaced by a "people who will come" and "who without having heard me will believe."

Fifth Ezra also introduces a metaphor not found in Justin, the figure of the mother: "The mother who bore them says to them, 'Go, my children, because I am a widow and forsaken. I brought you up with gladness, but with mourning and sorrow I have lost you, because you have sinned before the Lord God and have done what is evil in my sight" (2:2–3).[32] Who is the mother? Scholars generally agree that the author here is drawing on a familiar image found in the Jewish Scriptures, such as Isa 66, that depicts Jerusalem as the mother of Israel:

> Before she was in labor
>   she gave birth;
> before her pain came upon her
>   she delivered a son.
> Who has heard of such a thing?
>   Who has seen such things?
> Shall a land be born in one day?
>   Shall a nation be delivered in one moment?
> Yet as soon as Zion was in labor
>   she delivered her children.
> Shall I open the womb and not deliver?
>   says the LORD;
> shall I, the one who delivers, shut the womb?
>   says your God.
> Rejoice with Jerusalem, and be glad for her,

---

32. It would be instructive to trace the use of Jerusalem as a *nomen sacrum* in the early Christian manuscript tradition as another example of visualizing the *adversus Judaeos* tradition, but for the sake of space that project will need to be pursued at another time. It is also possible that "David" and "fathers/ancestors" (in the plural) may also emerge from a similar tradition, but that would be more difficult to demonstrate given that both could have roots in other christological or theological interests and concerns.

> all you who love her;
> rejoice with her in joy,
>   all you who mourn over her—
> that you may nurse and be satisfied
>   from her consoling breast,
> that you may drink deeply with delight
>   from her glorious bosom. (Isa 66:7–11; see Ps 87)[33]

The author explicitly invokes Jerusalem just a few verses after employing the figure of the mother: "Thus says the Lord to Ezra: "Tell my people that I will give them the kingdom of Jerusalem, which I was going to give to Israel" (5 Ezra 2:10). Graham Stanton observes, "The metaphor of a mother and her sons is repeated at 2.15; 2.17; and 2.31, but now it refers to the church and to Christians."[34] Theodore Bergren argues that there are two mothers in 5 Ezra 2: earthly Jerusalem (2:1–7) and "Mother Church" (2:15–32). This metaphor, which dominates the second half of 5 Ezra, is used to stress the finality of the separation of the church from Israel.[35]

Summary

In various ways, explicit and implicit, in the *adversus Judaeos* tradition, scriptural Israel is replaced by the church.[36] And much more is at stake than exchanging a single ethnic group for a multiethnic community. The term Ἰσραήλ (and Israelite), by and large in antiquity, was not a term used by non-Jews; it is in-group language. Israel/ite, according to James Dunn, "denoted a self-understanding in terms of election and covenant promise."[37] The term Ἰουδαῖος did not convey this same significance, at least not consistently; it was a way to differentiate Jews from other ethnic

---

33. Paul knows and cites this tradition in Gal 4:26.
34. Stanton, *Gospel for a New People*, 262.
35. Theodore A. Bergren, "Two 'Mothers' in 5 Ezra 2:1–32," *VC* 73 (2019): 440–62.
36. Our survey could be expanded to include examples from Irenaeus, Tertullian, Origen, and Cyprian, but Barnabas, Justin, and 5 Ezra should suffice to establish the basic contours of the *adversus Judaeos* tradition.
37. James D. G. Dunn, *The Partings of the Ways: Between Christianity and Judaism and Their Significance for the Character of Christianity*, 2nd ed. (London: SCM, 2006), 192.

groups.³⁸ Ἰσραήλ represents the people constituted by God. The term is coterminous with what is called ethnic Israel, but that is not the point. Divine creation is the point.³⁹ These *adversus Judaeos* writers understood that point and were claiming Israel's benefits as God's chosen people for the community of Christ believers, replacing Israel's role as the divinely constituted people of God with the church.⁴⁰

In view of this clear trajectory of interpretation, especially the way in which Israel, Israel's Scriptures, and its interpretation were contested, is there any indication that such Christian theology was inscribed in the texts that Christians used and copied in the early centuries of the Christian movement? If so, of what significance might this phenomenon have for understanding both early Christianity and its manuscript tradition? We turn now to explore how and why Ἰσραήλ was visualized as a *nomen sacrum*.

3. Visualizing the *Adversus Judaeos* Tradition

As noted above, the four core *nomina sacra*—θεός, χριστός, Ἰησοῦς, κύριος—have been singled out by scholars who note their special treatment in early Christianity for reverential and devotional reasons. In fact, Schuyler Brown dubs these core four terms *nomina divina*, "divine names."⁴¹ In addition, investigations into the origins of the *nomina sacra* tend to focus on these core four *nomina divina*. According to some, the origins of the remaining terms beyond the core four, to which *Israel* belongs, radiated out later from the devotional practice of early Christians that had earlier resulted in the emergence of the core *nomina sacra*. Bruce Metzger, for example, affirms that the original *nomina sacra* were "extended to a vari-

---

38. Dunn, *Partings of the Ways*, 192. The sense of Ἰουδαῖος is not as clear-cut as often assumed. See Nathan Thiel, "'Israel' and 'Jew' as Markers of Jewish Identity in Antiquity: The Problems of Insider/Outsider Classification," *JSJ* 45 (2014): 80–99.

39. We are grateful to Professor Beverly Gaventa in helping us articulate this point.

40. Stanton argues that the metaphor of Jerusalem depicts the city as mother of both Israel and the church, thus underscoring the continuity (rather than discontinuity) between the two (*Gospel for a New People*, 262). Even if Stanton is correct (and Bergren wrong) regarding the author's *intention*, we shall see that the use of Jerusalem as a *nomen sacrum* does not affect our argument that its visual effect is to replace physical Jerusalem with the church as new Jerusalem.

41. Schuyler Brown, "Concerning the Origin of the *Nomina Sacra*," *SPap* 9 (1970): 7–19.

ety of other words that carried deep theological connotations."[42] But he does not specify what those "deep theological connotations" might be. Others conclude that there are connections between and among the core four and the other *nomina sacra*, though they "may have followed once the original significance of the first contractions had been lost."[43] But why must we assume a common explanation for the emergence of all fifteen *nomina sacra*, especially when there is such divergence in the terms? Can we tease out other possible reasons for the inclusion of the term *Israel* as a *nomen sacrum*?

A tertiary group of terms, so identified by Bokedal because the abbreviated form is used in 23 to 62 percent of their occurrence in seventy-four manuscripts from the second to fourth centuries, includes such varied terms as σταυρόω (62 percent), πατήρ (53 percent), ἄνθρωπος (45 percent), Ἰερουσαλήμ (44 percent), υἱός (36 percent), Ἰσραήλ (24 percent), and πνευματικός (23 percent).[44] Hurtado has a third group (based on what he thinks are not only abbreviated less consistently but "joined the list of sacred terms latest"), which includes πατήρ, υἱός, σωτήρ, μήτηρ, οὐρανός, Ἰσραήλ, Δαυίδ, and Ἰερουσαλήμ.[45] That a number of these terms did in fact grow out of an interest in, and devotion to, names associated with God or Jesus seems reasonable: terms such as πατήρ, ἄνθρωπος, and υἱός (from Bokedal's list) in addition to σωτήρ and Δαυίδ (from Hurtado's list) could be viewed as logical extensions of theological/christological terms.[46] But what of *Israel*? Was it a sacred term that appeared early in the manuscript tradition and that emerged in a Jewish Christian context as a sign of the honor and esteem attached to scriptural and ethnic Israel?[47]

---

42. Metzger, *Manuscripts of the Greek Bible*, 37.

43. Harry Y. Gamble, *Books and Readers in the Early Church: A History of Early Christian Texts* (New Haven: Yale University Press, 1995), 77.

44. Bokedal, *Formation and Significance*, 90. As we will see, these percentages mask the preponderance of occurrences for specific *nomina sacra* in specific manuscripts; see, e.g., the discussion of P.Beatty 6 (Rahlfs 963) and P75 below. Furthermore, Bokedal limits his analysis to New Testament manuscripts, while we have also included manuscripts of Christian OT texts.

45. Hurtado, "Origin of the *Nomina Sacra*," 655–56.

46. Likewise, πνεῦμα, found in Hurtado's and Bokedal's second subgroup, could be recognized as indicating some emerging and incipient Trinitarian interests.

47. Bokedal may reflect this view, although he does not specify Ἰσραήλ (*Formation and Significance*, 102–3). He connects Ἰερουσαλήμ with the nascent Christians' "strong sense of the OT and Jewish traditions" (quoting Hurtado), implying a very

We contend that the replacement of Israel with the church in the *adversus Judaeos* tradition provided the impetus for marking Ἰσραήλ a *nomen sacrum*, thereby visualizing a major facet of the *adversus Judaeos* tradition in the manuscripts of both Old and New Testaments. The simultaneous rise of the secondary *nomina sacra*, such as Ἰσραήλ, and of the *adversus Judaeos* tradition in the late first and early second centuries makes it reasonable to suppose that the two phenomena occurred in some kind of relationship to each other. *Nomina sacra* provided visual continuity between Christian writings and Jewish Scripture and asserted Christian ownership of these texts and their interpretation. The core four illustrated Christ-followers' devotion to God and Jesus, and the *nomen sacrum* for Ἰσραήλ visually represented the replacement of scriptural or ethnic Israel with the church, the entity that the *adversus Judaeos* tradition believed was the true Israel. What was at stake was the rejection of scriptural Israel (and their contemporary descendants) as the divinely constituted people of God in favor of the communities of Christ-followers. A look at the evidence of the use of *nomina sacra* for the word Ἰσραήλ, both the number of manuscripts and specific features of its use, supports this proposal.

The word Ἰσραήλ is contracted in forty-one manuscripts through the fifth century CE.[48] The following forms are found in manuscripts through the fifth century: (1) ιηλ in thirty-four manuscripts, which Traube suggests is the oldest form, and Anton Paap concurs;[49] (2) ισλ in eleven manu-

---

early date (pre-70 CE) for Ἰερουσαλήμ as a *nomen sacrum*, which runs counter to most other schemes, which place its emergence later in the second century. Bokedal's argument is based on an apparent misreading of Hurtado, who clearly does not include Ἰερουσαλήμ (or Ἰσραήλ) in the earliest group of words that were "regularly treated as *nomina sacra*" within Jewish-Christian circles in the first century (namely, θεός, χριστός, Ἰησοῦς, κύριος; see Hurtado, "Origin of the *Nomina Sacra*," 671–72).

48. We have consulted Traube, *Nomina Sacra*, and Paap, *Nomina Sacra in the Greek Papyri*. Manuscripts from the sixth century on almost invariably use the *nomina sacra* forms, so they have been excluded here.

49. It could be that name theology played a role in ιηλ becoming the *nomen sacrum* of choice for Israel in many manuscripts. The author of Epistle of Barnabas writes in 9.7–9 about the letters ιη bearing christological significance, and Justin writes about connecting the name Christ with the name Israel (*Dial.* 125.3–5, 134.6, 135.3). These two *nomina sacra* share two letters: ιη. Might such name theology contribute to the development of the *nomen sacrum* for Israel? These arguments do not seem unique to Justin or Barnabas: Justin appears to stand with a community of Christians behind him, and Barnabas writes that the gematria he teaches are one of his most certain teachings (see Barn. 9.9).

scripts, which Traube suggests may come from the Syriac; (3) ισηλ in four manuscripts; (4) ισρηλ in two manuscripts; (5) ισρλ in three manuscripts; ιελ once; ιαηλ once; and ισαηλ once. It occurs *only* in full (plene) in twenty-eight manuscripts before the fifth century. In seven manuscripts it occurs plene and in contracted form. A *nomen sacrum* form occurs in only one manuscript in the second century (P.Beatty 6), in ten manuscripts in the third century, in seventeen manuscripts in the fourth century, and in thirteen manuscripts in the fifth century (of course, variable dates for many manuscripts could change these numbers).

Chester Beatty Papyrus 6 (Rahlfs 963)

The earliest extant instance of the *nomen sacrum* ιηλ is found in P.Beatty 6 (Rahlfs 963), from the second century (fig. 10.1).[50] This LXX manuscript containing portions of Numbers and Deuteronomy has forty occurrences of ιηλ, potentially forty-one given one occurrence of ι[.]λ. It is written plene twice: Deut 29:9 (πας ανηρ ισραηλ') and 34:12 (εναντι παντος ισραηλ'). In both cases there seems to be no contextual reason to write the word plene as opposed to in *nomen sacrum* form. It is important to note how early this manuscript is, its likely Christian provenance,[51] and the consistency with which this word is contracted. In this manuscript, Ἰησοῦς is contracted as both ιη (the suspended form) and ιης for Joshua, pointing to the fact that its use for Jesus was so established by this time that it was carried over to LXX manuscripts in which Jesus was not the clear referent.[52] This evidence shows the inclination of the scribe to inscribe Christian theology to the text, perhaps even its interpretation (a christological typology between Joshua/Jesus).

---

50. Frederick G. Kenyon suggests second century. See Kenyon, ed., *The Chester Beatty Biblical Papyri: Descriptions and Texts of Twelve Manuscripts on Papyrus of the Greek Bible, Fasciculus V: Numbers and Deuteronomy* (London: Emery Walker, 1935). Roberts surveys the proposals from Kenyon and decides for second or third century, but perhaps late second ("Nomina Sacra Origins and Significance," 78–81). The Chester Beatty library in Dublin has second century.

51. The manuscript uses *nomina sacra* forms for Ἰησοῦς, κύριος, πνεῦμα, ἄνθρωπος, πατήρ, and Ἰσραήλ. Roberts argues for its Christian provenance on the basis that manuscripts of certain Jewish provenance from the early second century BCE to the early first century CE do not contract Ἰσραήλ ("Nomina Sacra Origins and Significance," 30).

52. Roberts, "Nomina Sacra Origins and Significance," 36–37; see also Frederick G. Kenyon, "Nomina Sacra in the Chester Beatty Papyri," *Aegyptus* 13 (1933): 6.

Scott Charlesworth notes that two other words in the less consistently contracted group of *nomina sacra* are also contracted in P.Beatty 6, although only a few times: πατήρ is contracted only two times out of twenty-three and ἄνθρωπος four times of twenty-three. Charlesworth argues that these six "slips" indicate the scribe is used to copying New Testament manuscripts and has intruded *nomina sacra* into this LXX manuscript. Thus the *nomina sacra* conventions in New Testament manuscripts are affecting copying of LXX manuscripts as well.[53] But what he does not account for here is why Ἰσραήλ is the opposite of these other two—why has it become more often contracted, like one of the core *nomina sacra*? Perhaps this word is more important, approaching the core category for this particular manuscript and/or its scribe. The consistent occurrence of Ἰσραήλ as a *nomen sacrum* suggests that P.Beatty 6 indicates an early use of the *nomen sacrum* for Israel and its *importance* as a *nomen sacrum* in the second century. Furthermore, it shows that this word was a *nomen sacrum* in the texts that were considered *Christian Scripture* to the early Christians and reflects the *adversus Judaeos* tradition of interpreting the church as the new Israel around the time that this tradition was beginning to flourish.

Hanna Papyrus (Mater Verbi 1; P75)

The next earliest occurrence of the *nomen sacrum* ιηλ is found in Hanna Papyrus (Mater Verbi 1; P75), dated to 175–225 (fig. 10.2).[54] In this manuscript θεός, Ἰησοῦς, χριστός, and Ἰσραήλ are contracted always with θς, ις, or ιης, χς, and ιηλ, respectively, while Ἰερουσαλήμ, ἄνθρωπος, κυριός, πατήρ, πνεῦμα, σταυρός, and σταυρόω with more or less irregularity.[55] Interestingly, πνεῦμα is only written plene at Luke 10:20, which James Royce takes as a slip in an otherwise universal use of *nomina sacra* for πνεῦμα.[56]

---

53. Scott D. Charlesworth, "Consensus Standardization in the Systematic Approach to Nomina 'Sacra' in Second- and Third-Century Gospel Manuscripts," *Aegyptus* 86 (2006): 64.

54. Victor Martin and Rodolphe Kasser, *Papyrus Bodmer XIV: Évangile de Luc chap. 3–24* (Geneva: Bibliotheca Bodmeriana, 1961). On the other hand, Brent Nongbri has marshalled arguments for pushing the *terminus ad quem* for P75 to the fourth century. See Nongbri, "Reconsidering the Place of Papyrus XIV–XV (P75) in the Textual Criticism of the New Testament," *JBL* 135 (2016): 405–37.

55. Martin and Kasser, *Papyrus Bodmer XIV*, 18.

56. Martin and Kasser, *Papyrus Bodmer XIV*, 1; James Royce, *Scribal Habits in Early Greek New Testament Papyri* (Leiden: Brill, 2008), 650 n. 182.

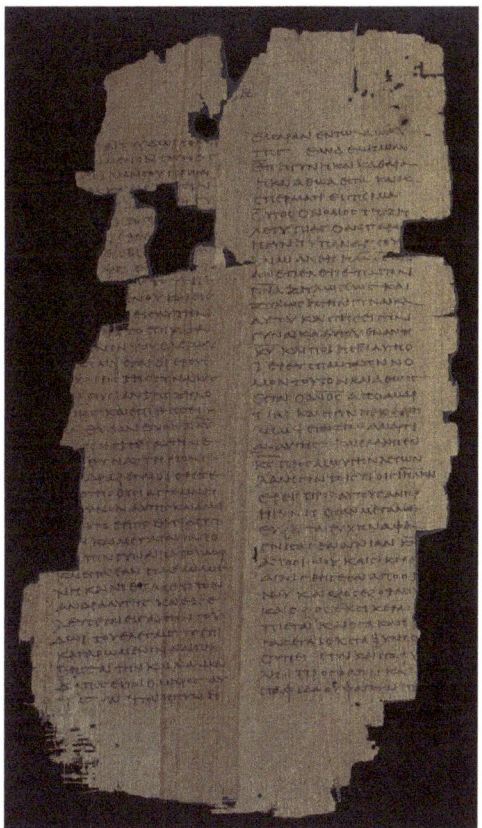

Fig. 10.1. Chester Beatty Papyrus 6 (Rahlfs 963), second century CE. CBL VI f9. Original size 33 cm x 19 cm. © The Trustees of the Chester Beatty Library, Dublin. Photograph by CSNTM. The highlighted detail shows the *nomen sacrum* ιηλ in line 23.

When it comes to the *nomen sacrum* ιηλ, there are seven instances, and (importantly) in every instance of this word extant in the manuscript it is contracted. In this manuscript Ἰσραήλ is marked as a sacred name as consistently as is θεός, Ἰησοῦς, and χριστός (and potentially also πνεῦμα), and more consistently than any other of the *nomina sacra*.[57] Charlesworth suggests such systematic use of the *nomen sacrum* ιηλ is the work of this scribe.[58]

Washington Manuscript 5 (Codex Washingtonensis)

Another important early papyrus is Washington Manuscript 5 (Codex Washingtonensis), a codex that dates to the middle or end of the third century and contains the Minor Prophets (Hos 1:10–Mal 4:6; see fig. 10.3).[59] In this manuscript *nomina sacra* are used consistently for κύριος, θεός, πνεῦμα, and ἄνθρωπος, but notably lacking for χριστός.[60] In this manuscript, Ἰσραήλ is abbreviated ιηλ forty-nine times but written plene in Amos 9:14 (ισρα]ηλ), Mic 1:14, and Mal 1:1. These three plene occurrences have no

---

57. As a point of comparison, we looked closely at the use of *nomina sacra* for πατήρ. In the John portion of the manuscript, the scribe uses the *nomen sacrum* for Israel irregularly, but in the Luke portion one could almost make a case that the scribe uses a *nomen sacrum* when πατήρ has a divine reference. For example, out of thirty-eight instances of πατήρ in Luke, in fourteen instances the context suggests a divine father is the reference, and in seven of these instances the scribe uses a *nomen sacrum*. On the other hand, in only one instance (Luke 11:11) the scribe uses a *nomen sacrum* when πατήρ refers to a human father, and that near another use of a *nomen sacrum* in 11:13 to refer to the divine father. This indicates that in P75 the use of *nomen sacrum* forms, especially those not part of the core group, indicates, unlike the evidence of some other manuscripts, that the *nomina sacra* are in a developmental stage so that the word appears as a *nomen sacrum* appropriate to its exegetical and/or theological context.

58. Charlesworth, "Consensus Standardization," 59. He further postulates that, given the lack of this *nomina sacra* form in P66, these two Bodmer manuscripts may have a different provenance, suggesting that P75 may not have originated in Egypt but traveled there, while P66 may have (in Panopolis).

59. See Henry A. Sanders and Carl Schmidt, eds., *The Minor Prophets in the Freer Collection and the Berlin Fragment of Genesis* (London: Macmillan, 1927), 11–12.

60. The terms πατήρ, μήτηρ, θυγάτηρ, and υἱός are also not abbreviated. Sanders and Schmidt discuss the *nomina sacra* in the introduction (*Minor Prophets in the Freer Collection*, 12). We note only exceptions of ἄνθρωπος plene at Mic 6:8 and πνεῦμα plene at Mic 2:11.

Visualizing the *Adversus Judaeos* Tradition

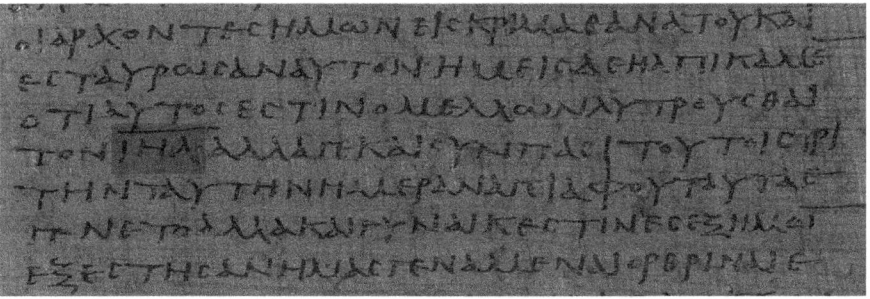

Fig. 10.2. Hanna Papyrus, third century CE. Mater Verbi 1. 2A.7r (with detail). Bodmer Papyrus XIV; P75; Luke 24:15–31. 26cm x 13 cm. Rome. Photograph by Vatican by permission of the Biblioteca Apostolica Vaticana, with all rights reserved. © 2016 Biblioteca Apostolica Vaticana. The highlighted detail shows the *nomen sacrum* ιηλ in line 19.

indication from context that they are any different from others. Notably, this manuscript only uses the *nomen sacrum* form ιλημ for Ἰερουσαλήμ in ten locations (and ιηλημ once) out of fifty-seven occurrences of the word, and almost all of them are in Zech 14.[61] The consistent use of the *nomen sacrum* ιηλ for Ἰσραήλ, alongside the *nomina sacra* for κύριος, θεός, ἄνθρωπος, and πνεῦμα, suggests that in this manuscript and for this scribe (or his exemplar), the word Ἰσραήλ (and Ἰερουσαλήμ to some extent) was theologically significant.

Papyrus Bodmer 24

Papyrus Bodmer 24 from the third or fourth century,[62] containing Pss 17–118, is another important text to consider, in which Ἰσραήλ is contracted as the *nomen sacrum* ιηλ in twenty-seven instances. There is systematic contraction of θεός, κύριος, χριστός, πνεῦμα, ἄνθρωπος, and Ἰερουσαλήμ (6x), while the words πατήρ and ματήρ are sometimes contracted (and υἱός never).[63] With respect to the use of the *nomen sacrum* for Ἰσραήλ, in thirty instances of the word only three are written plene, but two of these still have an overline when written in full (Pss 52:7, 58:6).

Papyrus Bodmer 5 and Papyrus Bodmer 10

Not only biblical manuscripts used *nomina sacra* forms, but also New Testament Apocrypha, such as the case of P.Bodmer 5, a manuscript of the Protevanglium of James from the third century (fig. 10.4).[64] Although the contracted forms of the *nomina sacra* vary, both ισηλ (15x) and ιηλ (5x) occur, while Ἰσραήλ occurs plene only twice. Thus, in this manuscript, too, the *nomen sacrum* for Ἰσραήλ joins the group that includes κύριος, θεός, Ἰησοῦς, χριστός, and πατέρων (while υἱός and Ἰερουσαλήμ are written

---

61. We note the *nomen sacrum* ιλημ at Zech 14:2, 8, 10, 11, 12, 14, 16, 17, 21; as well as Mal 3:4; and the form ιηλημ at Zech 9:10.

62. Dating of this manuscript is all over: late second century (Roberts), third–fourth century (Kasser-Testuz, Treu, Turner), and second–third century (Van Haelst); see Charlesworth, "Consensus Standardization," 64 n. 101.

63. See Rodolphe Kasser and Michel Testuz, *Papyrus Bodmer XXIV: Psaumes XVII–CXVIII* (Geneva: Bibliotheca Bodmeriana, 1967), 26–27.

64. See Michel Testuz, *Papyrus Bodmer V. Nativité de Marie* (Geneva: Bibliotheca Bodmeriana, 1958).

Visualizing the *Adversus Judaeos* Tradition 285

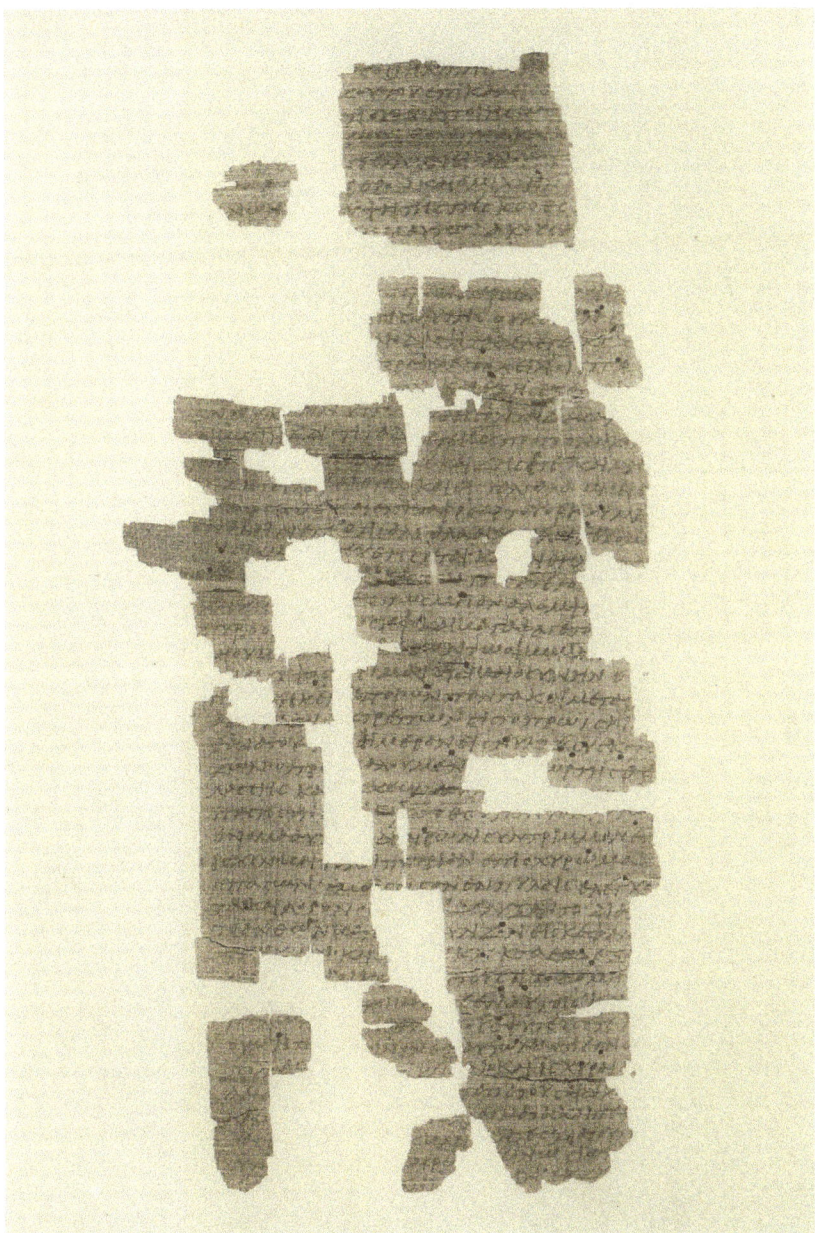

Fig. 10.3. Freer manuscript V on the Minor Prophets (Washington Manuscript 5). Henry A. Sanders, facsimile of the Washington manuscript of the Minor Prophets in the Freer collection, 1927. Freer Gallery of Art and Arthur M. Sackler Gallery Library Main Book Collection, Smithsonian Libraries, 224.048 1927 ff.

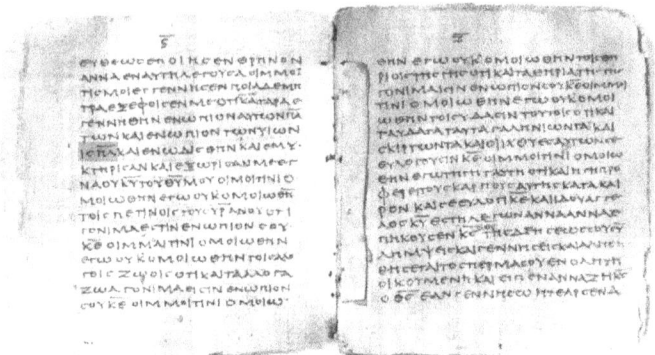

Fig. 10.4. Protevangelium of James 3.1–4.1 with the *nomen sacrum* ισηλ highlighted (P.Bodmer 5; Bodmer Composite Codex), late third–early fourth century CE. Bodmer Library, Geneva. Photograph by Fondation Martin Bodmer, Geneva.

plene). To this may be added P.Bodmer 10, a third-century manuscript of 3 Corinthians that renders Ἰσραήλ in both instances with a *nomen sacrum* form, once with ισρλ, once with ισρηλ.[65]

Papyrus Beatty 11 and Papyrus Leipzig 39

P.Beatty 11, from the fourth century, contains a fragment of Sirach (portions of chs. 36–37, 46) that contains the *nomen sacrum* ιηλ once, at 46:10:

οπως ιδωσιν] παντες οι υιοι ιηλ
οτι καλον το] πορευεσθαι οπισω κυ

---

65. See Michel Testuz, *Papyrus Bodmer X–XII. X: Correspondance apocryphe des Corinthiens et de l'apôtre Paul. XI: Onzième Ode de Salomon. XII: Fragment d'un Hymne liturgique* (Geneva: Bibliotheca Bodmeriana, 1959). Another third-century manuscript with the *nomen sacrum* ιηλ is P.Oxy. 17.2072, a fragment of an unknown Christian apology. The reconstructed context around ιηλ is as follows: "ο θεος υμας εσω]σεν απαξαπ[λως ... ου]κ αυτος δε αλλ[α ο υιος αυτου Ι(ησου)ς Χρ(ιστο)ς ο αποτα[ξαμενος τη δοξη και γενομενος σωτη]ρ τω Ι(σρα)ηλ και πα[σι τοις εθνεσι τοι]ς πιστευουσι [και συναλλαχθεισι δι αυ]του τω θ(ε)ω" ("God saved us ??? ... but not he himself but his son Jesus Christ the ??? in glory and who became a savior to Israel and to all the nations who believe and who ??? through him to God"). Both Χριστός and θεῷ are contracted as well (and potentially Ἰησοῦς). While this fragment may not shed much light on the issue at hand, it is at least an indication of the use of *nomina sacra* for Israel *outside* the biblical manuscript tradition and in the third century.

Other *nomina sacra* in this manuscript are ανω and ανων for ἄνθρωπος, κυ for κυριος, and υς for υιος. Interestingly, "sons of men" (υς ανων) uses a *nomen sacrum* in 36:28. The presence of these *nomina sacra* establishes a Christian provenance for this fragment.[66] Another fourth-century manuscript, P.Leipz. 39, containing portions of Pss 30–55, uses both ιηλ for Ἰσραήλ (4x) and ιλημ for Ἰερουσαλήμ (once) among the use of many other *nomina sacra* forms.[67]

Papyrus Beatty 12 and Papyrus Bodmer 13

In P.Beatty 12 is the *Homily on the Passion* by Melito of Sardis, dating to the fourth century (fig. 10.5).[68] The *nomen sacrum* form ισλ occurs twenty-three times, ιηλ once, and ισρλ once; in no cases is Ἰσραήλ written plene. The dominant use of ισλ is distinctive, and this manuscript is one of the first to do so (this use only occurs as early as the fourth century in our manuscripts). Compared to other *nomina sacra* in the same manuscript, the consistent use of the *nomen sacrum* forms for Israel stands out, since not even θεός is rendered always by a *nomen sacrum*.[69] Moreover, another manuscript of Melito (*Peri Pascha*), P.Bodmer 13, from the third or fourth century, also never writes Ἰσραήλ in full but uses contracted *nomina sacra* forms: the form ιηλ sixteen times, ισηλ six times, and ισαηλ once.[70]

---

66. Bokedal's comment is representative of many scholars' view regarding the significance of the *nomina sacra* for identifying the provenance of a manuscript: "The presence of any of the *nomina sacra* in a manuscript is itself a good indication of its Christian provenance. The selection and combination of these four to 15 names in effect immediately indicate a Christian context" (*Formation and Significance*, 107).

67. See C. F. Georg Heinrici, *Die Leipziger Papyrusfragmente der Psalmen*, vol. 4 of *Beiträge zur Geschichte und Erklärung des Neuen Testaments* (Leipzig: Dürr, 1903).

68. According to Campbell Bonner's critical edition. See Bonner, *The Homily on the Passion by Melito, Bishop of Sardis and Some Fragments of the Apocryphal Ezekiel*, Studies and Documents 12 (London, 1940), 9. Kenyon dates it to the fifth century ("Nomina Sacra in the Chester Beatty Papyri," 9).

69. See *nomina sacra* used regularly with θεός (with one exception), κύριος, πνεῦμα (with one exception), Ἰησοῦς, χριστός, and Ἰσραήλ, but only rarely in the case of πατήρ and ἄνθρωπος, and never for οὐρανοῦ, δαυειδ, Ἰερουσαλήμ, υἱός, σωτήρ, and μητήρ.

70. See Michel Testuz, *Papyrus Bodmer XIII. Méliton de Sardes, Homélie sur la Pâque* (Geneva: Bibliotheca Bodmeriana, 1960).

Fig. 10.5. Chester Beatty Papyrus, *Melito on the Passion*, fourth century CE, with the *nomen sacrum* ισλ highlighted. XII. CBL BP XII f.18. © The Trustees of the Chester Beatty Library, Dublin. Photograph by CSNTM.

When considering the importance of this witness to the use of the *nomen sacrum* for Israel, one should keep in mind the text at hand: Melito's *Homily on the Passion* has been widely viewed as part of the *adversus Judaeos* tradition, and perhaps one of the earliest (being written likely in the late second century). This is a quite early manuscript for that text and may give insight into its interpretation. Particularly, Melito gives an etymology of Israel in §81–82 (fig. 10.6).[71] The passage begins with the question of the name *Israel*: "Who called thee Israel?" the preacher asks (τον ισλ σε καλεσαντα;), to which the preacher answers:

συ δε ισλ [ο]υ-
χ ευρεθησ, ου γαρ ειδεσ τον θεον, ουκ ενοη-
σασ τον κυριον, ουκ ηδεισ, ω ισλ, οτι ουτοσ [εσ-
τιν ο πρωτοτοκοσ του θεου, ο προ εωσφορ[ου
γεννηθεισ

But thou wast not Israel, for thou didst not see God, thou didst not perceive the Lord; thou knewest not, O Israel, that this is the firstborn of God, *this is* he who was begotten before the morning star. (Bonner)

While the etymology about seeing God may not be accurate, the importance of the name *Israel* is clearly an issue for Melito, and perhaps the scribe has picked up on that. We suggest that this scribe, rewriting this homily by Melito, likely chose the *nomen sacrum* form for *Israel* due to theological significance, and perhaps that significance is to be found in the text being copied. Although this manuscript certainly does not stand at the origins of the various *nomina sacra* for Israel (which lie most likely in the first half of the second century), it does provide an example of the inscribing of Christian theology in a text that happens to have something to do with early Christian conceptions of Israel's significance.

Vaticanus and Sinaiticus

The important codices Vaticanus and Sinaiticus from the fourth century should also be considered here.[72] For the most part, Vaticanus uses Israel

---

71. This explanation later influences Hippolytus. On this see Bonner, *Homily on the Passion*, 60.
72. See Traube, *Nomina Sacra*, 66–71, 108. Traube details occurrences of *nomina*

Fig. 10.6. Chester Beatty Papyrus, *Melito on the Passion*, fourth century CE, with the *nomen sacrum* ισλ highlighted twice. XII. CBL BP XII f.19. © The Trustees of the Chester Beatty Library, Dublin. Photograph by CSNTM.

in plene, but when it does contract it uses the ισλ form.⁷³ Sinaiticus uses ισλ mostly but also ισηλ, and ιηλ. The presence of ισλ as a contracted form (even if inconsistently) in these major codices is noteworthy.

Papyrus Oxyrhynchus 13.1602

Finally, from the late fourth century is P.Oxy. 13.1602, a homily to monks, in which the *nomen sacrum* ιηλ occurs in line 3.

στρατιωται Χυ ακουσατε πο
σακις εκ χειρος ανομων ο
θς ερρυσατο τον Ιηλ. και με
χρι ου τα προς τον κν ετη
ρουσαν ουκ απεστη απ αυτο:

Soldiers of Christ, hear how often God delivered Israel from the hand of the lawless, and while they kept the things pertaining to the Lord He did not withdraw from them—for he saved Israel [literally, "him," αυτον] from the hand of Pharaoh the lawless.⁷⁴

One notices that a few other words are written using *nomina sacra*: Χριστοῦ as Χυ, θεός as θς, and κύριον as κν. The context is God's deliverance of Israel and how that translates into God's deliverance now available in Christ.

4. Conclusion

In sum, there is ample evidence that Israel as a *nomen sacrum* occurs regularly in early Christian manuscripts; and in some manuscripts, it appears very consistently and on a par with the four core *nomina sacra* (θεός, κύριος, χριστός, and Ἰησοῦς). The presence of the *nomen sacrum* for Ἰσραήλ occurs in both biblical manuscripts (of both Testaments) and early manuscripts of adjacent Christian literature, suggesting a coherent early

---

sacra in these two manuscripts according to hand, which is a wealth of data. See also Dirk Jongkind, *Scribal Habits of Codex Sinaiticus* (Piscataway, NJ: Gorgias, 2007).

73. Bokedal notes that Vaticanus is the exception that proves the rule with *nomina sacra*: this manuscript only uses *nomina sacra* for θεός, κύριος, χριστός, and Ἰησοῦς (*Formation and Significance*, 90–91).

74. Text and translation follow Bernard P. Grenfell and Arthur S. Hunt, eds. and trans., *The Oxyrhynchus Papyri* (London: Egypt Exploration Fund, 1919), 13:23–25.

Christian theology of Israel, at least in some quarters of early Christianity, some of which transcribed Christian manuscripts. We suggest that the impetus for this phenomenon was not some vague theological connection to the four core *nomina divina* but rather was a visual signature expressing the burgeoning *adversus Judaeos* tradition that was flourishing in the second and third centuries.

Furthermore, the "*nomina sacra* ... contributed to a distinct Christian textual identity of the Scriptures in relation to the synagogue."[75] The very presence of the *nomina sacra* in a text visually stamped that manuscript as Christian, an important factor in the struggle between Jews and Christians for the possession of the Scriptures. With regard to the *nomen sacrum* for Ἰσραήλ, its use reflects the attempt in the *adversus Judaeos* tradition to replace scriptural/ethnic Israel with the church.

Finally, while there is evidence in the cases of P.Beatty 6 (Rahlfs 963) and Hanna Papyrus to conclude the scribe (or his exemplar) consistently and consciously employed *nomina sacra* appropriate to the contextual content of the manuscript, in many other cases, the textual phenomena suggest that scribes were instructed to insert the *nomen sacrum* for Ἰσραήλ (as well as other *nomina sacra*) at every (or most) occurrence(s), regardless of whether their use was relevant to its immediate context. In either case, the function of the abbreviated form of Ἰσραήλ is best understood as a visual expression of the replacement tendencies of the *adversus Judaeos* tradition. This conclusion is supported by the fact that it is Ἰσραήλ, which we pointed out refers to the divinely constituted people of God (and not just an ethnic group), and not Ἰουδαῖος (which typically is an ethnic signifier), that is marked as a *nomen sacrum*. Ἰσραήλ carries a certain theological weight that Ἰουδαῖος does not, even though the struggle in the second century was with these ethnic Jewish communities.

We are still left with the problem of the social function of this visual phenomenon. Who exactly was viewing? This is not a problem peculiar to the specific instance of Ἰσραήλ as a *nomen sacrum*; it is true of all the *nomina sacra* and other visual phenomena of manuscripts, a point observed but not pursued by Hurtado: "the *nomina sacra* should be looked at as a particular instance of early Christian interest in visualizing forms of piety, not only for scribes and readers, but perhaps also for a wider public

---

75. Bokedal, *Formation and Significance*, 109; see also Hvalvik, *Struggle for Scripture and Covenant*.

of occasional onlookers."[76] But what conditions might have provided the opportunity of viewing for such a "wider public"? In this limited space, we can only offer some preliminary and exploratory observations in hopes they will spur others to engage the issue.

Harry Gamble observes that the manuscript as "a physical object is also a social artifact."[77] What was/were the social context(s) of these early Christian manuscripts that contained the *nomina sacra*? Based on extant evidence, the preferred format for early Christian manuscripts was the codex or book form. The shift from the scroll to the codex was a "peculiar" move, especially because the "codex of leaf book was not recognized in antiquity as a proper book."[78]

The innovative technology of the codex could have invited intrigue over and interest in the physical format of the text among listeners/hearers (Christ-followers or "outsiders") in a liturgical context who might wish to get a closer look at the codex after worship services. Several scholars have moved in this direction. Eldon Epp suggests that traveling Christian leaders utilized the portable codex as part of the "respected visitor's 'props'" that "would be strikingly visible to congregations visited."[79] For Epp, the codex was "a new and memorable property of early Christian leaders" that

---

76. Hurtado, *Earliest Christian Artifacts*, 99. As we have already observed and in view retrospectively of the harm done by replacement theology over subsequent centuries—especially the twentieth—we judge, *pace* Hurtado, this particular visualization should hardly be judged a "form of piety." Elsewhere Hurtado observes that "the *nomina sacra* registered solely as visual phenomena and could be experienced solely by those who read (or otherwise viewed?) the manuscripts in which they were written" ("Meta-Data," 158).

77. Gamble, *Books and Readers*, 43.

78. Gamble, *Books and Readers*, 49. Factors proposed to account for the Christian preference of the codex over the scroll include portability (codices were easier to transport than scrolls), accessibility (codices were easier to locate passages in than were scrolls), that the codex accommodated a larger number of writings to be collected into one continuous text for wider distribution (the corpus Paulinum and the Tetraevangelium), and that the codex form of their Scriptures allowed the early Christian communities to distinguish themselves from their Jewish counterparts (and facilitated the parting of the ways). None of these suggestions, on their own, have garnered scholarly consensus. The literature is voluminous; see, inter alia, Kenyon, *Chester Beatty Biblical Papyri*; Colin H. Roberts and Theodore C. Skeat, *The Birth of the Codex* (London: Oxford University Press, 1987); Hurtado, *Earliest Christian Artifacts*.

79. Eldon J. Epp, "The Codex and Literacy in Early Christianity and at Oxyrhyn-

"quickly became a trademark of early Christian teachers and preachers."[80] Furthermore, the codex proved useful when

> traveling teachers required a portion of the Septuagint, an apostolic letter, or a gospel that might serve evangelistic purposes or deeply felt needs for paraenesis and edification in the life of a developing but vibrant church. Then, once used in an impassioned, life-altering context by a person of accepted authority, the codex became a memorable attribute and acquired a symbolic value.[81]

Along similar lines, Stanton proposes that Christian messengers and travelers "experimented with … codices" and "would have readily appreciated the advantages."[82] Stanton further argues, "The earliest Christian experiments with the codex took place at a time when Christians were adopting a distinctive identity as a *tertium genus* over against both Judaism and the pagan world."[83]

In these scenarios, it is easy to imagine a wider audience for the *nomina sacra* (along perhaps with an explanation of their function if needed) than the small pool of lectors responsible for public reading.[84] For traveling teachers eager to demonstrate the church's distinctive christological

---

chus: Issues Raised by Harry Y. Gamble's *Books and Readers in the Early Church*," *CRBR* 10 (1997): 21.

80. Epp, "Codex and Literacy," 24.

81. Epp, "Codex and Literacy," 26.

82. Graham Stanton, "The Fourfold Gospel," *NTS* 43 (1997): 337–38.

83. Stanton, "Fourfold Gospel," 338–39.

84. Such a scenario would not necessitate the production of literary texts of aesthetic quality; as Gamble notes, "there is little to indicate that Christians had an aesthetic regard for their literature"; but neither, we should note, "do they seem to have a cultic attitude toward their books" that might have inhibited a wider viewing of their texts beyond the worship leaders or even the Christ followers (*Books and Readers*, 78). Furthermore, the aforementioned example of Barn. 9.7–9 suggests that the author presents the use of letters of Jesus's name ιη as something his readers needed to know and understand (9.7–9), as if the readers would find the particular collocation of letters to be significant. This presumes that even among communities of Christians the text itself was revered, and even more so particular letters that were in some sense sacred, or at least marked out as different from others when they were combined together. This would be true even if an early Christ-follower could not read; they would still see the line over the letters, thereby marking it different from the other letters and possessing possible "magical" significance.

message, the core four *nomina sacra* (θεός, χριστός, Ἰησοῦς, κύριος) would have been a striking and memorable *visual* symbol. And to establish, as Stanton says, the church's identity as a *tertium genus*, codices containing Ἰσραήλ as a *nomen sacrum* would have served that purpose equally well.[85] These observations regarding the probable *reception* of the *nomina sacra* (and the codex form in which they were embedded) do not diminish the argument regarding their compositional function; it is only a matter of the extent to which this visual phenomenon was observed.[86]

In our opinion, that the use of Ἰσραήλ as *nomen sacrum* emerged from the theological/christological motives of the core four *nomina sacra* (θεός, χριστός, Ἰησοῦς, κύριος), as many have claimed, can only be true if this visualization of Ἰσραήλ is viewed as Rosemary Ruether's anti-Jewish "left hand" of those christological commitments.[87] Nuanced expressions of supersessionism in the New Testament and early Christian writings were hardened into replacement theology by the presence of Israel as one of the *nomina sacra*, since ethnic Israel is *visually* replaced by the true/spiritual Israel, the Christian community, via the *nomen sacrum*. In this case, a picture paints much more than a thousand nuanced words.

Clarifying the effects and functions of such textual phenomena can lead to a deeper understanding of the motives of early Christians. Such historical descriptions are relevant for modern Christian communities,

---

85. Even if the medium that visualized a literal replacement of Israel and contemporary Jews with the "true" Israel had blunted any nuances regarding the relationships between Jews and Christ-followers. As a rough analogy, one might consider the effects of the use of PowerPoint technology in churches and classrooms in its early days, when the medium risked overwhelming the message!

86. As Hurtado observes, "In the presence or absence of these scribal phenomena we might have indications of how individual Christian texts were regarded in the second and third centuries by the scribal devices deployed" ("Meta-Data," 162). In this light, the very fact of the existence of the *nomina sacra* might suggest for those manuscripts in which they occur the probability that they were intended for wider viewing than by those responsible for their public reading.

87. A phrase she uses in "Anti-Semitism in Christian Theology" and an argument she developed in her monograph that appeared in the same year. See Ruether, "Anti-Semitism in Christian Theology," *ThTo* 30 (1974): 366; Ruether, *Faith and Fratricide: The Theological Roots of Anti-Semitism* (New York: Seabury, 1974). Details of her argument did not go unchallenged, but she opened an important, if painful, line of inquiry. Ruether died on May 21, 2022. We wish to acknowledge gratefully her singular and significant contributions to Jewish-Christian dialogues and to feminist theology. *Requiescat in pacem.*

although that relevance is not always edifying. The case of Israel as a *nomen sacrum* that emerged from and materially depicted the *adversus Judaeos* tradition of the early church adds another dimension to the complex, conflicted, and controversial struggle between Christ-followers and Jews in the early centuries of the Common Era. That history is agonizing. But as George Santayana noted long ago, those who cannot remember the past are doomed to repeat it.[88]

Works Cited

Allert, Craig D. *Revelation, Truth, Canon and Intepretation: Studies in Justin Martyr's Dialogue with Trypho*. VCSup 64. Leiden: Brill, 2002.

Bergren, Theodore A. *Fifth Ezra: The Text, Origin and Early History*. SCS 2. Atlanta: Scholars Press, 1990.

———. "Gentile Christians, Exile, and Return in 5 Ezra 1:35-40." *JBL* 130 (2011): 593–612.

———. "Two 'Mothers' in 5 Ezra 2:1–32." *VC* 73 (2019): 440–62.

Bokedal, Tomas. "Notes on the *Nomina Sacra* and Biblical Interpretation." Pages 263–96 in *Beyond Biblical Theologies*. Edited by Heinrich Assel, Stefan Beyerle, and Christfried Böttrich. Tübingen: Mohr Siebeck, 2012.

———. *The Formation and Significance of the Christian Biblical Canon: A Study in Text, Ritual and Interpretation*. London: Bloomsbury, 2014.

Bonner, Campbell. *The Homily on the Passion by Melito, Bishop of Sardis and Some Fragments of the Apocryphal Ezekiel*. SD 12. London, 1940.

Brown, Schuyler. "Concerning the Origin of the *Nomina Sacra*." *SPap* 9 (1970): 655–73.

Charlesworth, Scott D. "Consensus Standardization in the Systematic Approach to Nomina 'Sacra' in Second- and Third-Century Gospel Manuscripts." *Aegyptus* 86 (2006): 37–68.

Dinkler, Erich. "Älteste christliche Denkmäler: Bestand und Chronologie." Pages 176–78 in *Signum Crucis: Aufsätze zum Neuen Testament und zur Christlichen Archäologie*. Tübingen: Mohr Siebeck, 1967.

---

88. On the other hand, Santayana's quote suggests that those who do remember the past cannot avoid its tragic repetition. Christianity may have an inherent kind of supersessionism, but that need not be expressed as complete replacement. In other words, replacement theology is one expression of supersesssionism, but supersessionism need not entail complete replacement (see Longenecker, "On Israel's God," 38–44).

Donaldson, Terence L. *Jews and Anti-Judaism in the New Testament: Decision Points and Divergent Interpretations*. Waco, TX: Baylor University Press, 2010.

———. "Supersessionism and Early Christian Self-Definition." *JJMJS* 3 (2016): 1–32.

Dunn, James D. G. *The Partings of the Ways: Between Christianity and Judaism and Their Significance for the Character of Christianity*. 2nd ed. London: SCM, 2006.

Ehrman, Bart D., ed. and trans. *The Apostolic Fathers*. Vol. 2, *Epistle of Barnabas, Papias and Quadratus, Epistle to Diognetus, The Shepherd of Hermas*. LCL. Cambridge: Harvard University Press, 2003.

Epp, Eldon J. "The Codex and Literacy in Early Christianity and at Oxyrhynchus: Issues Raised by Harry Y. Gamble's *Books and Readers in the Early Church*." *CRBR* 10 (1997): 15–37.

Falls, Thomas B., trans. *Dialogue with Trypho*. Edited by Michael Slusser. SFC 3. Washington, DC: Catholic University of America Press, 2003.

Gager, John G. *The Origins of Anti-Semitism*. Oxford: Oxford University Press, 1983.

Gamble, Harry Y. *Books and Readers in the Early Church: A History of Early Christian Texts*. New Haven: Yale University Press, 1995.

Grenfell, Bernard P., and Arthur S. Hunt, eds. and trans. *The Oxyrhynchus Papyri*. Vol. 13. London: Egypt Exploration Fund, 1919.

Heath, Jane. "*Nomina Sacra* and Sacra Memoria before the Monastic Age." *JTS* 61 (2010): 516–49.

Heinrici, C. F. Georg. *Die Leipziger Papyrusfragmente der Psalmen*. Vol. 4 of *Beiträge zur Geschichte und Erklärung des Neuen Testaments*. Leipzig: Dürr, 1903.

Hurtado, Larry W. *The Earliest Christian Artifacts: Manuscripts and Christian Origins*. Grand Rapids: Eerdmans, 2006.

———. "The 'Meta-Data' of Earliest Christian Manuscripts." In *Identity and Interaction in the Ancient Mediterranean: Jews, Christians and Others; Essays in Honour of Stephen G. Wilson*. Edited by Zeba A. Crook and Philip A. Harland. Sheffield: Sheffield Phoenix, 2007.

———. "The Origin of the *Nomina Sacra*: A Proposal." *JBL* 117 (1998): 655–73.

———. "The Staurogram in Early Christian Manuscripts: The Earliest Visual Reference to the Crucified Jesus?" Pages 207–26 in *New Testament Manuscripts: Their Texts and Their World*. Edited by Thomas J. Kraus and Tobias Nicklas. Leiden: Brill, 2006.

Hvalvik, Reidar. *The Struggle for Scripture and Covenant: A Purpose of the Epistle of Barnabas and Jewish-Christian Competition in the Second Century*. WUNT 2/82. Tübingen: Mohr Siebeck, 1996.

Jongkind, Dirk. *Scribal Habits of Codex Sinaiticus*. Piscataway, NJ: Gorgias, 2007.

Kasser, Rodolphe, and Michel Testuz. *Papyrus Bodmer XXIV: Psaumes XVII–CXVIII*. Geneva: Bibliotheca Bodmeriana, 1967.

Kenyon, Frederick G. *The Chester Beatty Biblical Papyri: Descriptions and Texts of Twelve Manuscripts on Papyrus of the Greek Bible, Fasciculus V; Numbers and Deuteronomy*. Edited by Frederick G. Kenyon. London: Emery Walker, 1935.

———. "Nomina Sacra in the Chester Beatty Papyri." *Aegyptus* 13 (1933): 5–10.

Kok, Michael. "The True Covenant People: Ethnic Reasoning in the Epistle of Barnabas." ScRel 40 (2011): 81–97.

Kraft, Robert A. "The Epistle of Barnabas: Its Quotations and Their Sources." PhD diss., Harvard University, 1961.

Lieu, Judith M. *Image and Reality: The Jews in the World of the Christians in the Second Century*. Edinburgh: T&T Clark, 1996.

Longenecker, Bruce. "On Israel's God and God's Israel: Assessing Supersessionism in Paul." *JTS* 58 (2007): 26–44.

Mach, Michael. "Justin Martyr's *Dialogus cum Tryphone Iudaeo* and the Development of Christian Anti-Judaism." Pages 27–48 in *Contra Iudaeos: Ancient and Medieval Polemics between Christians and Jews*. Edited by Ora Limor and Guy G. Stroumsa. Tübingen: Mohr Siebeck, 1996.

Martin, Victor, and Rodolphe Kasser. *Papyrus Bodmer XIV: Évangile de Luc chap. 3–24*. Geneva: Bibliotheca Bodmeriana, 1961.

Metzger, Bruce M. *Manuscripts of the Greek Bible: An Introduction to Paelaeography*. New York: Oxford University Press, 1981.

Nongbri, Brent. "Reconsidering the Place of Papyrus Bodmer XIV–XV (P75) in the Textual Criticism of the New Testament." *JBL* 135 (2016): 405–37.

Paap, Anton H. R. E. *Nomina Sacra in the Greek Papyri of the First Five Centuries A.D.: The Sources and Some Deductions*. Leiden: Brill, 1959.

Paget, James Carleton. *The Epistle of Barnabas: Outlook and Background*. WUNT 2/64. Tübingen: Mohr Siebeck, 1994.

Parkes, James. *The Conflict of the Church and the Synagogue: A Study in the Origins of Antisemitism*. Philadelphia: Meridian Books, 1961.

Richardson, Peter. *Israel in the Apostolic Church*. Cambridge: Cambridge University Press, 1969.
Roberts, Colin H. "Nomina Sacra Origins and Significance." Pages 26–48 in *Manuscript, Society and Belief in Early Christian Egypt*. Oxford: Oxford University Press, 1979.
Roberts, Colin H., and Theodore C. Skeat. *The Birth of the Codex*. London: Oxford University Press, 1987.
Royce, James. *Scribal Habits in Early Greek New Testament Papyri*. Leiden: Brill, 2008.
Ruether, Rosemary. "Anti-Semitism in Christian Theology." *ThTo* 30 (1974): 365–81.
———. *Faith and Fratricide: The Theological Roots of Anti-Semitism*. New York: Seabury, 1974.
Sanders, Henry A., and Carl Schmidt, eds. *The Minor Prophets in the Freer Collection and the Berlin Fragment of Genesis*. New York: Macmillan, 1927.
Sandmel, Samuel. *Anti-Semitism in the New Testament?* Philadelphia: Fortress, 1978.
Skarsaune, Oskar. "Scriptural Interpretation in the Second and Third Centuries—Except Clement and Origen." Pages 373–442 in *Hebrew Bible / Old Testament: The History of Its Interpretation*. Vol. 1. Edited by Magne Sæbø. Göttingen: Vandenhoeck & Ruprecht, 1996.
Soulen, R. Kendall. *The God of Israel and Christian Theology*. Minneapolis: Fortress, 1996.
Stanton, Graham. "The Fourfold Gospel." *NTS* 43 (1997): 317–46.
———. *A Gospel for a New People: Studies in Matthew*. Louisville, KY: Westminster John Knox, 1992.
———. "Justin Martyr's Dialogue with Trypho: Group Boundaries, 'Proselytes' and 'God-Fearers.'" Pages 263–78 in *Tolerance and Intolerance in Early Judaism and Christianity*. Edited by Graham N. Stanton and Guy G. Stroumsa. New York: Cambridge University Press, 1998.
Steck, Odil H. *Israel und das gewaltsame Geschick der Propheten*. Neukirchen-Vluyn: Neukirchener Verlag, 1967.
Testuz, Michel. *Papyrus Bodmer V. Nativité de Marie*. Geneva: Bibliotheca Bodmeriana, 1958.
———. *Papyrus Bodmer X–XII. X: Correspondance apocryphe des Corinthiens et de l'apôtre Paul. XI: Onzième Ode de Salomon. XII: Fragment d'un Hymne liturgique*. Geneva: Bibliotheca Bodmeriana, 1959.

———. *Papyrus Bodmer XIII. Méliton de Sardes, Homélie sur la Pâque.* Geneva: Bibliotheca Bodmeriana, 1960.

Thiel, Nathan. "'Israel' and 'Jew' as Markers of Jewish Identity in Antiquity: The Problems of Insider/Outsider Classification." *JSJ* 45 (2014): 80–99.

Traube, Ludwig. *Nomina sacra: Versuch einer Geschichte der christlichen Kürzung.* Munich: Beck'sche Verlagsbuchhandlung, 1907.

Tuckett, Christopher M. "'Nomina Sacra': Yes and No?" Pages 431–58 in *The Biblical Canons.* Edited by Jean-Marie Auwers and Henk J. de Jonge. Leuven: Leuven University Press, 2003.

Williams, A. Lukyn. *Adversus Judaeos: A Bird's-Eye View of Christian Apologiae until the Renaissance.* Cambridge: Cambridge University Press, 1935.

Early Christians and Their Theological Symbols in Ostia Antica

Bruce W. Longenecker

Long ago, a mosaic installer in Rome's port city of Ostia was given the job of installing a mosaic floor in one room of a popular bath complex of the ancient city—a complex now referred to as the Baths of Neptune (region 2, insula 4). In the process of replacing the carpet of white tesserae that had originally covered most of the room, this craftworker also inserted small shapes into the mosaic, using black tesserae, causing the shapes to stand out from their context. Those shapes did not conform to the generic style of geometric patterning one might expect to see in standard mosaic ornamentation. Nor were they capturing epic scenes, divine beings, or heroic figures of Greco-Roman mythology—as was the case in other rooms of the bath complex. Instead, these relatively small shapes were uncoordinated, idiosyncratic, and cryptically presented.

They were, in fact, Christian symbols of various kinds. Giovanni Becatti, former director general for antiquities and fine art, demonstrates this in his two-part volume, *Scavi di Ostia, 4: Mosaici e pavimenti marmorei*.[1] In fact, these symbols give us a window onto the artistic self-presentation of early Christians living in Ostia—a city in which some Christians were martyred in the mid-third century.

In this essay, I canvass the symbols, since they remain underappreciated artifacts of early Christian history. I then reconstruct the archaeological

---

I would like to express my appreciation to Jan Theo Bakker for offering helpful suggestions at an early stage of my thinking about this subject. Any deficiencies that remain are my own.

1. Giovanni Becatti, *Scavi di Ostia, 4: Mosaici e pavimenti marmorei*, 2 vols. (Rome: Libreria dello Stato, 1961). The excavations of the bath complex were in 1888 (under Rodolfo Amedeo Lanciani) and 1909/1910 (under Dante Vincenzo Vaglieri).

and artistic contexts of the room, proposing how the room served a social function within the spa of the bath complex. Moreover, I place the installation of these mosaic symbols in the religious context of early Ostian Christianity, proposing the arrangements and motivations for undertaking this initiative. Along the way, I offer some fresh reflections on these matters and offer new interpretations for certain aspects of the symbols, interpretations that dovetail with what we know about the experiences of early Christians in Ostia Antica.

Becatti provided photos of most of the mosaic symbols.[2] He also provided his own drawings of those symbols, shown here as figures 11.1 and 11.2. Figure 11.1 shows the placement of the symbols within the mosaic flooring. Figure 11.2 depicts the symbols themselves, extracted from their mosaic context and grouped for ease of presentation. Figure 11.3 shows the room in which the symbols appear.[3]

1. Anchoring the Interpretative Register of the Mosaic Figures

Becatti identifies the symbols presented in figure 11.2 as Christian symbols. Some of the symbols are not exclusively Christian. For instance, an ivy leaf, a phoenix, a *gamma* cross—these are common stock within ancient symbols, even though they could also be adopted for Christian significance.[4] Other symbols in the mosaic flooring resonate most clearly

---

2. See Becatti, *Scavi di Ostia, 4*, vol. 2, TAV 196–TAV 198.

3. I have adjusted Becatti's figures in three ways. First, the *gamma* cross in the upper row (to the right of the central drinking cup) has been turned ninety degrees counterclockwise, in order to ensure that the *rho* (which is to give the impression of the head of the crucified one) is toward the top, rather than leaning to the right, as in Becatti's figure. Second, in his drawing of the figure between the *gamma* cross and the leaf at the top right, Becatti closed up one of the curved lines, whereas all of the curved lives are open rather than closed at the end (at least in this version of the symbol; see discussion of the other variation of this symbol, especially in note 54 below). Third, the second figure from the left on the bottom row has been turned 90 degrees counterclockwise, in order to place the five double appendages in the order of the human body (in the symbol's placement within Becatti's diagram), instead of lying to the right.

4. Becatti repeatedly claims that each of these symbols can be shown to appear in other Christian artifacts. While that might be true, the real point is that one symbol seems almost certainly to be a Christian symbol, and that symbol itself, together with others that are suggestively Christian, anchors the interpretation of other symbols that, on their own, would seem to have less claim to being symbols of Christian devo-

Early Christians and Their Theological Symbols 303

Fig. 11.1. Becatti's sketch of the placement of the symbols in room 6. Source: Giovanni Becatti, *Scavi di Ostia, 4: Mosaici e pavimenti marmorei* (Rome: Libreria dello Stato, 1961), 1:52. Used by permission of Parco Archeologico di Ostia Antica.

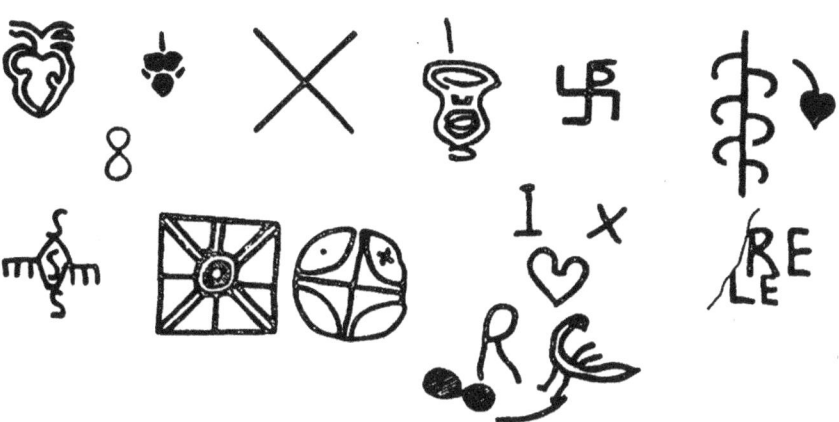

Fig. 11.2. Becatti's sketch of the symbols. Source: Giovanni Becatti, *Scavi di Ostia, 4: Mosaici e pavimenti marmorei* (Rome: Libreria dello Stato, 1961), 1:52. Used by permission of Parco Archeologico di Ostia Antica.

Fig. 11.3. Room 6, looking east toward Via dei Vigili. Photograph courtesy of Klaus Heese.

in a register of Christian significance, and one of them is most unlikely to be anything other than a Christian symbol. It is this symbol that locks down the Christian register for some of the more ambiguous symbols elsewhere in the room. For this reason, I will foreground it in this section of the essay. In the next section, I will discuss the other symbols in the order that they appear within Becatti's diagram (fig. 11.2).

The symbol of primary interest appears on the lower left of figure 11.2, as photographed in figure 11.4. In the mosaic floor, this symbol covers 37 x 35 centimeters or 14.5 x 13.8 inches.[5] To the uninitiated eye, it appears to be a bizarre collection of lines and scribbles. But that impression cloaks its ingenuity. This is because the mosaic pattern spells the Latin word *Iesus*, or "Jesus," at least twice and probably four times, doing so along the two axes of an equilateral cross. It is constructed in the following fashion, from left to right (see also fig. 11.5):

---

tion. For non-Christian *gamma* crosses in Ostia, for instance, see Becatti, *Scavi di Ostia, 4*, vol. 2, TAV 47, TAV 63.

5. All measurements that appear in this essay are taken from Becatti, *Scavi di Ostia, 4*, 1:52–59.

Fig. 11.4. Key mosaic. Photograph courtesy of Klaus Heese.

1. The letter *I* is formed by a single vertical stroke.
2. The letter *E* is formed by two vertical strokes.
3. The letter *S* appears in the middle of the mosaic, where the vertical and horizontal lines of the cross meet.
4. The letter *U* is placed below the center *S*.
5. The final letter *S* is placed below the *U*.

This same pattern is then repeated from other side with inverse procedures. The center *S* does double duty, with the second *U* appearing upside-down and above the center *S*, and with the second final *S* appearing above the second *U*. An overstroke is added to the *I* and the *E* in each of their occurrences, connecting them to the vertical letters (although see the next patterning of the letters, where this overstroke is part of the letters themselves).

In fact, the same word could have been spelled out in the same cross formation but using slightly different formations for the first two letters. In this option, the letters *I* and *E* lay on their side as a ligature, without the need for an overstroke joining them (see fig. 11.6). In this scenario, the name *Iesus* is again spelled twice, in the shape of an equilateral cross.

This symbol lies at the approximate center of the symbols in the mosaic flooring. It is as if this symbol holds the interpretative register for all the symbols that are embedded around it. The surrounding symbols serve, in

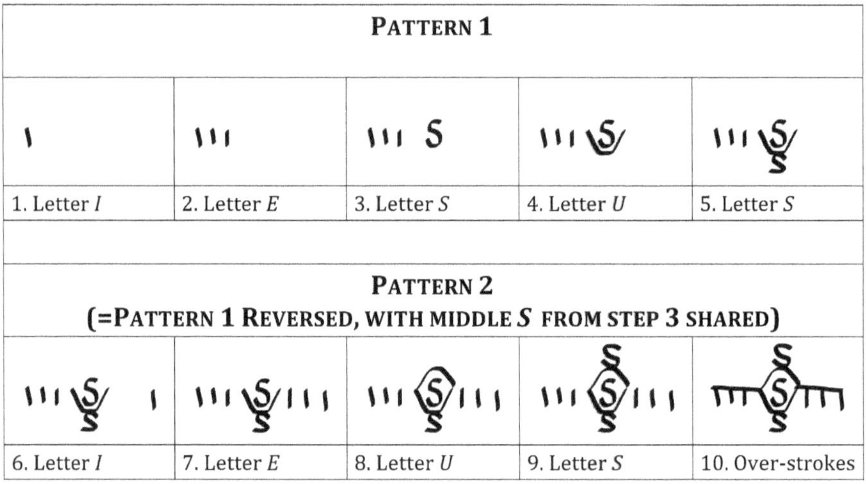

PATTERN 1				
\	\\\	\\\ S	\\\ ⓢ	\\\ ⓢ/S
1. Letter *I*	2. Letter *E*	3. Letter *S*	4. Letter *U*	5. Letter *S*

PATTERN 2 (=PATTERN 1 REVERSED, WITH MIDDLE *S* FROM STEP 3 SHARED)				
\\\ⓢ/S \	\\\ⓢ/S ///	\\\ ⓢ ///	\\\ ⓢ/S ///	⊓⊓ ⓢ/S ⊓⊓
6. Letter *I*	7. Letter *E*	8. Letter *U*	9. Letter *S*	10. Over-strokes

Fig. 11.5. Ostian *Iesus* mosaic, built stage by stage. Created by author.

PATTERN 3				
—	⊓⊓	⊓⊓ S	⊓⊓ ⓢ	⊓⊓ ⓢ/S
1. Letter *I*	2. Letter *E*	3. Letter *S*	4. Letter *U*	5. Letter *S*

PATTERN 4 (=PATTERN 3 REVERSED, WITH MIDDLE *S* FROM STEP 3 SHARED)			
⊓⊓ ⓢ/S —	⊓⊓ ⓢ/S ⊓⊓	⊓⊓ ⓢ ⊓⊓	⊓⊓ ⓢ/S ⊓⊓
6. Letter *I*	7. Letter *E*	8. Letter *U*	9. Letter *S*

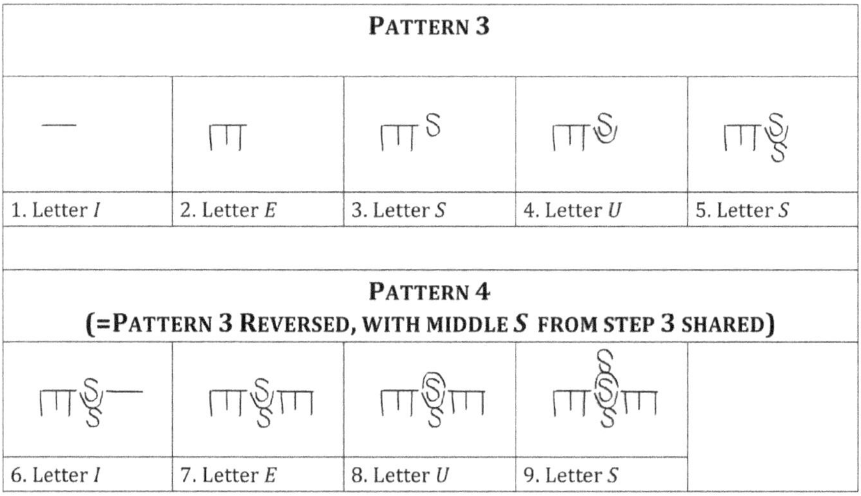

Fig. 11.6. Alternative version of the Ostian *Iesus* mosaic, built stage by stage. Created by author.

a sense, to amplify the theological significance of this symbol, which captures both ingeniously and cryptically the crucified Jesus.

2. Interpreting the Other Symbols

In light of the creative cross-shaped symbol containing the name Jesus, other symbols around that centerpiece need also to be interpreted. Here I follow the order of Becatti's diagram (fig. 11.2), from top left to top right, then along the bottom row in the same direction.

Top row, from left to right:

1. At the top right is the mosaic of a bunch of grapes, 30 centimeters or 11.8 inches tall. In the context of Christian symbols, a bunch of grapes is likely to allude to the wine of the Eucharist.[6] Another bunch of grapes, of roughly the same dimensions but a different composition, appears two symbols to the right of this one.

2. Between and slightly below the two grape bunches is a figure (18 cm or 7 in long) that Becatti has positioned as if it were an 8 shape, which of course in the Roman world is not the number eight. But Becatti's vertical orientation of this symbol is probably wrong. A figure much the same appears on the bottom line of the figure next to a phoenix. There it lies on its side (∞) in relation to the phoenix, which is then the probable orientation for the other occurrence of this shape. Becatti thinks these are the cursive version of the letter *M*, which itself is the common symbol for *mille*, one thousand. As such, he thinks it alludes to the resurrection, just as the phoenix (in one version of the myth) is restored to life after one thousand years of its normal life cycle.[7] This is probably right, but there may be more to it than that.[8] In the earliest centuries of Christianity, a reference to one thousand would almost invariably invoke millenarian

---

6. For a bunch of grapes having a eucharistic significance, see the tomb of Eutyches, which dates to 179/180 CE; Bruce W. Longenecker, *The Cross before Constantine: The Early Life of a Christian Symbol* (Minneapolis: Fortress, 2015), 114–17.

7. In some earlier occurrences, this shape does not lie on its side but is placed vertically, as "8." In these instances the reference to one thousand (by means of a cursive *M*) is not evident. In the horizontal formation, a gesture toward *mille* is probable.

8. My thanks to David Wilhite for pointing out to me the potential of the horizontal double circle to connote millenarian interests among early Christians.

references, since millenarianism had a discernible foothold in the early centuries of the Christian era.[9] In this view, there will be one thousand years of Christ's reign free from the influence of Satan. This aspect of the mosaic will be discussed further in section 7 below.

3. Next in Becatti's figure is a *chi*, the first letter of the Greek *Christ* (Χρίστος), each of its lines being 48 centimeters or 18.9 inches in length. Note, of course, that since there is no overarching orientation to the collective symbols, this symbol could also reference the cross of Christ (here an equilateral cross, +). Presumably both meanings could be in play simultaneously, simply by switching one's mental orientation toward the symbol.

4. Near the *chi* in the mosaic, and next to it also in Becatti's figure, is a drinking vessel. The mosaicist ensured that its circular shape could not be misinterpreted. An *I* was placed directly above the vessel (giving these symbols a height of 34 cm or 13.4 in). The combination is likely to reference a eucharistic drinking cup, with the *I* being the first Latin letter of the name *Jesus* (*Iesus*) or the first Greek letter of that name (Ἰησοῦς).

5. To the right of the eucharistic cup is a *gamma* cross 18 centimeters or 7 inches in length.[10] The *gamma* cross is named after the Greek letter *gamma*, which in its uppercase form looks like an upside-down *L* (Γ). To form a *gamma* cross, the *gamma* shape is repeated four times, with each *gamma* touching the others at right angles at their base, the four bases meeting at the center. This, then, has the appearance of a swastika, an ancient symbol predating Christianity that was later used for despicable purposes in the first half of twentieth century. Even in the Christian era this symbol is not necessarily Christian. It was a common symbol in the ancient world. The addition of the letter rho (P) to the *gamma* cross makes it explicitly specify a crucifixion. This is, then, a strange formation of a staurogram—a depiction of a crucified person (i.e., Jesus Christ), which is usually depicted with the *rho* superimposed on an equilateral cross (+) or

---

9. Eusebius admits as much, despite opposing the view himself (*Hist. eccl.* 3.39.11–13). He speaks of "so many of the Church Fathers" having adopted this view. As Charles E. Hill has shown, however, the extent of millenarianism (or chiliasm) was not as widespread as scholars have frequently thought. See Hill, *Regnum Caelorum: Patterns of Millennial Thought in Early Christianity*, 2nd ed. (Grand Rapids: Eerdmans, 2001).

10. A second *gamma* cross, but without the *rho*, also appeared in the mosaic flooring. Becatti notes that it measured 17 x 19 cm or 6.7 x 7.5 in. It was also twice the thickness, being two tesserae thick instead of one, as in the *gamma* cross with the staurogram added to it.

a *tau* cross (T). This unusual symbol seems to suggest an allusion to the crucifixion of Jesus. It was embedded in the mosaic close to other symbols referencing the cross of Jesus.

6. The symbol to the right of the *gamma* cross in Becatti's reconstruction is extremely difficult to interpret apart from its length at 51 centimeters or 20 inches. Besides the fact that it is hard to make sense of the symbol, there is the added complication that there are two versions of the symbol in the mosaic, and they differ in some ways. The version that Becatti reproduces in his diagram has curved lines that do not close up (see fig. 11.7), whereas in the other version (which he does not reproduce in his drawing) the curved lines do close up. Becatti thought these must somehow represent branches of a palm tree. I think the two versions work against this view, and I make a tentative proposal below (see footnote 54), which can be suggested only after accounting for other aspects of the mosaic.[11]

7. Next to this symbol the mosaicist placed a leaf (see fig. 11.7), 24 centimeters or 9.4 inches in length. It seems to be an ivy leaf. Becatti notes that ivy leaves sometimes adorned Christian tomb monuments. Perhaps, but this gives us little insight into its theological significance.[12] I have no view as to the symbolic significance of this leaf—which is inconsequential to the main argument of this essay, other than serving to give the orientation of the obscure symbol that it sits next to (as discussed below).

---

11. Elsewhere I considered the idea that it might borrow from the symbol associated with Asclepius—a snake wrapped around a rod. In this light, it would be depicting Jesus Christ as a deity of healing (Longenecker, *Cross before Constantine*, 78 n. 6). I no longer think this is likely. The closed-curved version prevents the possibility of a continuous line winding its way up the center line, since the close of one line does not correspond to the start of the next closed curve on the other side of the center line. This happens repeatedly. The open-curved version gives the impression that the curves are moving down, not up, as would be expected if this were a snake moving up the rod.

12. Ivy has little foothold within the Judeo-Christian tradition, never being mentioned in the Hebrew Bible or the New Testament. It is mentioned a few times in ancient Jewish literature (2 Macc 6:7, 3 Macc 2:29; see also 2 Macc 10:7, Jdt 15:12), often in its typical association with Dionysus.

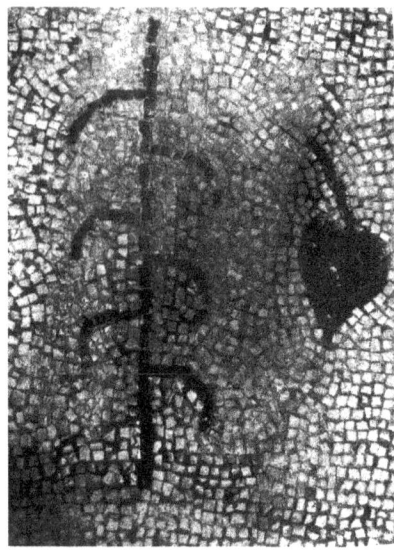

Fig. 11.7. Obscure symbol. Source: Giovanni Becatti, *Scavi di Ostia, 4: Mosaici e pavimenti marmorei* (Rome: Libreria dello Stato, 1961), vol. 2, TAV 197. Used by permission of Parco Archeologico di Ostia Antica.

Bottom row, from left to right, starting with the second symbol:

1. The second symbol on the bottom row is one of the larger symbols, being a square of 40 centimeters or 15.7 inches in height and width (see fig. 11.8, right side). Its main shape involves a combination of two shapes found elsewhere in the mosaic flooring. An equilateral cross (+) forms the central spine, with the Greek letter *chi* (X, the first letter of the Greek word Χριστος) superimposed over it. Obviously other things are also included beyond the cross and *chi*. First, a border is added to enclose the *chi* and cross shapes, giving the square an eight-point outer ribbon. Second, the center has been adjusted so that, rather than being the place where the cross and *chi* are shown to intersect, a circular deflector of the evil eye appears instead. Third, five of the eight lines of the combined *chi* and cross are doubled in order to capture five main appendages of the human body: the central head, two outstretched arms, and two outstretched legs. The artistry is intriguing because the addition of the human appendages complicates the symbolism. The outstretched legs conflict with the cross symbol, being a stylized way of placing a human body within the inner structure of the mosaic figure itself.[13] The outstretched arms would sug-

---

13. The posture is slightly reminiscent of crucifixions in which the legs are apart, but even in those instances, the legs straddle the centerpiece, with nails driven through the ankles into the center spike.

Early Christians and Their Theological Symbols   311

Fig. 11.8. Two cross-based symbols. Photograph courtesy of Klaus Hesse.

gest a top crossbar, as in a *tau* cross, even though the middle horizontal line is indicative of an equilateral cross.[14] This symbolic complexity is not without precedent in the catalogue of early Christian art—even at this early period.[15]

2. The circular symbol that Becatti places to the right of the square symbol was positioned immediately to the west of the square *chi*-and-cross symbol just discussed, being of a similar size (37 cm or 14.5 in; see fig. 11.8, left side). (On the other side of the square *chi*-and-cross symbol, but slightly farther away, was the *gamma* cross discussed above.) Here again an equilateral cross forms the central spine of the symbol. Becatti suggests that the four shapes surrounding the cross are olive leaves. He is probably right. The leaf to the top right on Becatti's diagram has a *chi* (again, referencing Χρίστος), so that both the square symbol (discussed above) and this rounded symbol have a cross and a *chi* within them. Becatti's diagram

---

14. A *tau* cross (T) was embedded elsewhere in the mosaic, being 11 cm high and 9 cm wide (or 4.3 x 3.5 inches). Becatti's diagrams of the symbols and the flooring do not register this *tau* cross, but it is shown in a photograph in TAV 196 in *Scavi di Ostia, 4*, vol. 2.

15. For instance, Christian rings from the third century frequently combine *tau* crosses with equilateral crosses. The overlapping of symbolism was not deemed problematic, as further evidenced by the placement of a *rho* to create an awkward staurogram within the double-crossed ring. See, e.g., Longenecker, *Cross before Constantine*, fig. 5.9 (three examples).

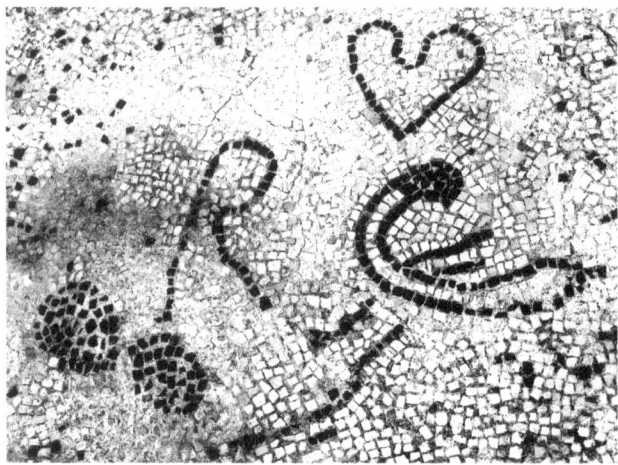

Fig. 11.9. Resurrection symbols. Photograph courtesy of Klaus Hesse.

depicts the leaf to the top left as having a central point of focus. Actually, all three of the leaves that are not marked by the *chi* share this feature. It is not clear what those central points might reference, although the best estimate is that they share the basic characteristic of the center of the square symbol and are, then, further evil-eye deflectors.

3. Six figures appear together in Becatti's next cluster of symbols. At the top are the letters *I* and *X*, no doubt the first letters of the Greek Ἰησοῦς Χρίστος. We have already seen each letter standing separately within the mosaic; in this instance, however, they are brought together to reference "Jesus Christ."

4. Below them in Becatti's diagram (but quite separate in the mosaic flooring) is collection of other symbols (see fig. 11.9). At the top of them is another leaf, evidently—this time without a stem (unlike the leaf discussed above). Becatti explains this as a commonly used symbol in Christian funerary inscriptions. Even if that is so, it does not explain the signification of the symbol. I have no explanation as to its import.

5. Below the leaf are other symbols that seem to cohere around the notion of resurrection. The key to them is the bird that appears there. Although it is poorly formed, the bird (28 cm or 11 in in height) is probably not a dove, which would be more rounded in its body shape; Becatti is probably right to propose that it is a phoenix, the mythic bird with a restorable life. The parallel with the resurrected Christ (and his followers?) is obvious. Becatti suggests that this is what the letter *R* (22 cm or 8.5 in

Fig. 11.10. Four letters. Source: Giovanni Becatti, *Scavi di Ostia, 4: Mosaici e pavimenti marmorei* (Rome: Libreria dello Stato, 1961), vol. 2, TAV 197. Used by permission of Parco Archeologico di Ostia Antica.

tall) is doing next to the phoenix: it references the resurrection (*resurrectio*). This again seems correct. Below this we find another double-circled figure, as discussed above in relation to the number one thousand. Again, this seems to represent the one thousand years of a phoenix's mythical life, before its rebirth, but it probably also reinforces a millenarian expectation about the thousand-year reign of Christ that was soon to come, an expectation that had currency among some Christians at this time.

6. Finally, four letters appear on two lines (see fig. 11.10). These were laid next to the outer black ribbon at the south of the room. The two letters on the top line are *RE* (14 cm or 5.5 in tall); the two on the lower line are *LE* (10 cm or 3.9 in tall). Becatti thinks the top letters are the start of the word *resurrectio* ("resurrection"), but he has no idea what the letters on the lower line are doing or why they are lined up so that the *L* slightly precedes the placement of the *R* in the line above it. In section 7 below, I offer an interpretation of this cryptic formation of four letters.

Having surveyed the various symbols of this mosaic flooring, two further observations are in order. First, this flooring does not exhibit a *chi-rho*—the symbol of the first two Greek letters of "Christ," which became tremendously popular among Christians with the coming of the Constantinian era. Ostia offers evidence of *chi-rho* symbols in the post-Constantinian Christian era, but there are none in this flooring.

Second, there is something of a cautious character about these symbols. The name *Jesus* is hidden in a pattern undiscernible to the uninitiated eye; crosses are often dressed up with other shapes that deflect from them;

letters are cryptically presented that convey no obvious meaning. Some symbols that are not distinctively Christian are sometimes given a Christian reference, but never a definitively explicit one; an *R* for *resurrectio* is placed next to a common phoenix, an *I* for *Iesus* or Ἰησοῦς is placed above a cup, a common *gamma* cross is used to form a curious staurogram (as opposed to a more explicit staurogram using an equilateral or *tau* cross).

These, then, are not the symbols of Christians living in a world where they felt legally secure in their devotion.[16] As such, it is not only the cautious hesitancy that is notable; the very fact that Christian symbols are being placed in public is itself somewhat remarkable. This is especially the case because of the likelihood of Christian martyrdoms in Ostia during the mid-third century (see section 5 below).

It is important to place these Christian symbols within their architectural, artistic, and social contexts. In section 3 below, the architectural and artistic aspects are considered, allowing a proposal in section 4 as to the social context of room 6 within the spa section of the bath complex. These observations become important later in the essay when considering the installation of these Christian symbols within the Baths of Neptune.

3. The Renovation of Room 6 in Context

Ostia Antica, the harbor city of Rome in the early Common Era (replacing Puteoli in that role), lay about 25 kilometers or 15.5 miles southwest of the imperial city on the mouth of the Tiber River. The city had two dozen bath complexes, varying in size and provision. These were places of high social priority within the ancient world. "Much of the life of the town went on in the baths, whose social importance can hardly be overestimated."[17]

The bath complex referred to as the Baths of Neptune was given that name by archaeologists because of the large mosaic of Neptune in what has been named room 4 of the complex (see fig. 11.11 below for the demarcation of rooms relevant to this study). The east side of the com-

---

16. Becatti dates them to "the period in which there had not yet been a full official recognition of the new religion but Christianity had already deeply penetrated Roman society" (*Scavi di Ostia*, 4, 1:58–59, my translation). He thinks this allows for a date between 250 and 350. I think the data favors a pre-313 date, as noted in various footnotes in section 7 below.

17. Inge Nielsen, *Thermae et Balnea: The Architecture and Cultural History of Roman Public Baths* (Aarhus: Aarhus University Press, 1990), 146.

plex was dedicated to bathing, with the standard layout for a Roman spa, with customers proceeding from the frigidarium to the tepidarium to the caldarium as they moved northward from the main entrance at the southeast of the complex. The west side of the complex was dedicated to the palaestra, where patrons could participate in physical exercise, massage, and competition, with a shrine for the imperial cult prominently placed in the middle of the palaestra's western colonnade.[18] Only a few Ostian baths had palastrae, and this one was notable for its size. The Baths of Neptune, whose footprint was extremely large at approximately 67 x 67 meters or 220 x 220 feet, must have been one of the more prestigious bath complexes and was likely to have been operated by the city.[19]

At the time of interest for our purposes, repairs were needed to the drainage system leading out from the spa rooms. This required compromising the flooring of room 6 in order to access the subterranean drains.[20] After the repairs were completed to the drains, the flooring was reinstalled, and mosaics needed to be laid.[21]

---

18. Fikret K. Yegül, *Baths and Bathing in Classical Antiquity* (New York: Architectural History Foundation, 1992), 68.

19. Edward Adams notes that the smaller bath complexes, *balnea*, "were privately owned establishments, but open to the public, while city authorities owned and ran the large *thermae*" such as the Baths of Neptune. See Adams, *The Earliest Christian Meeting Places: Almost Exclusively Houses?* (London: T&T Clark, 2013), 174. It used to be said that the Baths of Neptune owe their current layout to Emperor Hadrian, who sponsored the renovation of baths originally built in the first century during the time of Emperor Claudius. But the inscription listing Hadrian's donation of two million sesterces (CIL 14.98) has now been shown to pertain not to the Baths of Neptune but the Baths of the Marine Gate (my thanks to Jan Theo Bakker for pointing this out). See Marcello Turci, "Le iscrizioni delle Terme di porta Marina rinvenute da Gavin Hamilton: Nuovi dati per la contestualizzazione di CIL XIV, 98 e CIL XIV, 137," in *Ostia, l'Italia e il Mediterraneo. Intorno all'opera di Mireille Cébeillac-Gervasoni*, ed. Maria Letizia Caldelli, Nicolas Laubry, and Fausto Zevi (Rome: Collection de l'École française de Rome, 2021), 133–45.

20. This is Becatti's interpretation (*Scavi di Ostia*, 4, 1:53). This interpretation makes sense of certain features of the flooring, especially the scar in the black border in the northwest section of the room.

21. Repairs were done elsewhere at other times within the bath complex, none of which are pertinent to our study. See, e.g., Theodora Leonore Heres, *Paries: A Proposal for a Dating System of Late-Antique Masonry Structures in Rome and Ostia, AD 235–600* (Amsterdam: Rodopi, 1982); and her earlier studies: "Una ricerca sulla storia edilizia delle Terme di Nettuno ad Ostia Antica (II,4,2): nel periodo post-adrianeo,"

With these observations, we need to consider the mosaic decor on the floor of room 6. As is evident from the places where the floor was not disturbed by the renovations to the drains, the room's original decor involved a double ribbon of black tesserae that highlighted the extremities of the floor around all four walls of the room—a ribbon 17 centimeters or 6.7 inches in width, with a wider outer band and a narrower inner band. This black fringe bounded the white tesserae that covered the rest of the floor. In its repaired state, the floor mosaic was not a reproduction of the original pattern. This goes beyond the insertion of symbols; the new mosaic floor had some black tesserae peppered in randomly among the predominately white tesserae, and the black fringe was not carried on in the same fashion. The original double ribbon of black tesserae around all four walls of the room was reduced to a single (and less elegant) black band along the south and east walls of the room, along with the glaring oddity that there was no attempt to replicate a band of any kind all along the north wall of the room.

The quality of materials used for the renovated section of the flooring was inferior to the original materials. The original tesserae are smaller than the replacement tesserae, which are therefore less ornate while also being more irregular in shape.[22] The inferior materials, however, matched what must be deemed the inferior artistic skills of the renovator.[23] For instance, the mosaicist did not stick strictly to a straight line when constructing the black outer ribbons in the southeast corner of the room. Similarly, when repairing a small section of the black double ribbon in the northwest section of the room, white tesserae were used instead of black, in a way that only draws attention to the second-rate character of the relaid mosaic.

One way or another, the repaired mosaic floor of room 6 was of an inferior artistic quality. Previously, a carpet of white tesserae was bounded by a double-edged black ribbon in a simple and aesthetically pleasing effect. After the repairs, the mosaic flooring had a confused, inelegant, splotchy appearance, whether the eye fell to the disjointed outer perimeter

---

Meded 40 (1978): 93–112; "La storia edilizia delle Terme di Nettuno (II,4,2) ad Ostia: lo sviluppo nei secoli IV–V," *Meded* 41 (1979): 35–42.

22. Becatti, *Scavi di Ostia, 4* 1:52.

23. In private correspondence, Jan Theo Bakker assures me that this is not an uncommon phenomenon in the mosaics of Ostia Antica. See Bakker, "3.4—The Restorations of the Mosaics and the Masonry," Ostia Antica, https://tinyurl.com/SBL4830y.

of the room or the middle of the room, where bizarre shapes interrupted the flooring of white tesserae peppered with black.

4. The Function of Room 6 within the Spa

Consideration now needs to be given to the social function of room 6 within the bath complex, taking into account both architectural and artistic features (see fig. 11.11 for the room demarcation used in this essay).

Room 6 (with dimensions of 14 x 9 m or 46 x 29.5 ft) has an external doorway, giving it access to the street now known as Via dei Vigili. While we should imagine some form of passage between the spa and the larger civic context being possible by way of this room, this was not a main entrance. In fact, the width of the doorway was roughly half the width of the official entry corridor in the southeast corner of the complex.[24] This doorway in room 6 was not specially decorated; it was simply a low-grade functional doorway.

Room 6 also had potential to serve as a passageway from the frigidarium of room 5 to the tepidarium of room 7. Customers could pass into room 7 directly from room 5, but room 7 could also be accessed from room 5 through room 6. Although room 6 allowed passage between those rooms, its primary function lay elsewhere. Any movement between rooms 5 and 7, for instance, required only the two doorways in the southwest corner of room 6; and movements between room 6 and the street involved only a sliver of the room's space along its southern strip. Accordingly, roughly three-quarters of the room lies beyond any purposes allowing movement. Room 6 must have had some function beyond the movement of people.

If the room was not primarily about movement, neither was it about enterprise. Shops were located at the southern end of the bath complex, and three shops (and a staircase) were located directly to the north of this room, with doorways out to the street. Room 6, however, does not have any semblance to those shops, whether in its much larger size or its much narrower doorway.

From these observations it would seem relatively easy to discern the room's function. I propose that room 6 is perfectly situated and suited

---

24. Some think the main entryway was from the south, through a narrower entryway next to a stairway. I think this unlikely.

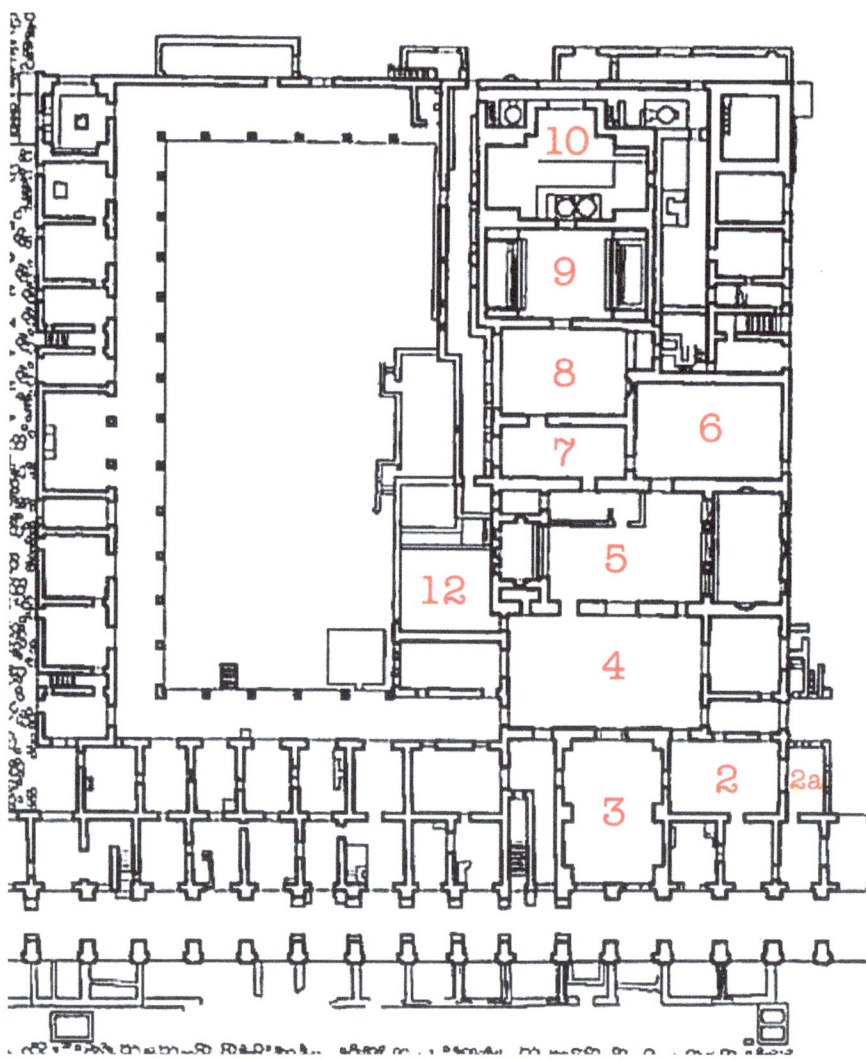

Fig. 11.11. Plan of the Baths of Neptune. Source: Parco Archeologico di Ostia Antica, https://gisnadis.parcoarcheologicostiantica.it/ (with room numbers added).

to serve as a waiting room for slaves attending to their masters as they (their masters) moved into the tepidarium (rooms 7 and 8) and caldarium (rooms 9 and 10). Slaves would generally not have accompanied their masters into those rooms, which were prime social position within the spa. To have slaves milling around in those rooms would have added congestion unnecessarily and been socially unappealing. Slaves would have accompanied their masters through rooms 3 and 4 (at least). Masters would have disrobed in room 4 (or perhaps also in room 5). It was the slave's job to take his master's clothing and guard it, together with other items (e.g., clothing for exercise, towels, oils, perfumes, sponges, and strigils for scraping oil and impurities from skin). Once a slave was given the master's clothing, he was to remove himself from the main rooms within the spa, needing to be out of sight but within earshot.

Room 6 is ideally located for that, whether slaves' masters were in the frigidarium to one side of room 6 or the tepidarium and caldarium to the other side. Moreover, should a master require something from his slave while in any of those rooms, the slave (being called on by his master) could reach him quickly and remove himself from the scene just as quickly. Or perhaps a functionary of the complex was stationed at the doorway between rooms 6 and 7, to act as a go-between—conveying the wishes of masters to their slaves on call in room 6 and delivering things to the masters that had been held or retrieved by the slaves. Further, should the master require his slave to leave the complex for some purposes (i.e., to retrieve something or someone), the slave could slip out through the ordinary doorway of room 6, without having to pass through the other rooms where masters were mixing and without having to pass through the entry hallway precisely when free(d)men might have been entering the premises.[25] When a slave's master exited the caldarium and tepidarium and returned to the frigidarium of room 5, his slave would have heard his voice coming from room 7, perhaps even seeing him through the doorway between rooms 6 and 7—positioning himself to meet his master with his clothing, either in room 5 or perhaps room 4.

In every way, then, room 6 is ideally suited as a waiting room for slaves, to be used by them when their masters were using the inner rooms of the spa. When the original architects were planning the layout of the

---

25. Adams, *Earliest Christian Meeting Places*, 176: "Food and drink could be purchased in *popinae* located outside and brought into the bathhouse."

spa, they took account of the marked social distinction between slave and free, ensuring that one room within the spa could contain slaves as they waited for their masters. This is probably why the room was nonetheless relatively large. The success of the bath complex required a good customer base, and free(d)men would inevitably have at least one slave in tow. The spa needed to have somewhere for the potentially numerous slaves to retreat to, to avoid cluttering up the spa's social space and detracting from the spa's ornamentation. It is unlikely, then, that masters would have moved from room 5 into room 7 by way of room 6; that room was for those perceived as socially inferior.

The decor of room 6 fits perfectly within this scenario, as evident in the mosaic patterns within the spa. The eastern side of the bath complex is distinguished, wherever feasible, with mosaic flooring featuring aquatic images.[26] Note the following:

1. In the toilet room (room 2a, an annex of room 2), a mosaic flooring depicts a Nilotic scene, including a crocodile chasing a pygmy and a riverboat transporting amphorae.[27]
2. The floor of the room 3 features a mosaic of Amphitrite, the Greek goddess of the sea, riding on a hippocampus (a mythical seahorse). Also depicted with Amphitrite is a cupid and Tritons, referencing mosaics in rooms 4 and 5, respectively.
3. The cupid of room 4 associates Amphitrite with her husband, Neptune (or Poseidon, as the Greeks knew him), the deity of the sea, who is depicted in the central room 4 (the *apodyterium*) with the largest mosaic in the spa. The Neptune mosaic is full of marine images. Even the cupids of this mosaic (referencing the cupid of the Amphitrite mosaic) are shown riding dolphins.
4. The mosaic of room 5 (the frigidarium) amplifies the Tritons of the Amphitrite mosaic, expanding their number to fill the floor mosaic. The Tritons were fish-tailed sea deities in the entourage of Neptune who represented the deity Triton, the son of Neptune and Amphitrite.

---

26. See Becatti, *Scavi di Ostia*, 4, vol. 2, TAV 118, 124–33.
27. The crocodile/pygmy portion was no doubt intended humorously, with crocodile about to bite the pygmy's exposed bottom. Presumably exposed bottoms were not infrequent in the latrine. See Becatti, *Scavi di Ostia*, 4, vol. 2, TAV 118.

An aquatic theme, then, consistently runs throughout the mosaic flooring in four rooms on the eastern side of the bath complex (rooms 3 to 5), including even the most inglorious room of that section (i.e., the toilet of room 2a). The same theme, however, does not continue beyond those rooms. For instance, room 12 adjoins room 4 and is the main passage from the east section (where the spa is based) to the west section's exercise palaestra. Like rooms 2 through 5, room 12 also has a pictorial mosaic flooring, but that mosaic breaks with the aquatic theme. Instead of mythical figures associated with the sea, the mosaic floor of room 12 depicts human athletes in competitive action, appropriately referencing the main activities of the palaestra, into which the room leads.

Room 6 also breaks from the aquatic motif. It is not the case that the mosaic changes to a different theme, as in the change to athletic images in the flooring of room 12; instead, the attempt to thematize the mosaic drops out altogether. This room is, then, mosaically unadorned, with white tesserae carpeting the floor (until, of course, the renovation work, when small black tesserae were sporadically embedded into the renovated mosaic). In terms of social prominence, then, room 6 needs to be placed lower than the toilet of room 2a.

This feature of the decor in room 6 (i.e., the absence of a predominant mosaic) makes perfect sense when seen in light of the proposed social function of the room. Prior to arriving at the tepidarium of room 7 in the bathing side of the complex, freemen/freedmen walked on mosaics linked by aquatic mythological figures. Since room 6 was the waiting room for slaves attending to their masters, a mosaic motif was not inserted into the floor mosaics. Those who were free/freed had their social prominence reinforced by the themed mosaics; those who were enslaved had their social insignificance reinforced by the absence of themed mosaics in the room dedicated to placing them out of the way but within serviceable distance. Room 6 was not a place for free(d)men; the mosaic flooring advertised that clearly.

With this, we have a significant piece of the puzzle in place for interpreting the situation in which Christian symbols were embedded within the flooring of room 6. As we move toward that interpretation, we need also to consider aspects of the early history of Christianity in Ostia.

5. Aspects of Early Christianity in Ostia Antica

A full survey of Christianity in Ostia is not intended here; that has been done by others.[28] According to Russell Meiggs, for instance, "the literary tradition suggests that, by the middle of the third century, Christianity was firmly rooted" in Ostia.[29] It is not necessary to review all the data here. Instead, I want to capture only a few key moments that seem to be both relatively stable historically and potentially pertinent to this study—in particular: (1) the self-advertisement of an association in the late second century and (2) the martyrdom of some Christians in the late third century.

Adjacent to the grounds of the main theater is the Forum of the Associations (Piazzale delle Corporazioni; see fig. 11.12). This large space was easily and openly accessible. It enabled various guilds both to market their wares to the public and, more importantly, to allow long-distance traders and shippers to connect with people who shared their ethnic and/or trade identities.

The second of these stations, on the southeastern side, advertised its guild in the mosaic pavement (CIL 14.4549). The identifying mosaic has three lines, the first two of which are placed within the frame of a *tabula ansata*, while the five letters of the third line fall below the *tabula* (see fig. 11.13). The first two lines of the mosaic read (with spaces added and an *ET* ligature in the second line):

---

28. See Paul-Albert Février, "Ostie et Porto à la fin de l'antiquité," *MEFR* 70 (1958): 295–330; and especially Russell Meiggs, *Roman Ostia* (Oxford: Clarendon, 1973), 388–403, 518–31. See also Maria Floriani Squarciapino, "Considerazioni su Ostia cristiana," *StudRom* 27 (1979): 15–24 (translated into English by Jan Theo Bakker at https://tinyurl.com/SBL4830z). Most recently, see Douglas Boin, *Ostia in Late Antiquity* (Cambridge: Cambridge University Press, 2013), esp. 75–80, 114–19, 155–64, 167–80, 219–28.

29. Meiggs, *Roman Ostia*, 390. Elsewhere he says, "it seems probable that Christianity made little headway at Ostia during the second century, but spread widely during the economic distress of the third century" (392; the view that third-century Ostia experienced economic hardship is debated). It is nonetheless also important to note, as Boin says, that "Christianity did not alter the shape or appearance of the third-century town" (115). He may press too far, however, when claiming that Christians are "absent from the material record" until later centuries (115–16); nowhere does Boin interact with the Christian symbols of room 6 in the Baths of Neptune, for instance.

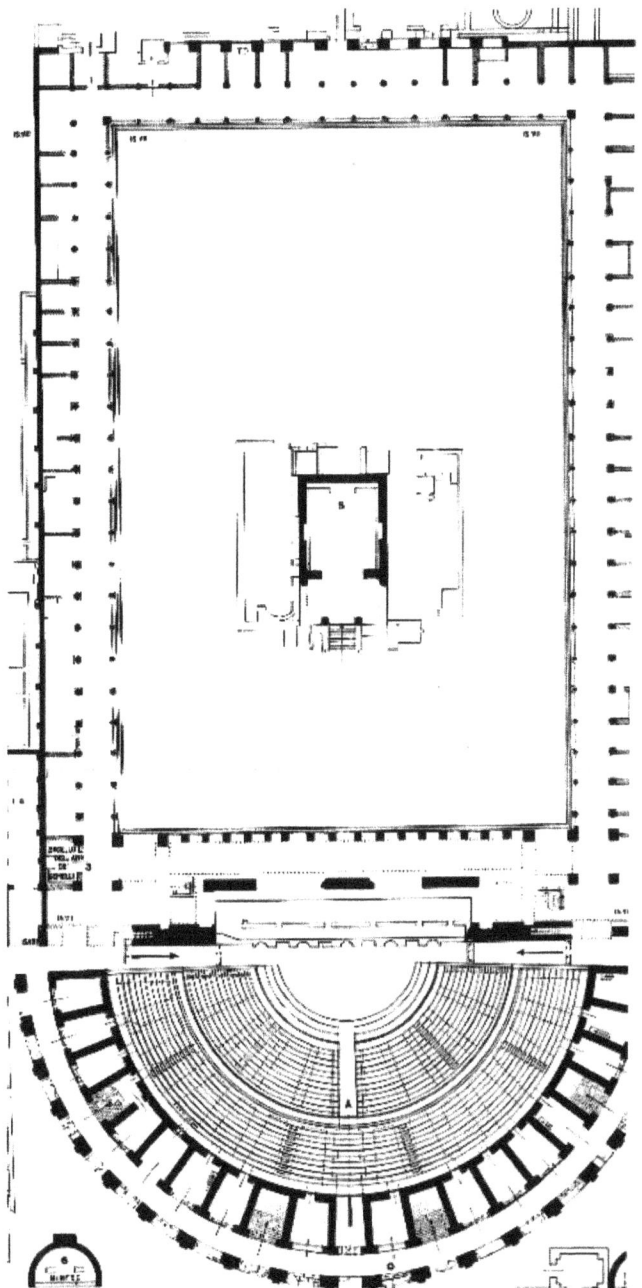

Fig. 11.12. Diagram of the Forum of the Associations adjacent to the theater. Source: Parco Archeologico di Ostia Antica, https://gisnadis.parcoarcheologicostiantica.it/.

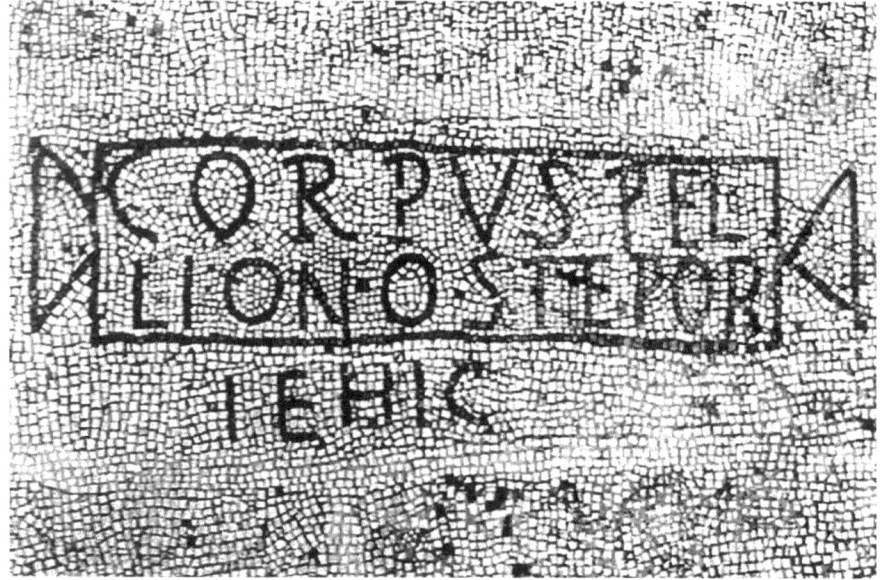

Fig. 11.13. Mosaic advertising the association of the furriers. Source: Giovanni Becatti, *Scavi di Ostia, 4: Mosaici e pavimenti marmorei* (Rome: Libreria dello Stato, 1961), vol. 2, TAV 189. Used by permission of Parco Archeologico di Ostia Antica.

CORPUS PEL
LION OST ET POR

Initially it was hard to make out the third letter from the right end of the first line, but the best interpretation has it not as a *T*, as in *corpus tellion[ariorum]* (an occupation otherwise unknown in the ancient world) but as a *P*—*corpus pellionum*, the association of furriers.[30] An Ostian inscription from the time of Marcus Aurelius's reign (161 to 180) heralds the *genius* of this association (CIL 14.10). Accordingly, the first two lines of the mosaic, falling within the *tabula ansata*, identify a particular association—the *corpus pellion[um]* that was based in Ostia and in Ostia's sister port nearby, Portus (*Ost[iensium] et Por[tensium]*). Here we see an association whose members were drawn from both neighboring cities.

---

30. Jan Theo Bakker suggests that this is less likely to be about clothing than about leatherwork for ship sails. See Bakker, "Statio 2," Ostia Antica, https://tinyurl.com/SBL4830aa. This is just one page in his extensive website on Ostia, an invaluable resource. I adopt his view in this section of this essay.

The five letters below the tabula ansata are clear: *IEHIC*. Some have wondered, however, whether the first letter, *I*, may originally have been a *T* that was later adjusted to an *I* (for some reason). The way the mosaicist has laid the tesserae allows for that possibility. In this interpretation, the third line is adding to the final word within the *tabula ansata*, so that the end of the second line and the first two letters of the third line together would read *Porte[nsium]*. There are some weaknesses in this proposed reconstruction, however. First, there would be no need to extend the stem of *Portensium* into a third line; everyone with even the most basic degree of literacy would have filled in the letters after *POR* easily enough, in view of the word's link to the three-letter abbreviation of Ostia just before it (*Ost[iensium]*). Second, if the first two letters of the third line were to be an extension of the word at the end of the second line, that third line should have been placed within the *tabula ansata*, presumably lowering the bottom of the *tabula ansata* to include space for the third line. Evidently the mosaicist did not think the third line was part of the material to be included within the *tabula ansata*. Even if he were mistaken about that, it would have been easy enough to fix the situation immediately upon discovering the mistake, moving the letters up and the extent of the *tabula ansata* down. Third, the white tesserae above the letter *I* are of the same quality and size as the white tesserae around them, suggesting that they are original to the setting. Evidently, then, the first two letters of the third line are not a continuation of the last word in the *tabula ansata*. They stand outside the tabula, and there is no reason to think that the first of the five letters once read *T* instead of *I*.

How, then, is the third line to be interpreted? Clearly the last three letters form the word *HIC*, "here." That just leaves the first two letters for interpretation: *IE*. Jan Theo Bakker is probably correct to see them as the first two letters of the name *IESUS*. The phrase "Jesus here" is probably not a plea for Jesus to assist in the business. More likely it advertises to those entering Ostia that getting connected to a group of Christians can be done through this particular association of furriers, leatherworkers. The mosaic was laid in the final decade of the second century.[31]

---

31. It is interesting to note that the station next to theirs (station 1) was for the association of the *stuppatores* (dealing in the caulking to pack between timbers and decking of ships). In the third century this association replaced their associational temple with a mithraeum. See Jan Theo Bakker, "Regio I—Insula X—Tempio Collegiale and Mitreo di Fructosus (I,X,4) (Guild Temple and Mithraeum of Fructosus),"

There is precedent for a single association adopting Christ devotion. This scenario best explains the origins of Christ devotion in Thessalonica in the year 50 or so.[32] As a consequence of their adoption of an exclusive form of Christ devotion, those early Christ-followers subsequently experienced persecution of some kind, as Paul's letter to them makes clear (1 Thess 1:6; 2:2, 14; 3:3–4). The Ostian association of leatherworkers may not have been persecuted for adopting Christianity, but the fact that they did not spell out the name *IESUS* in full might indicate some hesitation on their part. They were not completely secretive; people must have known of their devotion to their unconventional deity. But neither were they drawing overt attention to their devotion. Somehow people in search of Christian fellowship needed to be alert to this abbreviated form of advertising devotion to Jesus. It is notable that the same cautious approach to presenting Christianity in mosaics is on display both in this station in the late second century and in room 6 of the Baths of Neptune in the late third or early fourth century.

One other key episode in the story of Ostian Christianity needs to be registered, one that occurred during the reign of Emperor Claudius Gothicus (268–270), or perhaps earlier, during the reign of Trebonius Gallus (251–253).[33] This is the martyrdom of Aurea and other Christians. Many fictional adornments have been added to story of their deaths over the centuries, but the elaborated story is unlikely to have been fabricated de novo.[34] It would appear that Aurea, from an aristocratic family based

---

Ostia Antica, https://tinyurl.com/SBL4830ab. So the first two stations were populated by associations pertaining to the shipping industry with a notable commitment to a particular deity. My thanks to Jan Theo Bakker for pointing this out to me.

32. This estimate derives from teasing out the historical situation outlined in 1 Thess 1:7–9. On this, see especially Richard S. Ascough, "The Thessalonian Christian Community as a Professional Voluntary Association," *JBL* 119 (2000): 311–28; with updated discussion in Bruce W. Longenecker, "Configuring Time in Roman Macedonia: Identity and Differentiation in Paul's Thessalonian Christ Group," in *Greco-Roman Associations, Deities, and Early Christianity*, ed. Bruce W. Longenecker (Waco, TX: Baylor University Press, 2022), 289–308.

33. Boin offers a plausible explanation for the dating disparity (*Ostia in Late Antiquity*, 218). Since later tradition linked Constantine to Claudius, the martyrdoms needed to be moved to the time of Trebonius Gallus. This would tip the balance to Claudius being the emperor during the time of the Ostian martyrdoms.

34. Meiggs holds the view that later elaborations were "firmly rooted in actual events" that provided the basis for those later developments (*Roman Ostia*, 391). In the medieval version of the story, Aurea is referred to as Aura. For a recent survey of scholarly views regarding the historicity of Christian martyrdom accounts, see David L. Eastman, "Mar-

in Rome, was removed to Ostia because her Christian devotion was an offense to her family's identity. While living on an estate outside the city, she supported Ostian Christians, including Cyriacus, the bishop of Ostia.[35] She refused marital obligations, committed herself to chastity, provided food and clothing to those who had recently been baptized, and refused to participate in emperor worship. In due course, Aurea was accused of practicing magic (a rhetorically grounded charge) and was martyred for her Christian devotion, probably being drowned in the sea with a heavy stone tied around her neck. Her assets were seized by a local magistrate. Other Christians seem also to have been martyred at this time, including Cyriacus (who was killed in prison), a few leading ecclesiastical figures, and possibly some converted prison guards who were beheaded near the Arch of Caracalla, at the front of the theater on the Decumanus—not far from station 2 of the Forum of the Associations.[36]

Traditions also exist about the martyrdom of Christians in Portus.[37] Evidently Ostia and Portus were locations where Christians were insecure against social pressures and persecution, prior to the Constantinian legalization of their religion. This is not to suggest that Ostian Christians prior

---

tyrdom between Fiction and Memory," in *Cambridge History of Ancient Christianity*, ed. Bruce W. Longenecker and David E. Wilhite (Cambridge: Cambridge University Press, 2023), 372-95. On networks of spies keeping a lookout for social miscreants (including Christians) in the Roman imperial era, see Rose Mary Sheldon, *Intelligence Activities in Ancient Rome: Trust in the Gods but Verify* (New York: Routledge, 2005).

35. We know of a later bishop of Ostia by the name of Maximus, whom Constantine summoned to Rome in October 313 (see Meiggs, *Roman Ostia*, 391). In 336, the bishop of Ostia consecrated the new pope, setting a precedent for many years to come.

36. Meiggs concludes "that there was a group of martyrs executed near the theater, and that the leaders of the Ostian church, including the bishop, were involved" in this loss of life (*Roman Ostia*, 520). In the fourth century, a Christian shrine was erected on the Decumanus at the southeast corner of the theater, almost midpoint between the purported site of the martyrdoms of the prison guards and station 2 in the Forum of the Corporations. For the development of things Christian around this area, see Franz A. Bauer, "Stadtbild und Heiligenlegende. Die Christianisierung Ostias in der spaetantiken Gedankenwelt," in *Die spaetantike Stadt und ihre Christianisierung*, ed. Gunnar Brands and Hans-Georg Severin (Wiesbaden: Reichert, 2003), 43-62.

37. See especially Meiggs, *Roman Ostia*, 518-31. In the mid-third century, Cyprian (ca. 210-258), the bishop of Carthage, noted that Christians originating from North Africa and arriving at Portus received a welcome reception from Christians living in that city (*Ep.* 21.4).

to that time necessarily kept their Christian identity wholly concealed from others. But they must have been judicious about the extent and manner in which they presented themselves beyond their associational meetings.[38]

To go much further into the data is either unnecessary for our argument or meets with uncertainties about dating. For instance, it is tempting to think that the mosaic flooring at the entrance of the House of the Fish (at region 4, insula 3, entryway 3) is material evidence for pre-Constantinian Christianity in Ostia. The mosaic in the house's doorway features a drinking vessel with a symbol of a fish embedded in it, with two fish also appearing at the base of the vessel (see fig. 11.14). As some have proposed, it is possible that the vessel is a reference to the eucharistic cup, with fish being a common pre-Constantinian symbol among Christians who identified as fish devoted to the divine *ichthys* ("fish"; ιχθυς; ι = Jesus; χ = Christ; θυ = God's son; ς = savior).[39] The mosaic was positioned so that those leaving the house (as opposed to entering the house) encountered it in its proper orientation. If these are Christian symbols, they might have served to remind Christians of their identity as they left a corporate worship service. But when was this mosaic installed? Some scholars date the renovation in the house to the mid- to late third century, while others date it to the mid-fourth century, which seems more likely.

At some point within this timeline, a mosaicist inserted Christian symbols into the mosaic flooring in the Baths of Neptune. We need now to try to envisage the situation in which this might have transpired.

---

38. In this regard we can consider the case of a man named Felica, who may have been another Ostian Christian of this time period. He worked in the coin mint established by Maxentius in 308 or 309. According to the inscription on his tombstone, he had been *pr[a]epositus mediastinorum de moneta officina prima* ("the superintendent of the menial slaves for the first workshop of the mint"). Since the mint was closed in 313 and this is how his public career is noted, he must have died in that role between 309 and 313. The inscription also claims that he is *in pace in fide dei* ("in peace, in the faith/trust of God"). Although we cannot be certain, this is likely to refer to his Christian devotion. See Jan Theo Bakker, "The Mint of Maxentius," Ostia Antica, https://tinyurl.com/SBL4830ac.

39. Meiggs considers the arguments against a Christian interpretation of this mosaic to be weak (*Roman Ostia*, 400). I grant that, but the mosaic itself is better dated to a fourth-century renovation of the house.

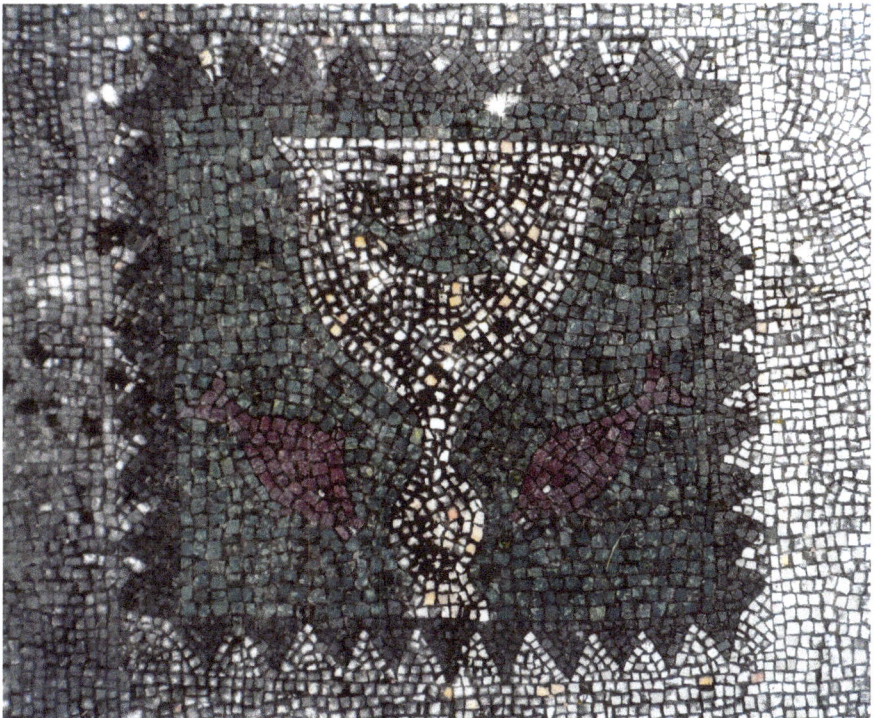

Fig. 11.14. Mosaic in the doorway of the House of the Fish. Photograph by author.

6. Interpreting the Situation

We now have the pieces in place for postulating the situation in which a collection of Christian symbols, most of them oblique, were embedded in the mosaic flooring in the waiting room for slaves in Ostia's prestigious Baths of Neptune. Becatti's guess is that a rogue mosaicist took the occasion to advertise his (presumably "his") own religious convictions in the mosaic flooring.[40] Exuberant in his faith, the mosaic installer could not hold himself back from making public what to him was most important in life.

I do not think this view is convincing. If the mosaicist was so exuberant, why are the symbols rather enigmatic? If we are to imagine a single mosaicist going beyond the remit of his brief, we have also to imagine

---

40. Becatti, *Scavi di Ostia*, 4, 1:53–54.

that he put his livelihood at risk. His roguish unprofessionalism would have given him a reputation as someone who was not trustworthy in his responsibilities. Moreover, if his initiative resulted in the mischievous formation of a mosaic unacceptable in its artistic appeal, the manager of the bath complex could very easily have hired another mosaicist to dig out the offending symbols and replaced them with white tesserae—a simple job that would not have taken long nor cost very much. Evidently no one imagined that the black mosaic symbols had been placed there cunningly, connivingly, and illegitimately. That they remained in place undercuts the force of the rogue mosaicist interpretation. No matter how we approach it, Becatti's scenario does not work.

While it is easy to disagree with Becatti's proposal, it is not at all easy to come up with a counterproposal. This is because the situation is so unusual. We might readily imagine Christian symbols being installed within household mosaics, as some have proposed for Ostia's House of the Fish, for instance. But this flooring is within the public arena, not within a privately owned residence. Moreover, its symbols seem largely to be enigmatic or disguised. The space for thinking about possible scenarios for the installation of this flooring is very limited indeed.

In my view, we have to imagine two things: a group of Christians sponsoring the initiative and an acquiescent manager of the bath complex, who could also present the inclusion of cryptic shapes as an acceptable situation to those to whom he was accountable. At the center of all this, there must have been a financial arrangement of some kind. This is why it is best to imagine not simply a single rogue mosaicist but a group of Christians taking the initiative. The amount of the financial transaction/transactions must have been somewhat sizable, so the funds were more likely to have been donated by a group than an individual—especially a single second-rate mosaicist, who may not even have been a Christian himself.[41] The symbols themselves occasionally point to a corporate context, as in the eucharistic imagery of the grape clusters and the eucharistic cup. The *IESUS* cross shows such ingenuity that, whether originally devised by an individual or members of a Christian group, it would have been shared and appreciated by a group or groups of Christians.

---

41. The mosaicist may simply have been given some wax-tablet drawings of what the symbols should look like.

Perhaps, then, an association of Christians (whether the furriers of station 2 in the Forum of the Corporations, or a household group like those possibly gathering at some point in the House of the Fish, or some other scenario), or even an intracity collective (within Ostia) or intercity collective (between Ostia and Portus) of Christian associations, devised the strategy of implanting symbols into the mosaic flooring of room 6 when the repairs to the subterranean pipes were being carried out. With the manager of the baths being one of their own (in our preferred scenario), these Christians knew that the flooring of room 6 was being taken up and then relaid, and they spotted their opportunity to propose that they be designated as the sponsors for this part of the renovation.[42] To everyone's agreement, the mosaic flooring would not be overtly Christian, and there was probably no attempt to hide the knowledge that Christians had sponsored the flooring. But interpreting the symbols was not something just anyone could do; the symbols would have been suggestively significant primarily to Christians who might be in the know as to their interpretation. Additionally, since this was the waiting room for slaves, such an arrangement probably did not seem overwhelmingly problematic to anyone. When explaining the situation to any of his higher-ups (presumably the city aediles), the manager of the baths could tip the balance of the pros and cons in favor of the pros, since there was a financial incentive of some kind and since only slaves were the room's regular users.

Eventually, of course, the manager (whom we are imagining to be a Christian) would move off to another position of responsibility or die. But at the time of the installation of the Christian symbols, we must imagine him to have been a key figure at the intersection of this public space and the devotional interests of Ostia Christians. Once the installation was completed, the connection between room 6 and the sponsoring Christian association/associations might have continued into the future (especially with financial incentives in play), regardless of the manager's continued involvement.

But why would Christians want to do this? Most likely, the room functioned as an occasional meeting place for Christians outside the normal hours of business for the Baths of Neptune. With money changing hands for the privilege, Christians may have accessed the room in the predawn

---

42. This is easier to imagine for an association that could be named as such (for example, the association of furriers) than for a household group.

hours of the morning or in the early hours of the evening, after dusk, when the functions of the bath complex were not in operation.[43]

At least two comparanda are in view of this proposal. First, in the ancient world, philosophers and rhetors "probably met their students in exedrae and lecture rooms" in some of the larger bath complexes; Christ-followers meeting in a room within a bath complex would be a variation on that social practice.[44] Second, we know of a centurion, "Gaianus, also called Porphyrius," who sponsored the installation part of a mosaic flooring for a Christian meeting hall in Kefar 'Othnay (near Megiddo) in the early third century.[45] In that situation, Christ-followers were not apprehensive to be known as such, with even a Roman centurion identifying himself as a "brother" in their midst, as noted by the mosaic he installed.[46] Like the Christian mosaics in room 6 of the Baths of Neptune, the mosaics

---

43. Adams notes, "Members of an association might arrange to meet up in the baths before going to their banquet. The society of Diana and Antinous met in the baths before banqueting" (*Earliest Christian Meeting Places*, 177 n. 143). See also Dennis E. Smith, *From Symposium to Eucharist: The Banquet in the Early Christian World* (Minneapolis: Fortress, 2003), 128. Adams also notes, "Night-time bathing was rare. Usually public baths were closed by imperial or municipal order before dusk" (*Earliest Christian Meeting Places*, 177 n. 144). In his letters to Trajan, Pliny notes that he knows of Christians who meet before dawn on a particular day of the week to sing a hymn and commit themselves to an ethical lifestyle (*Ep.* 10.97).

44. Fikret K. Yegül, *Bathing in the Roman World* (Cambridge: Cambridge University Press, 2010), 126; see also Yegül, *Baths and Bathing*, 178. Gustav Hermansen argues that the Forum Baths at Ostia contained rooms specifically for the purpose of lectures and educational classes. See Hermansen, *Ostia: Aspects of Roman City Life* (Edmonton: University of Alberta Press, 1981), 84–85. Dio Cassius (*Hist. rom.* 68.15.3) refers to the Baths of Sura in Rome as a γυμνάσιον, and often instruction took place within *gymnasia*.

45. See especially Yotam Tepper and Leah Di Segni, *A Christian Prayer Hall of the Third Century CE at Kefar 'Othnay (Legio): Excavations at the Megiddo Prison 2005* (Jerusalem: Israel Antiquities Authority, 2006), 26, 31–35; Rebecca Runesson, "Centurions in the Jesus Movement? Rethinking Luke 7:1–10 in Light of the Gaianus Inscription at Kefar 'Othnay," *JBL* 142 (2023): 129–49.

46. Runesson, "Centurions in the Jesus Movement," 148–49: "this would suggest that the Christ cult was likely not a persecuted minority cult in this part of Galilee during this time, but rather a cult of at least some local popularity capable of awarding social capital to its patrons." Runesson proposes that Gaianus was not a Christ-follower himself, being instead an "external patron" (with the mosaic's identification of him as "our brother" ([ΑΔΕΛΦΟΣ ΗΜΩΝ] simply being a way of forging relational bonds between him and them). That issue falls beyond the scope of this essay.

in Kefar 'Othnay were installed for purposes of Christian meetings within an otherwise public building, in this case, one probably owned by "the Roman army itself or the state."[47]

The situation of Christians in Ostia may have been somewhat different from that of Christians in Kefar 'Othnay in at least one respect, however. Ostian Christians in the late third or early fourth century probably did not meet in room 6 for purposes of teaching and worship in their weekly gatherings. They probably met normally in other settings.[48] Room 6 offered them something they did not have in their ordinary surroundings, that is, access to water for ritual bathing, baptism. Note, by way of comparison, that when the Roman poet Apuleius describes the conversion of his main character, Lucius, to Isis devotion, he includes a scene in which Lucius undergoes initiatory purification in a spa, being taken by a priest of Isis to the nearest bath complex (*ad proximus balneas*; *Metam.* 11.23). The difference, of course, is that Lucius was completely free to adopt Isis devotion without social ramifications. What room 6 offered was not simply water but water within a fairly closed and secluded setting. There was water on the shore of the Mediterranean Sea, of course, and water in the Tiber River, but those were exposed contexts, open to all to see. By contrast, a bath complex provided water behind closed doors at certain times of the day.[49]

It seems most likely that an association of Christians, or a collective of Christian associations (perhaps in both Ostia and Portus), wanted to have access to room 6 in order to gather there collectively when baptizing new adherents to Christianity, with access to water in a situation that could nonetheless be restricted from public view prior to the opening, or after the closure, of the bath complex.[50] Christians probably did not use the room regularly, but when they did, they could access it (in col-

---

47. Temper and Di Segni, *Christian Prayer Hall*, 51.

48. Meiggs imagines that Ostian Christians may have "met and worshipped in the cemeteries outside the walls" of the city (*Roman Ostia*, 391).

49. There is no reason to think that this water would have been full of impurities. The caldarium in Pompeii's Stabian Baths has a drain, allowing the water to be emptied and refilled (perhaps several times daily). This suggests that people were aware of the issue and took steps to address it. Any baths that did not have a drain would have been serviced by slaves regularly, changing the water in some fashion. Apuleius could not have placed Lucius's purification in a spa if he imagined the water to be overrun with dirty sludge.

50. If Christ groups generally included approximately three dozen members, the occasions for baptizing new members were probably not all that frequent. This

laboration with the manager of the complex) through the doorway to the street rather than through the main entrance.[51] Once inside, they would be met by mosaic symbols of their own devising that testified in a somewhat veiled fashion to the faith that they had adopted, the faith that others had been martyred for. Beyond that, they could perform the initiatory ritual of baptism in a fairly secluded and secure context. It seems that this situation was worth their financial investment in a pre-Constantinian context and in the wake of the recent martyrdom of some of their fellow Christians.

7. Interpreting the Word Puzzle

At this point we have enough data to propose an interpretation of one part of the mosaic floor that has thus far been deemed too cryptic for comprehension. I am referring to the four letters tucked into the flooring next to the south wall of room 6—the *RE/LE* combination.

In order to interpret those letters most effectively, it will be helpful to take note of the historical resonances of another symbol within the mosaic flooring—that is, the cursive *M*, suggesting *mille* or one thousand, embedded twice within the flooring. As we saw in section 2 above, Becatti thought this simply resonated with the phoenix, since the phoenix is depicted next to one of the two cursive *M*s within the flooring. But as noted above, any gesture to the number one thousand within the early centuries of Christianity would call to mind a millenarian expectation that was well known, referencing the thousand years of Christ's reign, as depicted in Rev 20:2–6. In that passage, Christians are said to be raised with Christ in "the first resurrection," reigning on earth with their Lord in an age wholly free from the influence of the dragon (Satan) and the beast (the Roman empire).[52] But these are not just any Christians. These are specifically said to be those Christians who have been martyred for their devotion to Christ—in par-

---

increases the likelihood that a collective of Christian associations within Ostia (and Portus?) may have been involved in the mosaic initiative.

51. Presumably wooden benches were normally positioned around the outside the room for the slaves to sit on, and perhaps other benches were placed elsewhere within the room as well. These could easily have been moved into any configuration for any gatherings of Christ-followers. In the ancient world, furniture was frequently repositioned to match the purpose of the room at any given time.

52. This does not necessarily rule out a notion that the souls of Christians enjoy an afterlife prior to the resurrection of their bodies.

ticular, being martyred because they had not "worshiped the beast or its image" (Rev 20:4). Notice that this dovetails perfectly with the tradition about the martyrs of Ostia (and Portus, for that matter).[53] It is not much of a stretch to imagine that the Christians who devised these symbols were conscious of events that had recently transpired in their city, creating symbols (in particular, the two ∞ shapes) that articulated their faith in light of those recent tragedies.[54]

I propose that something similar is evident in the *RE/LE* combination of the mosaic flooring. Becatti suggests that the *RE* on the top line must reference the resurrection (*resurrectio*). This makes sense, in view of the prominence of the theme of resurrection represented by the phoenix, the *R*, and the ∞ symbol. Becatti had no idea what the *LE* might refer to. He noted, however, that the placement of those two letters (with an *E* also placed beneath the *R*) would suggest that the word *resurrectio* is being repeated vertically as well as horizontally. Again, this makes sense, but Becatti could not go further with his interpretation. If we are to go further, it would seem that we need to orient ourselves to these letters as being the start of a word puzzle, with the *RE* starting a horizontal and a vertical word (or an abbreviated word) that serves as the scaffolding for other words to be included in relation to it. This is much like an ancient word square. Of course, the words of a word square normally share left and right margins (as well as top and bottom margins), whereas the *L* would be placed one

---

53. It also helps to tip the date of these symbols to the pre-Constantinian period, when the ruling authorities could more easily be demonized as the minions of Satan.

54. If Christians were devising symbols in light of their millenarian commitments, it is possible that the virtually impenetrable symbol in the top right of Becatti's diagram should also be seen in that light. It is possible that we are to see a reference to fire in this symbol. The leaf that accompanies the symbol shows the orientation of the "flames" to be downward. Perhaps this is precisely how Ostian Christians interpreted Rev 20:9 (within the millenarian workbook of Rev 20:2–10). That verse reads, "They [the beast and the kings of the earth and their armies] came up across the whole earth and surrounded the saints' camp, the city that God loves. But *fire came down from heaven* and consumed them." Perhaps Ostian Christians were not simply looking forward to their own resurrection but also to divine retribution against their persecutors. (Again, a date prior to 313 is more likely in this case.) This interpretation can only be tentatively held, of course. But it does hold together both versions of this symbol, with the open-curved version more clearly showing the fire to be coming down from above (since the leaf next to it orients both figures in the direction drawn by Becatti) and the closed-curve version better capturing the flames of fire.

column to the left of the *R* (and therefore also one row above the *R* to its right). But such a variation is what the placement of the letters calls for in this instance, with the mosaic word puzzle being more like a modern crossword puzzle.

What happens if we try to populate a word puzzle on the basis of the *RE* and *LE*? Sticking with Becatti's view that the *RE* is probably the start of *resurrectio*, we have to assume that that word is abbreviated within the proposed word puzzle, otherwise the word puzzle would be far too long to be manageable. I propose a word puzzle using the abbreviated form *RESUR*; filling out the *LE*, I propose *LEVARE*, which would seem to be the most natural word to couple with *resurrectio*. The interesting thing about this is, the *U* of *RESUR* and the *R* of *LEVARE* appear next to each other, leaving space for an *A* to be added before them and an *EA* after them, giving us the name of Ostia's famous martyr, *AUREA*. (And with this we can see why the full word puzzle was not written out; it would have drawn attention to a well-known woman recently killed by civic authorities for being a disrupter of society.)[55] After that, the addition of an *N* and an *S* (in two locations) easily completes the puzzle (see fig. 11.15).

Fig. 11.15. Proposed content of the word puzzle. Created by author.

---

55. Hiding the name of a hero thought by others to be a social deviant again suggests a pre-Constantinian date.

Ancient word puzzles rarely made smooth sense. Popular Latin word squares testify to this, such as the *Roma* word square (*Roma, amor, olim, Milo*) or the *rotas* word square (*rotas, opera, tenet, Arepo, sator*). The same is true for the *logos* word square discovered in Smyrna, dating to the late second through mid-third century (using the Greek words μῆλον, ἡδονή, λόγος, ὄνομα, νήσας).[56] By comparison, this proposed combination of words fares quite well as a semantic unit. Granted, the proposed word puzzle does not result in textbook Latin worthy of the poets of Greco-Roman epic. But it has some linguistic traction nonetheless. Some of the words have different semantic possibilities, depending on their contexts. This results in some flexibility in determining what a word puzzle of this kind might convey.

1. *RESUR:* as an abbreviated form of the noun *RESURRECTIO*, the case is unspecified and will depend on other components within the word puzzle.
2. *LEVARE:* a verbal form, present infinitive active, "to raise," "to support"; or a gerund, "raising," "supporting"; or a second-person imperative passive, "be raised," "be supported."
3. *SANES:* a verbal form, second-person singular present subjunctive active from *sano* ("heal," "correct") "you should heal," "may you correct"; alternatively (according to the Perseus Search Tools) an adverb, "soberly," "sensibly," "reasonably," "discretely."
4. *AUREA:* a nominative proper name, "Aurea"; or an ablative expressing either personal agency (without the preposition *ab*) or ablative of accompaniment (without the preposition *cum*), so "by Aurea" or "with Aurea."
5. *RES:* a noun form, either nominative singular ("thing," "matter," etc.) or plural nominative/accusative ("things," "matters," etc.); or a verbal form, second-person singular present subjunctive active from *reor* ("regard," "deem," "reckon," "consider," "judge"), "may you regard," "may you reckon," "may you judge," etc.).

There is room to move around within these words if we are looking for some semblance of semantic coherence from them. Two main options

---

56. On this, see graffito T9.6 in Roger S. Bagnall et al., *Graffiti from the Basilica in the Agora of Smyrna* (New York: New York University Press, 2016).

seem to be these: (1) *Aurea, sanes res; levare resurrectioni*: "Aurea, may you heal [correct] matters (for us); be raised for the resurrection." Here *Aurea* is taken as a nominative, *sanes* as verb, *res* as an accusative plural noun, and *levare* as a passive imperative. (2) *Sanes res, levare Aurea resurrectioni*: "May you regard [us] soberly, [God], raising [us] with Aurea for the resurrection." Here *sanes* is taken as an adverb, *res* as a verb, *levare* as a gerund, and *Aurea* as an ablative of accompaniment.[57]

Both of these possibilities would seem to be perfectly plausible sentiments for Ostian Christians of the late third or early fourth century. If there was a millenarian posture among Ostian Christians, however, the first possibility would seem to be the more likely of the two. If Ostian Christians were millenarians, they were not expecting to be raised with their beloved martyrs in the first resurrection, making the second possibility less likely. But the first possibility is suggestive of a situation in which Ostian Christians were counting on the martyred Aurea (her soul now exalted with the powerful, crucified-but-resurrected Jesus Christ) to be their advocate, helping to set right their situation in a city where she and others had been martyred. Here we see something of the early cult of the martyrs embedded in the mosaic flooring of room 6, with Ostian Christians of the late third or early fourth century calling on their local martyr to support and protect them in what the martyr herself well knew to be a dangerous context.

This was precisely what early Christians often held to be true: "While the ordinary dead were unable to assist the living, early Christians believed that martyrs and confessors who refused to deny or recant their Christian faith during episodes of persecution were in an exceptional class," precisely because "by virtue of their privileged position, they were able to petition Christ for mercy" for those in need.[58]

Of course, in all this we are in the unenviable position of postulating possible words for a possible word puzzle based solely on four given letters. But this is not wholly fanciful. This is what we have to work with,

---

57. Much the same meaning emerges if *levare* is understood as an infinitive.
58. Robin M. Jensen, "Power, Authority, the Living and the Dead," in Longenecker and Wilhite, *Cambridge History of Ancient Christianity*, 633–58, here 638. Jensen is here speaking in particular of Tertullian's (early) view regarding the martyrs' involvement in the forgiveness of sins—a view shared with many others. With that connotation in play, the verb *sanes* in our reconstructed word puzzle might shift more toward "heal us" or "restore us" rather than "correct our situation."

since the *RE/LE* combination itself suggests that we have the beginning of a word puzzle. And neither is this surprising. We have already seen that Christians in Ostia enjoyed creative word assemblage, as in the four occurrences of the name *Jesus* embedded in the shape of an equilateral cross (figs. 11.5 and 11.6 above). The *RE/LE* word puzzle is simply another example of their theological interest and creative ingenuity.

It also suggests (together with the millenarian interpretation of the symbol one thousand) that the memory of those recently martyred Ostian Christians had significantly shaped those Christians who sponsored the mosaic floor in room 6 of the Baths of Neptune. As Douglas Boin notes, "The memories of their martyrdom must have fostered a distinct sense of community among Ostia's Late Antique Christians."[59] Boin suggests that this coalescing of Christian identity around the martyrs of Ostia is especially notable in the fifth and sixth centuries, when the traditions of the martyrs were being narratively elaborated.[60] The mosaic floor in room 6 of the Baths of Neptune, however, gives us reason to peg that interest to a much earlier time, the late third or early fourth century.

Conclusion

In the late third or early fourth century, some Christians in Ostia undertook an initiative enabling them to have symbols of their faith installed in the renovated mosaic flooring of room 6 in the Baths of Neptune. There seems not to have been an evangelistic purpose in their plan; no one was teaching early Christianity to passersby in the room. By day, the room was the overflow room for slaves waiting while their masters enjoyed the waters and social setting of the spa. No one really cared much about the decor of a room dedicated to keeping slaves out of sight. But at times, either after or before the spa's normal hours of operation, some Christians from Ostia probably paid to access room 6 and the bathwaters in rooms adjacent to it. As these Christians gathered in room 6, they encountered symbols that they had devised in their regular weekly meetings, symbols that represented their faith. These symbols featured Jesus Christ, his cross, and his eucharistic wine and cup, and articulated the Christians' confidence in the resurrection of Christ and of his followers. The power

---

59. Boin, *Ostia in Late Antiquity*, 217.
60. See Boin, *Ostia in Late Antiquity*, 218–36.

of the crucified deity might protect them from those who would seek to harm them. But these Ostian Christians knew from experience that harm often came to the followers of the crucified one. Events that had recently transpired in Ostia and Portus illustrated that alarmingly. But these Christians also seem to have believed, based on what they read in Revelation 20:2–6, that those who were martyred for their commitment to Jesus Christ would be raised in a special resurrection, to reign with Christ for a thousand years in a world devoid of Satan and the beast of Rome. If the attempt to reconstruct the word puzzle (above) has merit, Ostian Christians seem to have imagined that the martyred Aurea was now a powerful advocate on their behalf, in view of her exalted position in the presence of their resurrected deity. This was the story Christians in Ostia must have articulated as they immersed new initiates into the waters of the Baths of Neptune, where theological symbols installed in the mosaic flooring of room 6 helped to reinforce commitment to a deity beyond the deities of the Roman imperial order.

Works Cited

Adams, Edward. *The Earliest Christian Meeting Places: Almost Exclusively Houses?* London: T&T Clark, 2013.

Ascough, Richard S. "The Thessalonian Christian Community as a Professional Voluntary Association." *JBL* 119 (2000): 311–28.

Bagnall, Roger S., Roberta Casagrande-Kim, Akin Ersoy, Cumhur Tanriver, and Burak Yolaçan. *Graffiti from the Basilica in the Agora of Smyrna.* New York: New York University Press, 2016.

Bakker, Jan Theo. "3.4—The Restorations of the Mosaics and the Masonry." Ostia Antica. https://tinyurl.com/SBL4830y.

———. "The Mint of Maxentius." Ostia Antica. https://tinyurl.com/SBL4830ac.

———. "Regio I—Insula X—Tempio Collegiale and Mitreo di Fructosus (I,X,4) (Guild Temple and Mithraeum of Fructosus)." Ostia Antica. https://tinyurl.com/SBL4830ab.

———. "Statio 2." Ostia Antica. https://tinyurl.com/SBL4830aa.

Bauer, Franz A. "Stadtbild und Heiligenlegende. Die Christianisierung Ostias in der spaetantiken Gedankenwelt." Pages 43–62 in *Die spaetantike Stadt und ihre Christianisierung.* Edited by Gunnar Brands and Hans-Georg Severin. Wiesbaden: Reichert, 2003.

Becatti, Giovanni. *Scavi di Ostia, 4: Mosaici e pavimenti marmorei*. 2 vols. Rome: Libreria dello Stato, 1961.

Boin, Douglas. *Ostia in Late Antiquity*. Cambridge: Cambridge University Press, 2013.

Eastman, David L. "Martyrdom between Fiction and Memory." Pages 372–95 in *Cambridge History of Ancient Christianity*. Edited by Bruce W. Longenecker and David E. Wilhite. Cambridge: Cambridge University Press, 2023.

Février, Paul-Albert. "Ostie et Porto à la fin de l'antiquité." *MEFR* 70 (1958): 295–330.

Heres, Theodora Leonore. "La storia edilizia delle Terme di Nettuno (II,4,2) ad Ostia: lo sviluppo nei secoli IV–V." *Meded* 41 (1979): 35–42.

———. *Paries: A Proposal for a Dating System of Late-Antique Masonry Structures in Rome and Ostia, AD 235–600*. Amsterdam: Rodopi, 1982.

———. "Una ricerca sulla storia edilizia delle Terme di Nettuno ad Ostia Antica (II,4,2): nel periodo post-adrianeo." *Meded* 40 (1978): 93–112.

Hermansen, Gustav. *Ostia: Aspects of Roman City Life*. Edmonton: University of Alberta Press, 1981.

Hill, Charles E. *Regnum Caelorum: Patterns of Millennial Thought in Early Christianity*. 2nd ed. Grand Rapids: Eerdmans, 2001.

Jensen, Robin M. "Power, Authority, the Living and the Dead." Pages 633–58 in *Cambridge History of Ancient Christianity*. Edited by Bruce W. Longenecker and David E. Wilhite. Cambridge: Cambridge University Press, 2023.

Longenecker, Bruce W. "Configuring Time in Roman Macedonia: Identity and Differentiation in Paul's Thessalonian Christ Group." Pages 289–308 in *Greco-Roman Associations, Deities, and Early Christianity*. Edited by Bruce W. Longenecker. Waco, TX: Baylor University Press, 2022.

———. *The Cross before Constantine: The Early Life of a Christian Symbol*. Minneapolis: Fortress, 2015.

Meiggs, Russell. *Roman Ostia*. Oxford: Clarendon, 1973.

Nielsen, Inge. *Thermae et Balnea: The Architecture and Cultural History of Roman Public Baths*. Aarhus: Aarhus University Press, 1990.

Runesson, Rebecca. "Centurions in the Jesus Movement? Rethinking Luke 7:1–10 in Light of the Gaianus Inscription at Kefar 'Othnay." *JBL* 142 (2023): 129–49.

Sheldon, Rose Mary. *Intelligence Activities in Ancient Rome: Trust in the Gods but Verify*. New York: Routledge, 2005.

Smith, Dennis E. *From Symposium to Eucharist: The Banquet in the Early Christian World*. Minneapolis: Fortress, 2003.

Squarciapino, Maria Floriani. "Considerazioni su Ostia cristiana." *StudRom* 27 (1979): 15–24.

Tepper, Yotam, and Leah Di Segni. *A Christian Prayer Hall of the Third Century CE at Kefar 'Othnay (Legio): Excavations at the Megiddo Prison 2005*. Jerusalem: Israel Antiquities Authority, 2006.

Turci, Marcello. "Le iscrizioni delle Terme di porta Marina rinvenute da Gavin Hamilton: Nuovi dati per la contestualizzazione di CIL XIV, 98 e CIL XIV, 137." Pages 133–45 in *Ostia, l'Italia e il Mediterraneo. Intorno all'opera di Mireille Cébeillac-Gervasoni*. Edited by Maria Letizia Caldelli, Nicolas Laubry, and Fausto Zevi. Rome: Collection de l'École française de Rome, 2021.

Yegül, Fikret K. *Bathing in the Roman World*. Cambridge: Cambridge University Press, 2010.

———. *Baths and Bathing in Classical Antiquity*. New York: Architectural History Foundation, 1992.

Contributors

Gregory M. Barnhill (BA, Lee University; ThM, Dallas Theological Seminary; ABD, Baylor University) is a history teacher at Briarwood Christian School in Birmingham, Alabama. He has published articles in the *Journal for the Study of Paul and His Letters* (2020), *Catholic Biblical Quarterly* (2020), *Journal of Theological Interpretation* (2018), and *Journal for the Study of the New Testament* (2017), and he is coauthor (with Mikeal C. Parsons) of an essay in *TC: A Journal of Biblical Textual Criticism* (2019).

Eric J. Brewer (BA, Whitworth University; MDiv, Regent College; ThM, Duke Divinity School) is a doctoral student in Baylor's Graduate Program in New Testament. He has authored an essay in *Greco-Roman Associations, Deities, and Early Christianity* (2022) and forthcoming articles in the *Journal for the Study of the Old Testament* and the *Journal of Theological Studies*. He is working on a dissertation on Greco-Roman friendship in the Gospel according to Luke.

Jeffrey M. Dale† (BA, Andrews University; MTS, Candler School of Theology, Emory University; PhD [posthumous], Baylor University) published articles in *Conversations with the Biblical World* (2018) and *Journal of Biblical Literature* (2022). He was working on a dissertation titled "Microcosm of God's Final Victory: Paul's Vision in 1 Corinthians for a Community amid Cosmic Conflict in Greco-Roman Context."

Zen Hess (BA, Huntington University; MTS, Duke Divinity School) is a doctoral student in Baylor's Graduate Program in New Testament. He has published in *Christian Century* (2021), *The Other Journal* (2017), *Journal for the Study of the New Testament* (forthcoming), and *Currents in Biblical Research* (forthcoming).

Heidi J. Hornik is professor of Italian Renaissance and baroque art history and department chair at Baylor University. This paper resulted from a seminar given on art-historical methodology in Mikeal Parsons's graduate seminar. Hornik's book *Michele Tosini and the Ghirlandaio Workshop in Cinquecento Florence* (2009) is the first biography on the Mannerist painter. Hornik and Parsons coauthored the three-volume Illuminating Luke series (2003–2008) and *The Acts of the Apostles through the Centuries* (2017), and they coedited *Interpreting Christian Art* (2004). Her most recent solo-authored book is *The Art of Christian Reflection* (2018), and her most recent coedited volume (with Ian Boxall and Bobbi Dykema) is *The Art of Biblical Interpretation: Visual Portrayals of Scriptural Narratives* (2021). She is cochair of the Society of Biblical Literature Bible and Visual Art program unit.

Jeffrey M. Hubbard (BA, Biola University; MAR, Yale Divinity School) is a doctoral student in New Testament at Baylor University. He has published articles in *Journal of Greco-Roman Christianity and Judaism* (2020), *Journal for the Study of the New Testament* (2022), *Harvard Theological Review* (2022), *Studia Philonica Annual* (2022), *Vigiliae Christianae* (2023), *Novum Testamentum* (2023), and *Journal of Theological Studies* (forthcoming).

Robin M. Jensen is the Patrick O'Brien Professor of Theology at the University of Notre Dame, where she also holds concurrent appointments in classics and art history and is a fellow of the Medieval Institute. Her most recent book, *From Idols to Icons: The Emergence of Christian Devotional Images in Late Antiquity*, was published by the University of California Press in 2022.

Bruce W. Longenecker is professor of Christian origins and W. W. Melton Chair at Baylor University. He is the author or editor of some two dozen books, including *Greco-Roman Associations, Deities, and Early Christianity* (2022), *In Stone and Story: Early Christianity in the Roman World* (2020), *The Cross before Constantine: The Early Life of a Christian Symbol* (2015), and *Remember the Poor: Paul, Poverty, and The Greco-Roman World* (2010).

Mikeal Parsons is University Distinguished Professor and Kidd L. and Buna Hitchcock Macon Chair in Religion, Baylor University, where he has taught since 1986. He is author of the Paideia commentaries on Luke and Acts (2008, 2015) and coauthor, with Heidi J. Hornik, of the Illuminating Luke trilogy (2003–2008) and *The Acts of the Apostles through the Centuries* (2017).

Christian Sanchez (BA, Southwestern Assemblies of God University; MPhil, St. Mary's College, University of St. Andrews) is a doctoral student in Baylor's Graduate Program in New Testament. He has an article in *Journal of Theological Interpretation* (forthcoming) and an entry on "Zacchaeus" for the *Brill Encyclopedia of Early Christianity* (forthcoming).

Natalie Webb (BA, Howard Payne University; MDiv, Truett Seminary; MA, Baylor University) is senior pastor, University Baptist Church, Austin, Texas. She is author of "Powers and Protection in Pompeii and Paul," in *Early Christianity in Pompeian Light* (2016) and coauthor (with Todd D. Still) of an essay in *The T&T Clark Handbook to Social Identity and the New Testament* (2014).

Jason A. Whitlark is professor of New Testament in the Honors College, Baylor University, where he has taught since 2006. He is the author of *Getting Saved* with Charles H. Talbert (2011). He is also the author of several articles and books on the Letter to the Hebrews, including *Inventing Hebrews* with Michael W. Martin (2018) and *Resisting Empire* (2014).

David E. Wilhite is professor of historical theology in Baylor University's Truett Seminary, where he has taught since 2007. His books include *The Gospel according to Heretics* (2015) and *Ancient African Christianity* (2017), and he has coedited a series on the reception of Paul in early Christianity (T&T Clark) and (with Bruce Longenecker) the *Cambridge History of Ancient Christianity* (2024).

Ancient Sources Index

Hebrew Bible/Old Testament

Genesis
- 12 — 55
- 14 — 95, 131
- 17:4 — 55
- 17:21 — 90
- 18 — 79–81, 85, 89–91, 102
- 18:1 — 94
- 18:1–2 — 94
- 18:1–5 — 79
- 18:6–9 — 94
- 18:7 — 86
- 18:10 — 90
- 25:23 — 90
- 28:10–19 — 88
- 28:12 — 88
- 28:13 — 90
- 44 — 223
- 45 — 223
- 48:12–20 — 90

Exodus
- 20:3–5a — 25
- 24:10 — 165
- 32:1–25 — 27
- 32:32 — 165
- 33:11 — 27
- 33:20 — 27

Leviticus
- 26:1 — 44

Numbers
- 14:10 — 93

Deuteronomy
- 5:7–9 — 25
- 9:15–21 — 27
- 29:9 — 279
- 34:12 — 279

Judges
- 2:16–23 — 27

1 Kings
- 3 — 222
- 3:16–28 — 222

Nehemiah
- 9:18 — 27

Psalms
- 23 — 61, 150
- 30–55 — 287
- 52:7 — 284
- 58:6 — 284
- 87 — 275
- 106:19–20 — 27
- 110:4 — 131
- 115 — 26
- 115:4 — 26

Jonah
- 1:17 — 10
- 2:1 — 7

Isaiah
- 40:11 — 148–49
- 44 — 26
- 44:9 — 26

-347-

Isaiah (cont.)
53	267
66:7–11	275

Jeremiah
23	166
23:16–17	169

Ezekiel
34	164, 166, 170
34:1–10	167
34:3	164
34:3–4	169
34:4–6	170
34:10	170
34:11	148, 170
34:13–14	148
34:15	167
34:15–31	167
34:16	148, 170
34:23–24	148
34:23–25	148

Daniel
7:9	164
7:13	164
13	214

Hosea
1:10	282

Amos
9:14	282

Micah
1:14	282
2:11	282
6:8	282

Zechariah
9:10	284
14	284
14:2	284
14:8	284
14:10	284
14:11	284
14:12	284
14:14	284
14:16	284
14:17	284
14:21	284

Malachi
1:1	282
3:4	284
4:6	282

Deuterocanonical Books

Judith
15:12	309

Wisdom of Solomon
7:27	222
14:8–31	27

Sirach
36–37	286
36:28	287
46	286
46:10	286

1 Maccabees
13:51	122

2 Maccabees
6:7	309
10:6–7	122
10:7	309

3 Maccabees
2:29	309

Ancient Jewish Writers

Josephus, *Antiquitates Judaicae*
15.333	115

Josephus, *Bellum judaicumn*
3.469	115

Josephus, *Vita*	115	25:31–46	170
		27:64	240
Philo, *De Abrahamo*		28:4	240
119–122	94	28:23	240
Philo, *De Legibus*		Mark	
3.74	122	8:1–13	218
		10:13–16	195
Philo, *De posteritate Caini*		10:24–25	155
142	115	10:29–30	155
163	115		
		Luke	
Philo, *De sacrificiis Abelis et Caini*		2:41–52	18
90	115	3:8	159, 162
		6:36	195
Philo, *De Somniis*		10:20	280
2.225	115	11:9–13	195–96
		11:11	282
Philo, *Quis rerum divinarum heres sit*		11:13	282
305	115	11:29–32	7
		15	167, 170
New Testament		15:1	166
		15:3–7	166
Matthew		15:4–7	9
3:8–9	159, 162	15:5	148
6:9	194	15:6	149
7:9–13	196	15:7	169
9:2	196	18:15–17	195
9:22	196	19:1–10	184
9:29	196	24	22
12:40–41	7		
15:32–39	218	John	
16:3–4	7	1:12	195
16:12	22	1:17–18	165
16:18–19	20	2	209
18:1–5	195	2:1–11	218
18:3	195	4	73
18:3–4		6	209
18:4	195	6:1–14	218
18:12–13	148	6:25–59	217
19:13–15	195	6:33	217
19:14	195	6:51	217
24:15–28	254	10	61, 165
24:29–30	254	10:11	147, 149, 162, 165–66
25	169	10:11–12	169

John (cont.)
  10:11–16   9
  10:12   165
  14:9   28

Acts
  5:30   242
  7:39–43   27
  10:39   242
  13:29   242
  17:24–29   27
  27:29   115
  27:30   115
  27:40   116

Romans
  1:7   195
  1:20   46
  6   73
  8:14–17   195
  8:24–25   126
  8:35   217

1 Corinthians
  1   255
  10:7   27
  13:13   126
  15:19   113
  15:32   113

2 Corinthians
  5:4   39
  5:17   73

Galatians
  3:13   242
  3:27–28   73
  4:26   275
  6:15   73–74

Ephesians
  1:2   195

Philippians
  2:7   39

  2:8   243

Colossians
  1:15   27

1 Thessalonians
  1:6   326
  2:2   326
  2:14   326
  3:3–4   326
  4:13   187–88, 191

1 Timothy
  1:17   27
  6:16   27

Hebrews
  1:5–14   125
  2:5–9   125
  3:1   131
  3:5   128
  3:6   126
  4:12   128
  5:1–10   124
  5:5–7   125
  5:6   125
  5:6–10   125
  5:7   125
  5:7–8   125
  5:11   124
  6   125
  6:1–8   160
  6:4–6   129
  6:6   129
  6:8   128
  6:11   126
  6:12   125
  6:13–14   125
  6:13–17   125
  6:15b   125
  6:18   126
  6:18–19   114, 120
  6:18–20   109–10, 117, 124, 136–37
  6:19   115
  6:20   131

7:1	131	Acts of John	
7:4–10	131	26–27	34
7:11–25	125	98	247
7:16	131	99	245, 249
7:19	126		
7:20–21	131	Acts of Peter	
8	130	37–38	237
8:13	130	38	243
9:13–14	130	38–39	246
10:23	126		
10:26	129	Acts of Thomas	
10:29–31	129	25	61
11:1	126	27	61
11:17	125	104	60
11:17–19	125, 185	121	60
11:19	125	132	61
11:20	128	139	60
11:27	27	149–153	60
11:37	128		
12:2	125	Ambrose, *De excessu fratris sui Satyri*	
12:7	195	1.9	187
		2.96	83
1 Peter			
2:22	242	Ambrose, *De obitu Valentianiani consolation*	
1 John		45	187
5:21	25	48	187
Revelation		Ambrose, *De officiis ministrorum*	
1:14	154	21	195
3:4–5	154		
6:11	154	Ambrose, *De sacramentis*	
7:9	154	4.24–25	213
7:9–14	122		
14:13	119	Apocalypse of Elijah	
19:11–16	170	3.2–4	254
20:2–6	340		
20:2–10	335	Apocalypse of Peter	
20:4	335	16	254
20:9	335		
		Apocalypse of Pseudo-Methodius	
Other Christian Writings		14.4	254
Acts of Andrew		Arnobius, *Adversus nations*	
54	236	8.8.9–10	31

Athanasius, *Contra gentes*
  2.34   47

Athanasius, *De incarnatione*
  14   46
  17   245

Athanasius, *De officiis ministrorum*
  2.8.40–47   222
  2.8.46–47   223

Athanasius, *Epistula ad Marcellinum de interpretatione Psalmorum*
  22   115

Athanasius, *Epistulae festales*
  10   214–15, 217–18, 220–21, 225–27
  10.1   217–18
  10.1–2   216
  10.2   217–18
  10.3   224–25
  10.3–4   216
  10.4   222–23
  10.4–8   216
  10.5   223
  10.8   218, 220
  10.9   219
  10.9–11   216
  10.11   218
  10.12   216

Athanasius, *Orationes contra Arianos*
  3.26   220
  3.33   220

Athenagoras, *Legatio pro Christianis*
  15   30

Augustine, *Confessions*
  9.7   227
  9.13.36   213
  9.14   191
  9.27–37   191
  9.29   191
  9.29–32   191
  9.31   191

Augustine, *Contra Julianum*
  6.23   29

Augustine, *Contra Maximinum Arianum*
  2.26.5   84

Augustine, *De civitate Dei*
  16.29   84

Augustine, *De consensus evangelistarum*
  1.10.15–16   43

Augustine, *De moribus ecclesiae catholicae*
  1.34   44

Augustine, *De trinitate*
  2.11.20   84, 86, 102
  8.7   42

Augustine, *De vera religione*
  49   195

Augustine, *Epistles*
  92.1   187
  102   16
  140.9–11   195

Augustine, *Homilae*
  172   187, 192
  172.3   191
  173   187, 192
  340A.1   195

Augustine, *Sermons*
  198.10   44

Basil, *Epistulae*
  93   210

Berlin-Strasbourg Apocryphon
  5.1–14   250
  8.31   250

Ancient Sources Index

8.35	250	Commodian, *Instructiones adversus gentium deos*	
9.10	250	30	163
Calvin, *Institutes*		35	243
1.11.13	25	Coptic Apocalypse of Peter	
1 Clement		81–83	249
1.3	128	Cyprian, *Ad Quirinum testimonia adversus Judaeos*	
5	128		
5.4	128	1.14	170
17.1	128		
17.5	128	Cyprian, *De catholicae ecclesiae unitate*	
21.1	128	8	170
21.9	128		
27.2	128	Cyprian, *De habitu virginum*	
31.3	128	1	170
36.1–5	128–29		
37.5	128	Cyprian, *De lapsis*	
42–44	128	4	170
47	128		
63	128	Cyprian, *De opera et eleemosynis*	
66	128	23	169
Clement of Alexandria, *Excerpta ex Theodoto*		Cyprian, *Epistulae*	
22.4	246	8.1.1	169
42.1–43.1	246	8.2.1	169
		21.4	327
Clement of Alexandria, *Paedagogus*		43.5.1	169
1.5.16–17	196	51	169
1.5.17	196	51.2.1	169
1.9	149	55	169
3.11	32	55.15.1	170
3.11.59	116	68.4.1	170
		69.5.1	170
Clement of Alexandria, *Protrepticus*		71	170
4	30	71.2.2	170
4–7	31	74.12	170
Clement of Alexandria, *Stromateis*		Dance of the Savior	
4.17	128	1.11	250
5.5	28	4.18–19	247
		Didache	
		7.1	73

Didascalia Apostolorum
10	62
16	62
24	62
26	62

The Discourse of the Savior on the Mystery of the Cross
5	
7	243
8	252

Encomium of Mary Magdalene
17.3	243

Ephrem, *Commentary on the Diatessaron*
2.2	66
2.21c	65
4.3	64
12.17	64, 73
13.1	64, 72

Ephrem, *Hymni de Epiphania*
1.1	66
1.4	66
5	64
5.9–11	71
11.6	64, 72

Ephrem, *Hymni de fide*
3.4	66
5.3–4	63
10.20	64, 72

Ephrem, *Hymni de ieiunio*
5.1	66

Ephrem, *Hymni de nativitate*
1.5–6	65
1.15–16	66, 73
5.1	66
17.6	66, 73
17.12	66, 73
21.6	65
24.12–13	65

Ephrem, *Hymni de virginitate*
5.3	65
7	63
7.2	63
7.5	63
7.6	63
8	63
16.9	66
17.10	64, 73
20.12	65

Ephrem, *Hymns on the Church*
51.8	243

Epiphanius, *Letter to Theodosius* 41

Epiphanius, *Panarion*
7.36.1	131
27.6.9–10	35
55.1.1–5	131

Epistle to the Apostles
16	254

Epistle of Barnabas
4.6–7	269
4.6–8	269
4.8	269
4.14	267
5.2	267, 269
5.6	269
5.8	267
5.13	242
6.7	267–68
8.1	242, 267
8.1–3	267–68
8.3	267
8.5	242
8.7	268–69
9.2	267
9.7	269, 272
9.7–9	242
9.9	278
10.10	269
11.1	267

12.1	251	Gospel of Nicodemus	
12.2	267–69	8.1	251
12.2–3	272		
12.5	267–68	Gospel of Peter	
12.5–7	242	10.38–42	237
13.5	269	10.39	251
14.1–4	269	10.41–42	250
16.5	267		
16.5–9	269	Gospel of Philip	
		80	243
Eusebius, *Demonstratio evangelica*		84	249
5.9	83, 85	105	246
		Gospel of Truth	
Eusebius, *Historia Ecclesiastica*		18.24–31	242
3.3.6	151		
3.15–16	128		
3.16	127	Gregory of Nazianzus, *Orationes*	
3.25.4	151	7.1	187
3.38.1–3	128		
4.22	127	Gregory of Nyssa, *De virginitate*	
5.4.1–3	131	23.6	115
5.6.2–3	128		
5.8.7	151	Gregory of Nyssa, *Oration on Meletius* 38	
5.26.1	131		
		Hippolytus, *De antichristo*	
Eusebius, *Praeparatio evangelica*		59	116, 245
1.5.8	115		
		Hippolytus, *Refutatio omnium haeresium*	
Eusebius, *Vita Constantini*		7.32.7	35
3.49	4		
		Ireneaus, *Adversus haereses*	
5 Ezra		1.2.4	246
1:24	273	1.3.5	246, 249
1:35–37	274	1.4.1	249
2:2–3	274	1.25.6	34
2:10	275	3.3.3	127
2:15	275	3.3.4	131
2:15–32	275	5.16.3	243
2:17	275	5.19.2	243
2:31	275	5.21.1	122
Firmicus Maternus, *De errore profanarum religionum*		Irenaeus, *Epideixis tou apostolikou kērygmatos*	
13.4	30	34	245, 249
		36	195

Irenaeus, Epideixis tou apostolikou (*cont.*)
43	82
44	82
45	83
96	195

Jerome, *Commentariorum in Matthaeum libri IV*
18.3–4	195

Jerome, *Epistulae*
39.1	189
39.1–2	189
39.3	187–88
39.5	189
39.6	187, 190
39.7	190
48	211
71	211
107	227

John Chrysostom, *Ad populam Antiochenum de statuis*
16.2	115

John Chrysostom, *Ad Theodorum lapsum*
1.2	115

John Chrysostom, *De Lazaro*
1.10	115

John Chrysostom, *De sancto Meletio Antiocheno*
3	38

John Chrysostom, *Homiliae in epistulam ad Colossenses*
8.5	190

John Chryostom, *Homiliae in epistulam ad Hebraeos*
11.3	115

John Chrysostom, *Homiliae in epistulam ii ad Thessalonicenses*
1.1	115
6	187, 190
6.2	175

John Chrysostom, *Homiliae in Genesim*
25.22	115

John Chrysostom, *Homiliae in Joannem*
62.4	190

John Chrysostom, *Homiliae in Matthaeum*
31.5	187, 190
62.4	195–96

John of Damascus, *Fide*
4.11	243

John of Damascus, *First Apology* 40

Justin Martyr, *1 Apology*
9	29, 31
20	31
55	118, 245
60.1–7	249
63	131

Justin Martyr, *Dialogue with Trypho*
3.1	148
11.2	130
11.3	130
11.5	270
13.1	130
19.4	131
25.6–26.1	271
26.1	270
29.2	270
33.1–2	131
34.3	271
36.1	131, 143
36.2	143
42.1	131
42.4	270

56.10–11	82	Passion of Perpetua and Felicity	
82.1	271	2.1	155
116.3	270	4.8	151, 154
119.5	271	4.9	155, 164
123.9	271	11	164
125.3	271	11.3	164–65
125.3–5	278		
125.5	272	Paulinus, *Carmina*	
127.4	82	27.542–597	45
134.5	271		
134.6	271, 278	Paulinus, *Epistles*	
135	270	32.2–4	45
135.3	270, 278		
135.6	272	Polycarp, *Letter to the Philippians*	
		3.2	128
Martyrdom of Pionius		5.3	128
13.8	251	8.1	242
		9.2	128
Martyrdom of Polycarp		11.4	128
22.2–4	132		
		Procopius of Gaza, *Commentarii in Genesim*	
Melito of Sardis, *Homily on the Passion*			
81–82	289	18	84
Minucius Felix, *Octavius*		Pseudo-Hippolytus, *Paschal Homily*	
8.4	29	29	246
19	31	51.10–12	247
24.5–8	29	51.26–40	239
27	30	51.38–39	245
29.7–8	245	56	248
Nicephorus, *Adversus Epiphanium*		Pseudo-Tertullian, *Refutatio omnium haeresium*	
18.79	41		
		2:91–92	131
Origen, *Commentarius in Canticum*			
2.8.8	83	Shepherd of Hermas, Visions	
		5.1.1	150, 154, 156
Origen, *Contra Celsus*		5.1.2	151, 168
2.55	237	5.1.3	151
2.58	237	5.1–4	148
4.31	29	5.1.7	151
6.36	243	6.4–5	129
		25.7	129
Origen, *De principiis*			
2.11.6	245		

Shepherd of Hermas, Mandates
31.1-7   129

Shepherd of Hermas, Similitudes
2   163
9.27   148
98.3   130
103.5-6   129

Sibylline Oracles
6   250
6.26-28   252
8.244-246   254

Tertullian, *Ad Nationes*
1.12   118, 245

Tertullian, *Adversus Judaeos*
13   243

Tertullian, *Adversus Marcionem*
40.20.2-4   245

Tertullian, *Apology*
12.3   245
16.7   245
22.6   30
23.16   29
46.4   31

Tertullian, *De corona militis*
3.3   164

Tertullian, *De fuga in persecutione*
11.1   165
11.2   165

Tertullian, *De idololatria*
1   30
1.1   31
3-4   28
4   30
8   30
11.7   29
15   30

21-22   30

Tertullian, *De Oratione*
16.2   156
29   145

Tertullian, *De paenitentia*
4-5   166
7   166-67
8   166

Tertullian, *De praescriptione haereticorum*
20.2   160
32.1-2   160
32.6   160
36.4   160

Tertullian, *De Pudicitia*
3   166
7-10   167
7.1   160, 166
7.2   166
7.4   166
7.6   166-67
7.8-17   167
7.18   167
10.12   159-60, 166
10.12-13   159
13.7   166
14.27   160
20.2   160

Tertullian, *De spectaculis*
8.10   30
23   28, 30

Theodore of Mopsuestia, *Homiliae Catecheticae*
12   68
13   67
14   68

Theodoret, *Commentarii in Isaiam*
14.577   115

Ancient Sources Index

Greco-Roman Literature

Appian, *Historia Romana*
11.56 — 111, 116

Apuleius, *Metamorphoses*
11.23 — 333

Aulus Gellius, *Noctes Atticae*
3.6.1–3 — 122

Cicero, *De republica*
2.5 — 112

Dio Cassius, *Historia Romana*
68.15.3 — 332

Epictetus, *Fragments*
30 — 114

Euripides, *Fragments*
866 — 111

Euripides, *Hecuba*
79–81 — 111

Euripides, *Helena*
277–279 — 114

Galen, *De venae sectione adversus Erasistratum*
11.182.13 — 114

Galen, *Synopsis librorum suorum de pulsibus*
9.432.10 — 111

Heliodorus, *Aethiopica*
4.19 — 114
7.25 — 114

Livy, *Ab urbe condita*
28.44.7 — 112

Lucan, *De bello civili*
2.23 — 180

Lucian, *Juppiter tragoedus*
51 — 114

Plato, *Leges*
12.961c — 111

Pliny the Younger, *Epistulae*
10.97 — 332

Plutarch, *Consolatio ad uxorem*
10–11 — 188

Plutarch, *De fortuna Romanorum*
323a — 112

Plutarch, *Solon*
19.2 — 111

Propertius, *Elegies*
2.22.41 — 111

Seneca, *Ad Marciam de consolation*
7 — 189

Seneca, *Epistles*
99.1–2 — 175

Sententiae Pythagoreorum
14 — 114
135 — 114

Servius, *In Vergilii Aeneidos commentarii*
6.218 — 180

Silius Italicus, *Punica*
7.24 — 114

Sophocles, *Fragments*
685 — 111

Statius, *Silvae*
4.2.15 — 113

Stobaeus, *Anthologus*		2.4246	117
3.1	114	2.4435	120
3.2	114	2.6540	117
4.46	114	3.6556	117
		3.6568	117
Suetonius, *Gaius Caligula*		3.6576	117
32.2	122	3.6581	117
		3.6673	117
Tacitus, *Annales*		3.6680	117
2.49	112	3.6718	118
		3.6875	118
Veleius Paterculus, *Historia Romana*		3.7167	120
2.103	112	3.7223	117
		3.7230	117
Papyrus and Epigraphic Data		3.7260	117
		3.7314	117
Bodmer Papyri		3.7315	117
5	284	3.8039	120
10	284, 286	3.8068	120
11	286	3.9290	119
24	284	4.9453	117
		4.9494	118
Chester Beatty Papyri		4.9506	119
6	277, 279, 292	4.9644b	117
11	286	4.999b	118
12	287	4.10698a	120
13	287	4.10698b	120
		4.10714	117
Corpus Inscriptionum Latinarum		5.12891	108, 118
14.10	324	5.12892	108, 118
		5.12900	108, 118
Hanna Papyrus	280	5.13269b	118
		5.13528	118
ICUR		5.13971	117
1.705	117	5.14187	117
1.1592	121	5.14284	117
1.1872	117	5.14525	117
1.1778	117	5.14751	117
1.2233	117	5.14845	117
1.2569	120	5.14982	117
1.2680	117	5.15108	120
1.2745	117	5.15146	118
1.2898`	117	5.15221	117
1.4027	120	5.15223	117
2.4212	108	5.15246a	117–18

5.15246c	121	10.27057	
5.15360	108, 118		
6.17138	117	Leipzig Papyri	
6.17232	117	39	286–87
7.18794	117		
7.19260	118	Oxyrhynchus Papyri	
7.19875a	120	13.1602	291
7.20429	121	17.2072	286
7.20622	118		
8.20998	118	Papyrus Berolinensis	
8.21026	118	22220	243, 252
8.21072	118		
8.21077	118		
8.21084	118		
8.21553	118		
8.22429	118, 121		
8.22792	118		
8.22817	118		
8.22865	118		
8.23243	118		
8.23285	122		
8.23308	118		
9.23780	118		
9.24417	118		
9.24615	120		
9.24931	118		
9.25005	118		
9.25068	118		
9.25116	121		
9.25118	121		
9.25119	118		
9.25145	118		
9.25428	118		
9.25465	118		
9.25515	118		
9.26027	118		
9.26038	118 ,121		
9.26041	118		
9.26300f	118		
9.26303	118		
10.26497	118		
10.26515	120		
10.26519	120		
10.26541	118		
10.26545b	118		

Modern Authors Index

Abbe, Mark B. 18
Adams, Edwards 51–52, 70, 315, 319, 332
Alborino, Verena 205
Alexander, Paul J. 40
Allert, Craig D. 270
Allison, Dale C. 238
Andreescu-Treadgold, Irina 97
Ascough, Richard S. 326
Attridge, Harold W. 115, 122,
Awes-Freeman, Jennifer 144, 149
Backhaus, Knut 130
Bakke, Odd M. 195
Baghos, Mario 214, 216, 227
Bagnall, Roger S. 337
Bakker, Jan Theo 316, 322, 324–25, 328,
Barnard, Leslie 82
Barnes, Timothy 40, 214–15
Bassett, Sarah E. 97
Bauer, Franz A. 327
Becatti, Giovanni 301–4, 307–14, 316, 320, 324, 329, 334–35
Beck, Roger 58
Berger, Teresa 164
Bergren, Theodore A. 273, 275–76
Beyschlag, Karlmann 160
Biesen, Kees den 64, 65,
Bigham, Steven 40
Bingham, D. Jeffrey 132
Birk, Stine 192,
Bischoff, Friedrich 110
Bisconti, Frabrizio 123, 133,
Black, Matthew 239
Boardman, John 10
Bobichon, Philippe 82, 143
Boeft, Jan den 41
Boin, Douglas 323, 326, 339
Bokedal, Tomas 265, 277, 291–92
Bolyki, János 247
Bonner, Campbell 287, 289
Botti, Giuseppe 135
Boulnois, Marie-Odile 80–81, 93
Bowes, Kimberly Diane 211
Bradley, Keith R. 175
Braham, Allan 91
Brakke, David 242, 246
Braunfels, Wolfgang 93
Bremmer, Jan N. 236, 247, 251
Brendel, Otto 93
Brenk, Beat 91, 95
Brent, Allen 116, 159
Brock, Sebastian 65–66
Brown, Katherine R. 97
Brown, Raymond E. 127
Brown, Schuyler 276
Brubaker, Leslie 40
Bucur, Bogdan Gabriel 80–81, 83–87, 91, 94, 96–98, 100, 144, 151
Bunge, Gabriel 80–81, 86–88, 91, 93–94, 97–102,
Bunge, Marcia J. 195
Burke, Tony 243, 250, 252
Burkert, Walter 188
Burns, Dylan M. 243
Burns, J. Patout, Jr. 133, 135, 144–45, 168, 152, 154, 160
Butler, Rex D.
Cabrol, Fernand 149
Cairnes, Douglas 113
Camplani, Alberto 214, 227
Carletti, Carlo 120–21, 126

Modern Authors Index

Carroll, Maureen 176
Castelli, Emanuele 108–9, 114, 116–17, 120, 133
Cecconi, Paolo 163
Cerrato, John A. 116
Chadwick, Henry 28
Charlesworth, Scott D. 280, 282, 284,
Chase, George Henry 110
Clark, Mark Edward 112–13
Clarke, Graeme W. 169–70
Clauss, Manfred 57
Claassen, Jo-Marie 176
Collins, John J. 252
Connolly, R. Hugh 62
Corbeill, Anthony 181
Correia, Alice 14
Costache, Doru 214, 216, 227
Couzin, Robert 100, 177–78
Cross, Frank L. 212
Cumont, Franz 58, 113, 182
Dael, Peter C. J. van 183
Daniélou, Jean 237, 245, 251
Davies, Jon 189
Deichmann, Friedrich Wilhelm 182, 184, 194
Dekkers, Elgius 156
Deleeuw, Patricia 60
Di Segni, Leah 332–33,
Dijk, Stephen J. P. van 212
Dimas, Stephanie 192
Dinkler, Erich 264
Dirven, Lucinda 52, 63, 73
Doerfler, Maria E. 193
Donaldson, Terence L. viii, 265, 266, 272
Dresken-Weiland, Jutta 150, 186–87
Dunn, James D. G. 275–76
Eastman, David L. 326–27
Ehrman, Bart D. 129, 251, 267
Elliot, J. Keith 251, 254
Elsner, Jaś 44–45
Ennabli, Liliane 135–36
Epp, Eldon J. 293–94
Evans, Ernest 159
Evans, John 111
Fahey, Michael A. 170

Falls, Thomas B. 143, 270
Farber, Allen 18
Farina, William 152
Fears, J. Rufus 112
Feldmeier, Reinhard 195
Ferguson, Everett 52, 60, 62–63, 67–68
Février, Paul-Albert 322
Finney, Paul Corby 28, 108–9, 123, 144, 158, 205
Florovsky, Georges 40
Fliegel, Stephen N. 4, 9
Forbes, Greg 148
Foster, Paul 237–38, 251
Frank, Georgia 237
Fretheim, Terence E. 195
Füglister, Robert L. 255–56
Fulkerson, Laurel 113
Gager, John G. 265
Gagetti, Elisabetta 204
Galavaris, George 212
Galvao-Sobrinho, Carlos 122
Gamble, Harry Y. 277, 293–94
García Márquez, Gabriel 238
Gardner, Iain 246
Garstad, Benjamin 254
Gaventa, Beverly Roberts 195
Geffcken, Joh 252
Gero, Stephen 39
Gibbon, Edward 26, 31, 44
Giulea, Dragos-Andrei 239
Glorie, Frater 42
Golden, Mark 175
Goodacre, Mark 238
Goodenough, Erwin R. 56, 82, 86–88, 97–98, 115, 134
Gordon, Richard 57, 188
Grabau, Joseph 191
Gray, Patrick 130
Gregory, Andrew F. 127–28, 130
Grenfell, Bernard P. 291
Grossman, Janet Burnett 18
Grypeou, Emmanouela 80–81, 84
Gundry-Volf, Judith 195
Guyon, Jean 107, 122
Gwynn, David M. 215

Hägg, Henny Fiskå 196
Hahneman, Geoffrey Mark 163
Haldon, John 41
Harley-McGowan, Felicity 144–45, 186, 240
Harnack, Adolf von 163
Hartog, Paul 128
Hauck, Robert John 151
Heath, Jane 264
Heine, Ronald E. 160
Heinrici, C. F. Georg 287
Heres, Theodora Leonore 315
Hermansen, Gustav 332
Herrin, Judith 102
Heschel, Abraham J. 9–10
Hill, Charles E. 132, 309
Hill, Edmund 42
Hillhorst, Antoon 251
Hofer, Andrew 148
Holderness, Graham 233–34
Holl, Karl 40
Holmes, Michael 128, 150
Hope, Valerie M. 188
Hopkins, Clark 51
Horn, Cornelia B. 195–96
Hornik, Heidi J. 2, 9, 16, 18, 21–22, 32, 152
Horton, Fred L. 95, 131
Hubbard, Jeffrey M. 82
Hunt, Arthur S. 291
Hurtado, Larry W. 239, 263–64, 277–78, 292–93, 295
Huskinson, Janet 177, 179–80, 182, 185–86, 188, 192–94
Hvalvik, Reidar 267, 269, 292
Irvine, Christopher 233, 242
Jäggi, Carola 102
Jashemski, Wilhelmina F. 4
Jefferson, Lee M. 144, 194
Jensen, Robin M. 2, 32, 51, 59, 67, 72, 74, 80–81, 86, 88, 91, 93, 97, 99, 101, 103, 109, 122, 133, 135, 144, 145, 149–50, 152, 168, 177, 185–87, 194, 196, 213, 240–41, 243–44, 246, 252, 253, 338

Jongkind, Dirk 291
Junod, Éric 247
Kaestli, Jean-Daniel 247
Kariatlis, Philip 214, 216, 227
Kasser, Rodolphe 280, 284
Kennedy, Charles 116, 118–19
Kenyon, Frederick G. 279, 287, 293
Kessler, Herbert L. 54–55
King, Margaret 176
Kitzinger, Ernst 28, 40
Klaver, Sanne 71
Klauck, Hans-Josef 113
Klauser, Theodor 145
Kleiner, Diana E. E. 5
Klijn, Albertus F. J. 62
Kloos, Kari 84
Knight, David J. 97
Knott, Betty L. 177
Koch, Guntram 180, 185, 188, 205–8, 218
Koester, Craig R. 127–28
Kok, Michael 269
Konstan, David 189
Kraeling, Carl H. 51, 54–55
Kraft, Robert A. 267
Kuder, Ulrich 209–10, 218
Landau, Brent 250, 252
Lattimore, Richmond 188
Layton, Bentley 242, 246
Lazreg, Nejib Ben 147
Leader-Newby, Ruth E. 204, 206
Leclercq, Henri 149
Leemans, Johan 214
Leynaud, Augustin-Fernand 133–35, 145, 148
Lieu, Judith M. 266, 270
Lieu, Samuel N. C. 246
Lipinsky, Angelo 97
Loerke, William C. 91, 93–94
Longenecker, Bruce W. 118, 245, 265, 296, 307, 309, 311, 326–27, 338
Longfellow, Brenda 4
Lorenz, Rudolf 214–15, 217
Louth, Andrew 80
MacDonald, Dennis Ronald 236, 245

Modern Authors Index

MacDonald, Margaret Y. 195
MacDougall, Elisabeth Blair 4
Mach, Michael 270
MacKendrick, Paul L. 145
Madec, Goulven 43
Mango, Cyril A. 39, 41
Maraval, Pierre 40
Marsengill, Katherine 32
Martens, John W. 195
Martin, Michael W. 125
Martin, Victor 280
Marucchi, Orazio 117
Mattingly, David J. 147
Mattingly, Harold 111
Mazzoleni, Danilo 123, 133
McCarthy, Carmel 63
McClendon, Charles B. 54, 56, 58
McColl, Donald A. 2
McLachlan, Elizabeth Parker 211–12
McVey, Kathleen E. 63, 65–66
Meier, John P. 127
Meijering, Eginhard P. 46
Meiggs, Russell 322, 326–28, 333
Mell, Ulrich 68–69
Merdinger, Jane E. 159
Metzger, Bruce M. 264–65, 276–77
Miazzo, Lucia 207
Milburn, Robert 4, 19
Miles, Margaret R. 91, 94–95
Miller, Patricia Cox 35
Mingana, Alphonse 67
Mitchell, Nathan 210
Moffitt, David M. 125
Morey, Charles R. 204–5, 209–10
Mountain, William J. 42
Murray, Mary Charles 39–40, 147, 168
Murray, Robert 64
Myers, Susan E. 61
Nelson, Jinty 102
Neusner, Jacob 56, 87
Nicolai, Vincenzo Fiocchi 107, 123–24, 132–33
Nielsen, Inge 314
Nongbri, Brent 280
Norris, Russell Bradner, Jr. 246

Osborn, Eric 159
Osiek, Carolyn 148, 150, 152
Ostrogorsky, Georg 40–41
Paap, Anton H. R. E. 264, 278
Parkin, Tim 175
Parkes, James 269
Pearson, Birger A. 133
Peppard, Michael 51–52, 63, 71, 73–74, 150
Perassi, Claudia 112
Pesthy, Monika 236–37
Pierce, Joanne M. 212
Pitra, Jean B. 39
Post, Paulus Gijsbertus Johannes 183
Potthoff, Stephen E. 134
Prieur, Jean-Marc 246
Rad, Gerhard von 79
Rahner, Hugo 215
Ramage, Andrew 5
Ramage, Nancy 5
Rawson, Beryl 176
Rebillard, Éric 153, 190, 251
Reynolds, Benjamin E. 164
Richardson, Peter 267, 273
Richlin, Amy 181
Roberts, Colin H. 264, 279, 284, 293
Roberts, Erin 109
Rokéah, David 82
Rossi, Giovanni Battista de 121
Roth, Dieter T. 239
Royce, James 280
Ruether, Rosmary 295
Runesson, Rebecca 332
Russel, Ben 179
Rutgers, Leonard V. 107
Sanders, Henry A. 282, 285
Sanders, E. P. 237
Sandmel, Samuel 265
Schiller, Gertrud 240, 244
Schmidt, Carl 282
Schönborn, Christoph von 40
Sena Chiesa, Gemma 204–8, 220–21
Serra, Dominic E. 71, 73
Sheldon, Rose Mary 327
Sichtermann, Hellmut 180, 188

Siragan Arlen, Jesse 190
Skarsaune, Oskar 82, 105, 130, 272–73
Skeat, Theodore C. 293
Slavazzi, Fabrizio 204–8
Slusser, Michael 143, 270
Smith, Dennis E. 332
Snoek, Godefridus J. C. 210, 229
Snyder, Graydon F. 51, 70, 149
Sode, Claudia 39
Soulen, R. Kendall 272
Spain, Suzanne 91, 94–95
Speck, Paul 39
Spieckermann, Hermann 195
Spickermann, Wolfgang 188
Spier, Jeffrey 123–24, 149
Spigel, Chad 54
Spurling, Helen 80–81, 84
Squarciapino, Maria Floriani 322
Stanton, Graham 270, 273, 275–76, 294–95
Steck, Odil H. 273
Stewart-Sykes, Alistair 158
Stirling, Lea M. 136
Stone, David L. 147
Strehlke, Brandon 91
Studer-Karlen, Manuela 177, 182, 186
Taft, Robert, Jr. 210
Taylor, Catherine C. 89
Tepper, Yotam 332
Testuz, Michel 284, 286–87
Thiel, Nathan 276
Thompson, Glen L. 215
Thunberg, Lars 80
Thunø, Eric 213, 244
Tilley, Maureen A. 133–34
Timmermann, Achim 255–56
Todorova, Rostislava 93–94
Tornau, Christian 163
Toynbee, Jocelyn M. C. 180
Trakatellis, Demetrios Christ 82
Tränkle, Hermann 160
Traube, Ludwig 264, 278–79, 289
Treadgold, Warren 97
Tronchin, Lamberto 97
Tronzo, William 88

Tucker, Mark 92
Tuckett, Christopher M. 127–28, 264
Turci, Marcello 315
Usher, Mark D. 252
Verheyden, Joseph 130
Vermaseren, Maarten J. 57
Vieillefon, Laurence 144–45
Visonà, Giuseppe 239, 248
Waldner, Katherina 188
Walker, Hazelden 212
Walker, Susan 180
Wang, Xueying 190
Weitzmann, Kurt 54–55
Wenham, Gordon 79
White, L. Michael 51, 57–58
Whitlark, Jason A. 122, 125, 127
Wilhite, David E. 144, 159–60, 163, 327, 338
Williams, A. Lukyn 267
Winkler, Gabriele 60, 62
Wilpert, Joseph 33
Wisniewski, Robert 35, 208, 212
Wischmeyer, Wolfgang 3
Wixom, William D. 3
Wright, David F. 193
Yegül, Fikret K. 315, 332
Zahn, Theodor 162
Zanker, Paul. R. 5, 110.

Subject Index

Abraham, 32, 55, 79, 81–83, 85–86, 90–91, 94–95, 97, 100–1, 125, 131, 143, 159, 185, 270–72
Adam and Eve, 32–33, 65–66, 72–73, 182–85, 194, 243
adoration of the magi, 34, 183–86
Adversus Judaeos, 263–66, 268, 272–76, 278, 280, 289, 292, 296
anchor/ἄγκυρα/*ancora*, 32, 107–27, 132–37
aniconism, 28–29, 32
afterlife, 122, 187–88, 197, 334
Arianism, 102, 214–16, 219, 226–27, 253
baptism/baptismal font, 32, 52–53, 59–64, 66–69, 71–74, 129–30, 156, 186, 193–94, 253, 333–34
Bodmer Papyrus/I, 282–84, 286–87
Carpocratians, 34
Carthage, 30, 135–36, 159–60, 163, 168–70, 327
catacombs
    Via Latina, 81, 86, 102
    Roman, 107–8, 110–11, 114, 117–20, 122–24, 126–27, 132–33, 136–37, 152–53
    Hadrumetum, 133–36, 144–45
Chester Beatty Papyrus/I, 241, 279, 281, 288, 290
childhood as a metaphor, 194–96
children, 175–97
Christ
    with apostles, 48, 209
    healing, 183, 193
    ministry of, 52, 64, 71
    miracles, 209, 218

Christ Teaching, 2, 16–19
Christ with Sts. Peter and Paul, 20, 36
christological, 4, 15, 38–39, 46, 80–87, 90–91, 94, 96–103, 151, 164, 210, 226, 236, 242, 255, 274, 277–79, 294–95
christomorphization, 234, 236, 238, 240 249, 255–56
Cleveland Museum of Art, 2–7, 11–12, 157, 161
Codex
    Sinaiticus, 289, 291
    Vaticanus, 289, 291
    Washingtonensis, 282, 284
Communion, 60, 62, 100–2, 160, 166, 187, 210, 213, 216–18, 226, 228, 256
    in early Christian art, 209, 307
    home, 210–12, 228
Constantine, 4, 9, 137, 187, 214, 245, 249, 326–27
Contrapposto, 5, 7, 13, 18
cosmic/cosmos, 52–58, 60, 63, 65–74, 167, 236, 238–39, 245–50
docetic, 249–50
Diogenes figure, 15
Doryphorus, 5, 6
Eden, 89, 182, 184–85, 243
epitaphs, 113, 135, 177–78, 182, 188
Eucharist. *See* Communion
Euelpistos (Euelpistus), 121
festal letters, 213–15, 217–18, 220–21, 225–28
golden calf, 26–27
graven images, 25–29
Good Shepherd, 2, 5–8, 13–14, 146, 153, 157, 161

The Good Shepherd with Jonah and the Whale, 8
hand gestures, 181, 183–85, 192, 210
Hanna Papyrus, 280, 283, 292. *See also* P75
Hermes, catacomb of, 109, 134–35
Hermes/Hermes Criophorus, 7, 123, 147, 149–51
hope/*spes*/ἐλπίς, 3, 16, 109–15, 120–26, 136–37, 187–88, 193, 197
icon, 32, 45, 47, 91, 120, 123
iconoclasm, 26, 40
idol, idolatry, 25–28, 30–31, 47, 62, 69, 165
image (veneration of), 26, 30, 34, 37, 44, 208
Israel/Ἰσραήλ, 56, 71, 144, 162, 164–65, 167, 169–71, 263, 267–78, 280, 282, 286–87, 289, 291–92, 295–96
Jonah, 2–4, 7, 10, 13, 15–16, 32, 123, 156, 193
Jonah Marbles, 2–4, 7, 10, 16
  Jonah Cast Up, 9, 12–14
  Jonah Praying to God, 9, 11, 13–14
  Jonah Swallowed, 9–11, 13–14
  Jonah under the Gourd Vine, 9–10, 12–14
judgment of Joseph, 205, 214, 223–24
judgment of Solomon, 205, 221
Last Judgment, 19, 21
Lycomedes, 34, 38
mandorla, 91, 93–94, 97, 99
manuscript, 132, 238–39, 245, 263–64, 273–74, 276–80, 282, 284–87, 289, 291–93, 295
Mary/Mary with child, 21, 35, 41, 47–48, 66, 73, 93, 186, 205–6, 218–21, 226, 256
Melchizedekians, 131
Michelangelo, 13–14, 19, 21
Milan, 16, 170, 204, 207, 211, 213, 227–28
millenarianism, 307–8, 313, 334–35, 338–39
Mithras/Mithraism/Mithraeum, 53, 57–60, 74, 325

Moses, 27, 32–33, 55, 64, 69, 89, 93–94, 143, 165–66, 168, 248, 268–69, 272
mourning, 176, 180–81, 186–87, 190–91
narrative image/s, 34–35
nomina sacra, 238–39, 263–65, 274, 276–84, 286–96
omnipresence, 236, 245, 255
orant, 13
Orpheus, 9, 147
Ostia Antica, 6, 301–40
  association of furriers, 324
  Aurea, 326–27, 336–38, 340
  Baths of Neptune, 301, 314–15, 318, 322, 326, 328–29, 331–32, 339–40
  Forum of the Associations, 322–23, 327
  House of the Fish, 328–29, 331
  martyrs, 29, 36, 122, 164–65, 327, 335–36, 338–39
  word puzzle, 334–40
Oxyrhynchus, 291
P75, 277, 280, 282–83
parousia, 248, 253–54, 258
Perpetua, 147, 152, 154–55, 162–65
personification, 236, 240
portrait/s, 3–5, 21, 32, 34–35, 37–38, 44–47, 168, 179, 182–84
Raphael, 14–15
relics, 35, 37, 44, 47 203, 205–8, 212, 229
reliquary, 203–4, 206–8, 211, 213, 228–29, 245
replacement theology, 266, 293, 295–96
resurrection, 13, 16, 68, 73, 115, 125–26, 151, 185, 190, 234, 236–38, 240, 244, 250–52, 258, 307, 312–13, 334–35, 338–40
sacrifice of Isaac, 98–99, 184–86, 193–94
saints, 8, 26, 32, 35, 37, 40–42, 44–45, 47–48, 109, 226, 272
salvation, 3, 13, 42, 60, 62, 112, 115, 117, 125, 128, 206, 217, 222, 226, 243, 248, 254, 256, 258
Santa Maria Maggiore, 81, 90–97, 99, 102–3
San Vitale, 81, 97–99, 101–3

www.ingramcontent.com/pod-product-compliance
Lightning Source LLC
Chambersburg PA
CBHW042225010526
44111CB00045B/2954

sarcophagus, 18–20, 43, 71, 150, 154, 156, 176–94, 196–97, 205, 215, 240, 242
Second Commandment, 28
second coming. *See* parousia
sheep, 3, 5, 7, 9, 61, 72, 100, 124, 130, 145, 148–49, 154, 165–67, 169–70, 248
shepherd, 2, 5, 7, 9, 13, 15–16, 18, 52, 61, 64, 69, 72, 123, 134–35, 143–45, 147–52, 154–56, 158–71, 206,
Study for a River God, 14
supersessionism, 265–66, 295–96
symbols/symbolism, 32, 34, 65, 107–8, 110, 115–19, 122–24, 132, 135–36, 182, 208, 218, 270, 301–5, 307–14, 316, 321–22, 328–31, 334–35, 339–40
synagogue, 53–57, 59–60, 74, 271, 292
theophany, 83–84, 90, 94, 143, 164–65
Three Pairs of Portrait Busts of an Aristocratic Couple, 3–4
three youths in the fiery furnace, 205, 224–26
trinitarian, 46, 63, 80–81, 83–86, 89–90, 93–94, 102–3, 265, 277,
typology/types, 7, 15, 64, 83–84, 87, 185, 223, 242, 251, 266–68, 279
visual culture, 46, 263
Washington Manuscript. *See* Codex Washingtonensis